# Chinese American Literature since the 1850s

The Asian American Experience

*Series Editor*
Roger Daniels, University of Cincinnati

*A list of books in the series appears at the end of this book.*

# Chinese American Literature since the 1850s

Xiao-huang Yin

**Foreword by Roger Daniels**

University of Illinois Press

Urbana and Chicago

The Angel Island poems in chapter 1 are reprinted by permission
of the University of Washington Press.

© 2000 by the Board of Trustees of the University of Illinois
Manufactured in the United States of America
∞ This book is printed on acid-free paper.

Library of Congress Cataloging-in-Publication Data
Yin, Xiao-huang.
Chinese American literature since the 1850s / Xiao-huang Yin ;
foreword by Roger Daniels.
p.   cm. — (The Asian American experience)
Includes bibliograhpical references (p.   ) and index.
ISBN 0-252-02524-5 (alk. paper)
1. American literature—Chinese American authors—History and criticism.
2. American literature—20th century—History and criticism.
3. American literature—19th century—History and criticism.
4. American literature—Chinese influences.
5. Chinese Americans—Intellectual life.
6. Chinese Americans in literature.
I. Title.
II. Series
PS153.C45Y56   2000
810.9'8951—dc21   99–6512
CIP

C 5 4 3 2 1

*To my family and friends*

# Contents

*Illustrations follow page 156*

# Foreword
Roger Daniels

Ethnic literature in the United States—literature that focuses on an ethnic group or on a group of persons of color—was long largely ignored by scholars when not despised. That is clearly no longer the case: the Modern Language Association now issues bibliographies of various kinds of ethnic literature.[1] In addition, since 1974 a scholarly journal, *MELUS,* has been published by the Society for the Study of the Multi-Ethnic Literature of the United States.

Most ethnic literature has been written in English, but some significant works of American ethnic literature have been written in languages other than English. The most notable author of such literature, the Norwegian American Ole E. Rolvaag (1837–1931), insisted, "We can call these works . . . emigrant literature, but then we give the child a wrong name. For they are not that: they are American literature in the Norwegian language."[2] His *Giants in the Earth* (1927) is one of the first works in American literature to be translated from another language to achieve wide readership in the United States and be welcomed into the general literary canon.

If this and a few other works of American literature by Europeans had floated into the mainstream before World War II—one thinks also of Abraham Cahan—Asian American literature remained almost literally a sealed book until after that war. Even its most brilliant and celebrated practitioner, Maxine Hong Kingston (b. 1940), could write that Jade Snow Wong (b. 1922), author of *Fifth Chinese Daughter* (1950), the first widely read work of Asian American literature, was "the Mother of Chinese American Literature," not realizing that the woman who recreated herself as Sui Sin Far had preceded Wong by more than half a century.[3]

Although we have had a scholarly account of Asian American literature since 1982 and by the 1990s began to have complex literary criticism of it, only with this volume are we provided a comprehensive history of Chinese American literature, including important path-breaking work on American literature written in Chinese.[4] Its author, Xiao-huang Yin, China-born and raised and Harvard-educated, is representative of that echelon of Asian-born scholars who are helping to revamp and move Asian American studies from a marginal position toward the leading edge of global scholarship. A cultural historian with links to more than one discipline as well as to more than one culture, Yin catalogs, classifies, and analyzes virtually all forms of Chinese American writing from the post–Gold Rush years through the 1980s. In doing so he has not only helped to excavate a buried past but also contributed to a more acute perception of an often-misunderstood present. Although there is no such thing as a "last word" in scholarship, *Chinese American Literature since the 1850s* will surely be the place from which much future scholarship will start.

## Notes

1. Relevant here is King-Kok Cheung and Stan Yogi, *Asian American Literature: An Annotated Bibliography* (New York: Modern Language Association of America, 1988).

2. As cited in Dorothy B. Skardal, *The Divided Heart: Scandinavian Immigrant Experience through Literary Sources* (Lincoln: University of Nebraska Press, 1974).

3. See chapter 3 of this volume as well as an earlier volume in this series: Annette White-Parks, *Sui Sin Far/Edith Maude Eaton: A Literary Biography* (Urbana: University of Illinois Press, 1995). The quotation is from Maxine Hong Kingston to Amy Ling, April 28, 1988, quoted in Ling, *Between Worlds: Women Writers of Chinese Ancestry* (New York: Pergamon Press, 1990), 120.

4. Elaine H. Kim, *Asian American Literature: An Introduction to the Writings and Their Social Context* (Philadelphia: Temple University Press, 1982). For literary criticism, see, for example, Sau-ling Cynthia Wong, *Reading Asian American Literature: From Necessity to Extravagance* (Princeton: Princeton University Press, 1993), and Lisa Lowe, *Immigrant Acts: On Asian American Cultural Politics* (Durham: Duke University Press, 1996).

# Preface

When I completed my dissertation on the sociohistorical context of early Chinese American writing in the fall of 1991, I never imagined that it was only the beginning of what would develop into a long-term project. In addition to rewriting many parts of the original manuscript, I expanded my study to include contemporary Chinese American literature and publications by Chinese immigrants in their native language. Although these new subjects now account for about half the book, I have kept my discussions focused on the sociohistorical aspects of Chinese American writing. As a cultural historian and an Asian Americanist, I tend to see the literature as a product of Chinese American life, recording and reflecting the hardships Chinese have experienced, the struggle they have made, and the success they have achieved since they first settled on the "Gold Mountain" in the mid-nineteenth century.[1]

A few issues related to Chinese-language materials discussed in this volume need to be explained. Unless otherwise noted, I have translated all the Chinese sources, both primary and secondary. To maintain consistency, I have spelled Chinese names according to the Chinese custom, which places one's family name before the given name, and have romanized Chinese characters based on the *pinyin* system, with the following exceptions: the word *Canton* and other names, terms, and titles that are customarily used in the Chinese American community. ("Canton" is the European rendering of the name in local Chinese dialect; it becomes "Guangzhou" in *pinyin*. I chose to say with "Canton" because it is the more traditional and familiar usage.) For readers' convenience and to save space, in most cases I have only cited English translations of Chinese titles in the text while placing the romanization in the notes and bibliography. Those who have questions about Chinese names, terms, and titles are referred to the Chinese-language bibliography and glossary.

I have listed in the bibliography most of the titles and works mentioned in the notes, although spatial considerations prevent me from fully acknowledging every work of relevant intellectual interest, or even all the works I have consulted. The bibliography is, therefore, selective, with the criteria for inclusion being those works particularly significant to my study.

### Note

1. "Gold Mountain" is a nickname that Chinese immigrants have used for the United States. Historically, America has been known to the Chinese as a "mountain of gold" both because of the nineteenth-century gold rush in California and the nation's image for being a land of opportunity.

# Acknowledgments

The publication of this book provides a much-needed opportunity to reiterate my gratitude to institutions and individuals that have supported and encouraged me over the years as I worked on this project. The Louis and Hermione Brown Humanities Support Fund at Occidental College, the Ethnic Studies Committee and Longfellow Institute at Harvard University, the Harvard-Yenching Institute, the Mrs. Giles Whiting Foundation, Smithsonian Institution, the National Endowment for the Humanities, the John Randolph Haynes and Dora Haynes Foundation, and the Massachusetts Historical Society have supported this project in the form of scholarships, faculty fellowships, summer stipends, research grants, and funds for publication.

Support from the Dean of the Faculty's Office and the Remsen Bird Lectureship at Occidental College allowed me to invite several prominent Chinese and Asian American writers to campus and interview them at length: Maxine Hong Kingston, Frank Chin, Amy Tan, Jade Snow Wong, and Wendy Law-Yone. Their views and opinions on Chinese American literature helped sharpen my thinking.

Portions of chapters 2, 3, and 5 in earlier versions have appeared in *Origins and Destinations: Forty-one Essays on Chinese America, Arizona Quarterly,* and *Multilingual America: Transnationalism, Ethnicity, and the Languages of America.* I wish to thank the editors and publishers for their permission to use the material.

Among many scholars and friends who have helped me with this project, I am particularly grateful to Roger Daniels, editor of the Asian American Experience series at the University of Illinois Press and a leading historian of Asian Americans. Many of the ideas in this book were profitably exposed to his critiques, and the volume reflects his direction in great proportion. Stephan Thernstrom and Werner Sollors, academic advisers during my graduate studies at Harvard University, provided constant support and advice throughout the years. Without their directions and friendship, this project would have never been possible. Amy Ling of the University of Wisconsin at Madison read the manuscript with great care and shared her wealth of knowledge about Chinese American literature. Her insights helped me reach more nuanced analyses on many critical issues discussed herein. Yu Lihua, a Chinese immigrant writer renowned for her work on student immigrants, told me in detail about her life and writing during a lengthy interview and made an explicit summary of the development of Chinese-language publications in the United States since the 1950s. I also benefited enormously from the valuable comments made by Roderick MacFarquhar, Akira Iriye, Leo Ou-fan Lee, and Tu Wei-ming. Their knowledge of and interest in the Chinese diaspora and Asian Americans inspired me to take on this project.

I am grateful to the following friends and colleagues who generously read drafts, helped me revise the manuscript, or contributed their expertise: Warner Berthoff, Thomas Schwartz, Marc Shell, Adrienne Tien, Marian Demos, Joseleyne Slade, Marjorie Fletcher, Steven G. Kellman, Alex Kuo, Merle Goldman, Tony Saich, Nancy Hearst, Wellington K. K. Chan, David Axeen, Eric Newhall, Lynn Dumenil, Norman Cohen, Rebecca Chien, Sue Fawn Chung, Shan Te-hsing, Qian Jun, Zhang Ziqing, Franklin Ng, Huck Gutman, Gary Kulik, L. Charles Laferrière (Sui Sin Far's grandnephew), Caroline and Shelton Beatty, and Patricia Arkin. I also thank my students at Occidental College and Harvard University. Their enthusiastic response to my questions and lectures on Asian American studies has been a constant source of inspiration.

My final thanks go to my wife, Xiaoling Hong, and my son Lu, who shared my joys and frustrations in working on this project. It is their unfailing belief in my ability to complete this book that gave me confidence and sustained me through the most difficult phase of the writing.

# Chinese American Literature since the 1850s

# Introduction

This book is a study of Chinese American literature in English and Chinese, with an emphasis on sociohistorical interpretations.[1] Covering the period from the 1850s to the 1980s, it attempts to trace the origins and development of Chinese American literature in English and Chinese, to discuss its broader social implications and cultural context, and to examine the diversity of styles and subject matter that make up the literary scene of the Chinese American community. In doing so, I have tried to provide answers to the following questions: To what extent is the writing a product of the experience of Chinese immigrants and their descendants in the "Gold Mountain" throughout history? What is the relationship between the text and its broad sociohistorical backgrounds? And how different is the literature from that of other ethnic and minority groups?

To illuminate changes and continuity of the Chinese American experience as revealed through their writing, I include in this study not only the contemporary but also the early phase of Chinese American literature, such as works written by Chinese immigrants in the nineteenth century. Although going as far back as one can in the search for a Chinese American cultural heritage may be regarded as a quest for the "usable past"—a well-known phrase attributed to Van Wyck Brooks, referring to the study of American Puritan writing—reviewing these "forgotten pages" allows an in-depth understanding of an important part of the Chinese American legacy and an appreciation of the complexity and diversity of the Chinese experience in American society. Thus, it helps people see more clearly the progress of the Chinese American community since the mid-nineteenth century and better understand how deeply the Chinese, as an American ethnic group, are rooted "in this land."

I have also included in this study works written by Chinese immigrants in

their native language. Although most critical studies of Asian American literature, for various reasons, tend to cover only works written in English, it is time
to consider the creative expertise, aesthetics, and enduring, multifaceted themes
of Chinese-language writing.[2] While remaining largely unknown to the general
public, its impact on the Chinese American community cannot be underestimated. It provides social stability for new immigrants and is enormously popular
among Chinese Americans. The many volumes of Chinese-language literature
on display in Chinatown bookstores throughout the United States are clear evidence of the genre's powerful influence in the community. Given that around
70 percent of Chinese Americans are immigrants and more than 80 percent,
including those who are native-born, speak some Chinese at home, it is inexcus-
able to ignore work written in the Chinese language in a sociohistorical study of
Chinese American literature.[3]

In examining the growth and development of Chinese American literature I
have deliberately moved between literary study and discussion of sociohistorical background. My study is intended both as an investigation into how the literature reflects the changing experience of the Chinese in America and their
cultural perspectives in successive eras and as an analysis of the artistic integrity
of their writing. That twofold approach is important. If the cultural and historical context of Chinese American writing is unfamiliar, the literature is likely to
be misunderstood and unappreciated. One example is Lee Yan Phou's autobiography, *When I Was a Boy in China* (1887). The author's strenuous endeavor
to improve the image of the Chinese represents a conscious attempt to correct
distortions of China and Chinese civilization in popular American culture in the
late nineteenth century. The book is largely a response to, and defense against,
the discriminatory Chinese Exclusion Act (1882), which prohibited Chinese
immigrants to enter the United States and denied them citizenship on the
grounds they were an "unassimilated" race with an inferior cultural tradition.

The defense of Chinese civilization constitutes a major theme in most early
Chinese American works, appearing and reappearing with peculiar vitality in the
writing. If readers are unable to understand this aspect of Chinese American
history, they are likely to dismiss Lee's autobiography as simply an ethnocentric
and "yellow-supremacy" statement. Therefore, a study of the writing of Chinese
Americans must simultaneously include an analysis of their experience in the
United States. In fact, many Chinese American writers insist on including passages of history in their work, even in their creative writing, for fear the general
audience's unfamiliarity with Chinese American history may cause misunderstanding. As Maxine Hong Kingston explains, "The mainstream culture doesn't
know the history of Chinese Americans. . . . That ignorance makes a tension for

me, and in the new book [*China Men*] I just couldn't take it anymore. So all of a sudden, right in the middle of the stories, plunk—there is an eight-page section of pure history. It starts with the Gold Rush and then goes right through the various exclusion acts, year by year."[4]

There is another reason to study the sociohistorical aspects of Chinese American writing. Although individual authors are affected by personal backgrounds, Chinese American writers, taken as a whole, are concerned with issues indigenous to the Chinese American community and are acutely sensitive to problems that affect Chinese American life. Consequently, their writing, as Elaine H. Kim finds, functions as a social statement and historical document and reaches beyond the realm of literary merit and artistic values. It provides unique access to understanding the sensibilities of members of a frequently misunderstood minority group.[5]

In other words, what makes it an additional appreciated asset is that Chinese American literature, autobiographical and fictional alike, contains authentic knowledge and factual accounts of Chinese American life and presents a version of the Chinese experience and feelings typical of the period. That the authors actually lived the lives they describe makes their narratives reliable and informative. For instance, Lee Chew's autobiographical sketch, "The Life Story of a Chinese Laundryman" (1906), shows how the social and economic conditions of the time shaped his life in America and excluded Chinese immigrants from most occupations, restricting them from more decent styles of living. That Lee Chew, like numerous other Chinese laundrymen, had never done washing in the old country but learned the trade in America is not only highly ironical but also demonstrates that laundry was not a "standard Chinese business." As Lee Chew bitterly points out, it was a "woman's job" forced on male Chinese immigrants because they had no other choice.

Similarly, the Tong (Tang) war has long been a highly publicized issue in popular American literature. Despite the large quantity of publications on the subject, few books presented so clear a picture or explored the social origins of the Tongs as did Pardee Lowe in the autobiographical *Father and Glorious Descendant* (1943). Based on his father's involvement as a "pie" (a lucrative target) in Tong fighting, Lowe presents a kaleidoscopic look at the Tong organizations in the Chinese American community that is authentic and free of the societal distortion commonly seen in works by mainstream American writers. Because he witnessed major events depicted in his book, Lowe's account provides a window into an important aspect of Chinese American life in the early twentieth century. It is a sharp contrast to the melodramatic or sensational portrayal of bloodthirsty Chinese hatchetmen in books such as *Tong War!*, which is a clearly fabricated, perhaps fraudulent tale.[6]

Lowe's analysis is also insightful in terms of the Tongs' social origins and development in the Chinese American community. The institutional structure of Chinese secret societies was originally brought to the United States by immigrants from rural regions in China. Under American conditions, however, they were dramatically transformed. According to Lowe's personal observation, Tongs thrived in America during the late nineteenth and early twentieth centuries in part because their activities created a counterculture to the establishment of the Chinese community. As a secret organization, Tongs provided working-class Chinese immigrants with a sense of belonging and mutual support in the "bachelor society." They also provided protection in a strange land when traditional Chinese leadership failed to deal with problems that plagued the community in the late nineteenth and early twentieth centuries. It is significant that Lowe's explanation of the emergence and development of Tongs in the Chinese American community presents a partial parallel to the origins of secret societies in mainstream American culture.[7]

While focusing on sociohistorical interpretations, I have analyzed the artistic values of Chinese American writing. The literature is by no means merely historical documentation or anthropological writing per se. Its values as a social statement are absorbing, but its qualities as literature are equally enlightening. My analysis not only helps an audience perceive the sensibility and subtlety of Chinese American writing as a literature but also reveals how "Americanized" or "un-Americanized" the authors are.

The concept that "Orientals" are perpetual foreigners has led many readers to think that Chinese American literature, like the pidgin English spoken by "Ching Chong Chinamen," is virtually foreign writing. That misinterpretation has manifested itself in a belief that Chinese American authors inherited the cultural tradition of their old country. In reality, that concept is misleading. Stylistically, Chinese American writers from the very beginning were influenced by mainstream culture. That they, particularly the native-born, write in the same way as their peers in society at large demonstrates that, stylistically, they have been thoroughly Americanized.

One example of how critics have misread the literature concerns the prevalent view that Jade Snow Wong's use of third-person narrative in her autobiographical novel *Fifth Chinese Daughter* (1950) originated from Chinese literary tradition. By examining carefully the prose style of her work, we find what has really influenced Wong are American autobiographical works such as Henry Adams's *The Education of Henry Adams* and Richard Wright's *Black Boy*. Moreover, the fact that earlier Chinese American writing is in the realm of American-style realism and largely of an autobiographical nature, a genre virtually nonexistent in traditional Chinese literature, reveals that Chinese American writers are more "Americanized" than critics have realized. It remains true to this day. Maxine Hong Kingston, for example, has remarked that in writing *The Woman Warrior* she was more influenced by William Carlos Williams's *In the American Grain* than the "exotic" literary tradition of China, as some mainstream critics suggest.[8]

A study of formal and stylistic features of Chinese American literature can thus enhance understanding of the extent of mainstream culture's impact on the Chinese American experience. Of course, critics' misjudgment does not occur only in the case of Chinese American authors. There is a general tendency to view ethnic American writing as bearing the traits of "foreign" literature; take, for example, the controversy over Mario Puzo's *The Godfather*. Although a critic claims the book is an Italian-style novel, scholars from Italy have argued that it is a "very American book," closer to the work of Mark Twain than the critic maintains.[9]

Consisting of seven chapters, this book begins with the appearance of the first major piece of writing in English by Chinese immigrants in 1852 and ends with the publication of Amy Tan's *The Joy Luck Club* in 1989. Organized chronologically, my discussion focuses on representative works that illustrate the social significance of Chinese American writing from different periods. The study is not an encyclopedic survey. My aim is to interpret how the writing reflects the changing experiences of Chinese in the United States rather than write a comprehensive and balanced literary history.

Chapter 1 analyzes some of the earliest Chinese American works. By piecing together documents from archival research and publications that have been rediscovered and placing them in a historical context to illuminate cultural patterns, I have tried to uncover the collective voice of early Chinese Americans—the "buried past." Historically, Chinese immigrants were often seen as being "unassimilable" because they refused to discard their heritage. But these writings show that if indeed they refused to adopt Anglo-American beliefs and behavior, it was mainly because they had been excluded from the "melting pot." As one Chinese American historian argues, "Assimilation does not depend solely on the predilections of the newcomers. It can only occur when members of the host society give immigrants a chance to become equal partners" to share in shaping the world in which they live.[10] Chinese immigrants were not given such a chance until the post–World War II era. Pleading for tolerance and protesting discrimination, the voices of early Chinese immigrants were bitter, angry, and appealing. Their desire for American citizenship shattered popular belief that Chinese immigrants were sojourners who had no intention of settling in America. Chapter 1 also includes poems written by Chinese detained at the Angel Island immigration station (1910–40). Although written in a somewhat later era, the poetry express moods and feelings similar to those reflected in other work discussed in the chapter.

Chapter 2 is a study of the work of "cultivated Chinese" during the late nineteenth and early twentieth centuries. Most were Chinese students and scholars who came to America for advanced education and then settled in the United States. As members of the "exempt classes," they were the predecessors of contemporary "uptown Chinese" (well-educated professionals who live in the suburbs rather than in Chinatowns).[11] I identify them as a separate group because their lives in American society were not always the same as those of immigrant laborers trapped in poverty and struggling for survival. Compared with their downtown compatriots, the cultivated Chinese were not bitter. They were treated with more tolerance and enjoyed more privileges than others from China, even during the exclusion era (1882–1943).[12] Concerned chiefly with how to improve the Chinese image, their writing aimed at introducing the fine qualities of Chinese civilization to the American public in the hope of winning more acceptance for Chinese immigrants.

The gap between cultivated Chinese and their working-class countrymen in terms of American experiences reveals how the "color line"—a term W. E. B. Du Bois coined to refer to divisions along racial distinctions—has sometimes been blurred by factors such as class differences and social status. Yet despite the fact that they were part of the exempt classes, cultivated Chinese were still targets of various forms of racial discrimination and haunted by their "Chinaman identity." Such was the experience of Lin Yutang, who recalled visiting his editor at a posh New York hotel. Upon entering the building, however, he was turned away by the doorman and forced to use the service entrance to gain readmittance.[13]

Chapter 3 is a discussion of Sui Sin Far [Edith Maude Eaton, 1865–1914], the first Chinese woman writer in North America. A towering figure among early Chinese American authors, Sui's work poignantly expresses the theme of cultural conflict and the consequences of acculturation in a way that reaches far beyond the realm of the Chinese American experience. Her writing also surpasses the Chinese cultural boundaries in that she is one of the few Chinese American writers who successfully depicted not only Chinese but also white Americans. Instances of such portrayal were rare in early Chinese American literature because racial segregation excluded most Chinese authors from having close contact with Caucasians. As a result, they had little chance to observe or become familiar with life in mainstream society. As a Eurasian, however, Sui's link with white Americans—"her father's race"—made her an exception. Large numbers

of Caucasian characters with divergent ethnic backgrounds appear in her stories. One can find Greek fishermen who befriended the Chinese, radical German
women suffragettes, arrogant "old stock" Yankees, and missionary workers dedicated to "the betterment of the condition and the uplifting of the young work-
ingmen of Chinese race who came to America."[14]

Chapter 4 concentrates on works by second-generation Chinese between the
1920s and the early 1960s. In contrast to first-generation Chinese, the focus of
their writing shifts to a search for a place in American life. Showing an intense
desire to enter mainstream society and speed the process of Americanization, it
suggests the way of thinking of the second generation during a specific historical period and provides a precious glimpse into the lives and minds of native-
born Chinese before the 1960s. If their perceptions of American life seem to
confirm rather than correct the stereotypical image of the Chinese as the "model
minority," however, it is because their work was written during a period all but
devoid of strong ethnic affiliations. Preoccupied with imitations of "American
models," they followed the course designated by the mainstream culture. As pioneers of "ABC" (American-born Chinese) authors, their writing represents a
transition from that of Chinese to Chinese Americans and breaks ground in an
era that provided no other alternative to the social trends.

Chapters 5 and 6 cover work written in Chinese by immigrant writers since
the 1950s.[15] Although they share with their counterparts who write in English
the same thematic concerns (e.g., the generation gap, cultural conflicts, desires
for personal freedom, and the struggle against prejudice), the subject matter of
their writing is more oriented toward the lives of immigrants. More significantly, their coverage of the Chinese American experience, especially controversial
issues such as the promises and perils of assimilation, interracial love affairs,
relationships between Chinese and other ethnic groups, conflicts among different segments of the Chinese community, and clashes between the opportunities
and temptations of America and the comforting but restricted immigrant community, is often different from English-language writing. Because Chinese-language writers seek affirmation and recognition only from readers in their own
community and do not worry about the response of the general reading public,
their portrayal of Chinese immigrant life is often more straightforward than that
found in the work of those who write in English. It also seems closer to reality.

In chapter 7, I focus on works by contemporary Chinese American writers,
especially on their efforts to create a distinctively Chinese American sensibility.
This chapter also sums up the changes and continuity of Chinese American literature throughout history. Chinese-language literature continues to express
strong concerns for the fate of immigrants in America, but the focus of the writ-

ing in English has shifted from a search for a place in mainstream life to an authentically Chinese American cultural identity. In discussing major issues that have affected the contemporary Chinese American literary scene, I have examined the "war of words" between Frank Chin and Maxine Hong Kingston. Most people view the dispute as a fight over gender issues, but in reality the controversy goes far beyond male-female divisions and is concerned with exposing conflicting views among Chinese Americans on the role of ideology in creative writing. I have chosen a nonprescriptive approach to present the Chin-Kingston debate, not because of reluctance to take a stand but rather because I believe there is truth to both sides of the argument.

Discussions within each chapter are arranged around the major themes that have dominated Chinese American writing throughout history. This organizational format allows me to focus on the subject matter of major works and the significant changes in the literature through periods. It also allows for a comparative examination of the texts and authors' backgrounds. In my discussion, I also make extensive use of reference works published in the Chinese language in China, Taiwan, Hong Kong, and other parts of the world to bring to light new material that hitherto has rarely been made available to American scholars. In addition, I examine the image of the Chinese in popular American culture in order to understand why the average American is likely more familiar with Fu Manchu and Charlie Chan than with Chinese Americans as ordinary human beings. The portrayal of "Orientals" in popular American culture has not only shaped the racial stereotypes of Chinese in the minds of millions but has also influenced the formation of Chinese American literature and affected the self-expression of Chinese American writers.

A synthetic and extensive study of Chinese American literature is greatly needed. By using an interdisciplinary approach and combining the work of ethnicity specialists with the findings of literary critics, I hope that this study will provide a new perspective from which to understand the social experience and cultural heritage of Chinese Americans. Although this book focuses only on representative works that illustrate the social significance and historical experience of Chinese Americans, especially in areas where problems of race, class, and gender are closely interwoven, other scholars may arrive at varying conclusions based on their pursuits of Chinese American cultural tradition. Given that Asian American studies has entered a new stage of development and faces challenges from emerging trends such as transnationalism and transculturalism, it is my hope that this volume will contribute to the progress in the discipline and promote a broad humanistic understanding of the interrelations between Asian American history and literature.

## Notes

1. I use the term *literature* in a broad sense, including not only "pure literature" such as poems and fiction but also letters, essays, newspaper articles, memoirs, and other forms of publications that have recorded the Chinese American experience within the larger literary universe.

2. For example, King-Kok Cheung and Stan Yogi have explained somewhat apologetically that they excluded work written in Asian languages in order to keep their book to a "manageable size." See Cheung and Yogi, comps., *Asian American Literature: An Annotated Bibliography* (New York: Modern Language Association, 1988), vi. Elaine H. Kim, for the same reason, also excluded literature written in Asian languages in her pioneering study of Asian American literature: *Asian American Literature: An Introduction to the Writings and Their Social Context* (Philadelphia: Temple University Press, 1982), xi–xix. Their criteria, although somewhat controversial, are understandable. It is virtually impossible for a single volume to cover work written in English as well as all the Asian languages. For lack of a better term, I use *Chinese-language writing* for work written in Chinese by Chinese Americans to differentiate it from literary work written in English by Chinese Americans.

3. Edna L. Paisano, *We the American . . . Asians* (Washington: Bureau of the Census, 1993), 3, 5.

4. Timothy Pfaff, "Talk with Mrs. Kingston," *New York Times Book Review,* June 15, 1980, 25. Most Asian American writers act in a similar way. For example, Jeanne Wakatsuki Houston, author of *Farewell to Manzanar* (1973), describes many historical details, including documents about the Japanese American internment during World War II, to help readers understand the Japanese American experience discussed in her book.

5. Elaine H. Kim, "Asian American Literature and the Importance of Social Context," *ABD Bulletin* 80 (Spring 1985): 34.

6. Eng Ying Gong and Bruce Grant, *Tong War!* (New York: Nicholas L. Brown, 1930). Judging from its style of narrative and numerous errors on Chinese cultural customs, I suspect the book was written by a non-Asian author using a Chinese pseudonym.

7. For example, as a contemporary historian concludes, millions of nineteenth-century American men joined secret societies such as the Freemasons, Odd Fellows, and Knights of Pythias because these organizations provided a fantasy world antithetical to prevailing religious and social practices and a means to oppose an increasingly liberal and feminized Protestantism. See Mark Carnes, *Secret Ritual and Manhood in Victorian America* (Berkeley: University of California Press, 1989). Of course, the development of the Tong in the Chinese American community is a more complicated issue than that of the secret societies in American culture. See Victor G. Nee and Brett de Bary Nee, *Longtime Californ':  A Documentary Study of an American Chinatown* (Stanford: Stanford University Press, 1986), 60–69, 80–92, 223–26; Lynn Pan, *Sons of the Yellow Emperor: A History of the Chinese Diaspora* (New York: Kodansha International, 1994), 117–24, 338–56; and Him Mark Lai, *Cong huaqiao dao huaren* [From overseas Chinese to Chinese Americans], (Hong Kong: Joint, 1992), 25–45.

8. Author interview with Kingston, Harvard University, Cambridge, Mass., March 7, 1990; see also Maxine Hong Kingston, "Cultural Mis-readings by American Reviewers," in *Asian and Western Writers in Dialogue,* ed. Guy Amirthanayagam (London: Macmillan Press, 1982), 55–65; and Kim, *Asian American Literature,* xvi–xviii.

9. Werner Sollors, *Beyond Ethnicity: Consent and Descent in American Culture* (New York: Oxford University Press, 1985), 12.

10. Sucheng Chan, *Asian Americans: An Interpretive History* (Boston: Twayne Publishers, 1991), xiv.

11. The Chinese Exclusion Act passed by Congress in 1882 stopped the entry of all Chinese except "scholars, students, merchants, officials, and tourists," who were termed "the exempt classes." William L. Tung, ed., *The Chinese in America: A Chronology and Fact Book* (New York: Oceana, 1974), 58–67; Christian G. Fritz, "Due Process, Treaty Rights, and Chinese Exclusion," in *Entry Denied: Exclusion and the Chinese Community in America, 1882–1943,* ed. Sucheng Chan (Philadelphia: Temple University Press, 1991), 25–56.

12. The "exclusion era" refers to the period between 1882, when Congress first passed the exclusion act to deny entry of Chinese immigrants, to 1943, when the act was finally repealed.

13. Lin Taiyi [Anor Lin], *Lin Yutang zhuan* [Biography of Lin Yutang], (Beijing: Zhongguo Xiju, 1994), 163. Lin Taiyi is Lin Yutang's second daughter.

14. Sui Sin Far [Edith Maude Eaton], *Mrs. Spring Fragrance* (Chicago: A. C. McClurg, 1912), 68.

15. I use the term *immigrant writers* to refer to Chinese immigrants who have settled in America and primarily written in the Chinese language.

*This is to certify that we, the undersigned, are good Chinamen and have lived in California and other parts of the United States, and that we have at all times been willing to abide by all the laws of the United States, and the States and Territories in which we have lived. And are now willing to deport ourselves as good law abiding citizens of Montana Territory, and ask but that protection that the liberal and good government of this country permits us to enjoy. We pay all our taxes and assessments, and only ask that the good people of Montana may let us earn an honest living by the sweat of our brow.*
—Ye Sing, Hob Hee, Ye Hob, and others, *Montana Radiator* (1866)

# 1

# Plea and Protest: The Voices of Early Chinese Immigrants

The writing of early Chinese immigrants is a record of plea and protest—a plea for tolerance and a protest against mistreatment and discrimination.[1] Responding to an unfriendly environment, the literature is a testament to a conscious effort on the part of Chinese immigrants to fight for survival and acceptance. While its value as literary production is immense, its significance as a sociohistorical document of the Chinese American experience is even greater. In order to understand and appreciate early Chinese American writing fully, it is necessary to consider the historical background of immigration from China to the United States during the mid-nineteenth century.

## Early Chinese Immigration and Its Background

The scarcity of reliable sources makes it difficult to determine exactly when and where the Chinese first came to North America. Although some individuals arrived in the New World as early as the eighteenth century, it was not until the Gold Rush years that Chinese immigration became large enough to have significant impact on American society. The discovery of gold at John Sutter's sawmill on January 24, 1848, precipitated a massive migration to California from all over the world, including a considerable number of adventurous souls from China. In fact, the Chinese were among the first groups who rushed to the mines in the Sierra Nevada. Chinese and American sources both report that on February 2, 1848, less than ten days after James Marshall discovered gold on the lower reaches of the American River, three Chinese—two men and a woman—arrived at San Francisco on the American brig *Eagle*. The men immediately went to the mines and were said to have discovered a piece of gold ore of some 240 pounds near the Moore's Flat.[2] Accounts of their fortune and glowing tales of the fabulous wealth to be had in California quickly traveled back to Guangzhou [Canton], the provincial capital of Guangdong [Kwangtung] province on the South China coast. As word spread in the Pearl River Delta around Canton, gold-seekers hurried to make plans to embark upon the voyage across the Pacific. There were 325 Chinese forty-niners [*Jinshan Ke,* or *Gam San Hak* (Gold Mountain travelers) in Cantonese] in 1849. A year later the number reached 789, and it grew to 2,716 in 1851.[3]

At the beginning of 1852, Peter Parker, a missionary ophthalmologist and the chief American diplomatic representative in Canton since 1846, wrote to the State Department that "the favorable reports of those who have returned to China, having been fortunate at the gold mountain, seem to have imparted a new impetus to the tide of emigration."[4] Parker's words soon became reality. In 1852 the number of Chinese who entered California took a quantum leap; 20,026 arrived in San Francisco, which the Cantonese called the "Big Port."[5] A popular folk song that circulated in the Pearl River Delta demonstrates the momentum of Chinese immigration to California at the time:

> In the second reign year of Haamfung [Xianfeng, 1852], a trip to Gold
>     Mountain was made.
> With a pillow on my shoulder, I began my perilous journey:
> Sailing a boat with bamboo poles across the seas,
> Leaving behind wife and sisters in search of money,
> No longer lingering with the woman in the bedroom,
> No longer paying respect to parents at home.[6]

Why Chinese immigration to California took such a sudden, dramatic increase in the early 1850s is an issue that needs further study. Remunerative wages and the prospects of the discovery of gold were, of course, the major factors, although several others also impelled the Chinese to break family ties and join the rush for the Gold Mountain. News of the great wealth in America reached the Celestial Empire at a time of disaster—what Arnold Toynbee called "a time of troubles." The situation was particularly catastrophic in Guangdong province, where the economy had never fully recovered from the ravages of the Opium War (1839–42). The ruling Manchu court, badly defeated in the war, was forced to sign a humiliating treaty, the Treaty of Nanjing [Nanking], on Britain's terms. In order to pay huge indemnities levied by the Western powers, the Qing [Ch'ing] regime increased taxes to eighteen times the customary rate in Guangdong province. Unable to pay the heavy taxation, farmers and peasants were forced by the government to sell their land and possessions. In addition, as China ceded Hong Kong to England and opened the port of Canton to Western merchants, foreign goods poured in and caused a rapid breakdown in the local commerce and economy. The competition with technologically more advanced Western merchandise resulted in massive bankruptcy for domestic industries such as textiles. People were reduced into destitution and strove desperately to find a way out. Many able-bodied men went abroad to try their luck.[7]

Another cause for mass emigration was the Taiping Rebellion (1851–64), the largest peasant uprising in modern Chinese history. By 1852 the rebellion, which started upriver in the neighboring province of Guangxi [Kwanghsi], had swept down along the Pearl River to Guangdong and left heavy destruction in its wake. Fierce battles between the rebels and government forces devastated land, uprooted the peasantry, and dislocated the economy and polity. To discourage peasants from joining the rebellion, the Qing regime adopted a policy of extreme terrorism, often executing indiscriminately all adult males in villages that supported the rebels. Chinese historians estimate that nearly twenty million people died throughout the country during the decade-long civil war. The bloody strife created political chaos, economic disaster, loss of life, and widespread suffering, especially in South China.[8] People in Guangdong province were forced to flee, and many refugees, driven from their homes by famine, economic hardships, and incessant warfare, chose to go abroad. For them, the process of relocation had already become a characteristic of their struggle to survive. The skills acquired during that struggle could easily be applied to emigration to a foreign land such as North America.[9]

The civil and foreign wars left another impact on Chinese emigration: They compelled the Qing regime to abandon its highly restrictive emigration law. Since its conquest of China in the mid-seventeenth century, the Manchu throne had forbade emigration under penalty of death. Section 225 of the *Da Qing luli* [Imperial laws of Great Quing], enacted in 1712, stipulates: "All officers of government, soldiers, and private citizens, who clandestinely proceed to sea to trade, or who remove to foreign islands for the purpose of inhabiting and cultivating the same, shall be punished according to the law against communicating with rebels and enemies, and consequently suffer death by being beheaded."[10]

The imperial decree was nullified, however, once the Taiping rebellion demolished the Qing regime's control of South China and Western countries obtained exterritorial privileges in treaty ports along the coast. Since the end of the Opium War, many Western companies had openly set up offices in Canton to recruit laborers to work abroad. The Manchu court was powerless to stop the emigration, and it was finally forced to repeal the law when Britain and France defeated China again during the second Opium War (1856–60).[11]

Chinese immigration to California became more regular and better organized after 1852. Vessel masters, many of whom worked for American companies, advertised exaggerated accounts of the unmined gold in California on placards and pamphlets.[12] Labor brokers also printed greatly overblown stories about the wealth in America and distributed them widely, as shown in the following circular:

> Americans are very rich people. They want the Chinaman to come and make him very welcome. There you will have great pay, large houses and food and clothing of the finest description. You can write to your friends or send them money at any time and we will be responsible for the safe delivery. It is a nice country, without Mandarins or soldiers. All alike; big man no larger than little man. There are a great many Chinamen there now, and it will not be a strange country. . . . Come to Hong Kong, or to the sign of this house in Canton, and we will instruct you.[13]

It has often been said that the majority of the early Chinese immigrants to California were contract laborers who did not have much personal freedom. That is not true. Chinese immigration to North America, from the very beginning, was voluntary. Although only a few Chinese immigrants to California were able to pay ships' fares themselves, usually by mortgaging farms, houses, or small possessions, the pool system and credit-ticket arrangements enabled potential emigrants to fund their journey. Families and relatives would collect money to send one son to America first. Then it would be his responsibility to help his brothers or relatives emigrate. Neighbors or newly returned immigrants would sometimes lend money to a potential emigrant, expecting that he would soon make a fortune and repay the debt.

Statistics show that historically about a third of the Chinese going to North America and Australia bought passage through the pool system.[14] Most, however, came under the credit-ticket system. Under that arrangement, an emigrant's passage was paid in advance by labor brokers and then deducted from his pay in the ensuing months after his arrival. The system was organized by Chinese middlemen in cooperation with American shipping companies. The fact that the arrangement required references who could guarantee that the emigrant would return his fare partly explains why most who used it came from a relatively small area in Guangdong. Until after World War II, more than 80 percent of the Chinese immigrants to America were from a region consisting of eight counties in the Pearl River Delta around Canton.[15]

Internal turmoil and economic hardships, favorable reports of wealth in America, effective trans-Pacific traffic, and the availability of cheap ships' fares all combined to create a dramatic increase in Chinese immigration to California in 1852. Thereafter, arrivals became more regular. By 1882, when Congress passed the Chinese Exclusion Act, the Chinese population in the United States had reached about 150,000. Including those who returned home, some 322,000 Chinese took the Gold Mountain trip from 1849 to 1882 before the exclusion law prohibited their entries.[16]

As many scholars have pointed out, early Chinese immigrants in the United States confronted grueling labor and racial prejudice. But despite the bitterness that characterizes much of the Chinese experience in the late nineteenth century, their initial arrival did not cause much negative response from mainstream Americans.[17] Most evidence points to a certain degree of welcome for Chinese immigrants when they first came to North America.

Before the Gold Rush years, when Chinese immigration was limited to a trickle of sailors, merchants, and domestics, average Americans considered them as curiosities. With a limited understanding of China and little contact with the "Celestials," Americans' opinions of the Middle Kingdom was naive. Of course, the belief that the Chinese, as the first Asian group to emigrate to the United States, were admired is misleading.[18] Yet the conclusion that from the first boatload they were seen as either exotic curiosities or deceitful, cunning barbarians is also questionable. Although prejudice lived side by side with opportunity in frontier towns and mining camps in general, free competition and tolerance prevailed in the first few years of the Gold Rush.[19]

Because the Chinese provided a much-needed labor force and brought with them "exotic rituals" of celebration, their initial arrival prompted great interest and was welcomed. In Fourth of July parades and other public ceremonies, for example, their displays were often the most elaborate and were applauded vigorously. On August 29, 1850, when the news of President Zachary Taylor's death reached San Francisco, the Chinese were invited to participate in that city's funeral ceremony. The thank-you note written by leaders of the Chinese community on the following day to "Hon. John W. Geary, Mayor of the City of San Francisco" indicates the then-friendly relationship between the Chinese and the local authorities:

> Sir: The "China boys" wish to thank you for the kind mark of attention bestowed upon them in extending to them an invitation to join with the citizens of San Francisco in doing honor to the memory of the late President of the United States, General Zachary Taylor. The "China boys" feel proud of the distinction you have shown them, and will always endeavor to merit your good opinion and the good opinion of the citizens of their adopted country. . . . Strangers as they are among you, they kindly appreciate the many kindnesses received at your hands, and beg leave, with grateful hearts, to thank you.
> Ah-Sing
> A-He
> in behalf of the China boys.[20]

The favorable reception toward the early Chinese immigrants can also be seen in a comment made by California governor John McDougal. Speaking to a public gathering in January 1852, the outgoing governor called the Chinese "one of the most worthy classes of our newly adopted citizens—to whom the climate and character of these lands are peculiarly suited."[21] McDougal's enthusiastic speech was a marked contrast to the Chinese Exclusion Act passed by Congress three decades later.

## A Plea for Tolerance: A Message from Chinese Community Leaders

Deteriorating political and economic conditions at home continued to push the Chinese to California throughout the 1850s. Unfortunately, few could have expected the fair treatment they received before 1852. On the contrary, as Chinese emigration increased dramatically, Californians' initial acceptance for the newcomers gave way to animosity. As one Chinese American sociologist points out, "Whereas the Chinese had been praised for their industry, their honesty, their thrift, and their peaceful ways, they were now charged with being debased and servile coolies, clannish, dangerous, deceitful, and vicious."[22]

The dramatic change in the attitude of San Francisco's leading newspaper, the *Daily Alta California,* is a good example of the change in public perception. In the spring of 1851 the newspaper was still warmly pro-Chinese. Celebrating that "a young Chinese community will grow up in our mountains . . . there will be the building of a bridge connecting the Sierra Nevada with the Chinese wall," the *Alta* informed readers that "they [Chinese immigrants] are amongst the most industrious, quiet, patient people among us. . . . They seem to live under our laws as if born and bred under them."[23] But only two years later, its tone had changed. In an editorial on May 21, 1853, it was the same newspaper that declared, "The Chinese are morally a far worse class to have among us than the Negro . . . they are not of that kind that Americans can ever associate or sympathize with. They are not our people and never will be."[24] After the early 1850s, as an increasingly negative image of Chinese immigrants came into being, racial prejudice against Chinese gradually permeated all levels of California society, and a crescendo of persecutive legislation began to build.

Surrounded by such a hostile atmosphere, Chinese immigrants had to speak out to defend themselves. Viewing the discriminatory laws and regulations as unfair and unjust, they addressed numerous complaints to the federal government, mainstream politicians, and local authorities.[25] Although most Chinese immigrants at this point were unable to write in English, Chinese merchants who had been educated in schools set up by American or Western missionaries in Hong Kong and Canton after the 1820s had a very good command of the language. Beginning in the 1810s, Chinese youths were also being sent to the United States for schooling by American missionaries.[26] As a result, the late nineteenth century saw continuous proclamations from Chinese immigrants against institutionalized racism and the hostile treatment they encountered in American society. Among the more significant are the "Letter of the Chinamen to His Excellency, Governor Bigler" (1852), "To His Excellency, Governor Bigler from Norman Asing" (1852), "Remarks of the Chinese Merchants of San Francisco, upon Governor Bigler's Message and Some Common Objections" (1855), "The Chinese Question from a Chinese Standpoint" (1874), "To His Excellency U.S. Grant, President of the United States: A Memorial from Representative Chinamen in America" (1876), "A Memorial from the Six Chinese Companies: An Address to the Senate and House of Representatives of the United States" (1877), "Why Should the Chinese Go?" (1878), "A Letter to San Francisco Board of Education" (1885), "The Chinese Must Stay" (1889), "The Chinese Six Companies" (1894), "Chinese Exclusion, a Benefit or a Harm?" (1901), and "My Reception in America" (1907).[27]

Most such statements were written by Chinese merchants, especially leaders of the Chinese Consolidated Benevolent Association (CCBA). Popularly called the Six Companies, the association consisted of self-help and protection groups analogous to similar organizations in other immigrant communities. Its leaders were almost exclusively well-established individuals and merchants, successful businessmen, and editors of Chinese-language newspapers. Providing various defense functions when the rights of individual Chinese immigrants were denied, the Six Companies constituted a de facto government that oversaw the Chinese American community throughout the era. Because of its leading position and connection with both the Chinese and American governments, it acted as the spokesman for Chinese immigrants.[28] What its leaders wrote represented the views of established members of the Chinese community as well as their strategy for dealing with racism.

In general, the writings are characterized by a conciliatory posture and desire to accommodate. The earliest and perhaps most influential is "Letter of the Chinamen to His Excellency, Governor Bigler." Because in many ways the letter represents the ideas and style that were to appear repeatedly in numerous similar works, it deserves careful examination of both its background and context.

The letter—a five-page essay—was written first as a direct response to the anti-Chinese campaign launched by then-governor, John Bigler. On April 23, 1852, Bigler, a former lawyer from Pennsylvania and "a man who had neither the capacity, the education or manners to grace the position," presented a special message regarding Chinese immigration to the California legislature.[29] It was the first official public announcement in American history on assumed "Chinese evils." In customary lawyer-politician style, Bigler strongly denounced "the present wholesale importation to this country of immigrants from the Asiatic quarter of the Globe" and attacked the Chinese as unlawful "coolies." In order to "check the tide of Asiatic immigration," he submitted two propositions: to use the state's taxing power to stop the entry of Chinese laborers and to petition Congress for take action prohibiting "coolies" from working in the mines.[30]

It is unclear whether Bigler's motive was to use the politically expedient speech to capture the newly emerged popular anti-Chinese mood for his reelection or, as he declared, "to enhance the prosperity and ensure the tranquillity of the State." His message, however, further agitated feelings against the Chinese and marked the beginning of the anti-Chinese movement in California and on the West Coast. His accusation that the Chinese were "coolies, unassimilated, and dishonest" echoed in anti-Chinese propaganda until the World War II era.

At first stunned by open hostility from one of the most powerful politicians in California, the Chinese community quickly gathered its wits and reacted to counter Bigler's allegations. Leaders of San Francisco's Four Great Houses—the predecessor of the Chinese Six Companies—immediately consulted with American advisers about how to deal with the crisis, and only six days later the United States saw its first significant publication by Chinese immigrants. On April 29, 1852, the articulate "Letter of the Chinamen to His Excellency, Governor Bigler" was published simultaneously in San Francisco's two mainstream newspapers, the *Daily Alta California* and *San Francisco Herald*. Its message was marked by subtle barbs and an understated refutation of Bigler's accusations as well as a dignified, restrained pleading for tolerance.[31] Well composed in concise and graceful English, it was favorably received and widely reprinted.[32] As a historical document and one of the most influential published works by early Chinese immigrants, the essay today still impresses readers with its sharpness of logic and subtlety of style.

Unlike traditional petitions by civilians to government officials in imperial China, the letter's opening was unusually straightforward:

> Sir: The Chinamen have learned with sorrow that you have published a message against them. Although we are Asiatics, some of us have been educated in American schools and have learned your language, which has enabled us to read your message in the newspapers for ourselves, and to explain it to the rest of our countrymen. We have all thought a great deal about it, and after consultation with one another, we have determined to write you as decent and respectful a letter as we could, pointing out to your Excellency some of the errors you have fallen into about us.[33]

Its direct, firm approach makes the letter drastically different from the roundabout way and humble style of a traditional Chinese petition. The smooth and elegant English as well as the unemotional, sober method of argument indicate that it was a work that only people who had dexterous writing skills, a keen sensitivity to the Chinese experience in California, and a profound knowledge of Western culture could produce. Therefore, a question arises, What was the background of the two men—Hab Wa and Tong K. Achick—who wrote the first published work by Chinese in America? Both were merchants representing leading Chinese trading companies in San Francisco and were, as they claimed in the letter, "educated in American schools." Although not much information exists about Hab Wa, surviving documents do shed some light on the background of Tong K. Achick, who was an influential figure in San Francisco's Chinese community during the 1850s.

A native of Xiangshan [Zhongshan] County near Canton, Tong Achick was head of Ton Wo and Company, one of the largest Chinese-owned businesses in the San Francisco Bay area in the 1850s. As a child, he attended the then well-known Morrison School founded by American missionaries in Macao [Aomen]. Among his classmates were Yung Wing, who graduated from Yale College in 1854, and Lee Kan, an eminent English translator and editor of *The Oriental,* one of the earliest Chinese-language newspapers, published in San Francisco during the 1850s. Educated in an American school since his childhood, Tong, like his class-mates Yung and Lee, was thoroughly at ease in English, which undoubtedly helped him become a leader of the local Chinese community during the Bigler episode. He not only coauthored the letter but was also elected by Chinese mer-chants to head a delegation to Sacramento to meet the governor. In the ensuing years he served as spokesperson for the Chinese community and frequently act-ed as interpreter and translator in court for the Chinese Six Companies. Two of his translations, both testimony of the leaders of the Six Companies, were pub-lished in 1853 and in 1854, which shows that Tong continued to be an impor-tant figure in the Chinese community.[34]

The writing of the letter might also have involved the efforts of the American consultants of Chinese immigrants. Despite the powerful anti-Chinese atmo-sphere that dominated the West Coast throughout the nineteenth century, indi-vidual acts of defiance by mainstream Americans on behalf of Chinese were not unusual. There were people—members of the clergy, philanthropists, business-men, and public officials—who either sympathized with the Chinese or were in-terested in seeing them be acculturated. One, the Rev. William Speer (1822–1904), was an "active and eloquent spokesman for the Chinese." A former Presbyterian missionary who worked in China for several years, Speer was sent by the Presby-terian Board of Foreign Mission in New York to open a mission in San Francisco's Chinese community in 1852. A talented writer and an eloquent lecturer, he pub-lished extensively on China and Chinese, frequently spoke out to defend Chinese immigrants, set up the first Sunday school for the Chinese in San Francisco in 1854, and helped found *The Oriental* in 1855.[35] In fact, missionaries remained friendly and supportive of Chinese immigrants throughout the years and were often the sole public defenders of the Chinese in California, although their mo-tives were subject to controversy. In addition to compassion and humanitarian beliefs, what undoubtedly interested them in Chinese immigrants was the possi-bility of Christianizing the "pagan strangers" and converting "heathens" in the Celestial Empire. As an early missionary writer observed, "These intelligent, apt, industrious, but heathen people, awakened her warm sympathy, and she earnestly desires that others should think and feel and work for them. Unless we bless them with our Christianity, they will curse us with the vices and wickedness of heathen-ism."[36] Despite such evangelical enthusiasm, the missionaries' help and friend-ship was a great assistance to Chinese immigrants in the struggle against racial prejudice, and they remembered that support throughout the era.[37]

Following its polite but firm opening, the letter wastes no time in counter-ing Bigler's accusations. With convincing facts, it exposes one by one the mis-conceptions of his message. A large proportion was directed to the issue of the "coolies," a term not previously applied to Chinese immigrants until Bigler did so. Since then, the word has become a stereotype for Chinese immigrants who were believed to engage in slave labor and undercut American workers' wages. Because the image greatly distorted the size and fearsomeness of the reality of Chinese immigration, it was natural that it be the first important issue addressed in the letter:

> You speak of the Chinamen as "Coolies," and, in one sense, the word is ap-plicable . . . but not in that in which you seem to use it. "Cooly" is not a Chinese word: it has been imported into China from foreign parts, as it has been into this country. What its original signification was, we do not know; but with us it means a common laborer, and nothing more. We have never known it used among us as a designation of a class, such as you have in view—persons bound to labor under contracts which they can be forcibly compelled to comply with. . . . If you mean by "Coolies," laborers, many of our coun-trymen in the mines are "Coolies," and many again are not. There are among them tradesmen, mechanics, gentry, and school masters. . . . None are "Coo-lies," if by that you mean bound men or contract slaves.[38]

The real issue, however, concerned whether Chinese immigrants had done anything for the economic development of the state. Bigler had accused them of making no financial contribution to the land to which they had immigrated. Worse—and presumably at the root of the prejudice—they were mere sojourn-ers who had arrived solely to bleed the local economy, seize jobs from white workers, and reduce American families to starvation. The Chinese bought no real estate and benefited no banks. Their money hardly circulated because the bulk of it was sent right back to China. Their true interest, according to Bigler, was to "dig the precious metal and carry it back to China." Regarding the allegation, the letter replies tactfully:

> The Chinamen are indeed remarkable for their love of their country. . . . They honor their parents and age generally with a respect like religion, and have the deepest anxiety to provide for their descendants. . . . With such feelings as these, many return home with their money. . . . But not all; others—full as many as of other nations—invest their gains in merchandise and bring it into the country and sell it at your markets. It is possible, sir, that you may not be aware how great this trade is, and how rapidly it is increasing, and how many are now returning to California as merchants who came over originally as miners.

Of course, the authors were somewhat evasive on this point and did not clar-
ify the issue of whether the Chinese were sojourners. It is common knowledge
that the majority of Chinese immigrants at this point did intend to return home
rather than settle in the United States. Most dreamed of striking it rich in the
Gold Mountain and returning to China as wealthy and respected men for the
rest of their lives. But the Chinese were not alone in such a dream. People who
emigrated from other parts of the world shared the same goal. Indeed, many
European immigrants also viewed themselves only as "temporary toilers" in
America.[39] During the last three decades of the nineteenth century, for example,
the proportion of Italian immigrants returning home from the United States
fluctuated between 11 and 73 percent; the majority left within a few years of their
arrival. Immigration records also indicate that more than half of the immigrants
from Hungary, Croatia, and Slovia returned to Europe between 1908 and 1914.[40]
In comparison, the figure is smaller for Chinese. Even during the era of free
immigration (1849–82), only about half of Chinese immigrants who entered the
United States returned to China.[41]

Thus, differences between Chinese and European immigrants in the issue of
the "sojourner mentality" were of degree rather than of kind. Moreover, even if
the majority of Chinese immigrants were dominated by a sojourner mentality
and wanted to "carry the precious metal back to China," few could truly realize
that dream. Instead of returning home quickly with a fortune, many failed to
make any money and lost their lives in the United States; they were delivered
home only as cremated remains or bones. When the French ship *Asia* sailed to
China from San Francisco in 1858, for example, its cargo included 321 sets of
bones of those who had died in the Gold Mountain.[42] The death rate was even
higher when Chinese immigrants were recruited to construct transcontinental
railroads during the 1860s. According to some Chinese-language sources, between 1863 and 1869, more than 10 percent of the fourteen thousand Chinese
workers hired by the Central Pacific Railway lost their lives to accidents or dis-
ease.[43] Joaquin Miller [Cincinnatus Hiner Miller], a popular frontier writer, in
his novel *First Fam'lies of the Sierras* (1876) provided a sentimental picture of a
special caravan—"the caravan of the dead"—whose work was to collect the remains of Chinese across the frontier and return them to their old home:

> Every five years there is a curious sort of mule caravan seen meandering
> up and down the mining streams of California, where Chinamen are to be
> found. It is a quiet train. . . . In this train or caravan the drivers do not shout
> or scream. The mules, it always seemed to me, do not even bray. This cara-
> van travels almost always by night, and it is driven and managed almost al-

together by Chinamen. . . . These mules, both in coming in and going out of a camp, are loaded with little beech-wood boxes of about three feet in length and one foot square. . . . This is the caravan of the dead.[44]

In order to solicit broad support for their cause, the authors of the letter appealed directly to the monetary interests of people in San Francisco, from local merchants who did business with the Chinese to government officials concerned with public revenues. Apparently with the hope of impressing readers, they elaborated on the financial contribution the Chinese had made to California's economy. Although that amount is impossible to calculate, "the sum must be very large."[45] As their contemporary testified, Chinese merchants in California during the 1850s and 1860s enjoyed a high reputation for business ability and contributing to the local economy.[46]

According to the letter, San Francisco's business profited considerably from Chinese customers. The high sale of boots is an obvious example: "[Every] Chinaman [bought] one or more pairs immediately on landing." In fact, miners' leather boots became the first and most common article of American dress that Chinese immigrants adopted, because they found that their homemade cloth shoes were "no footwear to be worn in the rugged, stony, and muddy placer mines." "The first outfit Tai Ming purchased was a pair of heavy leather boots," writes a Chinese American author of an immigrant who arrived in San Francisco in the fall of 1850.[47] A reporter likewise remarked, "Even the lowliest [Chinese] miner adopted American boots for his work."[48]

The letter then claimed that the local economy must also have benefited greatly from Chinese imports, because "we employed your ships in preference to any others, even when we could get them cheaper." For those interested more in land speculation than the "noble idea" of the white man's California, the letter pointed out the Chinese investment in San Francisco real estate: "In this city alone there are twenty stores kept by Chinamen, who own lots and erected the buildings themselves."

The question of veracity is another issue Bigler raised in his message. The Chinese could not be believed, he warned, because "they are indifferent to the solemn obligation to speak the truth which an oath imposes." On this matter the letter offered a subtle barb aimed at the hypocritical demagogue. "We do not deny that many Chinamen tell lies, and so do many Americans, even in Courts of Justice." In explaining differences between Chinese and American customs in swearing to the truth, the letter argued, "We do not swear upon so many little occasions as you do . . . we are good men; we honor our parents . . . we pay our debts and are honest; and of course [we] tell the truth." Indeed, even politicians who supported Bigler's anti-Chinese campaign at that time admitted that "the Chinese merchants are men of integrity and uprightness in their dealings, and the mass of laborers are industrious and frugal."[49]

As for Bigler's allegations that the Chinese seemed neither interested in nor capable of becoming American citizens, the letter provided factual details concerning Chinese immigrants' moral standards, living situations, business attitudes, and willingness to assimilate into society at large. According to the letter, by 1852 there were already Chinese individuals in San Francisco, Boston, New York, and New Orleans who had become naturalized American citizens and married "free white American women."[50] "If the privileges of your laws are open to us," the letter continued, "some of us will doubtless acquire your habits, your language, your ideas, your feelings, your morals, your forms, and become citizens of your country; many have already adopted your religion in their own;— and we will be good citizens."

Having made the pledge, the letter finally ended with a plea: "In concluding this letter, we will only beg your Excellency not to be too hasty with us, to find us out and know us well, and then we are certain you will not command your Legislature to make laws driving us out of your country. Let us stay here—the Americans are doing good to us, and we will do good to them."

Such is the context and style of the first important piece of writing by Chinese immigrants in the United States. In addition to composing the letter, leaders of the Chinese community made other efforts to appease the governor's anti-Chinese attitude. One of the most dramatic episodes concerned a meeting with Bigler. Shortly after publication of the letter, Tong K. Achick headed a good-will delegation of leading Chinese merchants to Sacramento to visit the governor. Acting within typical Chinese tradition, they brought gifts—"shawls of rarest pattern, rolls of silk of the costliest texture, and some. . . . seventy handkerchiefs of the choicest description"—to the man who they thought controlled their fate. Although their attempt to persuade the governor to give up his anti-Chinese campaign was a total failure, the trip at least taught the Chinese merchants one thing—the style of American politicians. Bigler accepted the gifts but continued his anti-Chinese campaign.[51]

The Chinese community headed by merchants also employed other strategies to quiet growing anti-Chinese cries. They tried to gain standing with local society in various ways, most noticeably with money. When missionaries had difficulty raising funds to build a church near San Francisco's Chinatown in 1853, leading Chinese businessmen contributed more than $2,000, an impressive sum in those days.[52] They also donated money to schools, fire companies, police, and public charities in San Francisco and elsewhere in California. Of course, the idea of using money to buy tolerance is neither new nor an original invention by Chinese in California. It is a standard practice of ethnic merchants throughout the world. Jews in Europe, Armenians in Turkey, East Indians in Africa, and the Chinese themselves in Southeast Asia have repeatedly resorted to this means throughout history.[53] That the Chinese had to adopt the same strategy to win acceptance in California, where most of the population was immigrants, was ironic, however.

Chinese leaders also suggested a more significant solution to the problem of intolerance. One of the propositions Bigler had advanced was to levy an extra tax on Chinese to "check the present system of indiscriminate and unlimited Asiatic immigration." In order to show their willingness to accommodate, Chinese community leaders endorsed that proposition. In the spring of 1853, testifying before the Committee on Mines and Mining of the California legislature, they promised to help collect the tax and even proposed that it be increased. Since then, the Foreign Miners' License Tax was chiefly aimed at the Chinese (the state legislature specifically translated the tax law into Chinese) and became a significant resource for the state. Although European and Mexican miners greatly outnumbered them, by 1870, when amendments to the federal constitution nullified the law, Chinese immigrants were estimated to have paid 98 percent of the $491 million collected through the tax. It accounted for half of all the taxes collected in California and represented more than 10 percent of the state's total revenues during the two decades. When railroad construction drew away Chinese miners in the 1860s, many mining districts in California lamented the loss of that labor supply because revenues had been greatly reduced.[54]

At the very outset, the writing of the Chinese in the United States was a plea for tolerance. Although few publications from leaders of the Chinese community were as well written, the pleading tone and strategy of accommodation contained in "Letter of the Chinamen to His Excellency, Governor Bigler" were played out in most of the early work by Chinese immigrants. Unfortunately, the letter-writing effort as well as subsequent actions bore little fruit. Despite repeated pleas, the negative attitude of the larger society toward Chinese immigrants remained unchanged throughout the era. The ensuing decades saw anti-Chinese propaganda grow quickly, and legal discrimination followed proportionately.

In terms of the Chinese American experience, however, the letter was of special significance. It marked the first attempt by Chinese immigrants to employ a language not their own to express themselves and use their constitutional right to defend their interests. Within that context, the letter is a vivid fragment of Chinese American cultural history and represents a landmark in the struggle of Chinese immigrants against racial prejudice.

## Angry Voices: Protests and Complaints of the "Undistinguished" Chinese Immigrants

The relatively small Chinese population in the United States in its early days consisted largely of immigrant laborers inclined to return to their homeland. Living in an adverse environment and preoccupied with daily work, they had little time or desire to raise their sights beyond limited economic success; therefore, their point of view on the immigrant experience was rarely presented in writings published in America. That does not mean, however, that they remained completely silent about the struggle for survival in the Gold Mountain. Despite cultural obstacles and language barriers, they managed to express their feelings in various written forms. There are letters, journals, newspapers, and other writings that have survived. Although these texts have not gained much notice, they are a vivid record of the diverse lives of Chinese immigrants in goldfields, railroad construction camps, and segregated urban ghettos. The writings are often highly informal but construct a social history of early Chinese immigrants. Moreover, as attempts to convey indomitable courage and strength in the face of privation and loneliness they add personal dimension to a collective history of struggle and triumph.

Compared to the pleading tone and restrained attitude that characterized the writing of leaders of the Chinese American community, the work of average Chinese was often more outspoken and emotional. Perhaps because of contacts with working-class Americans, they seemed influenced by the concept of equality. As a result, ordinary Chinese immigrants—miners, railroad workers, farmhands, laundrymen, artisans, and small merchants—exercised a greater degree of defiance and showed a stronger group consciousness in demanding fair treatment than their more established leaders.

Such a phenomenon is not unique to the Chinese American community. As Kurt Lewin, a social psychologist, has pointed out, it is the general tendency for minority leaders, particularly those of underprivileged ethnic groups, to be marginal to their own people. The economic success or professional attainments of these minority leaders make them relatively acceptable outside the group, hence they are not always reliable as strategists and spokespeople for their own groups. They tend to be accommodating because they depend on mainstream society for recognition. Too, their policy of accommodation and posture of negotiation have frequently collided with attitudes of defiance and resistance from the rank and file of their own ethnic groups.[55]

"A Letter to San Francisco Board of Education," written by an individual Chinese in 1885 to protest educational segregation, is a case in point. Widely reported by the local press, the letter created a statewide sensation. Because it pinpointed an aspect of social life that had been greatly biased against the Chinese, it became one of the most important works by Chinese immigrants against racial discrimination during the late nineteenth century.

The author of the letter, Mary Tape, was a Chinese orphan from Shanghai who came to the United States with missionaries at the age of eleven and was brought up by the San Francisco's Ladies' Relief Society.[56] Her husband, Joseph Tape, also emigrated to California at an early age. Having learned English at a church-sponsored Sunday school, he served, in addition to working as an expressman and drayman, as an interpreter for Chinese labor contractors. To some extent, the couple was not a true part of the Chinese immigrant community. They were thoroughly Americanized in language, dress, and life-style and had converted to Christianity. The fact that they lived outside Chinatown and their children played with white children demonstrates their intention and eagerness to assimilate into the larger society. Despite their Americanization, however, they were treated by the society with which they sought to associate in the same way as were most other Chinese immigrants. When they tried to enroll their daughter Mamie in the neighborhood public school in 1884, she was denied entry, just like other Chinese children. Although there was abundant evidence to show that Mamie was native-born and spoke English more fluently than Chinese, the San Francisco Board of Education continued to reject her application to enter the school. Backed by the state superintendent of education, the board even resolved that any principal or teacher who admitted "a Mongolian child" would be subject to immediate dismissal.[57]

What the Tapes' daughter encountered was not a new experience for Chinese children. Throughout the era, access to American public education remained a contested issue in California. Although the Chinese were regular tax-payers, their children, native-born or not, were denied entry to public schools because of their status as "aliens." For decades, the only education available for them, apart from Chinese-language schools set up by the Six Companies, was through Sunday schools in or near Chinatown that churches sponsored because missionaries realized that learning English was a prerequisite to understanding the Gospel. When their battle against discriminatory education was lost in the 1870s, the Chinese in San Francisco, led by the Six Companies, accepted Sunday schools as a solution to the education problem.[58] The Tapes were not satisfied with that, however. Sunday schools were inconvenient for their children because the family did not live in Chinatown. Moreover, they did not want to be treated as second-class citizens. The couple refused to bow their heads and accept rejection. They took their case to court.

The case caused a sensation throughout the city because by then the number of Chinese children in San Francisco had increased to such a degree that local authorities could no longer afford to ignore the situation. Many residents were shocked to learn that nearly a thousand Chinese children were shut out of the schools.[59] Both the San Francisco superior court and the California Supreme Court ruled in the Tapes' favor on the basis that "[to] deny a child, born of Chinese parents in this State, entrance to the public schools would be a violation of the law of the State and the Constitution of the United States."[60]

Despite the favorable verdict, however, Mary Tape's efforts to enroll her daughter in a public school failed. The board of education circumvented the ruling by establishing a separate school for Chinese children in a rented room above a grocery store in Chinatown. In response, Mary Tape wrote the board a scathing protest. Dated April 8, 1885, her letter was read before the board and reprinted in full in the local press. It reads in part:

> Dear Sirs: I see that you are going to make all sorts of excuses to keep my child out off the Public Schools. Dear sirs, Will you please tell me! Is it a disgrace to be born a Chinese? Didn't God make us all!!! What right! have you to bar my children out of the school because she is a Chinese Descend. They is no other worldly reason that you could keep her out, except that I suppose, you all goes to churches on Sundays! Do you call that a Christian act to compel my little children to go so far to a school that is made in purpose for them. . . . You have expended a lot of the Public money foolishly, all because of a one poor little Child. . . . It seems no matter how a Chinese may live and dress so long as you know they Chinese. Then they are hated as one. There is not any right or justice for them.[61]

In conclusion, Mary Tape declared defiantly, "May you Mr. Moulder [the San Francisco school superintendent], never be persecuted like the way you have persecuted little Mamie Tape. Mamie Tape will never attend any of the Chinese schools of your making! Never!!! I will let the world see sir What justice there is When it is govern by the Race prejudice men!" The letter, with grammatical errors and a plain style, was no match for the smooth and elegant messages of Chinese merchants. But Mary Tape's courage and her indignation in demanding justice marked a sharp contrast to the feeble protest and pleading tone of established leaders of the Chinese community.[62]

Another, perhaps more interesting, example of an angry voice is found in the autobiographical sketch of Lee Chew, a Chinese laundryman in New York. The "lifelet"—as its editor called it—appeared in a collection entitled *The Life Stories of Undistinguished Americans as Told by Themselves* (1906), edited by Hamilton Holt, a progressive and publisher of *The Independent*, "a secular, liberal journal of general interests" in New York.[63] Lee's story is perhaps one of the most significant and representative works by an ordinary Chinese immigrant in the exclusion era. Its factual content and mode of thought are typical of that of many working-class Chinese immigrants in America during this period.[64] For that reason, the lifelet has become an important document for the study of early Chinese American history and is frequently quoted in work about the Chinese American experience.[65]

There is no official record available about Lee's personal background owing to his humble origin. From his own account, we know he came from the Si Kiang area [the Xijiang River], part of the Pearl River Delta near Canton from which the bulk of the nineteenth-century Chinese laborers to America emigrated. Like many others, he began his career in America as a house servant and learned English in Sunday school in San Francisco. By working hard and saving virtually every penny, he managed to open a small laundry and finally settled in New York: "I was getting $5 a week and board, and putting away about $4.25 a week . . . I worked for two years as a servant, getting at the last $35 a month. I sent money home to comfort my parents . . . saved $50 in the first six months, $90 in the second, $120 in the third and $150 in the fourth. So I had $410 at the end of two years."[66] Lee's precise discussion on his finances, particularly the emphasis on budgeting skills, reveals how Chinese immigrant laborers managed their lives. It also permits comparisons of financial matters among immigrants from other parts of the world.

Despite his "humble" background, however, there is clearly a defiant tone in Lee's narrative. He forcefully expressed opinions that were generally held by his "undistinguished" countrymen, especially concerning the American public's misconceptions of his profession. To some extent, Chinese laundries had become landmarks in American cities by the late nineteenth century. An English visitor who traveled in the United States in the 1880s reported that most towns looked the same because they all had "the same wide streets, crossing at right angles . . . the same shops, arranged on the same plan, the same Chinese laundries with Li Kow visible through the window."[67]

Until the World War II era, laundering was a popular occupation for Chinese in the United States, and most Americans thought it was a typical Chinese business. Lee Chew argued forcefully, however, that Chinese laundries were an "American product." No laundries were in China at the time: "All the Chinese laundrymen here were taught in the first place by American women just as I was taught." According to Lee, the laundry business became a popular occupation for Chinese immigrants because it required little capital and was one of the few opportunities available: "Men of other nationalities who are jealous of the Chinese, . . . have raised such a great outcry about Chinese cheap labor that they have shut him out of working on farms or in factories or building railroads or making streets or digging sewers. He cannot practice any trade, and his opportunities to do business are limited to his own countrymen. So he opens a laundry when he quits domestic service."[68]

Life as a laundryman was full of hardship and humiliation, particularly in the West. Lee recalled that he and his friends suffered numerous harassments and were often driven by mobs from one mining camp to another: "We had to put up with many insults and some frauds, as men would come in and claim parcels that did not belong to them, saying they had lost their tickets, and would fight if they did not get what they asked for . . . many of the miners were wild men who carried revolvers and after drinking would come into our place to shoot and steal shirts, for which we had to pay. One of these men hit his head hard against a flat iron and all the miners came and broke up our laundry, chasing us out of town." Even in a cosmopolitan place such as New York, things were not necessarily better. Chinese laundrymen had to put wire screens over their businesses' windows because street boys often broke the windows "while the police seemed to think it a joke."

One of the frequent accusations leveled against Chinese immigrants was that they brought prostitution along with them. Most who wrote about Chinese immigrants in America, whether hostile or sympathetic, have echoed that charge. Sing-song girls and brothels became symbolic of Chinatowns in popular American culture.[69] Lee found that sinister misconception outrageous and argued fierily that prostitution was largely a result of institutionalized discrimination against the Chinese. He was, of course, not alone in his frustration and cynicism over alleged "Chinese vices." Responding to accusations made against "Chinese prostitution problems," a leader of San Francisco's Chinatown had commented sarcastically, "Yes, yes, Chinese prostitution is bad. What do you think of German prostitutes, French prostitutes, Spanish prostitutes, and American prostitutes? Do you think them very good?"[70] Moreover, contrary to the popular sensational stories about sing-song girls, the majority of prostitutes then active in Chinatowns, according to Lee, were "American ladies" who had both Chinese and white patrons. Because of the Chinese Exclusion Act, Lee pointed out, "In all New York there are less than forty Chinese women, and it is impossible to get a Chinese woman out here unless one goes to China and marries her there, and then he must collect affidavits to prove that she really is his wife. That is in case of a merchant. A laundryman can't bring his wife here under any circumstances." Consequently, the Chinese American community around the turn of the century remained predominantly a "bachelor society" that had an extremely unbalanced sex ratio. In 1900 the sex ratio between Chinese men and women was 12:1 in California; in Boston the ratio was 36:1; in New York, 50:1; and 19:1 in continental America.[71]

Because of language barriers and racial segregation, Chinese immigrants, especially laborers, were rarely understood and accepted by the larger society. Hence there was little chance for them to marry women of other ethnic groups. Although there were no laws against intermarriage between Chinese and Caucasians in most eastern states, Americans in general appeared to oppose such marriages until the 1960s.[72] Even Jacob A. Riis, whose enthusiastic desire for urban reform was shown in the classic *How the Other Half Lives* (1890), was dismayed at contacts between white women and Chinese men. Talking about Chinese immigrants, he sounded like a bigoted nativist: "I am convinced that he [a Chinese] adopts Christianity, when he adopts it at all, as he puts on American clothes, with what the politicians would call an ulterior motive, some sort of gain in the near prospect—washing, a Christian wife, perhaps, anything he happens to rate for the moment above his cherished pigtail."[73] To be sure, the comment did not represent Riis's well-intentioned reform urge, yet if he, a progressive and an immigrant himself, was biased against interracial marriages it is not hard to imagine how average Americans would treat the issue. "If Chinese marry American women," Lee observed, "there is a great outcry." Under such circumstances, he asked bitterly, "Is it any wonder, therefore, or any proof of the demoralization of our people if some of the white women in Chinatown are not of good character? What other set of men so isolated and so surrounded by alien and prejudiced people are more moral?"

It is interesting that the insider's perspective, while it serves to make Lee's story a strong protest against injustice in American society and demonstrates his "Chineseness," also reflects traces of his "Americanness." Lee's outspokenness and willingness to talk about his immigrant experience show that he had already undergone some Americanization. The value systems indicated by his defiant tone are compatible with the progressive tradition of American culture. It would be difficult to believe that he could make the same frank and critical statements without being familiar with the behavior and attitudes of American workers of the era, the "rough miners" and "tough railroad workers" who were his primary customers. Lee's problematic generalizations about other immigrants also reveal the influence of racial bias on ethnic American society. The comment that "Irish fill the almshouses and prisons orphan asylums, and Italians are among the most dangerous of men" is typical of immigrants' general tendency to consider their own respective groups better than others. Lee's opinions also coincide with prejudices displayed by other immigrants in the same volume, for example, Irish anti-Semitism and French hatred of Germans.[74]

Even compared with the "undistinguished Americans" from other countries, Lee's story stands out in one respect: He was virtually the only one who intended to return to his old home. The reason was simple: Unlike immigrants from Europe, Chinese were permanent aliens in America because they were denied the right to be American citizens. This proves that while faith in the American dream and its possibilities was widespread, it was not universal. To those of the "right race," America appeared to be the Promised Land and a utopian paradise, but immigrants of the "wrong race" must have felt disillusionment and despair as their notions of America, the land of freedom, clashed with reality. Lee's critical conclusion (also the ending of the first edition of Holt's book) illustrates the point: "More than half the Chinese in this country would become citizens if allowed to do so, and would be patriotic Americans. But how can they make this country their home as matters are now? . . . Under the circumstances, how can I call this my home, and how can any one blame me if I take my money and go back to my village in China?"[75]

Compared with the fulfilled expectations of progress (or at least some advancement) that many immigrants experienced in America, Lee's bitter statement was a strong contrast to optimistic "melting-pot" advocates. It seems to forecast the conclusion made by Nathan Glazer and Daniel Patrick Moynihan half a century later: The point about the melting pot is that it never happened.[76]

The unusually tormenting experiences and oppressive conditions that early Chinese immigrants encountered also caused their publications to reflect characteristics rarely seen in the writing of other immigrant groups. A sense of uncertainty pervaded their work, even in the most functional writing. An English-Chinese Phrase Book (1875) reflects that sense of insecurity.[77] Compiled by Wong Sam, a Chinese businessman affiliated with the Wells Fargo Bank in San Francisco, the 299-page phrase book was based on the practical experience of earlier Chinese immigrants in their dealings with mainstream Americans. Widely circulated, it taught English words and phrases of practical value in matters of work, self-defense, and everyday survival. Its carefully selected vocabulary made clear what sort of lives Chinese immigrants could expect. The section on "Names, Places, Etc.," for example, began with English words that were thought necessary for a Chinese immigrant to memorize: "pirate, robber or thief, rascal, swindler, kidnapper, gambler, enemy, murderer, criminal, missionary, preacher, physicians."[78] Even the sample letter contained in the book can be seen as warning newly arrived Chinese that economic prospects in the land of opportunity were not always as bright as they had envisioned:

I left San Jose full of expectation of getting work here, but after the lapse of two weeks without success, I have determined to set out for my old home [Canton]. I write this note to let you know of my intentions, and to thank you for the very kind manner in which you treated me; and be assured that wherever I may be I shall always think of you with kindness. I sail on the first of next month. Give my regards to all. Bidding you good-bye, I remain

Yours, truly,

Ah Ching[79]

Although the book includes sentences such as "I understand how to work. Have you any work for me to take home to do?" and "I will come for them to-morrow," most of its pages are full of lines considered critical for a Chinese immigrant's survival:

I cannot trust you.
I have made an apology, but still he wants to strike me.
He took it from me by violence.
He assaulted me without provocation.
He tried to obtain my baggage by false pretenses.
He claimed my mine.
He squatted on my lot.
He tries to extort money from me.
They are going to extort a confession from him by false pretensions.
The confessions were extorted from them by threats.
He cheated me out of my wages.
He defrauded me out of my salary.
He falsely accused me of stealing his watch.
They were lying in ambush.
He was murdered by a thief.
He was choked to death with a lasso, by a robber.
He committed suicide.
He was strangled to death by a man.
He was starved to death in prison.
He was frozen to death in the snow.
He tried to kill me by assassination.
He was shot to death by his enemy.
He wrongfully deprived me of my wages.
It was ill treatment.
Have you no way to take revenge?
He refused to pay the money which he owes me.
He won't dare to go home without a guard.
The immigration will soon be stopped.[80]

The wide range of vocabulary and phrases concerning harsh working conditions, violence, persecution, and death reveals why "a Chinaman's chance"—meaning "no chance at all"—became a familiar saying throughout the West and what kind of justice the Chinese could expect.[81] It proves indirectly that even before anti-Chinese sentiment gained momentum in the late 1870s, mistreatment of Chinese had already become common on the West Coast. Bret Harte, a local colorist and the foremost writer of frontier fiction, was aware of the situation and in "An Episode of Fiddletown" (1873) described how Ah Fe, a Chinese miner, was bullied on a trip to San Francisco:

> On the road to Sacramento he was twice playfully thrown from the top of the stage-coach by an intelligent but deeply intoxicated Caucasian. . . . At Hangtown he was beaten by a passing stranger, purely an act of Christian supererogation. At Dutch Flat he was robbed by well-known hands from unknown motives. At Sacramento he was arrested on suspicion of being something or other, and discharged with a severe reprimand—possibly for not being it, and so delaying the course of justice. At San Francisco he was freely stoned by children of the public schools; but by carefully avoiding these monuments of enlightened progress, he at last reached in comparative safety the Chinese quarters, where his abuse was confined to the police and limited by the strong arm of the law.[82]

Even the California State Legislature found in 1862 that "there [had] been a wholesale system of wrong and outrage practiced upon the Chinese population of this state, which would disgrace the most barbarous nation upon earth."[83]

The phrase book also contains some Christian teachings. Rather than listing them in a separate section, however, they were mixed with the phrases of Confucius and ideas about practical matters, as if to hint that Chinese readers could use them to defend themselves or help strike a bargain with white Americans when in trouble. Hence, as Chinese American scholars point out, one way to appreciate the literary sensibility of the phrase book is to recognize what its structure implies. It functioned as "an internal manual of strategy" to teach Chinese to use Christian views in responding to white Americans.[84] The sequence of the following sentences is fascinating and meaningful:

> Please give me now that portion of my wages which you have withheld from
>     me.
> Christ is our mediator.
> I am taller than he.

And:

> I was very lucky, because the stone almost struck me.
> Christians bear great trials.
> The man is very subtle.

And:

> No one can go to Heaven without
> being a Christian.
> I am thirsty.
> Some men have much riches.[85]

The use of Christian teachings as a vehicle for Chinese immigrants to communicate with mainstream Americans is significant. The author's unconscious (or perhaps conscious) revelation of how Christian values might work for Chinese immigrants is ironic and a matter of deep human interest. That Christian teachings were used by Chinese not as prayers but as ways to achieve higher esteem and improve their condition in an unfriendly environment presents a fascinating picture of the social experience of the Chinese in America. It also helps explain why there were so few conversions in the nineteenth century despite the time and energy missionaries devoted to converting Chinese immigrants. Although the Chinese were enthusiastic about attending Sunday school, their interest in Christianity rarely went beyond using it as the only available means to study English.

Faced with a disappointing number of Chinese converts, many missionaries finally gave up their attempts to recruit Chinese.[86] Although the reason is complicated, it must be strongly related to the mistreatment Chinese immigrants received in what was purportedly a "Christian nation," which made them suspect the value of Christianity itself. As Riis observed in *How the Other Half Lives:* "How shall the love of God be understood by those who have been nurtured in sight only of the greed of man?"[87]

## Song of Hearts of Sorrow: The Angel Island Poetry

> This place is called an island of immortals,
> When, in fact, this mountain wilderness is a prison.
> Once you see the open net, why throw yourself in?
> It is only because of empty pockets I can do nothing else.[88]

This is one of the poems written by Chinese held at the immigration station on Angel Island. Composed in a bitter tone and full of frustration and deep sorrow, the poems are testimony to the indignity the immigrants suffered at the detention center on Angel Island and provide a glimpse of a special chapter of Chinese American history.

Like Ellis Island in New York Harbor, where immigrants from Europe first saw America, Angel Island, situated in the middle of San Francisco Bay, was both a gateway and a barrier for Chinese entering the United States in the early twentieth century.[89] The Exclusion Act of 1882 did not completely halt Chinese immigration. In addition to the exempt classes, the act also allowed the entry of children of those Chinese who had acquired the right of residence in the United States before 1882. Moreover, when the San Francisco earthquake and fire destroyed the city's immigration records in 1906, a significant number of Chinese immigrants took the opportunity to claim American birth fraudulently. Under immigration laws, children, even if born abroad, of Chinese who were American citizens could claim citizenship and come to the United States. The right of derivative citizenship explains why more Chinese were admitted as American citizens between 1920 and 1940 than as aliens (52 percent as American citizens against 48 percent as aliens).[90]

Modeled after Ellis Island, Angel Island was used as a "filtering center" to hold Asian immigrants, primarily Chinese but also Japanese and Koreans, until their admissibility could be verified. At any given time between two and three hundred Chinese were detained there. During its three-decade-long existence, the immigration station processed around 175,000 Chinese entries and deported about 10 percent of that number.[91] The procedure usually took from several days to a few weeks, depending upon the backlog of cases and length of time involved in processing documents considered questionable. For those whose applications had been denied and were awaiting decisions on their appeals, the process could last several months or even two or three years.

Compared to the experience of others who immigrated to the United States, detention at Angel Island was humiliating for the Chinese—much worse than Ellis Island was for Europeans. The fact that Chinese immigrants called Angel Island a "Devil's Pass" indicates what sort of treatment they received there. The memory of being confined as common criminals upon arrival left residual scars on their psyches and shaped the impression that America was dominated by racism:

I am distressed that we Chinese are detained in this wooden building.
It is actually racial barriers which cause difficulties on Yingtai Island.

Even while they are tyrannical, they still claim to be humanitarian.
I should regret my taking the risk of coming in the first place.[92]

The poems demonstrate that if the majority of early Chinese immigrants were dominated by a sojourner mentality, it was caused by the fact that they had found, from the time they landed in America, that they were unwelcome. As a Chinese American sociologist points out, "Although historically many early Chinese immigrants did not intend to settle in America, how long their sojourner attitude lasted is still debatable. In addition, it is more probable that an interrelationship existed between white hostility and Chinese sojourning psychology, rather than a one-way casual relationship which has been assumed."[93]

Most of the detained swallowed their bitterness and awaited their fate in solitude, but many vented emotion by writing Chinese-language poems on the walls. Their worries and feelings of disappointment, indignation, frustration, self-pity, homesickness, and loneliness were captured in verse:[94]

Alas, yellow souls suffer under the brute force of the white race!
.   .   .   .   .   .
Like a pig chased into a basket, we are sternly locked in.
Our souls languish in a snowy vault;
we are really not even the equal of cattle and horses.
Our tears shower the icy day; we are not even equal to bird or fowl.[95]

More than 135 poems have survived.[96] Although most did not come to light until the 1970s, a few were published at the time they were written and appeared in various Chinese newspapers, journals, and books in the United States and China. Perhaps the earliest was printed by the *World Journal*, a Chinese-language newspaper in San Francisco, on March 16, 1910, only three months after the immigration center opened officially.[97]

For many detainees at Angel Island, their interrogation by immigration officials was harrowing. Chinese immigrants, regardless of the validity of their claims, were considered guilty of carrying false entry papers unless proven innocent. In order to screen applicants, authorities set up a board of special inquiry and established a system of interrogation for every newly arrived immigrant. The hearings usually lasted five or six hours over a period of three or four days, and immigrants were not notified of the results for several days.

The primary purpose of the inquiry system was to screen "paper sons."[98] Many who had valid claims were also denied entry, however, because the questions, devised to outwit and trap the immigrants, were often so absurd that even legitimate immigrants could be easily stumped.[99] As an immigrant recounts:

My deepest impression of Angel Island now was the rudeness of the white interrogators. They kept saying, "Come on, answer, answer." They kept rushing me to answer until I couldn't remember the answers anymore. . . . One strange question they asked me was: "What is your living room floor made of?" I replied, "Brick." They said, "Okay. What is the floor under your bed made of?" So I thought if the living room floor was brick, then the bedroom must also be brick. So I said, "brick!" They typed the answer down and didn't say anything. The next day, they asked me the same question and I replied, "Brick" again. They said my father had said it was dirt. What happened was that the floor was dirt at first, but later, after my father left for America, I changed the floor myself to brick.[100]

There are undocumented reports of suicides among the Chinese detained at Angel Island. The Rev. Edward Lee, who worked as an interpreter for the immigration service in the San Francisco Bay area in the 1920s and 1930s, recalled a newly arrived woman who heard that her entry was denied and she might be deported back to China. Feeling that would be a shame, she sharpened a pair of chopsticks, thrust them in her ear through to her brain, and died.[101]

It was understandable, then, that many immigrant poets expressed deep hatred toward immigration authorities and fiercely denounced the institutionalized racist policies. Angry and poignant in their directness and simplicity of language, the poems often contained a courage and indomitability rarely identified with Chinese immigrants:

The low building with three beams merely shelters the body.
It is unbearable to relate the stories accumulated on the Island slopes.
Wait till the day I become successful and fulfill my wish,
I will not speak of love when I level the immigration station![102]

Chinese immigrants resented not only the discriminatory inquiry system of Angel Island but also the deplorable living conditions there. The quality of the food was poor. The average cost per meal, 12 cents in 1911, had fallen to 8 cents in 1916 rather than rising with inflation.[103] Locked in overcrowded barracks filled with bunk beds, immigrants were allowed little freedom of movement and denied the right to meet visitors because immigration authorities feared collusion about the interrogation. Sanitary facilities were few. As a result, an immigrant who had been detained there recalled, "I soon became dirty and full of lice. After three months, I was called for interrogation. The inspector only asked me my father's name; then I was landed. The interpreter told me I was lucky, because the sight of lice crawling all over me caused the inspector to cut short questioning."[104]

In addition to poor food and miserable living conditions, there was also general indignation among the immigrants. In 1925 alone, troops had to be called in to stop two protest riots that had broken out in the detention center. The frequency of the outbreaks demonstrated frustrations and anguish caused by harsh treatment. The emotions were clearly reflected in the poems:

> I, a seven-foot man, am ashamed I cannot extend myself.
> Curled up in an enclosure, my movements are dictated by others.
> Enduring a hundred humiliations, I can only cry in vain.
> This person's tears fall, but what can the blue heavens do?

And:

> I thoroughly hate the barbarians because they do not respect justice.
> They continually promulgate harsh laws to show off their prowess.
> They oppress the overseas Chinese and also violate treaties.
> They examine for hookworms and practice hundreds of despotic acts.[105]

Chinese detained at Angel Island were aware that immigrants from other countries were processed and released within a much shorter time. They attributed the unequal treatment to the fact that China was a weak country unable to intervene on their behalf like other "fighting nations." As one remarked, "The Japanese detention quarters were next to ours. . . . They did not need to have hearings and were free to go ashore within twenty-four hours. That could be because the diplomacy of a strong nation forced lenient implementation of the immigration laws.[106] Lamenting the fate of China (e.g., "We Chinese of a weak nation / Can only sigh at the lack of freedom") thus became a major theme:

> I bought an oar and arrived in the land of the Gold Mountain.
> Who was to know they would banish me to Island?
> If my country had contrived to make herself strong,
> this never would have happened.
> Then when the ship had docked, we could have gone directly ashore.[107]

Such feelings compounded an increasingly strong national consciousness that had arisen among the Chinese since the overthrow of the Qing Dynasty in 1911. Therefore, some poems contained the defiant wish that China become a powerful nation and wreak vengeance on the United States:

> I beat my breast when I think of China and cry bitterly like Ruan Ji.
> Our country's wealth is being drained by foreigners,

causing us to suffer national humiliations.
My fellow countrymen, have foresight, plan to be resolute,
And vow to conquer the U.S. to avenge the previous wrongs![108]

Not all poems, however, possessed such a strong political tone. Many simply bemoaned the poet's personal situation and are infused with deep sorrow and self-pity:

Imprisoned in this wooden building, I am always sad and bored.
I remember since I left my native village, it has been several full moons.
The family at home is leaning on the door,
urgently looking for letters.
Whom can I count on to tell them I am well?[109]

Because early Chinese immigrants were dominated by a sojourner mentality, illusions of retiring one day to their home villages with small fortunes helped them endure hardships and mistreatment. Even while trapped in the detention center and waiting anxiously for court decisions, many still dreamed of making and saving money quickly to pay off debts and rejoin families in China:

There are tens of thousands of poems composed on these walls.
They are all cries of complaint and sadness.
The day I am rid of this prison and attain success,
I must remember that this chapter once existed.
In my daily needs, I must be frugal.
Needless extravagance leads youth to ruin.
All my compatriots should please be mindful.
Once you have some small gains, return home early.[110]

Unfortunately, few were able to make gains and return home early. No reliable return migration figures are available for the first half of the twentieth century, but dreams of China remained only dreams for most sojourners. A decade-long civil war following the overthrow of the Manchu court in 1911, Japan's invasion of China in the 1930s and 1940s, and the communist victory in 1949 all combined to shatter dreams of returning to China as wealthy "Gold Mountain travelers." Instead, many remained stranded in America's Chinatowns and lived out their miserable lives as poor and lonely bachelors. In one Chinese-language account, an old man in San Francisco's Chinatown has lost hope of returning home as a wealthy "Gold Mountain traveler" and expresses disillusionment:

"Let's go to America!
Let's go to America!
Let's go to America!"
The cries were sung out loudly and exaltingly. Thereupon America became
the utopia of my grandfather's generation. Now here I am in this paradise.
But where is it?[111]

In addition to such sentiments, there are also poems by those who sought to
tell their stories to fellow immigrants. So as to encourage detainees to likewise
endure hardships, these poems contain frequent references to the traditional
Chinese philosophy of self-control or allusions to famous heroic figures in Chinese history who faced adversity:

The male eagle is also easy to tame.
One must be able to bend before one can stretch.
.   .   .   .   .   .
Confucius was surrounded in Chen for seven days.
Great men exhibit quality,
Scholars take pride in being themselves.
Gains and losses are entangled in my bosom.
My restlessness is a sign of self-illumination.[112]

And:

I leave word for my compatriots not to worry too much.
They mistreat us but we need not grieve.
Han Xin was straddled by a bully's trousers yet became a general.
Goujian endured humiliation and ultimately avenged his wrong.
King Wen was imprisoned at Youli and yet destroyed King Zhou.
Even though fate was perverse to Jiang Taigong,
still he was appointed marquis.
Since days of old, such has been the fate of heroes.
With extreme misfortune comes the composure to
await an opportunity for revenge.[113]

One poet even compared the confinement of Chinese immigrants at Angel Island to that of Napoleon on Saint Helena Island:

This is a message to those who live here not to worry excessively.
Instead, you must cast your idle worries to the flowing stream.
Experiencing a little ordeal is not hardship.
Napoleon was once a prisoner on an island.[114]

In addition to displaying a wide range of knowledge, the poems are significant in another respect. Their images and diction indicate that their authors must have been well-versed in classical Chinese poetry.[115] Together with their rich allusions, the poems' literary craftsmanship shatters the stereotype that detainees at Angel Island were illiterate peasants who claimed citizenship by birth or by derivation. As one Eurasian writer discovered through frequent contacts with Chinese immigrant laborers at the time, "Many of the Chinese laundrymen I know are not laundrymen only, but artists and poets, often the sons of good families."[116]

The establishment of a *zizhihui* [self-governing association] by detainees at the immigration center in 1922 also suggests that a significant number of Chinese immigrants coming to America during the exclusion era were highly educated. As several Chinese American scholars have pointed out, although the idea of organizing a self-governing body for collective redress and maintaining self-order was nothing new, forming such a group under extraordinarily adverse circumstances was clear evidence that many detainees were politically progressive and knew how to provide mutual aid in a hostile environment.[117]

What makes the Angel Island poems appealing to an audience today is not only artistic excellence but also the fact that they portray the emotional responses of Chinese immigrants to racial prejudice, which makes them valuable in the study of the Chinese American experience. As a mirror that captures an image of the past, the poetry stands on its own and occupies a singular place in the writing of early Chinese immigrants. Symbolizing what their predecessors experienced, it is an important legacy to all Chinese Americans and proves that "in the vast iconography of the American experience a place must be found for Angel Island."[118]

## Notes

1. The epigraph is from John R. Wunder, "Law and Chinese in Frontier Montana," *Montana* 30 (Summer 1980): 20.

2. Li Chunhui et al., *Meizhou huaqiao huaren shi* [A history of Chinese immigration to North and South America], (Beijing: Dongfang, 1990), 115; Yang Guobiao, Liu Hanbiao, and Yang Anyao, *Meiguo huaqiao shi* [A history of the Chinese in the United States], (Guangzhou: Guangdong Jiaoyu, 1989), 45. Also see Jack Chen, *The Chinese of America* (New York: Harper and Row, 1980), 5, 11; and H. Brett Melendy, *The Oriental Americans* (New York: Twayne Publishers, 1972), 15.

3. Ronald Takaki, *Strangers from a Different Shore: A History of Asian Americans* (Boston: Little, Brown, 1989), 79.

4. Quoted in Roger Daniels, *Asian America: Chinese and Japanese in the United States since 1850* (Seattle: University of Washington Press, 1988), 14. A missionary doctor from Massachusetts, Peter Parker opened the first foreign hospital in China in 1835. Even Parker

used the term *Gold Mountain* to refer to America in his letter, showing how people in Canton received the news of the gold discovery in California. For a detailed discussion on Parker's activities in Canton, see Jonathan Spence, *To Change China: Western Advisers in China, 1620–1960*, rev. ed. (New York: Penguin Books, 1980), 34–56.

5. Him Mark Lai, Joe Huang, and Don Wong, *The Chinese of America, 1785–1980* (San Francisco: Chinese Culture Foundation, 1980), 20.

6. Contained in Marlon K. Hom, ed. and trans., *Songs of Gold Mountain: Cantonese Rhymes from San Francisco Chinatown* (Berkeley: University of California Press, 1987), 39.

7. Him Mark Lai, *Cong huaqiao dao huaren* [From overseas Chinese to Chinese Americans], (Hong Kong: Joint, 1992), 3–6; Li et al., *A History of Chinese Immigration to North and South America*, 22–37.

8. For discussions on the impact of the Taiping Rebellion on the Canton area, see Frederic E. Wakeman, *Strangers at the Gate: Social Disorder in South China, 1839–1861* (Berkeley: University of California Press, 1966).

9. It is necessary to point out that the Chinese immigration to California represented only a very small part of the extensive exodus from China to other countries, particularly to Southeast Asia. It is estimated that three million Chinese emigrated during the second half of the nineteenth century, and another five million went abroad in the first four decades of the twentieth century. In addition, some early Chinese immigrants to California were the Taiping rebels who fled from the Manchu regime's crackdown. Being politically more sophisticated than other immigrants, they provided the Chinese American community with leadership in the early days. See Lynn Pan, *Sons of the Yellow Emperor: A History of the Chinese Diaspora* (New York: Kodansha International, 1994), 1–57; S. W. Kung, *Chinese in American Life: Some Aspects of Their History, Status, Problems, and Contributions* (Seattle: University of Washington Press, 1962), 3–29; and Feng Ziping, *Haiwai chunqiu* [The Chinese diaspora], (Shanghai: Shangwu, 1993), 22–23.

10. Cited in Laura L. Wong, "Chinese Immigration and Its Relationship to European Development of Colonies and Frontiers," in *The Chinese American Experience: Papers from the Second National Conference on Chinese American Studies (1980)*, ed. Genny Lim (San Francisco: Chinese Historical Society of America, 1984), 40; and Li et al., *A History of Chinese Immigration to North and South America*, 63.

11. Huang Lianzhi, *Dongnanya huazu shehui fazhanlun* [The development of ethnic Chinese communities in Southeast Asia], (Shanghai: Shehui Kexue, 1992), 4.

12. From the very beginning, American merchants gained a virtual monopoly of the transportation of Chinese to California and made great profits from passage money. Documents of the China Trade such as the "Comstock File" (MS N-49.5, Massachusetts Historical Society) contain detailed records of the transportation of Chinese immigrants by American shipping companies. For additional information on this issue, see Kwang-Ching Liu, *Anglo-American Steamship Rivalry in China, 1862–1874* (Cambridge: Harvard University Press, 1962), 1–111; Robert J. Schwendinger, "Investigating Chinese Immigrant Ships and Sailors," in *The Chinese American Experience*, ed. Lim, 16–25; and Melendy, *The Oriental Americans*, 20–23.

13. Cited in Diane Mei Lin Mark and Ginger Chih, *A Place Called Chinese America*, rev. ed. (Dubuque: Kendall-Hunt, 1985), 5; and Li et al., *A History of Chinese Immigration to North and South America*, 82.

14. Lai, *From Overseas Chinese to Chinese Americans,* 5–6; Li et al., *A History of Chinese Immigration to North and South America,* 114. Also see C. F. Yong, *The New Gold Mountain: The Chinese in Australia, 1901–1921* (Richmond, Australia: Raphael Arts, 1977), 1–3; and Takaki, *Strangers from a Different Shore,* 35. The method was also very popular among the Chinese who went to Australia, which they called the "new gold mountain."

15. Lai, Huang, and Wong, *The Chinese of America, 1785–1980,* 11–21; Chen, *The Chinese of America,* 16–20; Hom, ed. and trans., *Songs of Gold Mountain,* 5–8.

16. Him Mark Lai, "The Chinese," in *Harvard Encyclopedia of American Ethnic Groups,* ed. Stephan Thernstrom (Cambridge: Harvard University Press, 1980), 218. Other scholars believe that the actual numbers might be larger; see, for example, Rose Hum Lee, *The Chinese in the United States of America* (Hong Kong: Hong Kong University Press, 1960), 11–13.

17. For information on violence and racial discrimination against Chinese immigrants in the nineteenth century, see *Chink! A Documentary History of Anti-Chinese Prejudice in America,* ed. Wu Cheng-Tsu (New York: World Publishing, 1972).

18. James Thomson, Jr., Peter Stanley, and John Perry, *Sentimental Imperialists: The American Experience in East Asia* (New York: Harper and Row, 1981), 4–7. For information on the attitude of average Americans toward Chinese immigrants in the early years, see Stuart C. Miller, *The Unwelcome Immigrant: The American Image of the Chinese, 1785–1882* (Berkeley: University of California Press, 1969), 3–15.

19. Ronald Riddle, *Flying Dragons, Flowing Streams: Music in the Life of San Francisco's Chinese* (Westport: Greenwood Press, 1983), 6–7. Also see Hom, ed. and trans., *Songs of Gold Mountain,* 8; and Harold R. Isaacs, *Scratches on Our Minds: American Views on China and India,* rev. ed. (Armonk: M. E. Sharpe, 1980), 111–12.

20. Contained in Pearl Ng, "Writings on the Chinese in California," M.A. thesis, University of California, Berkeley, 1939, 6. The thesis was published in 1972 by R and E Research Associates in San Francisco.

21. Cited in Melendy, *The Oriental Americans,* 28.

22. Betty Lee Sung, *The Story of the Chinese in America,* rev. ed. (New York: Macmillan, 1975), 42.

23. [San Francisco] *Daily Alta California,* May 12, 1851, 2 [hereafter cited as *Alta*]; also see Gunther Barth, *Bitter Strength: A Study of the Chinese in the United States, 1850–1870* (Cambridge: Harvard University Press, 1964), 158–159. Barth's work contains valuable information about Chinese immigrants in California during the 1850s, but he seems to overemphasize Chinese resistance toward assimilation without adequately analyzing the reason for such actions.

24. According to Mary Roberts Coolidge, a change in editorship of the *Alta* at the end of 1852 was a factor that led the newspaper to switch from its previous "pro-Chinese" stance to an anti-Chinese tone. Coolidge, *Chinese Immigration* (New York: Henry Holt, 1909), 58.

25. Despite their tendency to avoid confrontation with authorities, early Chinese immigrants never hesitated to use the American judicial system when necessary. For discussions on Chinese lawsuits against racial discrimination in the early era, see Charles J. McClain, *In Search of Equality: The Chinese Struggle against Discrimination in Nineteenth-Century America* (Berkeley: University of California Press, 1994), 1–6.

26. The earliest of these students on record are five Chinese boys who studied at the

Foreign Mission School in Cornwall, Connecticut, from 1818 to 1825. Doris Chu, *Chinese in Massachusetts: Their Experiences and Contributions* (Boston: Chinese Culture Institute, 1987), 36–37; Lee, *The Chinese in the United States of America,* 86–87; Lai, *From Overseas Chinese to Chinese Americans,* 59–60.

27. Hab Wa and Tong K. Achick, "Letter of the Chinamen to His Excellency, Governor Bigler," *Alta,* April 30, 1852, 2; Norman Asing, "To His Excellency Governor Bigler," *Alta,* May 5, 1852, 2; Lai Chun Chuen, "Remarks of the Chinese Merchants of San Francisco, upon Governor Bigler's Message and Some Common Objections," *The Oriental,* San Francisco, Feb. 1, 1855, 1. Also see Benjamin Brooks, *The Chinese in California* (San Francisco, n.p., 1877), 136–41; Lai Yong et al., "The Chinese Question from a Chinese Standpoint," in Otis Gibson, *The Chinese in America* (Cincinnati: Hitchcock and Walden, 1877), 285–92; Lee Ming How et al., "To His Excellency U. S. Grant, President of the United States: A Memorial from Representative Chinamen in America," in *Facts upon the Other Side of the Chinese Question,* ed. Augustus Layres (San Francisco, n.p., 1876), 20–24; "A Memorial from the Six Chinese Companies: An Address to the Senate and House of Representatives of the United States," in Julius Su Tow, *The Real Chinese in America* (Orange: Academy Press, 1923), 118–19; Kwang Chang Ling, "Why Should the Chinese Go?" [San Francisco] *The Argonault,* Aug. 7, 1878, 1; Mary Tape, "A Letter to San Francisco Board of Education," *Alta,* April 16, 1885, 1, in Victor Low, *The Unimpressible Race: A Century of Educational Struggle by the Chinese in San Francisco* (San Francisco: East-West Publishing, 1982), 199; Lee Yan Phou, "The Chinese Must Stay," *North American Review* 148 (April 1889): 476–83; Fong Kun Ngon, "The Chinese Six Companies," *Overland Monthly* 23 (1894): 519–21; Ho Yow, "Chinese Exclusion: A Benefit or a Harm?" *North American Review* 173 (Sept. 1901): 314–30; and Fu Chi Hao, "My Reception in America," *Outlook* 86 (Aug. 1907): 770–73.

28. For information about the Six Companies, see Victor G. Nee and Brett de Bary Nee, *Longtime Californ': A Documentary Study of an American Chinatown* (Stanford: Stanford University Press, 1986), 228–40, 272–77; and Lai, *From Overseas Chinese to Chinese Americans,* 25–45. For a brief yet explicit summary of the organization and function of the Six Companies, see Daniels, *Asian America,* 24–26. For discussions of the critical role played by the elite, especially big merchants, in the early Chinese American community, see Sucheng Chan, *Asian Americans: An Interpretive History* (Boston: Twayne Publishers, 1991), 29–30; 63–67; and L. Eve Armentrout Ma, "Chinatown Organizations and the Anti-Chinese Movement, 1882–1914," in *Entry Denied: Exclusion and the Chinese Community in America, 1882–1943,* ed. Sucheng Chan (Philadelphia: Temple University Press, 1991), 147–69.

29. Coolidge, *Chinese Immigration,* 55–56. For more recent characterizations of Bigler, see Barth, *Bitter Strength,* 145–47; and McClain, *In Search of Equality,* 10–12, 17–22.

30. John Bigler, "Governor's Special Message," *Alta,* May 1, 1852, 1. Only a few months earlier Bigler had expressed friendship for Chinese immigrants. As an anti-Chinese mood began to emerge among miners, however, he quickly changed his tone and tried to use the question of Chinese immigration to gain miners' vote. Coolidge, *Chinese Immigration,* 56; Barth, *Bitter Strength,* 145–46.

31. The essay was soon reprinted in a pamphlet by the *San Francisco Herald,* together with Bigler's message and two other documents, "Memorial to the Legislature on the Chinese Question" (May 1, 1852) and "To His Excellency, Gov. Bigler, from the Chinamen"

(May 16, 1852), under the title *An Analysis of the Chinese Question* (San Francisco: Office of the *San Francisco Herald,* 1852). It is perhaps the earliest published work on Chinese immigrants in the United States. I have found only two copies of the original pamphlet to have survived, one in the Huntington Library in Los Angeles and the other in the Essex Institute Library in Salem, Massachusetts.

32. Barth, *Bitter Strength,* 145, 149. Also see Loren W. Fessler, ed., *Chinese in America: Stereotyped Past, Changing Present* (New York: Vantage Press, 1983), 52–56.

33. Hab Wa and Tong K. Achick, "Letter of the Chinamen to His Excellency, Governor Bigler," in *An Analysis of the Chinese Question,* 5–8 (citations from this essay are quoted in the text).

34. For more information on Tong K. Achick, see *An Analysis of the Chinese Question,* 8, 10; *Instructions to Agents and Employees of Wells, Fargo & Co.'s Express* (San Francisco: Wells, Fargo, 1871), 95; Barth, *Bitter Strength,* 90, 98, 104, 146, 147, 251n21; McClain, *In Search of Equality,* 291n36; Him Mark Lai, "A Short History of the Jop Sen Tong," unpublished paper; and Lai, *From Overseas Chinese to Chinese Americans,* 16, 21.

35. Speer's sympathy for Chinese immigrants was clearly reflected in his six-hundred-page monograph, one of the best works on Chinese history and culture published in the United States during the nineteenth century. Speer, *The Oldest and Newest Empire: China and the United States* (Hartford: Scranton, 1870). For more information on Speer, see Michael L. Stahler, "William Speer: Champion of California's Chinese, 1852–57," *Journal of Presbyterian History* 48 (1970): 113–28; Barth, *Bitter Strength,* 159; and McClain, *In Search of Equality,* 19.

36. "Preface," in Margaret Kerr Hosmer, *You-Sing: The Chinaman in California: A True Story of the Sacramento Flood* (Philadelphia: Presbyterian Publication Committee, 1868); also see William F. Wu, *The Yellow Peril: Chinese Americans in American Fiction, 1850–1940* (Hamden: Archon Books, 1982), 25–27.

37. For more information on missionary activities in the Chinese American community, see Wesley Woo, "Chinese Protestants in the San Francisco Bay Area," in *Entry Denied,* ed. Chan, 213–45; Shih-shan H. Tsai, *The Chinese Experience in America* (Bloomington: Indiana University Press, 1986), 42–45; and Yong, *The New Gold Mountain,* 203–8, 214.

38. "Coolie" (or "cooley" as it was more commonly spelled at that time) is from "kuli," a Tamil word meaning hired, unskilled laborer. It was first used by Chinese merchants residing in Southeast Asia to refer to local aboriginals and imported laborers from India. For more discussions on the issue, see Pan, *Sons of the Yellow Emperor,* 45. Also see Li Yiyuan and Guo Zhenyu, eds., *Dongnanya huaren shehui yanjiu* [Chinese communities in Southeast Asia], (Taipei: Academia Sinica, 1985).

39. Roger Daniels, "The Asian-American Experience: The View from the 1990s," in *Multiculturalism and the Canon of American Culture,* ed. Hans Bak (Amsterdam: VU University Press, 1993), 136.

40. Quoted in Leonard Dinnerstein and David M. Reimers, *Ethnic Americans: A History of Immigration,* 3d ed. (New York: HarperCollins, 1988), 46, 159; and Thomas Sowell, *Ethnic America* (New York: Basic Books, 1981), 109. Also see Daniels, *Asian America,* 20.

41. Lai, "The Chinese," 219. Ronald Takaki estimates that the return rate for Chinese immigrants was about 47 percent during the free immigration period, whereas Stanford Lyman finds that more than 50 percent eventually went back to China. Takaki, *Strangers from a Different Shore,* 116; Stanford Lyman, *Chinese Americans* (New York: Random

House, 1974), 5. Also see Franklin Ng, "The Sojourner, Return Migration, and Immigration History," in *Chinese America: History and Perspective, 1987* (San Francisco: Chinese Historical Society of America, 1987), 53–72.

42. Chen, *The Chinese of America,* 121.

43. Feng, *The Chinese Diaspora,* 32. Also see Li et al., *A History of Chinese Immigration to North and South America,* 122–24; and Lai, *From Overseas Chinese to Chinese Americans,* 9, 20n9.

44. Joaquin Miller, *First Fam'lies of the Sierras* (Chicago: Jansen, McClurg, and Cox, 1876), 252–53.

45. Corinne K. Hoexter estimates that a third of the total custom duties at the port of San Francisco at the time were paid by Chinese merchants. Hoexter, *From Canton to California: The Epic of Chinese Immigration* (New York: Four Winds Press, 1976), 220.

46. Horace Davis, *Chinese Immigration: Speech of Hon. Horace Davis of California in the House of Representatives* (Washington: n.p., 1878), 5. Also see Yong, *The New Gold Mountain,* 45.

47. Chen, *The Chinese of America,* 119; Virginia Chin-lan Lee, *The House That Tai Ming Built* (New York: Macmillan, 1963), 37.

48. Quoted in Barth, *Bitter Strength,* 180.

49. Davis, *Chinese Immigration,* 5.

50. The letter did not specify the background of the "free white American women" who married Chinese or explain how the Chinese could receive American citizenship at this point. These issues are discussed in subsequent chapters.

51. "Curious Features of California Life," *San Francisco Herald,* June 6, 1852, quoted in Barth, *Bitter Strength,* 147. Also see *An Analysis of the Chinese Question,* 10–11; and Hoexter, *From Canton to California,* 39.

52. Barth, *Bitter Strength,* 166, 179.

53. Garth Alexander, *The Invisible China: The Overseas Chinese and the Politics of Southeast Asia* (New York: Macmillan, 1974), 61–64; Pan, *Sons of the Yellow Emperor,* 84–152, 225–45.

54. Barth, *Bitter Strength,* 142, 149–50; Coolidge, *Chinese Immigration,* 35–37; McClain, *In Search of Equality,* 12–24, 293n64; Takaki, *Strangers from a Different Shore,* 82; Wu, *Chink!* 11–25.

55. John Higham, "Introduction," in *Ethnic Leadership in America,* ed. Higham (Baltimore: Johns Hopkins University Press, 1978), 1–15.

56. For more information on Mary Tape's background, see Judy Yung, *Unbound Feet: A Social History of Chinese Women in San Francisco* (Berkeley: University of California Press, 1995), 48–49; and Ruthanne Lum McCunn, *Chinese American Portraits: Personal Histories, 1828–1988* (San Francisco: Chronicle Books, 1988), 41.

57. McClain, *In Search of Equality,* 136–44.

58. Victor Low, *The Unimpressible Race: A Century of Educational Struggle by the Chinese in San Francisco* (San Francisco: East-West Publishing, 1982), 13–111. Also see Liu Pei-chi [Liu Baiji], *Meizhou huaqiao yishi* [A history of the Chinese in America], (Taipei: Liming, 1976), 417–18.

59. Low, *The Unimpressible Race,* 48–78; Yung, *Unbound Feet,* 48–49.

60. Quoted in Low, *The Unimpressible Race,* 62. For more discussions on the court decision, see McClain, *In Search of Equality,* 136–144.

61. *Alta*, April 16, 1885, 1. Also see Low, *The Unimpressible Race*, 199. Even Mary Tape, whose English was considered exceptionally good among Chinese, could not write correctly. Thus it must have been difficult for most immigrants to express themselves in written form in English at this time.

62. Segregated schooling imposed on Chinese remained until the law was officially rescinded in 1906. But even after that, anti-Chinese elements continued to bar the Chinese children from attending white public schools. With public support, however, the Chinese finally succeeded abolishing the system in the 1920s. Thereafter, Chinese children were able to attend public schools with their white peers. Low, *The Unimpressible Race*, 112–32; Kai-yu Hsu and Helen Palubinskas, eds., *Asian-American Authors* (Boston: Houghton Mifflin, 1972), 14.

63. Chosen from among seventy-five previously published interviews in *The Independent*, the selections in the book represent a wide range of the "humble classes in the nation." It stimulated a great deal of interests among readers and continues to be favorably reviewed. Edmund Morris, "Books: Short and Simple Annuals," *The New Yorker*, June 11, 1990, 101–2; Werner Sollors, "Foreword: From the Bottom Up," in *The Life Stories of Undistinguished Americans as Told by Themselves*, ed. Hamilton Holt, 2d ed. (New York: Routledge, 1990), xi–xxviii.

64. Lee Chew's "lifelet" was first published under the title "Biography of a Chinaman" in *The Independent*, Feb. 19, 1903, 417–23. Although the lifelet may not have been actually written by Lee, there is no doubt about its validity. As the editor notes, in cases where a person was "too ignorant" or too busy to write, the story was recorded from interviews and then read to the person for approval. Although some life stories in the book may have been filtered, Lee's appears to be original. It has a distinctively Chinese-style narrative and contains accurate information on Chinese experiences in America as well as life back home. For example, Lee's elaboration of the utility of palm leaves in his hometown reveals detailed familiarity with daily life in the Pearl River Delta area that an outsider would not be likely to imagine. Lee's account can also be verified by comparing it with work written by Chinese immigrants in cooperation with American authors during the late nineteenth century, for example, *Story of a Chinese Boy in California* (1867) and *Uncle Sam-ee and His Little Chi-nee* (1879).

65. For example, Ronald Takaki cites Lee Chew's life story in seven places in his volume on Asian Americans; see Takaki, *Strangers from a Different Shore*, 34, 92, 94, 115, 125–27. Lee's story is also mentioned in Elaine H. Kim, *Asian American Literature: An Introduction to the Writings and Their Social Context* (Philadelphia: Temple University Press, 1982), 23.

66. Lee Chew, "The Life Story of a Chinaman," in *The Life Stories of Undistinguished Americans*, ed. Hamilton Holt (New York: Potts, 1906), 281–99. Citations from this essay are quoted in the text.

67. Quoted in Pan, *Sons of the Yellow Emperor*, 109–10.

68. For more information on the experience of Chinese laundrymen in America, see Paul P. C. Siu, *The Chinese Laundryman: A Study in Social Isolation* (New York: New York University Press, 1987), 8–136. Also see Chan, *Asian Americans*, 33–34; and Takaki, *Strangers from a Different Shore*, 92.

69. Lucie Cheng Hirata [Lucie Cheng], "Free, Indentured, Enslaved: Chinese Prostitutes in Nineteenth Century America," *Signs* 5, no. 1 (1979): 3–29. Also see Peggy Pascoe, "Gender Systems in Conflict: The Marriages of Mission-Educated Chinese American

Women, 1847–1939," in *Unequal Sisters: A Multicultural Reader in U.S. Women's History*, ed. Ellen Carol Dubois and Vicki L. Ruiz (New York: Routledge, 1990), 123–40.

70. Quoted in Gibson, *The Chinese in America*, 157. Like William Speer, the Rev. Otis Gibson was an active and enthusiastic supporter for the Chinese community in California during the nineteenth century. His book is one of the most comprehensive studies of Chinese immigrants in the early era.

71. Calculated from *U.S. Census: General Population Characteristics, 1900–1970* (Washington: Government Printing Office, 1971). It is noteworthy, however, that because Chinese women in America at this time were often hidden from census takers, their presence might be larger than indicated in census reports. Sue Fawn Chung, "Their Changing World: Chinese Women on the Comstock, 1860–1910," in *Comstock Women: The Making of a Mining Community*, ed. Ronald M. James and C. Elizabeth Raymond (Reno: University of Nevada Press, 1998), 203–28. For discussions on how immigration laws denied the entry of Chinese women, see Sucheng Chan, "The Exclusion of Chinese Women," in *Entry Denied*, ed. Chan, 94–146.

72. Paul R. Spickard, *Mixed Blood: Intermarriage and Ethnic Identity in Twentieth-Century America* (Madison: University of Wisconsin Press, 1989), 3–22; Betty Lee Sung, *Chinese American Intermarriage* (New York: Center for Migration Studies, 1990), 1–19.

73. Jacob A. Riis, *How the Other Half Lives* (New York: Hill and Wang, 1957), 68. Of course, the Chinese were not the only ethnic group Riis considered to be "low." Influenced by intolerance and racial prejudice of his era, he was also biased against other ethnic groups. In his words, Arabs were "dirty" (21); Germans, "clumsy" (21); Irish, "picturesquely autocratic" (16); and Italians, "born gamblers like the Chinese" (40). As for Jews, he said in many ways, "Money is their God" (79). Still, affected by the strong anti-Chinese sentiment at this time, Riis appeared to be more critical of the Chinese. The only positive thing he said of the Chinese was that they were "clean." Ironically, Riis's views on blacks were progressive and constituted a sharp contrast to his harsh attitude toward the Chinese and white ethnic groups.

74. See "The Life Story of a French Dressmaker" and "The Life Story of Irish Cook," in *The Life Stories of Undistinguished Americans*, ed. Holt, 61–76, 88–92.

75. Lee was considered fortunate by a southern black woman whose "lifelet" also appeared in *The Independent*. Responding to his conclusion, she said, "Happy Chinaman! Fortunate Lee Chew! You can go back to your village and enjoy your money. This is my village, my home, yet I am an outcast." See the 1990 edition of Holt, ed., *The Life Stories of Undistinguished Americans*, 220.

76. Nathan Glazer and Daniel Patrick Moynihan, *Behind the Melting Pot: The Negroes, Puerto Ricans, Jews, Italians and Irish of New York City* (Cambridge: MIT Press, 1963).

77. For more discussions of the significance of the book, see Jeffery P. Chan et al., eds., *The Big Aiiieeeee: An Anthology of Chinese American and Japanese American Literature* (New York: Meridian, 1991), 93–110.

78. Wong Sam and Assistants, *An English-Chinese Phrase Book Together with the Vocabulary of Trade, Law, etc.* (San Francisco: Cubery, 1875), 273. Wells Fargo Bank also published another widely circulated Chinese-English bilingual book: *Directory of Chinese Business Houses* (1878). Containing names and business addresses of more than eight hundred Chinese stores and companies in northern California and Oregon, the book is valuable for students of Chinese American business history.

79. Wong Sam and Assistants, *An English-Chinese Phrase Book,* 293.

80. Ibid., 12, 13, 14, 15, 18, 19, 20, 21, 22, 23, 24, 50, 51, 52.

81. For more information on violence against Chinese immigrants in the nineteenth century, see Roger Daniels, ed., *Anti-Chinese Violence in North America* (New York: Arno Press, 1978).

82. Bret Harte, "An Episode of Fiddletown," in *The Writings of Bret Harte* (Boston: Houghton Mifflin, 1896), 2:139. Harte also coined such phrases as "cheap Chinese labor" and "heathen Chinee." For discussions of the image of Chinese immigrants in Harte's writing, see Robert McClellan, *The Heathen Chinee: A Study of American Attitudes toward China, 1890–1905* (Columbus: Ohio State University, 1971), 47–52; and William Purviance Fenn, *Ah Sin and His Brethren in American Literature* (Peiping [Beijing]: College of Chinese Studies, 1933).

83. Quoted in Chan, *Asian Americans,* 48. To some extent, the experience of the Chinese in California in the late nineteenth century was worse than that of African Americans. Thanks to the outcome of the Civil War, blacks were allowed to testify in California in 1863, a decade before the Chinese were given the same right.

84. Jeffery P. Chan et al., "Resources for Chinese American Literary Traditions," in *The Chinese American Experience,* ed. Lim, 241–43.

85. Wong Sam and Assistants, *An English-Chinese Phrase Book,* 37, 114, 204.

86. Studies show that by 1892—forty years after the Rev. William Speer opened a mission in San Francisco's Chinatown—there were still fewer than two thousand Protestant converts among all the Chinese in North America, accounting for less than 2 percent of the Chinese population in North America at the time. The number of Chinese Catholics was even smaller. Lai, *From Overseas Chinese to Chinese Americans,* 140; Woo, "Chinese Protestants in the San Francisco Bay Area," 213–45.

87. Riis, *How the Other Half Lives,* 203.

88. Contained in Him Mark Lai, Genny Lim, and Judy Yung, *Island: Poetry and History of Chinese Immigrants on Angel Island, 1910–1940* (Seattle: University of Washington Press, 1991), 60. Hereafter, the numbers in parentheses are to this book. The book contains the Chinese text of the poems and the English translations. For a discussion of the difference between the Chinese text and English translation of the poems, see Shan Te-hsing, "An Island Where Angels Fear to Tread: Reinscribing Angel Island Poetry in Chinese and English," unpublished paper.

89. The immigration station was officially opened on January 21, 1910. Although facilities on Angel Island were deemed unfit for habitation, the station did not close until November 1940, when a fire destroyed its administration building. Roger Daniels, "No Lamps Were Lit for Them: Angel Island and the Historiography of Asian American Immigration," *Journal of American Ethnic History* 17, no. 1 (1997): 3–18.

90. Lai, Huang, and Wong, *The Chinese of America, 1785–1980,* 52.

91. Lai, Lim, and Yung, *Island,* 8, 16; Tsai, *The Chinese Experience in America,* 99–104.

92. Lai, Lim, and Yung, *Island,* 100.

93. Lucie Cheng Hirata [Lucie Cheng], "The Chinese American in Sociology," in *Counterpoint: Perspectives on Asian America,* ed. Emma Gee (Los Angeles: Asian American Studies Center, UCLA, 1976), 22.

94. Writing poems on prison walls or walls in public places is a common practice that has a long tradition throughout Chinese history. As an effective means to express one's

feelings in captivity, it can be traced back to ancient times, when people used brushes as writing tools. For example, in the sixteenth-century Chinese classic *Shuihu zhuan* [The water margin: Outlaws of the marsh], many of the captured rebels try to release their emotions by writing poems on the walls of their prison.

95. Lai, Lim, and Yung, *Island*, 141.

96. Most of the poems were scribbled on the walls of the detention center and were eventually covered by paint. However, some were first written with a writing brush, then carved into the wooden walls, and are still visible today. Some poems might have been written by one person and later revised by others, thus being a truly collective creation that represented common feelings of the immigrants. Ibid., 23–28.

97. See ibid., 138–46, for a translation of "Imprisonment in the Wooden Building." Throughout history, Chinese-language newspapers in America frequently published poems, stories, and other forms of literary work by immigrants about their American experiences (chapters 5–6).

98. Chinese immigrants who tried to enter the United States on the false claim that they were offspring of American citizens or permanent residents were called "paper sons" (sons of U.S. citizens on paper only). Yung, *Unbound Feet*, 3, 23, 106; Bill Ong Hing, *Making and Remaking Asian America through Immigration Policy, 1850–1990* (Stanford: Stanford University Press, 1993), 74; Lee, *The Chinese in the United States of America*, 300–307.

99. Typical questions were: "How many houses are there in your village?" "How many steps are there at the front door of your house?" and, "What was the location of the kitchen rice bin?" The inquiry system is vividly recaptured in *Carved in Silence* (San Francisco: Felicia Lowe Productions, 1987), a documentary film about the Angel Island immigration station. The film features archival footage and is based on interviews with former Chinese detainees and U.S. immigration officers.

100. Lai, Lim, and Yung, *Island*, 116.

101. Ibid., 22, 114; Frances D'Emilio, "The Secret Hell of Angel Island," *American West* 21 (May–June 1984): 44–51. Of course, the hearings were not always that terrible. Edward Lee also relates a story in which two young men were seeking admission as sons of a merchant: "They [the inspectors] asked the first applicant if there was a dog in the house. He said, 'Yes.' Later they asked the second if there was a dog in the house. He said, 'No, no dog.' The first applicant was recalled, and that question was put to him. He said, 'Yes, well, we had a dog, but we knew we were coming to the United States, so we ate the dog.'" Both were admitted because inspectors could find no discrepancies in their answers. Tsai, *The Chinese Experience in America*, 101.

102. Lai, Lim, and Yung, *Island*, 94.

103. Tsai, *The Chinese Experience in America*, 100.

104. Lai, Lim, and Yung, *Island*, 115.

105. Ibid., 60, 101.

106. Ibid., 96–97. Thanks to the Gentlemen's Agreement (1907–8), the Japanese were better treated than other Asian immigrants in the United States. However, there soon emerged increasingly strong anti-Japanese sentiment in American society. Roger Daniels, *Concentration Camps: North America, Japanese in the United States and Canada during World War II*, rev. ed. (Malabar: Robert E. Krieger, 1989), 1–25.

107. Lai, Lim, and Yung, *Island*, 86.

108. Ibid., 92. Ruan Ji (210–263 A.D.) was a prominent scholar during the Jin Dynasty.

109. Ibid., 152.

110. Ibid., 66.

111. Quoted in Mark and Chih, *A Place Called Chinese America*, 11.

112. Lai, Lim, and Yung, *Island*, 64. Confucius and his disciples once were surrounded by enemy troops on a lecture tour near the Chen Kingdom and were cut off from food supplies for seven days.

113. Ibid., 124. Han Xin (second century B.C.) rose from extreme poverty to become a famous general. King Goujian (fifth century B.C.) slept on firewood and tasted gall in order not to forget the bitterness and humiliation of his defeat. King Wen (twelfth century B.C.) once was held captive at Youli by King Zhou, but he escaped and later defeated Zhou. Lord Jiang (eleventh century B.C.) was a legendary figure whose talents were not recognized until he was seventy.

114. Ibid., 124.

115. Thirteen of the Angel Island poems have been anthologized in *The Heath Anthology of American Literature*, ed. Paul Lauter et al. (Lexington: D. C. Heath, 1994), 2:1755–62. The fact that they were selected by the *Heath Anthology*, a literary establishment, is a testament to their artistic value. Stylistically, almost all were written in the classical Chinese style of *Qi Yan* (a seven-character quatrain) or *Wu Yan* (a five-character quatrain). Some are imitative of similar work in traditional Chinese literature. For an analysis of the stylistic characteristics of the Angel Island poems, see Shan Te-hsing, "Yi wo ailun ru quanfu" [An island where angels fear to tread], in *Zaixian zhengzhi yu huayi meiguo wenxue* [Reexamining the relationship between politics and Chinese American literature], ed. He Wenjing and Shan Te-hsing (Taipei: Academia Sinica, 1996), 1–56.

116. Sui Sin Far [Edith Maude Eaton], "Chinese Workmen in America," *The Independent*, July 3, 1913, 57.

117. Lai, Lim, and Yung, *Island*, 19, 75, 78.

118. Daniels, "No Lamps Were Lit for Them," 18.

*Every fair-minded man can testify that the Chinese are the most law-abiding people in the community, that they are not easily provoked, but are patient (oh, too patient!) under insult and injury. They seldom appear in court-rooms in the character of prisoners. . . . Is it a crime to be industrious, faithful, law-abiding? wrong to coin one's honest toil into gold, and, instead of wasting one's earnings in drink and debauchery, to support wife and children therewith?*
—Lee Yan Phou

# 2

# The Writing of "Cultivated Chinese": Improving an Image to Win Sympathy and Acceptance

Early Chinese immigrants were not always so bitter, nor did they all live in poverty, disgrace, or humiliation.[1] While the majority suffered racial discrimination in the late nineteenth and early twentieth centuries, there were some who in general received fairly good treatment. These were the "cultivated Chinese," mostly students, who had been sent by the Manchu court, brought by missionaries, or came on their own for advanced education in America.[2] Although their presence in the United States represented only a small fraction of Chinese immigrants, they constituted a disproportionately large part of the literary voice of the early Chinese American community.[3]

The reason is not hard to understand. Although most Chinese immigrants during this period possessed neither the time nor means, either economic or social, to voice their views and beliefs, most of the students, sponsored by the Chinese government and missionary organizations or supported by their families' wealth, lived a fairly comfortable life. Moreover, because most received a good education in the United States and had sophisticated literary tastes they knew how to write and what audience to address.[4] Therefore, despite the fact they cannot be viewed as representative of Chinese immigrants, their writing composes the bulk of early Chinese American literature.

Unlike their countrymen who lived in segregated urban ghettos and remained outsiders to American society, most of the cultivated Chinese succeeded in assimilating into the mainstream of American cultural and intellectual life. To be sure, they were frustrated by racial prejudice and resented how Chinese immigrants were treated in America, but in general they rarely had the bitter experiences that Chinese laborers encountered every day and held social status that could never be dreamed of by their more "undistinguished" countrymen. The story of Liang Cheng [Sir Chentung Liang Cheng] is an example.

Liang was first brought by the Chinese Educational Mission to study at Phillips Academy in Massachusetts in 1872.[5] He later became a Chinese diplomat in the United States. At a time when most Chinese immigrants were deprived of the right of education and lived in desperation, Liang was awarded four honorary degrees from various prestigious American institutions, including Yale University and Amherst College, and was even knighted by Queen Victoria in 1897.[6] His portrait was hung in the Hall of Fame at the Phillips Academy at Andover alongside those of prominent American statesmen, scholars, and successful businessmen. It was an extraordinary honor for a Chinese during the exclusion era.[7]

Because the experiences of the cultivated Chinese differed greatly from that of average Chinese immigrants, it is understandable that the anger and frustration that filled the voice of their compatriots would rarely appear in their writing. In general, the work of the cultivated Chinese are characterized by intentions to bridge the racial and cultural gap between China and America. Apparently, their perception of the roots of racism differed from that of the majority of Chinese immigrants. They saw it as a result of total ignorance and common misconceptions about Chinese civilization on the part of the American public rather than as a product of social environment and economic conditions. Thus they believed that with knowledge there would come improved treatment of Chinese in the United States. To that end, they felt that they first of all needed to challenge and rectify negative views and stereotypes of China which then prevailed in American society. By disseminating correct information on various aspects of Chinese culture and society, they thought it possible to improve the image of their home-land and win sympathy and acceptance for Chinese immigrants. The books they wrote during the exclusion era were all of this nature: *When I Was a Boy in China* (1887) by Lee Yan Phou; *The Real Chinese in America* (1923) by Julius Su Tow; *My Country and My People* (1935) by Lin Yutang; and *A Chinese Childhood* (1940) by Chiang Yee [Jiang Yi].

Significantly, most of their writings are autobiographical—a sharp contrast to the Chinese literary tradition in which autobiography is virtually unknown and would be deemed egocentric. The choice of genre may be attributed to the fact that autobiography, compared to other kinds of literature, could be used more effectively to reveal their experiences in America and compare their lives in the United States and in China. In addition, educated in American schools, the authors had been exposed to Western literature, in which autobiography has a long tradition. Nevertheless, the fact that autobiography was a popular genre among them shows how far they had departed from the Chinese literary tradition.

Based on the experiences of the gentry class from which most of the authors came, their explanations of China focus primarily on the high culture of traditional Chinese society. They sought to present an attractive picture of Chinese civilization, particularly the more charming aspects of philosophy, religion, literature, and cultural traditions. In doing so, they hoped to arouse the benign curiosity of mainstream Americans who longed for the "exotic Oriental taste" and enhance China's image.

Although the picture they painted was often artificial and its views of Chinese society limited, their writing was a serious effort to introduce Chinese civilization to an American audience and defend it despite racial prejudice. Indeed, it was through their writing that many readers first learned of Chinese culture.[8] Lee Yan Phou's autobiographical account of his boyhood in China is an outstanding example of such writing.

### *When I Was a Boy in China:* An Attempt to Introduce Chinese Civilization to Americans

Born into a declining gentry-scholar family in Xiangshan [Zhongshan] County seventy-five miles south of Canton, Lee Yan Phou (1861–1938?) was brought to the United States to study by the Chinese Educational Mission in 1873. Although some aspects of his life are unknown, available documents reveal that he led a more colorful life than most of his fellow students in the Educational Mission. Having studied in grammar schools in Springfield, Massachusetts, and New Haven, Connecticut, he entered Yale College in 1880. When the Chinese Educational Mission was disbanded, Lee was recalled to China in 1882 but "made his escape" to the United States a year later and resumed his studies at Yale.[9] After graduating in 1887, he lived in various cities of the West and the South and finally settled in Wood Ridge, New Jersey, to become a businessman and newspaper editor. He was twice married—both times to white women—and active in local politics.[10] Such events were extraordinary for a Chinese immigrant during the exclusion era.

When the Lothrop Company in Boston asked him to write a book on China, Lee had lived in the United States for more than a decade and was frustrated by average Americans' stereotypes about China. "I still continually find false ideas in America concerning Chinese customs, manners, and institutions," he wrote. "Small blame to the people at large, who have no means of learning the truth except through newspapers or accounts of travelers who do not understand what they see in passing through our country. . . . Accordingly, what I tell in this series of articles about Chinese customs, manners and institutions may often contradict general belief."[11] That frustration motivated Lee to write his book.

Published in 1887, *When I Was a Boy in China* is an encyclopedic account of Chinese civilization. Covering such subjects as philosophy, education, literature, religion, ceremonies, family, food, and pastimes, the book provides a panoramic view of Chinese society and elaborates on many aspects of Chinese culture. The discussion of table manners, for example, is particularly detailed and amusing:

> The younger ones do not presume to sit till their elders are seated; then after making a show of asking permission to eat, when the elders gravely nod assent, the breakfast begins. Soup is taken first; then each person, holding the chopsticks in the right hand and the bowl of rice in the left, lifts his food to his mouth, pushes the lumps in with the sticks, alternating this motion with picking meat, fish or vegetables from the dishes which are common to all. One must take only from the side of the plate which is nearest to him, however. It is a breach of etiquette to reach over the opposite side. When one finishes, he bids the rest to "eat leisurely," which is our mode of saying "Excuse me!" The Chinese invariably wash their hands and faces after every meal. (30)

Although contemporary readers may weary of Lee's detailed elaboration of such trivial matters, there was a need for him to write so. Americans of his era, especially those of the middle-class who would be the potential audience of Lee's book, were more disturbed by the "strange" culture and actions of Chinese immigrants than by the issue of cheap labor. The Chinese custom of setting off firecrackers to celebrate the New Year and other holidays, for instance, was deemed a nuisance and fire hazard, and Chinese funerals, which had elaborate

ceremonies, often elicited only laughter and contempt from American specta-
tors. In the West, sacrifices to the dead—usually roast pig, chickens, rice, liquor,
and sweetmeats—were considered to be meals for Native Americans. A newspaper reporter in Nevada observed, "Many Indians made a delicious dinner from
the provisions customarily put by the grave of the dead Chinaman."[12] What the
reporter forgot or was too embarrassed to mention, however, was that white
Americans also appropriated food left after Chinese funeral ceremonies.[13]

The attempt to elucidate misunderstandings about China can also be seen
in Lee's explanation of why some cultural activities common in America did not
exist in China. For example, he explained that there was no such thing as social
dancing in China because Chinese were more conscious of "wasting time" than
Americans: "A Chinese gentleman would consider it foolishness and an insen-
sate waste of time to hop about and twirl around for a whole night. Amusements
requiring so much exertion are not his taste; and as for throwing his arm around
a girl's waist in the whirl of the waltz, a Chinese gentleman would not permit
himself such an indecorum" (39). For the same reasons of practicality, "Fishing
means work with the Chinese. A man, or boy, goes a-fishing simply for the fish,
and not for the fun." Lee then emphasizes, "And I am of the opinion that my
countrymen are right" (39).

For the most part, however, Lee intended to demonstrate that despite seeming differences between the "Middle Kingdom" and the United States there could
be points of compatibility between people of the two cultures. Using illustrations,
he explained in detail how Chinese institutions function and made comparisons
with those of other nations. In his opinion, Chinese society is essentially democratic, just as that of America, because "there is no such thing as caste in China,
in the sense that caste exists in India. In China, wealth, and literary and official
honors ennoble a family and can lift it from a lower to a higher plane" (20). Even
in daily life, Chinese and Americans shared many things. The book's cover, a
colorful picture of a Chinese boy flying a kite, is an indication that Chinese children played the same games as their American peers. Perhaps they even enjoyed
them more, because Chinese kites were better-made than American ones. Hence,
he suggested, "Kite-flying in America can be much improved. Kites should be
constructed of the Chinese shape" (35).

In order to ensure the book's acceptance, Lee described scenes that American readers might find exotic, foreign, or humorous. His discussion of a typical
Chinese classroom scene is a good example:

> It is six o'clock A.M. All the boys are shouting at the top of their voices, at
> the fullest stretch of their lungs. Occasionally, one stops and talks to some

one sitting near him. Two of the most careless ones are guessing pennies; and anon a dispute arises as to which of the two disputants writes a better hand. . . . All at once the talking, the playing, the shouting ceases. A bent form slowly comes up through the open court. The pupils rise to their feet. A simultaneous salutation issues from a dozen pairs of lips. All cry out, "Lao Se" [venerable teacher]! As he sits down, all follow his example. . . . Then one takes his book up to the teacher's desk, turns his back to him and recites. But see, he soon hesitates; the teacher prompts him. . . . A second one goes up, but poor fellow! He forgets three times; the teacher is out of patience with the third stumble, and down comes the ruler, whack! whack! upon the head. With one hand feeling the aching spot and the other carrying back his book, the discomfited youngster returns to his desk to re-con his lesson. (58–59)

The strong sense of humor in the depiction provides readers with a fascinating picture.

Here arises an interesting point. The narrative tone of the book is supposed to be Chinese, yet it is surprisingly Western. The influence of Western culture on Lee was so overwhelming that one might think the book was written by an American. His familiarity with English literature is authentic and impressive. For example, of the *erhu,* a traditional Chinese musical instrument, Lee writes that it can make melody in the hands of a skillful player but produces a sound "distinguished in the din like the witches' voices above the storm in *Macbeth*" when played by a stranger.

Moreover, readers can easily identify the traits of English literature in both the style and organization of the book. Despite the "Oriental taste" of its opening, Lee's text is surprisingly similar to a classic of his time: *David Copperfield.*[14] He must have had in mind "I Am Born," chapter 1 of that masterpiece, when he was put down the following: "On a certain day in the year 1861, I was born. I cannot give you the exact date, because the Chinese year is different from the English year, and our month being lunar, that is reckoned by the revolution of the moon around the earth" (7). The similarity between Lee's passage and Charles Dickens's betrays the extent of Lee's Westernization although he was still fluent in Chinese. The chapter also reveals that Chinese immigrant authors generally used the textbooks and fiction of their era in learning to write English, which is why their prose is usually formal and polished.

Because Lee was concerned to "present an accurate image of China," it was natural that he focus on matters he considered to have been deliberately distorted and try to correct them. His normally calm narrative tone changed when he discussed wild stories that American journalists spread about the fate of Chinese girls: "I am indignant that there should be a popular belief in America that Chinese girls at their birth are generally put to death because they are not wanted by their parents. Nothing can be further from the truth . . . I venture to say that in proportion to population and distribution of wealth that infanticide is as rare in China as it is in this country" (43).

Time and again Lee argued that Chinese civilization was not only similar to America's but also "superior" in many respects: "A 'poor relation' there [in China] is treated with much more consideration and affection than in this country. Generosity towards that class of unfortunates is so common, and its practice is so strenuously insisted upon, in the moral code of the Chinese, that it almost ceases to be an individual virtue—it is a national virtue" (44).

By explaining Chinese culture in such an idealized way, Lee would make readers feel that Chinese civilization was the better and more humane than American. Nevertheless, his writing should be put into sociohistorical context. This was the time many Americans "truly believed" that the Chinese were "inferior to any race God ever made" and also were "uncivilized, unclean, and filthy beyond all conception . . . lustful and sensual in their dispositions."[15] It was an immense blow to the self-esteem of Chinese immigrants to hear during the debate over the Exclusion Act that their culture was so inferior they could never match that of Western civilization.[16] With so much against them, it is small wonder that an educated Chinese like Lee would argue in this way. His was an obstinate voice intended to assure the American public of the excellence of Chinese culture and express a "defensive arrogance" to counter racial bias.

Lee's spontaneous expression of nostalgia served the same purpose. One of the most common accusations laid upon the Chinese at the time was that they lacked feeling and emotion. Even a progressive writer such as Jack London would claim that "the Chinese were a different race from mine" and that they were absolutely indifferent and insensitive.[17] Yet Lee's emotional account of his sad departure from home demonstrates that the Chinese had the same feelings as other races. He told us vividly how he felt heartbroken when he left his mother: "I bowed my head four times to the ground upon my knees. She tried to appear cheerful, but I could see that her eyes were moistened with tears. . . . She gave me some pocket-money and bade me be a good boy and write often" (96). Since Chinese then were labeled as lacking human feelings and holding life less dear than Caucasians, the sentimental description itself can be viewed as the author's subtle protest against racial bias.

Ironically, despite Lee's intentions and efforts to introduce Chinese culture to a general audience, the most interesting passages of his book are comments on life in America. Of course, as a member of the privileged Chinese Educational Mission, his experience in the "strange land" was very different from that of most

of his countrymen. Being totally unaware of the miserable fate of Chinese laborers in that very city, Lee claimed that "San Francisco in 1873 was the paradise of
the self-exiled Chinese" (106). That might be true for a person like him, "who
came to study under the auspices of the Chinese government and under the
protection of the American Eagle." But it was surely not the case for those subject to the anti-Chinese violence that was rampant under the same "American
eagle" at this time. Only two years earlier, an anti-Chinese riot in Los Angeles
had ended with the murder of nineteen Chinese "coolies."[18] Despite the drastic
difference in their backgrounds, however, Lee appeared to have experienced the
same cultural shock as his less-privileged countrymen: "It was a long time before I got used to those red-headed and tight-jacketed foreigners. 'How can they
walk or run?' I asked myself curiously contemplating their close and confining
garments. The dress of American ladies was still another mystery to me. They
shocked my sense of propriety also, by walking arm-in-arm with the men. 'How
peculiar their voices are! How screechy! How sharp!' Such were some of the
thoughts I had about those peculiar people" (99–100).[19]

If their dress stunned him, one cannot help wondering how he felt when he
actually met American women. The real embarrassment took place when Lee was
introduced to his American hostess: "She came after us in a hack. As I was pointed
out to her, she put her arms around me and kissed me. This made the rest of the
boys laugh, and perhaps I got rather red in the face. . . . It was the first kiss I ever
had since my infancy" (109).

The most dramatic parts of Lee's book, however, are his first impressions of
American civilization. The chapter, "First Experience in America," provides a
unique perspective on how nineteenth-century America was perceived by a
young boy from a "different shore." Ironically, Lee claimed that a train robbery
taught him what "American civilization really means." The statement is ironic
considering the pride American writers and artists took in railroads; the loco-
motive had become symbolic of progress and modernization in popular American culture.[20] The robbery occurred on Lee's first journey eastward across con-
tinent with fellow students and teachers from the Chinese Educational Mission:

> We were quietly looking out of the windows and gazing at the seemingly
> interminable prairies when the train suddenly bounded backward. . . . Our
> party, teachers and pupils, jumped from our seats in dismay and looked out
> through the windows for more light on the subject. What we saw was enough
> to make our hair stand on end. Two ruffianly men held a revolver in each
> hand and seemed to be taking aim at us. . . . Our teachers told us to crouch
> down for our lives. We obeyed with trembling and fear. Doubtless, many

prayers were most fervently offered to the gods of China at the time. Our teachers certainly prayed as they had never done before. One of them was overheard calling upon all the gods of the Chinese Pantheon to come and save him. . . . A brakeman rushed through with a lamp in his hand. He told us that the train had been robbed of its gold bricks by five men, three of whom, dressed like Indians, rifled the baggage car while the others held the passengers at bay; that the engine was hopelessly wrecked, the engineer killed; that the robbers had escaped on horseback with their booty. (107–8)

That the event left a powerful and lasting impact on Lee is obvious. After the agony and suspense were over, Lee declared in a sarcastic tone that "one phase of American civilization was thus indelibly fixed upon our minds." The remark also scores a neat point against those who believed that it was the Chinese who were lawless barbarians and would harm innocent Americans.

Although Lee's depiction of China is limited and artificial, his book is significant. The first volume written in English by a Chinese immigrant in America, it portrays Chinese people as exotic, quaint, and delicate rather than mysterious, evil, and threatening. Its humorous narration and informative discussion must have appealed to readers, because mainstream commercial publishers later published a series of books by authors from Asia, including Etsu Inagaki Sugimoto's *A Daughter of the Samurai* (1925) and New Il-Han's *When I Was a Boy in Korea* (1928).[21] In this sense, although Lee's book did not represent the early Chinese American experience, it did begin what would become a literary tradition that has been carried on through history.[22]

It is unfortunate that not all works of this nature reached the same level. Because most of the authors came from backgrounds of higher social status, they tended to write from a privileged vantage point. Their appeals for racial tolerance were primarily on behalf of their own. Sometimes they even appeared to allow discrimination against less-privileged countrymen and instead question the logic of prejudice against the educated elite. One example is *The Real Chinese in America* by Julius Su Tow, a former Chinese diplomat living in New York.[23] The book's title seems to imply that only members from the exempt classes could be considered as true representatives of China in America. In a whining, apologetic tone Tow explained that Chinese immigration was non-threatening and beneficial and tried to persuade readers that "real Chinese" (like him) had nothing to do with "Chinatown men," who were ignorant of the high culture of China's civilization. By emphasizing the concept of "real" Chinese, Tow implied that those coming as laborers and of humble background could not be considered as true Chinese. It is little wonder that now this book has been criticized by Chinese and Asian American scholars as an example of "yellow white supremacy."[24]

## America through the Spectacles of an Oriental Diplomat: Efforts to Impress the American Public

Ever since Crèvecoeur and de Tocqueville, it has been fashionable for foreigners to write on American life. Works such as *Letters from an American Farmer* and *Democracy in America*, from their first appearance, enjoyed tremendous popularity both in America and Europe because they were not only major contributions to the Western interpretation of the American civilization but also helped Americans better understand their nation. Influenced by this fashion as well as the Chinese literary tradition of writing of travel notes, cultivated Chinese immigrants often recorded impressions of American life and attempted discussions of its social and political system.

There is, however, an essential difference between the Chinese viewers and their Western counterparts. Their desire to comment on American life stems from the sense that doing so is an effective way to exhibit their sophisticated intellectual ability rather than to present critical views of American society.[25] The point is significant because few Americans believed that a Chinese could make the same insightful observations about American institutions that Europeans could. As Henry Pearson Gratton, editor of *As a Chinaman Saw Us*, observes, "It will be difficult for the average American to conceive it possible that a cultivated Chinaman, of all persons, should have been honestly amused at our civilization. . . . It is doubtless true that the masses of Americans do not take the Chinaman seriously . . . to many Americans, it was 'incomprehensible that a Chinaman can be educated, refined, and cultivated according to their own standards.'"[26]

What Chinese authors tried to do, therefore, was not introduce the American culture to their less-educated countrymen but demonstrate to the American public that "a Chinaman of cultivation and grasp of mind" could make the same "weighty expression of opinion on a multiplicity of American topics" as did Europeans.[27] They hoped that their carefully constructed comments on America would help rectify American prejudice and win acceptance for the Chinese. Works such as *America through the Spectacles of an Oriental Diplomat* (1914) by Wu Tingfang [Wu T'ing-fang], *Reminiscences* (1932) by the Rev. Huie Kin [Xu Qin], *An Oriental View of American Civilization* (1934) and *A Squint-eye of America* (1951) by Park No-yong [Bao Narong], and *The Silent Traveler in New York* (1950), *The Silent Traveler in Boston* (1959), and *The Silent Traveler in San Francisco* (1964) by Chiang Yee [Jiang Yi] were all written with that aim in mind.[28] The intention is also indicated by the fact that these works were written in English and thus meant primarily for an American audience; for few Chinese immigrant laborers in the United States could read the language effectively.[29]

Observations on American life by someone from the "Celestial Empire" held a certain appeal for the American public. As contacts between Chinese and Americans increased, many Americans were curious for views on their society by "Orientals" although they perhaps expected to reinforce their stereotypes of China through such writing. "The Orientals' experiences in American society," Gratton claimed, "have the hall-mark of actual novelty" and their traditions and egotism "add to the interest of the recital."[30] Such curiosity is part of the reason that Chinese observations about America in general were popular and often went through a second printing and enjoyed wide circulation.[31]

The single most influential and representative piece of such writing was Wu Tingfang's *America through the Spectacles of an Oriental Diplomat*. A prominent scholar and diplomat, Wu Tingfang (1842–1922) was born and grew up in a Chinese immigrant family in Singapore. Educated in British schools in Singapore and Hong Kong, he studied law in London during the 1870s and served as Chinese minister to the United States around the turn of the century (1896–1902, 1907–9).[32] A well-known orator and writer, he had already gained some publicity in America before the book was written. His previous works, including more than a dozen articles published in mainstream magazines such as *Harpers'*, the *Independent,* and *North American Review,* were well received, and he frequently spoke at various prestigious social organizations and institutions such as the Civic Forum in New York and at Harvard University. The book's appeal, however, lies not in Wu's reputation or his smooth English. Rather, it was his subtle comments and clever satire directed at American society that gave the book a peculiar engaging quality and made it especially arresting.

The book is well organized and consists of seventeen essays that record a wide range of American life at the turn of the century. In Wu's view, America was a commercial society where everything was carried on in a commercial way—from the presidential election campaign to the engagement of lovers. A typical example concerns the extraordinary employment of advertising. "If I should be asked what is most essential for the successful carrying on of business in America," Wu remarked, "I would say advertising." He found that "every book and magazine contains many advertisements."[33] Advertising had been applied to such an extent that businesses resorted to advertising to promote sales, colleges used it to enlarge student enrollment, and politicians relied on it to improve their images; and even proposals of marriages had been made and accepted through advertising. Every new invention, Wu observed, was employed to increase the effectiveness of advertising, including the newly invented telephone, "a great blessing to mankind" (68). If advertising continued to develop, Wu predicted, even "sweethearts can exchange their sweet nothings" through advertising (68). Considering the contemporary "advertising pollution" in American mass media, what Wu says here is insightful.

Being an astute observer, Wu was fully aware that America, "a most extraordinary country," was known for a unique, "unpressed jollity" and the carefree manners of its citizens (ix). Because social manners and revealing gestures were of interest to readers, recording American behavior became one of Wu's primary topics. Many things he noted were familiar enough to be ignored or considered common knowledge, but they became truly amazing under his skillful treatment:

> There freedom of speech and criticism are allowed to the extreme limit, and people are liable to be annoyed by slanders and libels without much chance of obtaining satisfaction; there you will see women wearing "Merry Widow" hats who are not widows but spinsters, or married women whose husbands are very much alive, and the hats in many cases are as large as three feet in diameter; there you may travel by rail most comfortably on palace cars, and at night you may sleep on Pullman cars, to find in the morning that a young lady has been sleeping in the berth above your bed. (viii)

According to Wu, paradoxes were an ironic part of American life. How, for example, could Americans engage in foxhunts and wear feathers on their hats while at the same time advocating the protection of wildlife and the worth of organizations such as the Society for the Prevention of Cruelty to Animals? Although Americans were proud of their culture and style, they worshipped the fashions of Europe. It was a nation of immigrants, but many called themselves "natives" and were prejudiced against those they considered as "aliens." Women could become lawyers and plead cases at court on behalf of male clients yet they were not allowed to vote. In order to save two or three minutes, Americans would spend "millions of dollars to build a tunnel under a river, or to shorten a curve in a railroad" (102), but in the end "many a man's life has been shortened" because of the deaths caused by constant hurry.

The paradoxical aspect of American life, according to Wu, was best reflected in how people addressed each other. There were, of course, no aristocrats, and "titles such as 'Excellency' [were] not often used because they are not consistent with American egalitarianism." Nevertheless, despite the idea that all men are created equal, vanity was strong in America, and "many people want[ed] to be more equal than others." Although they claimed "the plain democratic 'Mr.' suits them better than any other titles," Wu found that "'Mister' is too tame and flat for the go-ahead Americans. Hence many of the people whom you meet daily have some prefix to their names, such as General, Colonel, Major, President, Judge, etc. You will not be far wrong to call a man 'Judge' when he is a lawyer; or 'General' or 'Colonel' if he has served in the army" (90). Even a washerwoman would insist on being addressed as a "wash-lady," for "though neither the Federal nor the State Government has power to confer titles, the magnates do so."[34]

Being a progressive, Wu admired the democratic principles that govern the United States. In the two chapters, "American Government" and "American Freedom and Equality," he elaborated how institutions function and how they differ from those of other nations. In his opinion, America "fairly approximates the high ideas of democracy": "Its government is ideal, with a liberal constitution, which in effect declares that all men are created equal, and that the government is 'of the people, for the people, and by the people.' Anyone with ordinary intelligence and with open eyes . . . could not but be impressed with the orderly and unostentatious way in which it is governed by the local authorities, or help being struck by the plain and democratic character of the people" (4). Furthermore, Americans' high value on free inquiry, scientific experiment, and the application of the test of reason has become the dominant spirit in American life. Even American children are trained democratically so they become self-reliant and independent. They can correct their parents in front of strangers—and are encouraged by their parents to do so. "It is not his parent that he [a boy] obeys," Wu observed, "but expediency and the dictates of reason. Here we see the clearheaded, sound, common-sense business man in the making. The early training of the boy has laid the foundation for the future man" (106). The United States, he concluded, was the "most perfect society" in the world (viii).

Such exuberant praise might lead one to ignore the problems of the United States and leads to the suspicion that Wu did not truly understand the country. His motives for writing should be considered, however. His work was addressed to a mainstream audience as an attempt to help win better treatment for Chinese in American society. In addition, it is the projection of his ideal society that made him write in this way. He dreamed of the United States as being a place of democracy and modernization in the world that could be a model for China to follow. His writing appeared at a time when educated Chinese were warmly receptive to the idea of America being not only a land of opportunities but also one of progress. That illusion provided a comforting reason for them to remain rather than return to China.

While marveling at American democracy, Wu also felt that the American doctrines of pragmatism and absolute freedom sometimes permitted people to place self-interest and economic propositions in the position other nations assigned to morality. As a consequence, Americans seemingly were unrestricted by any conventional morality, and there emerged a phenomenon of "democratic cold-heartedness." For example, the idea of self-reliance was often carried to such an extreme that young people did not follow the universal custom of caring for old people. Wu was astonished to hear a young man declare that "as he was brought into this world by his parents without his consent, it was their duty to rear him in a proper way, but that it was no part of his duty to support them" (125).

Women, Wu commented, were so bold and independent that they did not behave like females. Drinking, smoking, and wearing men's clothing, they frequently "intimidate[d]" and "frighten[ed] away" potential husbands; thus many remained unmarried. Relationships among family members could be so liberal that they would surely be condemned as scandalous in other countries. Wu related a news report in which a Boston businessman had married his daughter-in-law after his son died in a train accident. "If a father is permitted to marry his deceased son's wife," he mused, "in fairness a son should be allowed to marry his deceased father's wife" (94). To someone from China, where a talk between father and daughter-in-law is considered inappropriate by Confucian tradition, it was indeed an unthinkable and shocking idea.

Racial policies during this period presented a thorny issue for most cultivated Chinese. They praised U.S. society as a "haven from the disillusionments of history" (81), but the fact that the nation they admired did not treat Chinese immigrants as equals was embarrassing. Nevertheless, despite what they had witnessed, heard about, and in some cases experienced, they rarely shared their more humble countrymen's anger toward racism. They feared that compelling, frank criticism and emotional directness on that sensitive issue would offend readers and contribute to more violent anti-Chinese campaigns. Thus many chose to remain silent and generally repressed their rage against racism. If they did make critical comments, their words were inhibited and reserved. Although the anonymous author of *As a Chinaman Saw Us* considered racism to be "the dark side" of American society, his writing contained only tactful and ambiguous criticisms of the problem. Park No-yong, in *An Oriental View of American Civilization,* wrote "as a friendly critic" who "understands both Oriental and Occidental civilizations" to challenge racial prejudice only because he felt it had been carried too far.[35] Others even blamed Chinese immigrants for their part in causing the discrimination. Without examining the impact of segregation on Chinese immigrants, for example, the Rev. Huie Kin, a Chinese Presbyterian minister in New York City, criticized residents of Chinatown in *Reminiscences* for remaining a "clannish people." In his view, adhering to traditional Chinese values and customs made them "an outlandish sight" and provided "gist for the anti-Chinese propaganda" in American society.[36]

So vital an issue, racism was unlikely to escape Wu's discussion. But unlike others, his comments on racism reveal that he had confronted the desolating consequences of the institution. Early in the book, he described segregation as being widely adopted in the South, where blacks were compelled to ride on separate cars and eat in separate restaurants.

What really differentiated Wu from other cultivated Chinese such as Park No-yong, however, was that he spoke openly and clearly against racism. Culturally and intellectually, he argued, the Chinese were as civilized as Anglo-Americans because they were the products of a rich and complex intellectual, moral, and artistic history. Pointing out that the idea of white superiority is illogical, he appealed to the rationality and common sense of the American public: "Our differences of color, like our differences of speech, are accidental, they are due to climatic and other influences. We came originally from one stock. We all started evenly, Heaven has no favorites. Man alone has made differences between man and man, and the yellow man is no whit inferior to the white people in intelligence" (180). Regarding the popular belief that the yellow race was inferior, he cited Japan's victory in the 1905 Russo-Japanese War as indicating that it was the "yellow race" that displayed superior intelligence in the conflict. "It is the hissing idea of greed, fear, envy, selfishness, ignorance and prejudice," he concluded, "that led to the emergence of anti-Chinese sentiment." He carried his argument so far that it begins to sound like an advocacy of the superiority of Asian civilization: "God made the world for all men, and if God has any preference, if God is any respecter of persons, He must surely favor the Chinese, for He has made more of them than any other people on the globe . . . I am sometimes almost tempted to say that Asia will have to civilize the West over again" (181, 183).[37]

Ironically, Wu began by attacking racism but arrived at a central formulation that was a version of the same racist theory he denounced. After pondering the issue of racial tension, he asserted that the only way to solve the problem was through interracial marriage. "There is no doubt that mixed marriages of the white with the yellow races will be productive of good to both sides," he insisted. "The offspring from such mixed unions inherit the good points of both sides" (185), thus becoming the best race.[38] Striving to prove his theory scientifically, Wu related several stories about Eurasians in Hong Kong being more successful in academics, business, and politics than either whites or Asians. The theory is, of course, pseudo-scientific, but considering its historical background it was an encouraging and progressive idea about a complicated issue.

Wu's book goes beyond being only a discussion of American life. He also described the contrasts between America and China. Through such comparisons he hoped that Americans would be able to appreciate the fine qualities of the ancient civilization that nurtured the Chinese. Contrasting American characteristics such as aggressiveness, speed, materialism, and orientation toward the future with the modesty, morality, and emphasis on tradition in Chinese life, Wu argued that the ideal must be based on the doctrine of the mean—somewhere between the two extremes. In the book, there is a discussion of the American attitudes toward money: "Most people in America are desirous of money, and rush every day to their business with no other thought than to accumulate it quickly. Their love of money leaves them scarcely time to eat, to drink, or to sleep; waking or sleeping, they think of nothing else. . . . You frequently hear of sudden deaths which doctors attribute to heart failure, or some other malady, but which I suspect are caused by the continual restless hurry and worry" (78, 152). He then advised not living at such a fast pace but rather relaxing and being more leisurely. After all, making money was not the sole purpose for one to live in this world. "Certainly one meets more old people in China than in America," Wu wrote; although Americans measure their lives by accumulation, the Chinese measure theirs by morality and thus are "happier and live longer" (164).[39]

It is obvious, however, that the frankness of Wu's comments was affected by his need to impress an American audience. This is true for almost all the writing by Chinese immigrants on America. Their delicate position in the United States, in addition to genuine courtesy and tolerance derived from traditional Chinese philosophy and fear of displeasing their readers, often prevented them from speaking their ideas frankly. Although Wu declared that he would "make frank and unreserved comments on America," his criticisms in general were politely muted, tangential, and innocuous except in the case of racism. When he did make a criticism, he tried to put it in a humorous way and serve the dual purpose of showing that Chinese are both "cultivated" and "good-willed."[40] Frequently, he apologized for even the most innocent remarks. His otherwise interesting comments were thus often spoiled by a constantly tentative, apologetic tone, such as in the following: "I offer this suggestion to the great American nation for what it is worth, and I know they will receive it in the spirit in which it is made. . . . It would be very bold, and indeed impertinent, on my part to suggest to my American friends that they should adopt the Chinese costume . . . I have enough faith in the American people to believe that my humble suggestion will receive their favorable consideration" (103, 142–43).

Wu's embellished view on American life, however, is not a uniquely Chinese phenomenon. After reading *Letters from an American Farmer,* George Washington thought its author's view of America was "rather too flattering."[41] Works about America were also part of the dedication of cultivated Chinese to the task of improving the image of Chinese immigrants and promoting cultural understanding of Chinese civilization. Therefore, it is not surprising to find superficial aspects of America life to be exhaustively covered in their writing. Although such observations do contain sober comments and insights, the essence of the American system receives less attention and criticism than it deserves.

Nevertheless, the writings of Wu and others like him are valuable documents in trying to understand what educated Chinese immigrants thought about the country and why they thought so, as the following remarks by Wu reveal: "Naturally, the new visitor thinks [Americans] the happiest people on earth, and wishes that his own country could be governed as happily. Until that lucky day arrives he feels that he would rather stay in free America than return to his native land" (82). Perhaps the wish that they "would rather stay in free America than to return to (their) native land" provided their real purpose in writing.

## *My Life in China and America:* The Story of an Americanized Chinese

Among works by the cultivated Chinese during this period, Yung Wing's autobiographical *My Life in China and America* (1909) holds a unique position.[42] Its significance is evident: among the earlier publications of Chinese Americans in English, it is the only one that has been translated into other languages (Chinese and Japanese), and it was reprinted in 1978.[43] It is valuable for what it tells about a legendary figure in Chinese American history. Yung was the first Chinese to be graduated from an American college (Yale, 1854).[44] He was also one of the earliest naturalized Chinese American citizens (1852).[45] One of the few Chinese who rose to prominence and gained distinction in both China and the United States during the late nineteenth century, Yung's extraordinary life makes the book a rich and valuable source of the social, cultural, and ethnic experience of early Chinese immigrants in America.

Contrary to the writing of other cultivated Chinese, Yung provided neither an exotic picture of Chinese culture nor witty comments and penetrating observations on American life. Although other authors enjoyed elaborating on the brilliance of Chinese civilization and felt proud of its superiority, Yung thought China had long been in decline and lagged far behind the West. Impressed by the miracles of American society, he believed the only way for China to survive was to allow its young people to receive an American-style education, which would enable them to use democracy to reform the "Middle Kingdom." There was not even any nostalgia or longing for the old country. For Yung, China meant poverty and oppression, which he had abandoned for good as a teenager. He remained a strong advocate for reform in China and spent much of his adult life working for progress there. But the calm tone of his discussion of China's destiny is more like an outsider's concern for an endangered old civilization facing "greedy foreign barbarians" rather than the fervent patriotism that burst from the pens of most native Chinese.

Nevertheless, the differences between Yung's book and those of other Chinese immigrant authors are not nearly as important as their similarities. For one thing, *My Life in China and America* also reinforces the effort to win acceptance for Chinese in America. Yung's photograph on the book's cover serves as an illustrating point. Wearing short hair, a Teddy Roosevelt moustache, and Western dress, he personifies what theories of racial bias claimed impossible: the adaptability of Chinese in America. By showing how Americanized a Chinese immigrant could be, Yung demonstrated that once "China boys" were given an opportunity, they were just as willing and able to "vote at the same polls, study at the same schools and bow at the same altar" as anyone else in America.[46] Hence they deserved to have the same place in the "melting pot" and be treated like other immigrants.

With regard to Yung Wing's time, that point is of particular significance. Mainstream Americans tended to think that Chinese immigrants were unassimilable because of the fundamental differences in the two cultures' beliefs about the nature of freedom and personal aspirations. It was thought that Chinese immigrants—intellectuals and laborers alike—could not understand or appreciate the liberal premises and principles underlying American values, let alone grasp the essence and intended meaning of the American system.[47] Yung Wing's successful integration into mainstream society exposed that such a popular belief was nothing but bigotry rooted in racism. His contribution to developing a U.S.-China relationship also showed that the good will America had invested in Chinese students was not without reward. "China boys" like Yung Wing were grateful and would return the generosity they had received when they had the opportunity.

Yung Wing [Rong Hong, 1828–1912] was born in a small village in South Guangdong, only four miles away from the Portuguese colony of Macao [Aomen].[48] Unlike most cultivated Chinese, he came from a poor peasant family. As a little boy he had already begun to help support his family by peddling homemade candy and gleaning rice in fields. That miserable childhood must have had a lasting impact and been a major factor in his being a progressive reformer, for whenever Yung recalled his life in China he seemed to feel a heavy sense of responsibility for redressing the wrongs of the system. His difficult childhood also explains why his book exposes an unjust society and a country in lamentable condition although other writing from China's elite is laced with romantic Chinese legends, shimmering fairy tales, and lyrical descriptions of old traditions and customs.

Western education was another significant element that formed Yung's progressive views by providing him with a new world and a new perspective. In 1835, when Yung was barely seven, his father sent him to study in a missionary school at Macao.[49] It was an unorthodox decision because at this point China was still proud of its ancient heritage and looked down upon Western education as being inferior and immoral.[50] Yung, too, admitted, "It has always been a mystery to me why my parents should take it into their heads to put me into a foreign school, instead of a regular orthodox Confucian school."[51]

Perhaps the influence of the nearby Portuguese colony led his parents to their decision. They might have calculated shrewdly that because Western influence was spreading it would be worthwhile to have a child study in a foreign school so he could bring fortune to the family in the future. Or the decision may have been based on financial considerations. Apart from being tuition-free, the school provided free boarding for children from poor families. In any case, the seemingly unorthodox decision proved vital to Yung's future. It allowed him to begin his "Pilgrim Journey," first to Monson Academy in Massachusetts and then to Yale College.

In 1846, when the Rev. Samuel Robins Brown, an American teacher at the missionary school, planned to return home, he decided to take three students with him. Yung was one. His enthusiasm for the chance to pursue American education was evident: "When he [Samuel Brown] requested those who wished to accompany him to the States to signify it by rising, I was the first one on my feet" (18). That was surprising, because few Chinese then had gone to the United States, and rumors abounded that Americans used Chinese children for medical experiments. The enthusiasm may have come from the fact that by then Western education had shaped Yung's personality and altered his mind. One example concerns his visit to Napoleon's tomb on his way to America. When the ship made a stopover at St. Helena, Yung "went over to Longwood where was Napoleon's empty tomb" and cut a few twigs from a large weeping willow that hung over the tomb to keep as souvenirs (22). Such romantic behavior surely differed greatly from most of his countrymen, to whom Napoleon was just another "barbarian" name.

Despite the modern stereotype of Chinese being quick at mathematics but slow at English, Yung, the first Chinese student enrolled in an American college, was just the opposite. He distinguished himself—excelling beyond many of his American classmates—in English but did miserably in mathematics:

In the Sophomore year, from my utter aversion to mathematics, especially to differential and integral calculus, which I abhorred and detested, and which did me little or no good in the way of mental discipline, I used to fizzle and flunk so often that I really thought I was going to be dropped from the class, or dismissed from college. . . . The only redeeming feature that saved me as a student in the class of 1854, was the fortunate circumstance that I happened to be a successful competitor on two occasions in English composition in my division. I was awarded the first prize in the second term, and the first prize in the third term of the year. (37–38)

Yung's bias against mathematics and his poor performance at the discipline add a sarcastic footnote to the modern myth of Chinese American whiz-kids.

Part of Yung's expenses at Yale were covered by members of the Ladies' Association, a charitable missionary organization in Savannah, Georgia. Considering the strong racial bigotry of the antebellum South at the time, particularly toward the education of blacks, that is surprising. No doubt the reasons are complicated, but the fact that Yung was the first Chinese to study at Yale College may help explain such unusual generosity. Throughout the nineteenth century, American missionaries were known for evangelical activities in China and considered the conversion of the Chinese in the United States to be part of those efforts. It is likely that Yung's potential value to the missionary cause that made him attract considerable attention.[52] Indeed, he was persuaded to return to China and join the American missionaries there as soon as he was graduated from Yale.

Contrary to the accusation that the Chinese could never be assimilated into American life, Yung had undergone a considerable degree of Americanization by the time he was graduated from Yale in 1854. Although he had only lived in the United States for seven years, he had been influenced by American ideas and Western education for nearly twenty, since he first entered the Morrison School at the age of seven. Tangible evidence, both physical and cultural, of his American identity was conspicuous. Instead of maintaining his Chinese heritage, he cut his queue, dressed in modern Western clothes, converted to Christianity, and acquired American citizenship. He had so completely assimilated that "he had even almost entirely forgotten his native tongue."[53]

Defiance of his newly acquired "Christian character" also added credit to his Americanization. He related, for example, that he had beaten a Scot who had insulted him. The incident happened when Yung worked in Shanghai shortly after his graduation from Yale. His rival was "a stalwart six-footer and a sportsman," but Yung fought him without hesitation: "Although he stood head and shoulders above me in height, yet I was not at all abashed or intimidated by his burly and contemptuous appearance. . . . I struck him back in the identical place where he punched me, but my blow was a stinger and it went with lightning rapidity to the spot, without giving him time to think. It drew blood in great profusion from lip and nose" (70–71).

One might appreciate Yung's courage in taking the law into his own hands, considering that a frequent allegation of the time was that the Chinese were unable to fight. As Jack London observed, "I was familiar enough with the Chinese character to know that fear alone restrained them."[54] The self-satisfaction evident in Yung's recounting of the fight helps in understanding how much the event meant to him: "I was looked upon with great respect . . . no Chinese . . . had ever been known to have the courage and pluck to defend his rights, point blank, when they had been violated or trampled upon by a foreigner" (72).

To many newly naturalized American citizens, war provides the first opportunity to prove their patriotism. One well-known example concerns the heroic performance of the Irish in the Civil War, who "were Americans twice over—by their oath under the law, and by their sword in the war."[55] That is also true in Yung's case. When the Civil War broke out he volunteered to serve in the Union army although he was on an important mission for the Manchu court at the time: "I felt as a naturalized citizen of the United States, it was my bounden duty to offer my services as a volunteer . . . simply to show my loyalty and patriotism to my adopted country" (158–59).

What drove him to the battlefield was evidently not the ferment of abolitionism or even Unionism but rather a demonstration of patriotism. In Yung's eyes, the great war that tested the principle of democracy was merely an occasion to present evidence of loyalty to his adopted country. Such an attitude then was not uncommon among Chinese immigrants, many of whom felt strongly that military service would be an excellent way to win better treatment in America. In fact, Chinese immigrants have fought for their adopted country in every major war since they first settled in the United States in the mid-nineteenth century.

Yung was by no means the only Chinese who volunteered to serve in the Union army. According to a study based on documents at the National Archives, nearly fifty Chinese immigrants fought for the Union and shed blood on the battlefield during the Civil War.[56] When the Spanish-American War broke out, Chinese community leaders attempted to organize a Chinese Brigade, although the war ended before they mobilized.[57] A significant number of Chinese Americans, both immigrants and native-born, fought bravely for the United States during World War I. For example, Lee Yan Phou's two sons both served. His eldest, Amos, a first lieutenant in the U.S. Army, was killed in action at Berdenal in France in 1918, and his second son, Clarence, was a midshipman on convey duty on the U.S.S. *South Dakota* in the Atlantic.[58] Lou Sing Kee [Liu Chengji], from New York, received the Distinguished Service Cross in recognition of his courage and endurance in France in 1918.[59]

Unfortunately, if there emerged growing acceptance for other groups of immigrants because of their loyalty to the United States in war, the similar performance of Chinese did not affect public opinion. Rewards for Chinese patriotism were more ironic. During the Spanish-American War, for example, several dozen Chinese sailors aboard the U.S.S. *Olympic* who had fought in the battle of Manila Bay in 1898 were not allowed to leave the ship upon arrival in San Francisco. Although Admiral Dewey petitioned for special permission, it was rejected. Customs officials felt it "their duty to enforce the law [the Chinese Exclusion Act]."[60]

Curiously, Yung's American citizenship and loyalty to his adopted country did not hamper his concern for the progress of China. Although he was unsentimental about the old country, he staunchly supported reform and was involved in almost all the major political movements in China during his lifetime. Because he felt he understood two points of view and, to some extent, two epochs (to him, America stood for the new and China for the old), he thought he could play a significant role in helping China regenerate. Upon his first return, for example, he suggested that the leaders of the Taiping Rebellion then sweeping across China organize an American-style civil government and establish an American-style educational system, "making the Bible one of the textbooks" (109).

Yung's most important contribution to the modernization of China as well as to the development of the early Chinese American community was his effort to bring Chinese students to study in the United States. Because he felt that American education had unmistakably enlarged his "mental and moral horizon" and revealed "responsibilities which the sealed eyes of ignorance can never see," Yung saw it as essential to send other Chinese youths to be imbued with democratic values. They could then initiate a similar system when they returned to China. "I was determined that the rising generation of China should enjoy the same educational advantages that I had enjoyed," he recalled, "that through Western education China might be regenerated, become enlightened and powerful" (41). By persuading some of the most influential officials in China, he succeeded in organizing the Chinese Educational Mission in 1872, which brought 120 boys to study in the United States over the next decade. Because of the efforts he made toward the educational program, he has been deemed the "father of the education of Chinese in the United States."[61]

Yung's keen interest in the progress of China, however, appears to have originated more from a desire to improve the position of Chinese in the United States than from a concern for the destiny of his homeland. In his view, a weak China was the major cause of humiliation Chinese suffered in America. Had China been a world power, Yung maintained, the status of the Chinese in the United States would be much improved. Such opinions were almost unanimous among Chinese immigrants in America, no matter what their backgrounds. One can find, for example, that even the "undistinguished" laundryman Lee Chew argued, "It [the mistreatment of Chinese] is persisted in merely because China is not a fighting nation. The Americans would not dare to treat Germans, English, Italians or even Japanese as they treat the Chinese, because if they did there would be a war."[62]

To some extent, that point of view was justified by the fact that most Americans around the turn of the twentieth century had a more favorable impression of Japanese immigrants than of Chinese. "There is something bright and likeable about those men [the Japanese]," remarked an American businessman, "[they] are different altogether."[63] Eurasians of Chinese parentage sometimes claimed to have Japanese ancestry in order to gain higher social status.

Although reasons for this phenomenon are complex, central to them seems to be the fact that Japan had emerged as a world power and gained a measure of international prestige by the early twentieth century. As a result, it was able to protect the interests of Japanese immigrants in the United States.[64] In contrast, Chinese immigrants throughout history received little such support because China was weakened by deteriorating social and economic conditions and foreign invasion. Consequently, Chinese immigrants widely believed that a strong and progressive China would help them win acceptance, and an intense desire for a reform movement in China characterized the Chinese American community.[65] Various political organizations were set up for that purpose, Chinatowns across the United States became meeting places for revolutionary activities, and immigrants established several military academies in the United States to train fighters to overthrow the corrupt Manchu regime.[66] Even poor laundrymen identifed China's fortunes with their own and donated money to the revolutionary movement in China, just as Irish immigrants gave their life savings willingly to the Catholic Church. Both groups believed that a powerful motherland or an influential church would benefit and protect its people abroad.

Stylistically, Yung's writing, crowded with Western cultural and religious allusions and metaphors, symbolizes his American credentials. In condemning the tyranny of the Manchu regime, for instance, he denounced it as "unparalleled in the annals of modern civilization, eclipsing even the enormities and blood-thirstiness of Caligula and Nero" (55). Luke, Johan, Tacitus, and the French Revolution are a few among scores of figures and events he used to illustrate his views. He even used God to justify his argument, which is rare in Chinese American writing. Like Puritan historians, Yung saw God's glory everywhere and in everything—from the unexpected reward for his work in childhood, to his parents' decision to send him to a missionary school, to his witness of God's punishing a "sinned" sailor on a ship in the sea, to the mediation of his children's destiny.[67] Furthermore, the bookishness of his prose resembles the Puritan style of writing in its meticulous but monotonous elaboration. The fact that he incorporated so many features of Puritan writing into his leads to speculation that *My Life in China and America* was a conscious attempt to imitate the work of Puritan historians.

Yung's determination to be a "good American citizen" is uniquely strong among early Chinese immigrants, but that desire also presented him with the subtle problem of how to deal with racism. Throughout his 246–page book, he remained mute on the issue, mentioning it only briefly and attributing it to the outcome of "party factors and politics." His intended ambiguity on so heated a subject was suspicious and controversial among Chinese immigrants. As a result, "he could not fail to encounter, among his own people, prejudice, suspicion, and hostility."[68]

To some extent, the fact that Yung Wing deliberately ignored the issue is not difficult to understand. Because his life in America differed so drastically from the experience of most Chinese immigrants, he might have been inclined toward indifference to the plight of those who struggled for survival in segregated urban ghettos.[69] He lived in a time when anti-Chinese violence was most rampant, yet as a respected public figure he did not seem in any way victimized by racism. Rather, he might have gained advantages because of his race. The fact that his friends included prominent politicians, scholars, and businessmen such as Mark Twain and former President U. S. Grant is strong evidence that he "was very kindly treated by the good people everywhere" in America (49).

The most astonishing event of such treatment was Yung's marriage in 1875 to Mary L. Kellogg, a daughter of an old Yankee family in Hartford. Although anti-Chinese feelings throughout the country were gradually increasing during the decade, the marriage was warmly received by the local community. Ironically, it was the Chinese officials who strongly opposed the union and used the event as an excuse to dismiss Yung as co-commissioner of the Chinese Educational Mission. Most interracial marriages of the era seem to have brought more misfortune than happiness.[70] In Yung's case, however, the match was unusually successful. The harmony of the marriage may be attributed to the fact that he had succumbed to Anglo-American culture so completely that he and Mary Kellogg shared the same worldview. Their wedding ceremony, for example, was a Christian one, and instead of naming their children in the traditional Chinese way, as most Chinese immigrants then insisted, they gave them Anglo-American names—Brown and Bartlett—in memory of two missionaries who had been Yung Wing's mentors.

As an accurate account of the experience of one of the earliest Chinese immigrants in the United States, Yung Wing's autobiography records his lifelong effort to integrate himself into American society, an effort that spanned the period of free immigration and the exclusion era. Some view the book as a valuable document of a pioneering figure in Chinese American history who broke a new path for later generations through his success in American life; others consider it as representing a "submissive" and "Christian missionary tradition."[71] Both views are extreme. Yung only did what he could do under the circumstances in which he found himself. He came to the United States at a time when virtually no other Chinese did so and was educated entirely in American schools. Few Chinese have been put under such long, intense, and continual American cultural influence. Thus it is not surprising that Yung made immersion in American life his ultimate goal. Although he did not speak for the majority of early Chinese immigrants, his writing contains the experience of those who became objects of American missionary efforts. It provides affecting testimony of a Chinese journey seeking an opening into American life through being able to cope with American social, cultural, and religious values.

The books discussed in this chapter represent three different types of writing of cultivated Chinese in America during the exclusion era. Whether an introduction to Chinese civilization, views on American life, or a demonstration that the Chinese were capable of integrating into American society, they all served the same purpose: improving the image of the Chinese. They were conscious efforts to gain better treatment for the immigrants. They also share a sustained desire to win acceptance and sympathy from mainstream society. As pioneering works, their significance is particularly noteworthy. They helped rouse the American public's interest in Chinese culture and increase their understanding of China. Together with writings of later Chinese American authors, they are a cause for revising American perception of Chinese immigrants.[72]

There is always the temptation to exaggerate the books' role in improving the status of Chinese immigrants, but the efforts made by the authors are impressive. The change in the American image of Chinese immigrants did not come overnight but rather through a long and gradual process. Its impetus was in part because of the writing of cultivated Chinese immigrants. In that sense, their work constitutes landmarks in Chinese American literature and history. The authors' views of racism are limited but insightful. Ignorance of cultural differences is surely one of the major things that has led to prejudice against Chinese immigrants throughout history. As John Higham points out, "In the absence of other disturbing factors, Americans rated lowest the nationalities most conspicuously remote in culture and race."[73] It is also unfair to declare that only the cultivated Chinese wrote in this way. The same intention led the Jewish immigrant playwright Israel Zangwill to compose *The Melting Pot*.[74]

## Notes

1. The epilogue is from Lee Yan Phou, "The Chinese Must Stay," *North American Review* 148 (April 1889): 482. Lee sometimes spelled his name as "Yan Phou Lee" (Lee being his surname).

2. Beginning from the 1870s, a growing number of Chinese students came to America for educations financed by their families. In 1873, when the second group of the Chinese Educational Mission left for America, in addition to the government-sponsored students there were also seven students who had been sent by their families. More self-financed Chinese students and scholars came to the United States in the ensuing decades. Him Mark Lai, *Cong huaqiao dao huaren* [From overseas Chinese to Chinese Americans], (Hong Kong: Joint, 1992), 60–62; Gao Yang, *Dengho loutai* [Lights in the pavilions], (Taipei: Jingji, 1980), 2:554–55.

3. Between Yung Wing's graduation from Yale College in 1854 to the end of the Korean War in 1953, more than twenty-two thousand Chinese students and scholars studied in the United States. A significant number later settled in America. Harold R. Isaacs, *Scratches on Our Minds: American Views of China and India*, rev. ed. (Armonk: M. E. Sharpe, 1980), 68; Rose Hum Lee, *The Chinese in the United States of America* (Hong Kong: Hong Kong University Press, 1960), 86.

4. From the beginning, Chinese students tended to study at the more prestigious schools in the United States. Between 1872 and 1954, 80 percent of Chinese students were enrolled in twenty elite American universities, for example, Harvard, Columbia, Yale, and Stanford. Kwang-Ching Liu, *Americans and Chinese: A Historical Essay and a Bibliography* (Cambridge: Harvard University Press, 1963), 23–40; Thomas E. La Fargue, *China's First Hundred* (Pullman: State College of Washington Press, 1942), 1–66.

5. The Chinese Educational Mission (1872–81) was an official organization sponsored by the Manchu regime to provide an American education for a small number of highly selected Chinese boys (120 altogether) between 1872 to 1881. Ssu-yu Teng and John K. Fairbank, *China's Response to the West: A Documentary Survey, 1839–1923*, rev. ed. (Cambridge: Harvard University Press, 1979), 91–95; La Fargue, *China's First Hundred*, 1–66.

6. Doris Chu, *The Chinese in Massachusetts: Their Experiences and Contributions* (Boston: Chinese Culture Institute, 1987), 38–40.

7. Liang made a strenuous effort to help Chinese immigrants improve their conditions when he served as Chinese minister to the United States (1903–7). Lai, *From Overseas Chinese to Chinese Americans*, 74.

8. R. David Arkush and Leo Ou-fan Lee, trans. and eds., *Land without Ghosts: Chinese Impressions of America from the Mid-Nineteenth Century to the Present* (Berkeley: University of California Press, 1989), 1–12; Isaacs, *Scratches on Our Minds*, 63–96; La Fargue, *China's First Hundred*, 17–35.

9. Lee does not explain how he managed to return to the United States, but he was not alone in doing so. Approximately ten students of the Chinese Educational Mission returned to America after they were sent back to China. Lucy C. Yu, "Acculturation and Stress within Chinese American Families," *Journal of Comparative Family Studies* 15

(Spring 1984): 91; Peter Kong-ming New, "Footnotes on a Yankee Chinese: Letters of Shang-chow New, 1913–1917," *Amerasia* 11, no. 2 (1984): 81–95. Also see Ruthanne Lum McCunn, *Chinese American Portraits: Personal Histories, 1828–1988* (San Francisco: Chronicle Books, 1988), 24–25.

10. Lee wrote in 1922, "I was in the live poultry business. . . . As a side line I worked as associate editor of the Hasbrouck Heights (N.J.) *Newsletter* and was later on the *Enterprise* of East Rutherford. In connection with my newspaper work, I was drawn into local politics. Strange as it may seem, I was campaign manager for a man who aspired to be mayor of Wood Ridge." "Thirty-Fifth Year Record of the Class of 1887" (1922), Yale University Library, New Haven. Lee was last heard from in March 1938 on a trip to his native village near Canton. Thereafter, he disappeared—presumably killed during Japanese air raids on that city. Lee Yan Phou, the "Fiftieth Year Record of the Class of 1887" (1938), Yale University Library, New Haven. I am indebted to Anne Nahl, a doctoral candidate at the University of Wisconsin at Madison, for sharing with me the information she found in the Lee file at the Yale University Archives.

11. Lee Yan Phou, *When I Was a Boy in China* (Boston: Lothrop, 1887), 41 (subsequent page citations appear in parentheses).

12. *Gold Hill* [Nev.] *Daily News,* July 3, 1880, quoted in Gary BeDunnah, "A History of the Chinese in Nevada, 1855–1904," M.A. thesis, University of Nevada, Reno, 1966, 16.

13. Limin Chu, "The Images of China and the Chinese in the *Overland Monthly:* 1868–1875, 1883–1935," Ph.D. diss., Duke University, 1965, 72–78.

14. Whether Lee read *David Copperfield* is not known, but given that he was well educated in English literature it is quite possible that he did so.

15. Quoted in Mary Roberts Coolidge, *Chinese Immigration* (New York: Henry Holt, 1909), 96; and *The Chinese Experience in Arizona and Northern Mexico: 1870–1940* (Tucson: Arizona Historical Society, 1980), 4.

16. Elmer C. Sandmeyer, *The Anti-Chinese Movement in California,* repr. (Urbana: University of Illinois Press, 1973), 61–63, 68–69; Coolidge, *Chinese Immigration,* 96–108. Also see Zhang Yinhuan, "Chinese in America," in *Land without Ghosts,* trans. and ed. Arkush and Lee, 71–76.

17. Jack London, "The Yellow Handkerchief," in London, *Tales of the Fish Patrol* (New York: Macmillan, 1905), 225. Despite his progressive views on social problems, Jack London was known to be prejudiced against "Orientals." When criticized by friends because his bias was inconsistent with the socialist doctrine, London responded by pounding on the table and exclaiming, "What the devil! I am first of all a white man and only then a Socialist!" Quoted in Thomas F. Gossett, *Race: The History of an Idea in America* (Dallas: Southern Methodist University Press, 1963), 206. Also see William F. Wu, *The Yellow Peril: Chinese Americans in American Fiction, 1850–1940* (Hamden: Archon Books, 1982), 117–21.

18. Him Mark Lai, "The Chinese," in *Harvard Encyclopedia of American Ethnic Groups,* ed. Stephan Thernstrom (Cambridge: Harvard University Press, 1980), 220.

19. Henry James and William Dean Howells made smiliar comments about American women. See Warner Berthoff, *The Ferment of Realism: American Literature, 1884–1919,* repr. (New York: Cambridge University Press, 1981), 50–125.

20. Gary Kulik, "Representing the Railroad," *Gettysburg Review* 2, no. 3 (1989): 495–510.

21. Elaine H. Kim, *Asian American Literature: An Introduction to the Writings and Their Social Context* (Philadelphia: Temple University Press, 1982), 25–27.

22. Lee continued to write about China and Chinese immigrants after the book was published and became more outspoken in defense of the interests of Chinese immigrants. He argued eloquently, for example, that the Chinese, like other immigrants, had every right to come and settle in America: "Chinese immigrants never claimed to be any better than farmers, traders, and artisans. If, on the one hand, they are not princes and nobles, on the other hand, they are not coolies and slaves." Armed with facts and logic, Lee pointed out that it was nothing but bigotry rooted in nativism that had led Congress to pass the Chinese Exclusion Act. Lee, "The Chinese Must Stay," 476–83.

23. Julius Su Tow, *The Real Chinese in America* (Orange: Academy Press, 1923).

24. Frank Chin et al., eds., *Aiiieeeee! An Anthology of Asian-American Writers* (Washington, D.C.: Howard University Press, 1974), xi.

25. For a brief yet explicit analysis of this issue, see *Land without Ghosts*, trans. and ed. Arkush and Lee, 1–12.

26. Henry Pearson Gratton, ed., *As a Chinaman Saw Us: Passages from His Letters to a Friend at Home* (New York: D. Appleton, 1904), vi–viii. There is controversy over the identity of the anonymous author of these letters. Although some scholars suspect that the book might be a "patent fraud," Andre Chih, a prominent China scholar, has cited it as a primary source of information in his acclaimed *L'Occident "Chretien" vu par les Chinois vers la fin du XIXme siecle* [The "Christian" west as seen by the Chinese around the end of the nineteenth century], (Paris: Presses Universitaires de France, 1962). Judging from the book's narrative style, knowledge of Chinese life, and familiarity with the Chinese American experience, I agree that the author was Chinese.

27. Gratton, ed., *As a Chinaman Saw Us,* vi.

28. I put Chiang Yee's "silent traveler" series in the same group as those by Wu Tingfang and others. Although Chiang's works were published in a later period, they were written in the same style as those of earlier authors, and his comments on American society are similar to those made by Wu.

29. There is an impressive body of literature of travel notes published in China about America, but it has served a different purpose. Arkush and Lee, trans. and eds., *Land without Ghosts,* 1–12.

30. Gratton, ed., *As a Chinaman Saw Us,* vii.

31. For example, *America through the Spectacles of an Oriental Diplomat* went through a second printing within two months after publication. Even now, the Harvard University Library has three copies, evidence of the book's continuing popularity.

32. For more information about Wu Tingfang's background, see Linda P. Shin, "China in Transition: The Role of Wu T'ing-fang," Ph.D. diss., University of California, Los Angeles, 1970.

33. Wu Tingfang, *America through the Spectacles of an Oriental Diplomat* (New York: Frederick A. Stokes, 1914), 66 (subsequent page citations appear in parentheses).

34. Wu's comments on paradoxes in American national character—if indeed there is such a thing as national character—are not unique in Chinese writings on America. They had been made with some frequency before and are still being made. In *As a Chinaman Saw Us,* the author claims that it is "the paradox in American life" that left an unforgettable impression on him. Seventy years later the same issue was still keenly felt; see Liu Zongren, *Two Years in the Melting Pot* (San Francisco: China Books, 1984).

35. Park No-yong [Bao Narong], *An Oriental View of American Civilization* (Boston: Hale, Cushman and Flint, 1934), 9–43. Park made similar comments in his other works, such as *A Squint-eye View of America* (Boston: Meador, 1951). Park is sometimes thought to be Korean, perhaps because of the unconventional way he spelled his Chinese surname.

36. Huie Kin [Xu Qin], *Reminiscences* (Peiping [Beijing]: San Su Press, 1932), 28, cited in Kim, *Asian American Literature,* 31. Also see Lai, *From Overseas Chinese to Chinese Americans,* 61, 66.

37. Here again the influence of mainstream American culture on Chinese authors is evident. What Wu says in this passage echoes Abraham Lincoln's assertion that "God must love the common people because he made so many of them."

38. Here, Wu confronts the theory espoused by Herbert Spencer and others that "half-breeds" might be inferior to both stocks. See Stephen Jay Gould, *The Mismeasure of Man* (New York: Norton, 1981), 19–72.

39. Wu influenced other Chinese immigrant authors; for example, his views on the gap between the life-styles of Chinese and Americans were further developed and elaborated upon by Lin Yutang in the bestselling *The Importance of Living* (1937).

40. Wu appears to have been much more straightforward and even blunt in private conversations about prejudice against the Chinese in America. In a talk with a group of New York reporters, for example, he said angrily, "Why can't you be fair? Would you talk like that if mine was not a weak nation? Would you say it if the Chinese [immigrants] had votes?" *New York Tribune,* Nov. 28, 1901, quoted in Roger Daniels, *Asian America: Chinese and Japanese in the United States since 1850* (Seattle: University of Washington Press, 1988), 93.

41. Quoted in George McMichael et al., eds., *Anthology of American Literature* (New York: Macmillan, 1980), 1:381.

42. Some critics erroneously think that "Wing" is the author's surname. We know, however, from Yung Wing's Chinese name and his own account that "Wing" is his given name.

43. *My Life in China and America* was reprinted by Arno Press in 1978 as part of a series on the Asian experience in America.

44. Chinese students came to study in the United States earlier than Yung Wing, but he was the first Chinese (also the first Asian) to graduate from an American institution of higher learning. La Fargue, *China's First Hundred,* 17–35; Edwin Pak-wah Leung, "The Education of Early Chinese Students in America," in *The Chinese American Experience: Papers from the Second National Conference on Chinese American Studies (1980),* ed. Genny Lim (San Francisco: Chinese Historical Society of America, 1984), 203–10; Yan Zi, "Zhongguo liuxue di yi ren" [The first Chinese college student in America], [Beijing] *Renmin Ribao* [People's Daily], overseas ed., May 5, 1992, 8.

45. How Yung Wing received his citizenship is still deserving of study. Because of a 1790 federal law restricting the right of naturalization to "free white persons" only, Chinese immigrants were denied American citizenship until 1943, when the Chinese Exclusion Act was repealed. Yet there were reports of individual Chinese being granted citizenship, primarily on the East Coast where Chinese were treated with more sympathy than elsewhere. A few cases did occur in the West, however.

Gunther Barth mentions two Chinese who claimed to be naturalized American citizens in San Francisco in 1852; Jack Chen found that a Chinese cabin boy who settled in Lancaster, Pennsylvania, became a naturalized citizen in 1862; and Pardee Lowe reports that his father, an immigrant from Canton, acquired American citizenship in California in the late nineteenth century. According to Sucheng Chan, because of a loophole in the law there was no racial restriction between December 31, 1873, and February 18, 1875, with regard to citizenship. As a result, a number of Chinese immigrants were naturalized during this period. Gunther Barth, *Bitter Strength: A Study of the Chinese in the United States, 1850–1870* (Cambridge: Harvard University Press, 1964), 179; Jack Chen, *The Chinese of America* (New York: Harper and Row, 1980), 5; Pardee Lowe, *Father and Glorious Descendant* (Boston: Little, Brown, 1943), 3–4; Sucheng Chan, *Asian Americans: An Interpretive History* (Boston: Twayne Publishers, 1991), 47, 92. For more information on lawsuits involving the naturalization rights of Chinese immigrants, see Charles J. McClain, *In Search of Equality: The Chinese Struggle against Discrimination in Nineteenth-Century America* (Berkeley: University of California Press, 1994), 12, 70–73, 137–38, 163–64.

46. *Daily Alta California,* May 12, 1851, 2.

47. Stuart C. Miller, *The Unwelcome Immigrant: The American Image of the Chinese, 1785–1882* (Berkeley: University of California Press, 1969), 113–66.

48. Ceded from Guangdong [Kwangtung] province in 1557, Macao was the only colony that Western countries had on the border of China until Britain took over Hong Kong from China after the Opium War (1839–42).

49. The school was established by the London Missionary Society in memory of the British missionary Robert Morrison (1728–1834) and employed by American teachers. It was moved to Hong Kong shortly after the Opium War.

50. It was not until after China was defeated by Britain in the Opium War that most Chinese began to change their views on Western education and culture. Teng and Fairbank, *China's Response to the West,* 46–57.

51. Yung Wing, *My Life in China and America* (New York: Holt, 1909), 2 (subsequent page citations appear in parentheses).

52. Lo Hsiang-lin, "Yung Wing: First Chinese Graduate from a U.S. University," in *The Life, Influence, and the Role of the Chinese in the United States, 1776–1960: Proceedings, Papers of the National Conference Held at the University of San Francisco* (San Francisco: Chinese Historical Society of America, 1976), 207–15. Throughout the nineteenth century, southerners remained major supporters for missionary activities in China. For more information on the attitude of southerners toward Chinese immigrants and missionary movement in China, see Lucy M. Cohen, *Chinese in the Post–Civil War South: A People without a History* (Baton Rouge: Louisiana State University Press, 1984), 1–21; and Jane Hunter, *The Gospels of Gentility: American Women Missionaries in Turn-of-the-Century China* (New Haven: Yale University Press, 1989).

53. The Rev. Joseph H. Twichell, "Appendix," in Yung, *My Life in China and America,* 257.

54. London, *Tales of the Fish Patrol,* 226.

55. *Newburyport Herald,* Dec. 8, 1870, quoted in Stephan Thernstrom, *Poverty and Progress: Social Mobility in a Nineteenth Century City* (Cambridge: Harvard University Press, 1964), 174. For more information on performance of immigrants in the Union army during the Civil War, see William L. Burton, *Melting Pot Soldiers: the Union's Ethnic Regiments* (Ames: Iowa State University Press, 1988).

56. Linda Wheeler, "Forty-seven Chinese Men Served in the U.S. Civil War," *Washington Post,* May 12, 1999, A18; William Frederick Worner, "A Chinese Soldier in the Civil War," *Journal of the Lancaster County Historical Society* 25 (1921): 52–55. Chinese-language sources also report three Chinese immigrants—Zhen Yatong, Cao Guipeng, and

Woo Hong Neok [Wu Hongyu]—served in the Union army and navy and fought in New York and Pennsylvania during the Civil War. Lai, *From Overseas Chinese to Chinese Americans*, 163, 173, 328, 336; Chen, *The Chinese of America*, 5.

57. Corinne Hoexter, *From Canton to California: The Epic of Chinese Immigration* (New York: Four Winds Press, 1976), 251.

58. Lee Yan Phou, "Fiftieth Year Record of the Class of 1887," Yale University Library.

59. "Cosmopolitan Heroes," *New York Times*, May 4, 1919, sec. 2, 1. Also see Hoexter, *From Canton to California*, 253–54; and Lai, *From Overseas Chinese to Chinese Americans*, 164. More Chinese Americans fought in World War II. After Japan's attack on Pearl Harbor, more than a fifth of all adult males in the Chinese American population were enlisted or drafted into the armed forces and fought under the American flag in both the European and Pacific fronts. Eighteen percent of them were either wounded or killed in action. Chan, *Asian Americans*, 122. Also see Ronald Takaki, *Strangers from a Different Shore: A History of Asian Americans* (New York: Penguin Books, 1989), 372–73.

60. Carson City, Nev., *Morning Appeal*, Sept. 2, 1899, quoted in BeDunnah, "A History of the Chinese in Nevada," 78. Also see Him Mark Lai, Joe Huang, and Don Wong, *The Chinese of America, 1785–1980* (San Francisco: Chinese Culture Foundation, 1980), 53.

61. Quoted in Yan, "The First Chinese College Student in America," 8. Also see Lai, *From Overseas Chinese to Chinese Americans*, 60. Ironically, despite Yung's Americanization, his method of recruiting for the Chinese Educational Mission was similar to that of contract laborers. A favorite American indictment of the system of contracting for laborers is that it did not give recruits personal freedom. That was also the case with Yung, who required parents or guardians of students sign "a paper which stated that without recourse, they were perfectly willing to let their sons or protégés go abroad to be educated for a period of fifteen years, from the time they began their studies in the United States until they had finished, and that during the fifteen years, the government was not to be responsible for death or for any accident that might happen to any student." Yung, *My Life in China and America*, 184.

62. Lee Chew, "The Life Story of a Chinaman," in *The Life Stories of Undistinguished Americans as Told by Themselves*, ed. Hamilton Holt (New York: Potts, 1906), 297. Lee was not quite correct. The mass lynchings of eleven Italian immigrants in New Orleans in 1891 is a case in point. See John Higham, *Strangers in the Land: Patterns of American Nativism, 1860–1925*, rev. ed. (New York: Atheneum, 1985), 90–91. Most Chinese immigrants of the era, however, shared Lee's sentiment that the Chinese encountered more prejudice than other groups in America because China was a weak country. For more analyses of Chinese views on the relationship between their experiences in America and China's status in the world community, see Xiao-huang Yin, "The Growing Influence of Chinese Americans on U.S.-China Relations," in *The Outlook for U.S.-China Relations Following the 1997–1998 Summits*, ed. Peter H. Koehn and Joseph Y. S. Cheng (Hong Kong: Chinese University Press, 1999), 331–49.

63. Quoted in Sui Sin Far [Edith Maude Eaton], "Leaves from the Mental Portfolio of a Eurasian," *The Independent*, Jan. 21, 1909, 129.

64. An explicit summary of the issue appears in Roger Daniels, "The Japanese," in *Ethnic Leadership in America*, ed. John Higham (Baltimore: Johns Hopkins University Press, 1979), 36–63.

65. Some African Americans also attributed the plight of the Chinese in America to the absence of a powerful homeland to protect them. David J. Hellwig, "Black Reactions to

Chinese Immigration and the Anti-Chinese Movement: 1850–1910," *Amerasia Journal* 6, no. 2 (1979): 38.

66. Franklin Ng, "The Western Military Academy in Fesno," in *Origins and Destinations: Forty-one Essays on Chinese America*, ed. Munson A. Kwok and Ella Yee Quan (Los Angeles: Chinese Historical Society of Southern California and Asian American Studies Center, UCLA, 1994), 153–75; Lai, Huang, and Wong, *The Chinese of America, 1785–1980*, 62–65; Chan, *Asian Americans*, 96–97; Peter Kwong, *The New Chinatown* (New York: Noonday Press, 1987), 101.

67. The story of the sailer is reminiscent of William Bradford's vivid account of the death of a "profane" young seaman on the *Mayflower*'s voyage across the Atlantic. William Bradford, *Of Plymouth Plantation* (1630), reprinted in *Anthology of American Literature*, ed. McMichael et al., 36–37.

68. Twichell, "Appendix," in Yung, *My Life in China and America*, 257. There might be another reason for Yung's restrained attitude toward racism and his extravagant praise for the American system. Perhaps he desired to be the Chinese ambassador to the United States. It did not seem strange for a foreign citizen to be appointed a Chinese diplomat by the Qing regime. The Manchu court was so ignorant that most Chinese diplomats in America during the late nineteenth century were either permanent residents or citizens of the United States. Even foreigners were appointed Chinese diplomats, as in the case of Anson Burlingame. A friend of Abraham Lincoln's, Burlingame became American minister to Beijing (1861–67). After retiring from the American diplomatic service he was appointed by the Manchu throne as chief of a special mission of China to America and Europe in 1868. Frederick Wells Williams, *Anson Burlingame and the First Chinese Mission to Foreign Powers* (New York: Scribner's Sons, 1912), 146–57. Also see Wu, *America through the Spectacles of an Oriental Diplomat*, 41.

69. It is noteworthy that Yung Wing expressed strong sympathy for Chinese immigrants in South America when he was a member of the Chinese commission that investigated the "coolie trade" in the 1870s. By exposing the miserable conditions endured by Chinese contract laborers in South America and the Caribbean, Yung played a significant role in helping stop the notorious "coolie trade." Charles Desnoyers, "'The Thin Edge of the Wedge': The Chinese Educational Mission and Diplomatic Representation in the Americas, 1872–1875," *Pacific Historical Review* 61, no. 2 (1992): 241–63.

70. There are, of course, exceptions. In one case, a Chinese immigrant in the Midwest married a Swedish woman, and their union was successful. Daniels, *Asian America*, 89. In general, however, such cases are rare because of the strong prejudice against interracial marriages at the time. Even marriages between cultivated Chinese and white women often failed; Lee Yan Phou's first union with a white woman, for example, lasted only three years. Betty Lee Sung, *Chinese American Intermarriage* (New York: Center for Migration Studies, 1990), 1–19.

71. Chen, *The Chinese of America*, 13, 177–79; Jeffrey Chan et al., eds., *The Big Aiiieeeee: An Anthology of Chinese American and Japanese American Literature* (New York: Meridian, 1991), xii.

72. For a detailed analysis of the role of Chinese scholars in improving the American image of the Chinese, see Isaacs, *Scratches on Our Minds*, 63–96.

73. Higham, *Strangers in the Land*, 24.

74. Werner Sollors, *Beyond Ethnicity: Consent and Descent in American Culture* (New York: Oxford University Press, 1986), 66–99.

*I give my right hand to the Occidentals and my left to the Orientals,*
*hoping that between them they will not utterly destroy the insignificant*
*"connecting link."*
—Sui Sin Far

# 3

# The Voice of a Eurasian:
# Sui Sin Far and Her Writing

Thus Sui Sin Far [Edith Maude Eaton, 1865–1914], the first Chinese woman writer in North America, expressed both her feelings as a Eurasian and her keen desire to explain what kind of people Chinese Americans were.[1] Among early Chinese immigrant authors, she was virtually the only one who was engaged in writing imaginative literature rather than social-anthropological works. Owing to her talent and deep insight, she achieved great success. In a time of strong literary bias against writers of Chinese ancestry her work was carried by major literary journals and newspapers throughout the United States, including *The Century, Independent, New England, Overland Monthly,* and *New York Evening Post.* Thirty-seven of her previously published stories ("my dear children") later were collected in a volume entitled *Mrs. Spring Fragrance,* which won critical and popular acclaim.[2] As the publisher said in the *New York Times,* "Quaint, lovable characters are the Chinese who appear in these unusual and exquisite stories of our Western Coast—stories that will open an entirely new world to many readers."[3] The fact that Sui's work continues to be favorably reviewed by both mainstream and Asian American critics while the writing of most Chinese Americans of her time has faded testifies to the recognition and success she achieved.[4]

The significance of her writing, however, goes far beyond its literary success. In addition to her artistic accomplishment, Sui is also remembered for a conscientious effort to create a more objective image of Chinese Americans. Unlike her contemporaries, who were generally "China-oriented" and saw themselves as "cultural ambassadors," she was concerned with the lives of Chinese Americans. Her focus was on "those who come to live in this land": "In these days one reads and hears much about Chinese diplomats, Chinese persons of high rank, Chinese visitors of prominence, and others, who by reason of wealth and social standing are interesting to the American people. But of those Chinese who come to live in this land, to make their homes in America, if only for a while, we hear practically nothing at all. Yet these Chinese, *Chinese-Americans,* I call them, are not unworthy of a little notice."[5]

Probing deeply into Chinatown and the complex lives of its inhabitants, Sui unearthed a world that mainstream American writers either ignored or distorted. Her stories, composed in an intimate, descriptive tone and based on what she learned among Chinese immigrants, provide a panoramic, realistic view of the Chinese American community at the turn of the twentieth century. The issue of Chinese American identity, the contradictions between Westernized and tradition-oriented Chinese immigrants, the self-protective aspect of the Chinese community, the mental torment of Eurasians, and interracial marriage and its consequences are all ably examined in depth with responsiveness to the imperatives of her conscience.

The rich diversity of themes and subject matter in Sui's work transcends color, gender, and class, thus satisfying almost all the segments in the world of literary critics. While scholars of women's history admire Sui's feminist stance, those who advocate writers' social responsibilities praise her conscientiousness in speaking for Chinese immigrant laborers; still others are impressed by her exploration of the cultural conflicts in the Chinese American experience. In that sense, Sui seems peerless among her contemporaries, and her writing represents an unusual perspective in Chinese American literary history. It is not an exaggeration to say that Sui is one of the few writers whom virtually all Chinese American critics endorse. Despite harshly criticizing other early Chinese American authors, for example, Frank Chin and his colleagues have praised Sui as being "one of the first to speak for an Asian-American sensibility that was neither Asian nor white American. . . . Working within the terms of the stereotype of the Chinese . . . she presents 'John Chinaman' as little more than a comic caricature, giving him a sensibility that was her own."[6]

## Biographic Background and Style of Writing

Compared with most early Chinese American authors, Sui's status was special because she was Eurasian, yet her background, like that of others, also reflects some of the problems typically encountered by writers of Chinese ancestry at that time. In her lengthy, vividly written autobiographic essay "Leaves from the Mental Portfolio of an Eurasian," one can see the uniqueness of her experience as a half-Chinese as well as the experiences held in common with other Chinese writers in America.[7] A daughter of an English entrepreneur and a "very bright Westernized" Chinese woman, she was born in the County of Cheshire, England, in 1865. Her father, Edward Eaton, was from a family of considerable wealth. At the age of twenty-two, he went to Shanghai to further the family fortune.[8] It was there he met Sui's mother, Grace Trefusius. The romance must have been an unusual, dramatic one. As Sui remembered, "I am never tired of listening to the story of how she [her mother] was stolen from her home. She tells over and over again of her meeting with my father in Shanghai and the romance of their marriage" ("Leaves" 128).[9]

The marriage, however, may also have required a great deal of courage from the young couple. Sui's mother must have been pressured not to marry an Englishman. China then had not yet recovered from its defeat in the Opium War, and people resented the humiliation that Great Britain had brought to the "Celestial Empire."[10] Likewise, Sui's father, upon returning to England with a Chinese wife, may have encountered trouble with his family. Because England deemed China to be a "heathen country" in need of civilizing, it was natural that the couple would be frowned upon by the Eaton family as well as by society. Perhaps that was one reason they decided to leave a comfortable home in England and emigrate to America in 1871.[11]

This unique family background inevitably affected Sui's fate. For one thing, the prejudice against her mother's race also had strong impact on Sui's life. Growing up in a middle-class community in England, she experienced various forms of British bigotry against "Orientals" early in childhood:

When I look back over the years I see myself, a little child of scarcely four years of age, walking in front of my nurse, in a green English lane, and listening to her tell another of her kind that my mother is Chinese. "Oh, Lord!" exclaims the informed. She turns me around and scans me curiously from head to foot. Then the two women whisper together. . . .

I am at a children's party. . . . There are quite a number of grown people present. One, a white haired old man, has his attention called to me by the hostess. He adjusts his eyeglasses and surveys me critically. "Ah, indeed!" he exclaims, "Who would have thought it at first glance. Yet now I see the difference between her and other children. . . . Very interesting little creature!" ("Leaves" 125–26)

Such curiosity, no matter how innocent it might have been, surely hurt little Sui's feelings, but had she been aware that it was not an isolated phenomenon, she might have felt less pain. According to a story published in San Francisco's *Overland Monthly*, for example, children of an American family of the era were charging playmates money for a peek at the "exotic wife" of their Chinese servant.[12]

The "covert smiles and sneers" Sui encountered in Britain soon turned to outright discrimination after she emigrated at the age of six to Hudson City, New York, with her parents in 1871. Although she and her siblings were "English bred with English ways and manners of dress" and were shocked at the sight of "the real Chinese dressed in working blouses and pantaloons with queues hanging down their backs," they still became targets of local children: "[They] amuse themselves with speculations as to whether, we being Chinese, are susceptible to pinches and hair pulling. . . . There are many pitched battles, of course, and we seldom leave the house without being armed for conflict" ("Leaves" 127).

Such experiences made Sui understand at an early age the full force of the misery of being part of a "despised race." They also triggered an internal monologue described in one of the most powerful and moving passages of the autobiography: "I have come from a race on my mother's side which is said to be the most stolid and insensible to feeling of all races, yet I look back over the years and see myself so keenly alive to every shade of sorrow and suffering that it is almost a pain to live. . . . Why is my mother's race despised? I look into the faces of my father and mother. Is she not every bit as dear and good as he? Why? Why?" ("Leaves" 127).

Despite the initial shock and recoiling from first encountering the Chinese, Sui's estrangement was soon changed to a sense of recognition. Although her appearance allowed her to pass into mainstream American society, she chose to identify herself publicly with a people then treated contemptuously.[13] Throughout her life she remained fiercely proud of her Chinese heritage and never let an insult to the Chinese go unchallenged. That is especially apparent in a childhood fantasy of acting as Joan of Arc and sacrificing herself for a just cause: "I glory in the idea of dying at the stake and a great genie arising from the flames and declaring to those who have scorned us: 'Behold, how great and glorious and noble are the Chinese people!'" ("Leaves" 128).

Considering the then-frantic anti-Chinese atmosphere in America, her decision to defy prejudice rather than deny being Chinese suggests a sense of courage and integrity. This is particularly significant if we compare Sui's insistence on asserting her Chinese heritage with her sister Winnifred's disavowal of having Chinese ancestry and assuming a "Japanese identity."[14] As Sui pointed out in her autobiography, some Chinese Eurasians, "thinking to advance themselves, both in a social and business sense," chose to "pass as Japanese" because Americans "manifested a much higher regard for the Japanese than for the Chinese" ("Leaves" 131).[15]

Her consciousness of Chinese ethnicity is also underscored by her selection of a Chinese pseudonym, Sui Sin Far ("narcissus" in Cantonese dialect), which she insisted upon using in print as well as in real life.[16] Adopting a pseudonym, of course, is not unusual among writers, both in the West and the East, and the pseudonym often reveals a specific intention or concern. If Samuel Langhorne Clemens's pseudonym Mark Twain reflected his nostalgia for (and memory of) his career as a steamboat pilot on the Mississippi River, and if the famous Chinese writer Zhou Shuren's pseudonym Lu Xun showed his deep feelings for his mother and hometown, Sui's pseudonym reflected her affection for her mother's race.[17] The full extent of her intention to select the name comes home when one finds that "narcissus" in Chinese culture, unlike the Western legend, symbolizes dignity, elegance, and love for homeland.[18] Again, this forms a sharp contrast to her sister Winnifred, who, as a bestselling writer of "Japanese culture," adopted a Japanese pseudonym and traded her birthright for recognition and popularity.[19]

To some extent, Sui's ethnic consciousness is a result of her close relationship with her mother, whose love and nostalgia for China had a powerful impact on Sui's mind: "She [the mother] tells us tales of China. Though a child when she left her native land she remembers it well" ("Leaves" 128). As the eldest daughter and second child in an unusually large family (there were sixteen children, fourteen of whom survived), Sui began to help her mother take care of the family at an early age and was particularly close to her mother. Yet Sui's growing knowledge of Chinese culture may also have affected her choice: "Whenever I have the opportunity I steal away to the library and read every book I can find on China and the Chinese. I learn that China is the oldest civilized nation on the face of the earth and a few other things. At eighteen years of age, what troubles me is not that I am what I am, but that others are ignorant of my superiority" ("Leaves" 128).

When she became a freelance journalist and writer covering the Chinese American community, Sui spent a great deal of time on the Pacific Coast, particularly in Seattle, where she lived for a decade and worked at a Baptist mission teaching English to Chinese immigrants.[20] The city was not only her base during her most productive years but also the background of many of her best-known stories. Sui's frequent contacts with Chinese immigrants enabled her to learn firsthand about their lives and gather material. Her experiences also made her a part of the local Chinese American community: "My Chinese instincts develop. I am no longer the little girl who shrunk against my brother at the first sight of a Chinaman. Many and many a time, when alone in a strange place, has the appearance of even an humble laundryman given me a sense of protection and made me feel quite at home. This fact of itself proves to me that prejudice can be eradicated by association" ("Leaves" 131). The idea that environment and association can significantly affect ethnic consciousness was thus firmly rooted in her mind and became an important theme in her writing, especially in stories representing her major efforts in fighting against racial prejudice.

No matter how strong her Chinese instincts had developed, however, when she decided to express them in fiction she had to seek new literary themes and forms. Although by the late nineteenth century Chinese characters had appeared frequently in the work of popular West Coast writers, there was virtually no ready pattern for Sui to adopt. "Chinamen" were chiefly used as a rich source of local color to reinforce the exotic effects of tall tales.[21] As a result, the public expected "literature on Chinamen" to be either stereotypical or melodramatic. As William Purviance Fenn, author of *Ah Sin and His Brethren in American Literature*, notes, "[In] the glorious process of exploding old myths and of creating new ones, the Chinamen were bound to suffer, . . . They were strange and they were enigmatical; their appearance and ways added color to already too colorful backgrounds, and the difficulty of understanding them piqued the curiosity of American readers."[22]

Sui also recalled that in searching for a way to present her ideas she met "funny people" who suggested she play the role of a curio peddler and sell exotic Chinese culture: "They tell me that if I wish to succeed in literature in America I should dress in Chinese costume, carry a fan in my hand, wear a pair of scarlet beaded slippers, live in New York, and come of high birth. Instead of making myself familiar with the Chinese-Americans around me, I should discourse on my spirit acquaintance with Chinese ancestors" ("Leaves" 132). She was uninterested, however, in embracing a distant and foreign China to gain popularity.

Nor did she have any intention of appealing to the curiosity of the reading public. What she wanted to do was record and define the ethnic experience of Chinese Americans, so she dipped into the deeper currents beneath the surface of Chinatown. By exploring the lives of those humble, law-abiding immigrants and their children who shouldered the burden of daily toil in the United States, Sui drew an original, realistic picture that provided glimpses into their lives, thoughts, and emotions.

It is such an achievement that closely links Sui's writing with the social realities that Chinese were encountering and represents a major aspect of the early Chinese American literature. Even critics who were less than enthusiastic about the literary merit of her work were impressed by how well she had broken with tradition:

> Miss Eaton has struck a new note in American fiction. She has not struck it very surely, or with surpassing skill. But it has taken courage to strike it at all, and, to some extent, she atones for lack of artistic skill with the unusual knowledge she undoubtedly has of her theme. The thing she has tried to do is to portray for readers of the white race the lives, feelings, sentiments of the Americanized Chinese of the Pacific Coast, of those who have intermarried with them and of the children who have sprung from such unions.[23]

As a professional writer, Sui was aware of the importance of choosing language and tone that were appropriate for her themes. Brought up and educated entirely in the West, her style was inevitably influenced by Western literature, particularly by major English and American writers of the eighteenth and nineteenth centuries. The impact of Jane Austen, for example, is conspicuous. In Sui's stories about Chinese women, especially in "Mrs. Spring Fragrance" (the title story of her collection), the neatly arranged plot, unerring dialogue, satisfying romance, and likable heroines all show Austen's influence. Similarly, the symbols Sui employed are often so subtle that they are reminiscent of the work of Nathaniel Hawthorne and Henry James. Casual readers, or audiences unfamiliar with Chinese culture, might easily miss some of the subtleties in her stories. In "Mrs. Spring Fragrance," for example, the tradition-oriented husband is never referred to by his own name, Sing Yook, but by his wife's name: Mr. Spring Fragrance. It is an indication that the husband has been outshone by his Americanized wife and that his final submission to Mrs. Spring Fragrance in the cultural conflict is predictable.[24]

The subtlety of Sui's writing is also reflected in her use of background to reveal the inner world of her characters. In "The Wisdom of the New," for example, she indicates the culture shock a newly arrived Chinese woman is experiencing by describing a noisy, overcrowded American Chinatown that contrasts with the tranquility of the woman's native village in rural China:

> Streaming along the street was a motley throng made up of all nationalities. The sing-song voices of girls whom respectable merchants' wives shudder to name, were calling to one another from high balconies up shadowy alleys. A fat barber was laughing hilariously at a drunken white man who had fallen into a gutter; a withered old fellow, carrying a bird in a cage, stood at the corner entreating passersby to have a good fortune told; some children were burning punk on the curbstone. There went by a stalwart chief of the Six Companies engaged in earnest confab with a yellow-robed priest from the joss house. A Chinese dressed in the latest American style and a very blonde woman, laughing immoderately, were entering a Chinese restaurant together. Above all the hubbub of voices was heard the clang of electric cars and the jarring of heavy wheels over cobblestones. (*MSF* 62)

Because Sui actually lived in various Chinese American communities, her portrayal of this Chinatown seems truthful. The minute description provides details that existed nowhere else in popular American fiction, and the detailed web of facts about daily life that she provided created a realistic environment in which her characters could interact. That forceful sense of verisimilitude persuaded readers of the truth of the message she wished to convey.

Similarly, Sui's accurate description of Chinese tradition shows she was not only familiar with Chinese culture but also knew how to use it appropriately in regard to the personality of her characters. Although she had never been to China, she demonstrated extraordinary familiarity with Chinese literature, culture, history, and customs.[25] The naming of her characters is a good example. Most of the Americanized Chinese in Sui's stories, such as Lin Fu, Wou Sankwei, and Liu Kanghi, have "sophisticated" names. That suggests they are from educated backgrounds, and it in part explains why they tend to be less imbued with clan and regional loyalties, and are more willing to adopt mainstream American values.[26]

In her autobiography, however, Sui deliberately employed a simple vocabulary and style that yielded an earnest, straightforward, and purposeful narrative. Focusing on the development of her ethnic consciousness, she artistically organized the long article, making it highly readable. For example, her use of the present tense in descriptions of past occurrences strengthens her recollections and fortifies the flashback effect:

> I see myself again, a few years older. I am playing with another child in a garden. A girl passes by outside the gate. "Mamie," she cries to my companion, "I wouldn't speak to Sui if I were you. Her mamma is Chinese."

It is tea time, but I cannot eat. Unobserved I crawl away. I do not sleep that night. I am too excited and I ache all over. . . . Toward morning, however, I fall into a doze from which I awake myself, shouting: "Sound the battle cry; / See the foe is nigh."

The scene of my life shifts to eastern Canada. The sleigh which has carried us from the station stops in front of a little French Canadian hotel. Immediately we are surrounded by a number of villagers, who stare curiously at my mother as my father assists her to alight from the sleigh. ("Leaves" 126)

Certainly none of the other early Chinese American authors, most of them literary amateurs, would have employed such sophisticated narrative skills.

More significantly, by using a fictional experience as catharsis for a real-life one, Sui created a series of characters closely modeled on various aspects of her own life. In many cases she endowed favorite women protagonists with personal traits of her own, so the characters appeared to pursue the same commitments and ideals as she. "The Chinese Lily," for example, describes how a beautiful Chinese woman, "Sin Far," dies self-sacrificingly in order to save her lover's crippled younger sister who has been trapped in a fire. It is noticeable that the heroine bears the author's Chinese name and is also called "Chinese Lily."[27] Her noble death in the flames is highly comparable to Sui's childhood dream of dying in a fire for the sake of the Chinese people ("Leaves" 128). Obviously, what the author does here is to use Sin Far's martyr image as an incarnation of herself to bring her childhood fantasy into full light. Although the story is overly sentimental, its simple, direct manner provides sincerity and realism.

## Acculturation and Cultural Conflict

Sui's artistry enabled her to achieve literary success beyond the reach of most early Chinese American authors. What made her stories attract critical attention, however, was her portrayal of the conflict caused by cultural barriers between tradition-oriented Chinese and those who had become Americanized—an underlying theme throughout her work. Indeed, it was her exploration of the transformation of the Chinese American community under the pressure of acculturation that impressed critics. "Our readers are well acquainted with the dainty stories of Chinese life written by Sui Sin Far," noted the editor of *The Independent*. "The conflict between occidental and oriental ideals and the hardships of the American immigration laws furnish the theme for most of the tales and the reader is not only interested but has his mind widened by becoming acquainted with novel points of view."[28]

Even in what appeared to be a romantic light comedy she could introduce the issue of cultural clash and how it affected Chinese immigrants. The title tale in *Mrs. Spring Fragrance* and its sequel, "The Inferior Woman," are examples. Sharing the same heroine, the two stories focus on Mrs. Spring Fragrance, a thoroughly Americanized Chinese immigrant, and her friction with her husband, a traditional Chinese merchant. Unconventional but cheerful, energetic, and persistent, she is reminiscent of the lively Elizabeth in *Pride and Prejudice* or Meg in Louisa May Alcott's *Little Women,* a name by which friends refer to her. Although Mrs. Spring Fragrance refuses to wear Western dresses when she first arrives in the "strange land," she advances quickly in the process of Americanization. Soon she looks "just like an American woman" and "there are no more American words for her learning" (*MSF* 1, 14). Feeling unbound in the new environment, she becomes bold and even rebellious as she begins to make her own decisions rather than follow the whims of her husband. Her independence and defiance of Chinese tradition are further reflected in her strong belief in American-style individualism: Everyone should pursue his or her own happiness, no matter what others think. When Laura, a Chinese American girl, becomes depressed because her parents have betrothed her against her will to their friend's son (a common practice in traditional Chinese society), Mrs. Spring Fragrance encourages her to stand up against the pressure. With her enthusiastic help, Laura manages to overcome obstacles and marry the man of her choice. At a time when the major mission of a Chinese woman was to "bear children to the man and the man was master of all" (*MSF* 65), her behavior is extraordinary. By successfully challenging the role traditional Chinese culture designates for women, Mrs. Spring Fragrance, as her name implies, becomes a spring flower in blossom, refreshing those around her.

Taken out of context, the story reads like a social comedy and seems irrelevant to the realities of Chinese American life. "Perhaps the exotic, that could be traded on," a critic remarked, "at worst, the quaint, but hardly the struggle toward realism that is found in the pages."[29] The light, sparkling aspect of the story should not be overemphasized, however. Beneath the seemingly picturesque and placid surface of Mrs. Spring Fragrance's life are traces of cultural conflict that trouble not only her relationship with her husband but also the Chinese American community as a whole.

Sui raised the issue of the couple's cultural differences by describing the husband as a man who wears American clothes and socializes comfortably with people in the larger society yet maintains a traditional Chinese mentality (*MSF* 1–5). Despite his changed circumstances, he upholds the institution of Chinese marriage, which allows wives to be treated as selfless beings. His Chineseness is also illustrated by his critical views of American culture. In his opinion, his wife's favorite Western poems, such as Tennyson's *In Memorium* ("'Tis better to have loved and lost / Than never to have loved at all") are "detestable [and] abhorrable," and "the easy-going relationship" between men and women in America constitutes a source of evil that will ruin society (*MSF* 3, 21).

The subtle friction between the couple intensifies when the husband realizes that his wife's love of Western poetry has led her to adopt American ways of thinking and behaving. He is irritated when he learns that despite his disapproval she continues to meddle in Laura's life in order to ensure a free marriage rather than the one arranged by the girl's parents in the traditional way. He is also annoyed that his wife attended parties with men during a visit to San Francisco— an unthinkable practice for a woman in traditional Chinese society. As the influence of Americanization begins to threaten his authoritative position in the family, he becomes more intolerant of "the unwisdom of the American way of looking at things" (*MSF* 5).

To some extent, Mr. Spring Fragrance is justified in his distrust of American values and adherence to Chinese tradition. White Americans did maintain a double standard in their treatment of Chinese immigrants. He remembers well that he pays a dollar for a haircut whereas the price for a white man is only fifteen cents.[30] Too, his older brother was detained in an immigration center while visiting America, despite having all the legal documents required for his admission.

The friction between the couple, however, does not develop into open confrontation. The story ends on a note of optimism as the husband submits to his wife's views and they are finally reconciled. Yet what will eventually happen in the family is unclear. The jade pendant that Mr. Spring Fragrance buys for his wife at the end of the story indicates that he will not yield completely to her Americanization. Because jade in Chinese culture symbolizes loyalty to family and ancestors, it is clearly a signal he sends to remind his wife of her traditional obligations. The symbolic ending shows that Sui was aware that there is no single solution to the issue of acculturation and that the problem is intrinsic and complicated. Hence, an undetermined ending was in keeping with the social realities of the Chinese American community.

Mrs. Spring Fragrance is further developed as a symbol of progress against conservatism in a sequel, "The Inferior Woman," which contains a love affair roughly parallel to that in the first story. In the sequel, however, both lovers are Caucasian and Mrs. Spring Fragrance's conflicts are not with her husband but with her neighbor, Mrs. Carman, who is middle class and white. When her son falls in love with an "inferior" woman, a self-made "working girl," Mrs. Carman strongly opposes the match because the young woman was "not only uneducated in the ordinary sense, but her environment, from childhood up, [had] been the sordid and demoralizing one of extreme poverty and ignorance" (*MSF* 34–35).[31]

Influenced by Mrs. Spring Fragrance's "enlightening" mind, however, she changes her attitude.

Mrs. Spring Fragrance's success in helping two white American lovers achieve happiness constitutes a stimulating message that shows how successfully she had assimilated into mainstream society. Even more striking is her criticism of liberal, privileged suffragists' prejudice against working-class women, which is discussed thoroughly in the story. Apparently, Mrs. Spring Fragrance embodied a new type of Chinese American, and Sui wished to demonstrate through this shining example that Chinese women, although from one of the world's most traditional societies, were able to adjust well in a new environment and be even more progressive than their American counterparts. In that sense, the characterization of Mrs. Spring Fragrance can be seen as the author's challenge to then-popular stereotypes of Chinese sing-song women and slave girls.

Few cultural clashes in Sui's stories, however, end so amiably as that in "Mrs. Spring Fragrance." In most cases the conflict between being Chinese and being American becomes so extreme that it appears that differences can never be reconciled. Frequently, the hidden tension caused by acculturation simmers, and violence leads to tragedy. "The Wisdom of the New," for example, concerns the tragic disintegration of a Chinese American family and contains such tension.

The story revolves around a couple's conflicting attitudes toward "the Wisdom of the New" (American ways of living, thinking, and behaving). Unlike the couple in "Mrs. Spring Fragrance," here it is the wife who remains intensely Chinese. The story opens with Pau Lin arriving in America to join her husband, Wou Sankwei, an Americanized Chinese merchant.[32] A crisis soon results as Pau Lin finds herself unable to understand, much less appreciate, the "New Wisdom" her husband introduces to her. While her husband admires American values, she thinks they threaten the survival of Chinese tradition. The death of her newborn baby further worsens the problem. Because the husband had allowed a white woman to paint a picture of the baby boy, Pau Lin suspects that the Western-style painting cast an evil spell on her baby's soul and caused his death.

Facing an estranged husband and surrounded by a strange yet unfriendly environment, Pau Lin regards her six-year-old son, who grew up in China and accompanied her to America, as her only link to Chinese tradition and culture. Compounding her panic, her husband decides to send the boy to a public school outside Chinatown so he can be quickly Americanized. That decision becomes "the catalyst for Pau Lin's metamorphosis."[33] She believes that American education will not only force her son to submit to the "New Wisdom" but also sever her last link with the familiar Chinese world. In desperation she poisons the child—a last resort to defending her Chinese heritage and the boy's Chinese identity. "'He is saved,' smiled she, 'from the Wisdom of the New'" (*MSF* 84).[34]

The tragic ending is shocking, but it is the author's deliberate design. As Sui points out at the beginning of the story, America is a place where one gains and loses. The loss of the son and the family's disintegration thus can be considered a price the husband must pay for obtaining "the wisdom of the new." Although the story also dwells on the theme of cultural conflict, it is not in the same way as "Mrs. Spring Fragrance." Here, Sui's message is made by way of the tragedy: The price of Americanization may be so high that not everyone can afford or is willing to pay for it, and it is sometimes impossible for Oriental and Occidental ideas to compromise.

With slight changes, the idea that acceptance by one culture means rejection from the other and that Chinese and American cultures are mutually exclusive is also reflected in "The Prize China Baby." The story concerns a Chinese woman who uses mainstream American values in trying (but failing) to acquire position in a traditional Chinese family. When her husband wants to give away their baby daughter, the wife feels powerless to stop him. The traditional codes imposed on Chinese women—the Three Obediences, Four Virtues, or Seven Grounds—have stripped her of all rights.[35] At the suggestion of a white mission woman, however, she decides to enter the daughter in a baby contest sponsored by the Presbyterian Church on Christmas Eve. She hopes that if her daughter wins an "American" prize it will raise her status and change her husband's mind. The baby does win the first prize, "a shining gold bit." On their way home, however, the mother and daughter are run over by a butcher cart and killed.

Although the tale suffers from melodrama, the author's points are clear: One culture does not accept the other, and the East and the West are mutually exclusive. Undoubtedly, the deaths of the mother and daughter on their way back to Chinatown after winning the "American" prize are aimed at demonstrating that those recognized by a "foreign" civilization will be denied by the Chinese and any attempt to bring Western values into the Eastern tradition will be ultimately crushed. Because people are unable to synchronize the two different cultures, they will have to choose between them.

Such a conclusion does not seem much different than the root of then-popular racial bias that emphasized the incompatibility of the Chinese and American cultures. As Rudyard Kipling wrote, "Oh, East is East, and West is West, and never the twain shall meet." But while the racial bias considered the two to be mutually exclusive and Chinese culture inscrutable and subhuman, Sui held a different view. She believed the two could not be mixed because American culture valued individualism, free competition, and personal success, whereas Chinese tradition emphasized conformity, harmony, the importance of family, and community responsibility. To be sure, Sui, born and raised in the Anglo cultural and religious tradition (both of her parents were Presbyterian), admired the progress of Western society, and even thought of Americanization as meaning enlightenment. This is evidenced by her favorable portrayal and idealization of the Americanized Chinese such as Mrs. Spring Fragrance.

Sui never believed, however, that a Chinese immigrant had to "become a convert and shed his foreign, heathen ways" because to most Americans of that era, "[The] social foundations were not negotiable."[36] On the contrary, she argued convincingly that Chinese immigrants clung to their cultural tradition because it was the only source from which they were able to draw spiritual support in an alien environment. In a sense, the Chinese rejection of American values in favor of their own system was not much different from Irish immigrants' adherence to the Catholic religion or to Jews to Judiasm in similar circumstances.[37] Their persistence with Chinese culture and tradition was chiefly a result of the insecurity and loneliness they felt in a strange land. Instead of insisting that the Chinese abandon their non-Christian traditions in order to stay on in America, Sui maintained with sympathy that people have the right to make their own choices and keep their cultural heritage.

To some extent, this point of view resembles what Mark Twain expressed in *Roughing It* (1872). As one of the few mainstream American writers sympathetic to Chinese immigrants, Twain believed that Chinese culture should be allowed to exist in American society for reasons that he observed in his customary sarcastic tone:

> Ours is the "land of the free"—nobody denies that—nobody challenges it. (Maybe it is because we won't let other people testify.)
> [The Chinese] are a harmless race when white men either let them alone or treat them no worse than dogs. . . . They are quiet, peaceable, tractable, free from drunkenness, and they are as industrious as the day is long. . . . So long as a Chinaman has strength to use his hands he needs no support from anybody; white men often complain of want of work, but a Chinaman offers no such complaint; he always manages to find something to do. He is a great convenience to everybody—even to the worst class of white men, for he bears the most of their sins, suffering fines for their petty thefts, imprisonment for their robberies, and death for their murders.[38]

The difference between Sui and those biased against Chinese culture is seen even more clearly in her sympathetic and empathic depiction of traditional

Chinese who either failed in America or rejected Americanization. In popular American fiction of the period that group was almost always presented negatively. Exhibiting the worst traits of humanity, they appeared brutal, deceitful, stupid, superstitious, and mysterious. In addition, their minds were said to be filled with indecent ideas.[39] Sui, however, sought to emphasize the humane, civilized nature of their personalities. For her, these traditional Chinese were ordinary humans just like immigrants from any other country. In general, her depiction ranged between describing them as tragic figures crushed by cultural barriers and high-minded, righteously indignant defenders of Chinese values. In fact, compared to her idealization of the Americanized Chinese, her portrayal of traditional Chinese as individuals who have a normal range of human characteristics is even more convincing and realistic.

The Americanized Mrs. Spring Fragrance, for example, is endowed with positive characteristics yet her tradition-oriented husband is also presented as a man of integrity. Witty, honest, and pleasant, he searches in his own diligent and enthusiastic way for a door through which to enter society. The fact he holds "smoking parties" regularly to entertain his American and Chinese friends (*MSF* 11) is evidence that he knows how to enjoy life and is respected by those around him. Such a description contrasts sharply with traditional Chinese in popular American literature who possess no mental or physical sensitivity and are too inflexible to flourish in Western society.

Even the more negative traditional Chinese in Sui's stories are portrayed differently from those of popular American fiction. Rather than being sinister villains incapable of assimilation, they are presented as having human emotions and often being the innocent victims of their environment. In "The Prize China Baby," for instance, the traditional Chinese husband who wants to give his baby daughter away is not a cold-blooded villain or the perpetrator of a female infanticide. What he wants to do is to give the baby to a close friend, a childless doctor who wishes desperately for a child. Pau Lin poisons her son in "The Wisdom of the New" because she, suddenly brought from rural China to an American metropolis, is shocked by the cultural differences she has encountered. Driven mad by the American values her husband tries to impose upon her, she regards death as the only way of saving the boy from an American education she believes will demand that he deny his cultural heritage. By writing sympathetically of Pau Lin's tragedy as a result of emotional torment and psychological anxiety, Sui exposed the inhumane side of the process of Americanization.

Again, in "The Americanizing of Pau Tsu," a story about how a traditional Chinese wife who rejects a spouse's plan to Americanize her, there are no significant differences between them. The husband is said to be an efficient and successful merchant, but the wife, who refused to be anything but intensely Chinese, is also described as being intelligent, compassionate, and sensitive. Although her conviction that America is a sterile, oppressive, and spiritually bankrupt society might seem biased and narrow-minded, it is a product of personal concerns that are realistic and convincing within the context of the story. She dislikes American things because she is jealous of Miss Raymond, her husband's white friend, and realizes that his attempts to Americanize her have been prompted by the desire to redirect his love for an "untouchable" white girl to an "accessible" Chinese woman.[40] Thus, Pau Tsu's failure to integrate into American society is clearly the result of deliberate choice rather than a lack of ability.

Of course, Sui's Chinese characters are not without flaw. Her writing sometimes suffers from being too melodramatic, and there are occasional cultural inaccuracies. Pau Tsu, for example, considers divorcing her Americanized husband as a means of keeping her Chinese identity. Such behavior, as some critics argue, would contradict her personality. For a traditional Chinese woman, divorce was a great humiliation, and she would rather have committed suicide than face the social ridicule and mental torment that follow divorce.[41] Nevertheless, at a time when the Chinese were being portrayed as an identical, one-dimensional mass, Sui endowed them with sensibility and individual human characteristics in a way that was beyond her contemporaries. In general, her apt appraisal and penetrating portrayal of traditional Chinese were forceful and meaningful. It translated her dedication to and love of Chinese Americans into an inspiring challenge for readers, something that distinguished her writing from the American fiction of the day. This was recognized by critics in her lifetime. As early as in 1896, for example, *Land of Sunshine*, an influential Californian literary magazine, commented that Sui's stories had "an insight and sympathy which are probably unique. To others the alien Celestial is at best mere 'literary material': in these stories he (or she) is a human being."[42]

## Interracial Marriage and Eurasians

Interracial marriage or "miscegenation" (a term coined by the Irish-born American journalist David Croly and used more commonly in Sui's time than it is now) has long been a familiar phenomenon in American society. Because she was the product of such a marriage, Sui was naturally interested in the subject. As a result, readers find that an account of an interracial marriage, like that of cultural conflict, appears either as a secondary aspect or as a primary focus of almost all her major work.[43]

"The Smuggling of Tie Co" is not explicitly about intermarriage but suggests that issue. It involves a Chinese woman's unrequited love for a white American. Disguised as a man, Tie Co emigrates from China and works in a laundry in Canada. She then falls in love with Jack Fabian, a white border smuggler. When she finds that he is unemployed and has difficulty making a living, she decides to offer him a job: smuggling her into the United States. Unfortunately, they are discovered by the police after crossing the border. In order to spare Jack from being caught with evidence, Tie Co jumps from a bridge, committing suicide. Jack shows little emotion, however, when he later learns the truth; rather than being moved by her love and ultimate sacrifice he only ponders "over the mystery of Tie Co's life—and death" (*MSF* 193).

In stories written by mainstream American authors of the period, few interracial relationships ended happily, at least for non-whites. As Katharine D. Newman observes, "[The] forbidden love between young people of different races or religions is the American form of *Romeo and Juliet,* and only occasionally is there a happy ending." In almost all'cases it is fatal for the lover who has the "wrong" skin color: "Death is the only fair fate for these unmarriable victims."[44] Because Jack's failure to recognize Tie Co's affection gives her self-sacrifice no value, Sui's description of her death is in keeping with the literary trends of the time. But unlike then-popular American fiction that portrayed the Chinese who loved whites as being motivated by baser impulses such as lust or money, Tie Co's affection and sacrifice contrast sharply with the insensitivity of her white lover. Of course, Sui's account of her death makes her seem either unbelievably noble or extremely foolish. In real life, a Chinese woman who had made her way across the Pacific and earned a successful living in a male world would likely not have ended her life so easily on account of a man like Jack. But what the author intended was to use Tie Co's sacrifice to create an alternative image of Chinese who loved white Americans. The young woman's name also implies that she is to be viewed as a tragic figure.[45] Thus her death for the sake of an undeserving lover is implausible yet logical.

While interracial love is but a secondary theme of the story and fortifies the image of a self-sacrificing Chinese woman, the same topic is examined carefully in "The Story of One White Woman Who Married a Chinese" and its sequel, "Her Chinese Husband." As the titles suggest, the stories describe a union from the perspective of a white woman who contrasts her experiences as the wife of a white American with those as the wife of a Chinese immigrant. By all standards the stories are more complex than "The Smuggling of Tie Co" and were considered particularly interesting by critics during Sui's lifetime.[46]

Written in the first person, both stories are narrated by Minnie, a working-class white woman who has been deserted by her husband James Carson, "a very bright and well-informed" man who thinks her too ignorant to be his wife. Just when she feels "weary of working, struggling and fighting with the world" and is about to commit suicide, she is rescued by Liu Kanghi, a Chinese businessman who then marries her (*MSF* 111).[47] He kindly supports her and does everything to help her recover from the traumatic experience of her previous marriage. A thoughtful husband, he treats Minnie with respect and tenderness in sharp contrast to James's callous and brutal conduct, and there is no cultural friction between them. Liu, a member of the progressive Reform Club of the Chinese American community, has been thoroughly Westernized in every respect. As Minnie asserts, their union means "happiness, health, and development" (*MSF* 134).

Nevertheless, no matter how perfect the marriage is, it runs counter to one of the deepest taboos in American society at the time. That the predominant social trend appeared to perpetuate sentiment against intermarriage rather than encourage interracial contact is evidenced by various antimiscegenation laws of the era and by the manner in which the theme was treated in popular American fiction. As I have mentioned, none of the popular American stories about Chinese-Caucasian intermarriage written at this time took a positive tone. Frequently, the topic symbolized the "yellow peril" and was used to create a sense that the survival of the American nation was being threatened.[48]

Of course, not all white Americans of the period held such extreme views, but most would likely have agreed that Chinese-Caucasian marriages could morally corrupt Christian values and threaten the well-being of American society. As Minnie mentions, she and her husband often encountered "sneers and offensive remarks" because of their marriage. This is indicative of the strong disapproval from the public of the couple's behavior, particularly that of Liu. An "unmarriable Chinaman," he was seen as breaking a taboo and treading "on the forbidden ground." In that sense his death is inevitable.[49] Unlike then-popular American fiction in which Chinese who loved Caucasians were usually murdered by white mobs, however, in Sui's story Liu is killed by his own countrymen: "He was brought home at night, shot through the head. There are some Chinese, just as there are some Americans, who are opposed to all progress, and who hate with a bitter hatred all who would enlighten or be enlightened" (*MSF* 143).

To be fair, this is not pure fiction intended by the author for sensational effect. In Sui's time the bitterness and frustration felt by traditional Chinese made them sometimes assault their Americanized countrymen—those who had "betrayed" their ancestors.[50] The *Daily Alta California* reported in 1870, "It appears that hostile feelings exist on the part of some Celestials . . . against those . . . who have become so far Americanized as to have their queues cut off, and wear our dress." According to the same report, in one brutal fight alone, several Americanized Chinese in San Francisco's Chinatown were fatally wounded by their more traditional compatriots.[51] Nevertheless, one would suspect that the story's ending was deliberately designed by the author to suggest that the Chinese were in part responsible for the taboo against interracial marriage. That viewpoint would be satisfying for white readers worried about the consequences of miscegenation but unwilling to shoulder sole blame for enforcing the taboo. Similarly, the striking gap in social status between Liu, a successful and well-educated Chinese businessman, and Minnie, a working-class white too "ignorant" to be the wife of "a bright American," may also be a subtle hint arranged by Sui to appease the concern regarding miscegenation. After all, this is only a marriage between an "upper-class Chinaman" and a "lower-status" white woman.[52]

That Sui, a child born of a successful intermarriage, wrote of a Chinese-Caucasian marriage in this way constitutes a scathing satire on her parents' romance. Yet few of her stories about mixed couples have completely happy endings, they contain a different message on a deeper level.[53] In popular American culture, accounts of intermarriages that have ended tragically often symbolize divine trial or punishment to warn that miscegenation is grossly improper and that readers should stay away from such behavior. But in Sui's stories, tragic endings are consequences of how society victimizes lovers from different races, thus eliciting sympathy from the public to get rid of the taboo. What sets her stories apart are favorable descriptions of intermarriage. Liu and Minnie's marriage, for example, functions smoothly, demonstrating that Chinese men have the same feelings as white and, contrary to the widespread racist concept, that Chinese are capable of experiencing love. Furthermore, because the story shows how a white woman exhibits an explicit love for a Chinese man, it stands out as the only truly favorable depiction of marriages between Chinese and Caucasians at the time, thus closing the gap between races.

There is another significant aspect of the stories. At this time the truthful depictions of Chinese-Caucasian marriages as they actually existed were still a novelty, having a factual glimpse into such a union was a rare experience, and presenting the feelings and lives of such couples was a relatively new thing. In that sense, Sui's vivid account of the marriage reveals more about the daily lives of an intermarried couple in the late nineteenth century than can be found in large compilations of factual or sociological material. For these reasons, the two stories are among her most significant work. As late as 1952, for example, one critic noted, "So intimately does the author write of mixed marriage that one is tempted to believe she herself married a Chinese and was enabled in this way to get firsthand information."[54]

While the two stories are chiefly about intermarriage, they touch upon another familiar phenomenon of American society: children of mixed blood. At the end of the first story, Minnie expresses worry about the fate of her young son: "[As] he stands between his father and myself, like yet unlike us both, so will he stand in after years between his father's and his mother's people. And if there is no kindliness nor understanding between them, what will my boy's fate be?" (*MSF* 132).

That speech apparently reflected one of Sui's own concerns over the social dilemma imposed on Eurasians at the time. Unlike the case of mulattos, whom idealists often cite as fusing the cultural opposites that prefigure a "New World synthesis," Eurasians long challenged the melting pot theory.[55] Most of them had a difficult time juggling racial and cultural identities and experienced bigotry and rejection from both Caucasian and Asians, at least until after World War II. "[This] is the greatest loneliness—of not being totally accepted by any group," recalls a Chinese Eurasian. "I guess it's like being a stranger at every banquet, but never being the host."[56] In fact, Sui's personal predicament was typical of the mental torment experienced by most Eurasians of her era. Although she assumed a Chinese identity, she was troubled for a time during childhood by the issue of nationality:

> I am only ten years old. And all the while the question of nationality perplexes my little brain. Why are we what we are? I and my brothers and sisters. Why did God make us to be hooted and stared at? Papa is English, mama is Chinese. Why couldn't we have been either one thing or the other? . . . I do not confide in my father and mother. They would not understand. How could they? He is English, she is Chinese. I am different to both of them—a stranger, though their own child. "What are we?" I ask my brother. "It doesn't matter, sissy," he responds. But it does. ("Leaves" 127–28)

That mental torment is revealed partially in her stories about Eurasians. Perhaps because of her development of "Chinese instincts" later in life, most of Sui's Eurasian characters waver for a while between the "two conflicting halves" before finally throwing in their lot with the Chinese.

"Its Wavering Image," which concerns a Chinese Eurasian's choice of racial identity, is about such a phenomenon. As a daughter of a Chinese man and a white woman, Pan leads a pleasant life in Chinatown with her father after her mother's death. But tranquility and happiness are not part of her inner world. She is often lonely when she realizes that although the Chinese treat her kindly she is not truly one of them. The "mystery of her nature" is awakened when she meets Mark Carson, a young white reporter who seems fond of her. What she does not know is that he "would sell his soul for a story." He intends to use her to get an inside scoop on Chinatown. Falling in love with him, she tells Mark in confidence personal matters about the Chinese community. She is soon betrayed by Mark's publication of what she has related to him in trust, however. The bitter experience helps her choose a racial identity. When Mark demands an answer—"Don't you see you have got to decide what you will be, Chinese or white? You cannot be both"—she replies that she will be Chinese for the rest of her life (*MSF* 90).

Stylistically, the story has all the characteristics of Sui's writing. Its background, Chinatown, is depicted as allusively as Pan's wavering mind. That implies that her seemingly happy life is not truly rooted in the Chinese community and that subconsciously she searches for belonging. Even though the time sequence is disrupted by flashbacks, narration about Pan's life is detailed so readers have a vivid impression of her environment and daily routine to help them understand what it was like to be Eurasian in Sui's time and empathize with her sorrow and happiness.

## Racial Relations and Other Issues

Although Sui's view of cultural conflict and interracial marriage is somewhat affected by the social thought of her time, she leaves no room for doubt on where she stands on the issue of racism. From the beginning of her career as a journalist and writer, she used her pen to protest anti-Chinese prejudices; at times, she served as spokesperson for the Chinese American community. Minnie, the protagonist of "The Story of One White Woman Who Married a Chinese," may speak for Sui when she says, "My life's experience had taught me that the virtues do not always belong to the whites. . . . But for all the strange marriage customs of my husband's people I considered them far more moral in their lives than the majority of Americans" (*MSF* 125, 140). Indeed, Sui's gallant defense of Chinese Americans was widely recognized by them and earned their praise in her lifetime. She recalled in her autobiography: "My heart leaps for joy when I read one day an article signed by a New York Chinese in which he declares 'The Chinese in America owe an everlasting debt of gratitude to Sui Sin Far for the bold stand she has taken in their defense'" ("Leaves" 128). When she died in Montreal in 1914, the Chinese communities of Montreal and Boston placed a memorial at her tomb to express their gratitude and admiration for her dedication to the cause of Chinese Americans. The tombstone is carved with four large Chinese characters: *Yi bu wong hua* [a righteous person who never forgets Chinese and China].[57]

Compared with the emotional outbursts of some militant Chinese who denounced racism, however, Sui's criticism was tactful. In most cases, she used subtle satire, which she believed worked more effectively in soliciting the American public's support in changing the unfair immigration law that excluded Chinese. An exchange between Mr. Spring Fragrance and his white friend, a young and progressive reporter, is typical of that method:

> "Everything is 'high-class' in America," he [Mr. Spring Fragrance] observed.
>
> "Sure!" cheerfully assented the young man. "Haven't you ever heard that all Americans are princes and princesses, and just as soon as a foreigner puts his foot upon our shores, he also becomes of the nobility—I mean, the royal family."
>
> "What about my brother in the Detention Pen?" dryly inquired Mr. Spring Fragrance.
>
> "Now, you've got me," said the young man, rubbing his head, "Well, that is a shame—'a beastly shame,' as the Englishman says. But understand, old fellow, we that are real Americans are up against that—even more than you. It is against our principles."
>
> "I offer the real Americans my consolations that they should be compelled to do that which is against their principles." (*MSF* 12)

The barb in Mr. Spring Fragrance's sarcastic comments on those who paid only lip service to the principle of democracy is conspicuous yet the author veils it with humor and irony so her "white audience" could accept the criticism without offense.

Although Sui's protest against racism is usually composed of subtle satire and rational argument, at times it can also be open and direct. In the story "In the Land of the Free," she expressed frankly her indignation about the inhumane side of the exculsion law imposed on the Chinese. The story exposes how the Chinese Exclusion Act forces the separation of a Chinese woman from her young son, only because the child was born in China.[58] The boy, taken into custody by immigration authorities, "protested lustily against the transfer" and the mother cries heartrendingly. The process to clear the boy proves to be long and agonizing. Although she is assured that "there cannot be any law that would keep a child from its mother," it takes more than ten months for "the Great Government at Washington to send the answer" (*MSF* 167). During that period, an unethical white lawyer offers help. After charging $500, a colossal figure in those days, he claims to need more money to "hurry the government," thus squeezing the last penny from the mother, including her wedding ring. Ironically, when the little boy is finally released he has lost his Chinese identity. He wears Western clothes, speaks only English, has forgotten his Chinese name, and is unable to recognize his mother. He shrinks away when she arrives to bring him home and shouts, "Go 'way, go 'way!" (*MSF* 177). The ending dramatically highlights the irony of the title: It is in the "land of the free" that a Chinese child is stripped of his ethnic identity and a Chinese mother loses freedom to keep her own son. Although Sui's criticism appeared less militant than confrontational attacks upon racism, it carried heavier weight and was more powerful. Being well directed, it exposed the era's institutionalized racist policy against the Chinese.

It is noteworthy that Sui's view on the roots of racism was unique and her analysis of the complexity of the issue was insightful in light of the social background of her time. While many Chinese immigrants of that era held that racial prejudice was inherited in certain cultures and members of some ethnic groups were "born racist," Sui believed racial bias to be a product of social and environmental factors and that education rather than genetics made people racists.[59]

The idea is stated explicitly in "Pat and Pan," in which a white boy is raised in a household in Chinatown. When Pat's mother dies shortly after his birth, a Chinese couple kindly adopt him. Growing up in Chinatown, he speaks only Chinese, is inseparable from his little Chinese sister Pan, and feels proud of his Chinese heritage. In reality, that is not merely a fantasy. In the late nineteenth century, while there were Chinese orphans raised by missionaries, there are also accounts of Caucasian children being adopted by Chinese American families. As one "American son" of a Chinese couple recalled, "I don't know who my biological parents are, so I think I was pretty lucky. My mother dyed my hair, dyed my eyebrows to make me look Chinese. . . . [But] there were do-gooders, you know, prying into our affairs. They tried three or four times to take me away from my foster parents, to stick me in an orphan's home. But somehow my foster father had some kind of proof."[60]

Not all white children reared by Chinese could be so lucky as to stay on with their parents, however. As Ruthanne Lum McCunn points out, taking a Chinese child into a Caucasian family was considered an act of Christian charity and no one questioned the legitimacy of the adoption, yet Chinese couples who adopted white children often had them taken away by authorities.[61] Such is the fate of Pat. He is finally taken away by a missionary who finds it unthinkable for a white boy to grow up Chinese and wants to prevent the impact of Chinese "moral degeneracy" before it is too late. The change of environment proves significant in altering Pat's ethnic feelings. Living in a white world, he soon loses his Chinese consciousness and even becomes ashamed of his Chinese connection. "Get away from me! Get away from me!" he shouts when Pan comes to visit. "Poor Pat!" she says sorrowfully as she runs away, "He Chinese no more, he Chinese no more" (*MSF* 344).

Ironically, despite her assertion of Chinese pride and enthusiastic defense of Chinese Americans, Sui found that having a Eurasian background prevented her from being fully accepted by the Chinese. This made her realize that while remaining victims of racial discrimination and other mistreatment, the Chinese themselves sometimes were also biased against other groups. To some extent, traditional Chinese bigotry against "foreign barbarians" was accentuated by the racial prejudice that pervaded American society during the late nineteenth century. As a result, Chinese Americans distrusted people of other races, frowned at interracial marriage, and tended to reject Eurasians. As some of Sui's Chinese friends explained, "Full-blooded Chinese people [have] a prejudice against the half white" ("Leaves" 129).

Compared to their bias against the "half white," Chinese prejudice against the "half black" was even stronger.[62] The tragedy of Arlee Hen (1893–1985), the daughter of a Chinese father and a black mother, in Mississippi is one example. Although she was proud of her Chinese heritage and insisted that she "never did feel any difference from Chinese," she was not accepted by the local Chinese community during her lifetime. Even after death, her wish to be buried beside her Chinese husband was denied on the ground that the local Chinese cemetery was for "pure-blooded" Chinese only.[63] Such misplaced superiority made Sui muse, "Fundamentally, all people are the same. My mother's race is as prejudiced as my father's. Only when the whole world becomes as one family will human beings be able to see clearly and distinctly" ("Leaves" 129).

Apparently, it is this awareness that all people are the same in terms of racial bigotry that prompted Sui to write "The Gift of Little Me," which concerns a white woman's ethnic experience among Chinese Americans. After "her early hopes and dreams had one by one been lost," Jean McLeod, an "honest and serious spinster," volunteers to teach in a Chinatown school (*MSF* 106). Living in Chinatown for many years, she not only learns the Chinese language and adopts Chinese customs but also feels "in her Scotch heart" that she is part of the Chinese community. Her trust turns sour, however, and the illusion is shattered when she is accused of kidnapping a Chinese baby even though it was presented to her by Little Me, an innocent student, as the "greatest gift" for the Chinese New Year. The implication of the story seems double-edged. It indicates that racial bigotry exists not only among the oppressors but also among the oppressed. Yet McLeod's dedication to the education of Chinese children shows that even amid the intense anti-Chinese atmosphere of the time, there were "real Americans" who believed in racial equality and devoted themselves to improving the lot of Chinese immigrants.

Apart from the racial issue, the tale's description of the polarization of wealth and poverty in Chinatown is also striking. While students from rich merchants' families can offer gold figures as gifts to teacher, a poor worker's child has nothing to present but his baby brother. Such an exposure of class distinction between the rich and the poor is rare in early Chinese American writing and provides an example how social status sometimes blurred the color line in the Chinese American experience. Along with subtly criticizing the racial bias of the Chinese in the story, it reflects Sui's serious attempt to convey the true Chinese American community and her determination to confront and remedy its less attractive side in order to further its progress.

In spite of having adopted new social perspectives, however, Sui was not entirely free from the influence of popular belief in her generation. Once stereotypes are established and widely accepted, as a critic argues, it is difficult for anyone, no matter how broadminded and strong-willed, to dismiss them completely.[64] Despite attempts to break away from them, Sui occasionally fell prey to the stereotypes of the day and unwittingly repeated the racial pattern established by mainstream writers. Her portrayal of Chinese men is an example. In popular American fiction of the time, Chinese men are typically devoid of manhood or the traditionally masculine qualities of daring and physical strength. Sui's characterization of Chinese men seemingly inherits such a stereotyped image. Under her pen, the lack of passion and masculinity of Chinese men contrasts sharply with the ruddy, stalwart image of white men and the "rough elegance" they possess. This is revealed in the comparison made by Minnie in "Her Chinese Husband" between Liu and her white ex-husband James. To Minnie, Liu is the best man she has met and an ideal husband. That is not because he is attractive as a masculine or romantic figure, however, but because he is reliable and can provide the security that is vital for her survival "in a world which has been cruel to [her]." Although James is "callous and ruthless," he is "strong, tall, and well built" and possesses a masculinity and physical strength that Minnie does not perceive in Liu. Being "much more of an ardent lover than ever had been Liu," his passion, whether real or feigned, always sweeps Minnie off her feet (*MSF* 134). As she comments to James, "For all your six feet of grossness, your small soul cannot measure up to his [Liu's] great one" (*MSF* 130). The implication is obvious: Liu's spiritual or moral grandeur is appealing, but he is not James's equal in terms of physique and sexual prowess.[65] Even the causes of their deaths are used by Sui to reinforce the varying images of Chinese and white men. Liu is killed for his "enlightened and progressive mind," whereas James dies "of apoplexy while exercising at a public gymnasium" (*MSF* 131). Such a portrayal of Chinese men suggests that in some respects Sui was as bound by social conventions of the day as mainstream American writers.

As the first Chinese woman writer in North America, Sui Sin Far's accomplishment is extraordinary. The full extent of her contribution is impressive and stands out distinctively if we compare her stories with the "Chinatown tales" of popular American writers of her time. Of course, having to work within conventional boundaries, she was not perfect in her effort to "strike a new note." After all, she could not act much beyond her time. Nevertheless, within these boundaries she separated herself from the tradition and achieved a breakthrough that no "pure-blooded" Chinese did. Sui was virtually the first one who created in fiction a unique Chinese American sensibility caught between East and West, and her achievement deserves recognition. An epitaph Ralph Waldo Emerson dedicated to others may also apply to Sui. Such people, Emerson wrote, "speak to the conscience, and have that superiority over the crowd of their contemporaries, which belongs to men who entertain a good hope."[66] As a pathfinder in a trackless new territory, Sui Sin Far was such a person.

## Notes

1. The epigraph is from Sui Sin Far, "Leaves from the Mental Portfolio of an Eurasian," *The Independent*, Jan. 21, 1909, 132. For a new edition of Sui Sin Far's writing, see *Sui Sin Far: Mrs. Spring Fragrance and Other Writings*, ed. Amy Ling and Annette White-Parks (Urbana: University of Illinois Press, 1995). I am indebted to Amy Ling for correcting Sui Sin Far's birth date and for sharing her collection of the author's family and biographic documents. According to Sui Sin Far's *New York Times* obituary, her birth year was 1867, but Ling argues with evidence that she was born in 1865. "Edith Eaton Dead: Author of Chinese Stories under the Name of Sui Sin Far," *New York Times*, April 9, 1914, 11; Amy Ling, *Between Worlds: Women Writers of Chinese Ancestry* (New York: Pergamon Press, 1990), 183. Also see Annette White-Parks, *Sui Sin Far/Edith Maude Eaton: A Literary Biography* (Urbana: University of Illinois Press, 1995), 1–8.

2. Sui, *Mrs. Spring Fragrance* (Chicago: A. C. McClurg, 1912), (subsequent page citations to *MSF* appear in parentheses). Many of the stories in the volume share common characters, thus making the book similar to a loosely constructed longer work of fiction such as Sarah Orne Jewett, *The Country of the Pointed Firs* (1896).

3. "Sui Sin Far" [publisher's note], *New York Times*, July 7, 1912, 45.

4. Paul Lauter et al., eds., *The Heath Anthology of American Literature* (Lexington: D. C. Heath, 1994), 2:884–901; Emory Elliott, ed. *Columbia Literary History of the United States* (New York: Columbia University Press, 1988), 517; Maria Hong, ed., *Growing up Asian America: An Anthology* (New York: William Morrow, 1993), 21–28; and William F. Wu, *The Yellow Peril: Chinese Americans in American Fiction, 1850–1940* (Hamden: Archon Books, 1982), 54.

5. Sui Sin Far, "Chinese Workmen in America," *The Independent*, July 3, 1913, 56, emphasis added. Sui Sin Far was likely the first writer to use the term *Chinese-Americans* to refer to Chinese immigrants and their American-born descendants.

6. Frank Chin et al., eds., *Aiiieeee: An Anthology of Asian American Writers* (Washing-

ton: Howard University Press, 1974), xxi–xxii; also see Jeffery Paul Chan et al., eds., *The Big Aiiieeeee: An Anthology of Chinese American and Japanese American Literature,* (New York: Meridian, 1991), 111.

7. Sui Sin Far, "Leaves from the Mental Portfolio of an Eurasian," 125–32 (subsequent page citations to "Leaves" appear in parentheses). It is no accident that Sui's autobiography as well as many of her most impressive stories, such as "In the Land of the Free," "One White Woman Who Married a Chinese," and "Her Chinese Husband," were first published in *The Independent,* a progressive New York journal that advocated fair treatment to immigrants and also carried Lee Chew's life story.

8. "Edith Eaton Dead: Author of Chinese Stories under the Name of Sui Sin Far," *New York Times,* April 9, 1914, 11. According to the obituary, Sui's father "received $300,000" from his family when he went to "the Orient." It is reasonable to assume, however, that the figure was exaggerated to impress readers with the wealth of the family. Also see Sui Sin Far, "Sui Sin Far, the Half Chinese Writer, Tells of Her Career," *Boston Globe,* May 5, 1912, 1.

9. The family story has the couple meeting at an art exhibition in China when she was sixteen and he twenty-four. S. E. Solberg, "Sui, the Storyteller," in *Turn Shadows into Light: Art and Culture of the Northwest's Early Asian Community,* ed. Mayumi Tsutakawa and Alan Chong Lau (Seattle: Young Pine Press, 1982), 86.

10. It was not until the turn of the century, especially after the Boxer Rebellion (i.e., after 1900), that the Chinese attitude toward the West began to change. Before that, Chinese who associated with Westerners were contemptuously dubbed *Jia yangguizi* [Pseudo foreign devils] and condemned for having betrayed their ancestors.

11. According to Sui, her father's pursuit of a career as a landscape painter rather than as a businessman might also be one of the reasons that caused him to split with his family. Solberg, "Sui, the Storyteller," 86.

12. Limin Chu, "The Images of China and the Chinese in the *Overland Monthly,* 1868–1875, 1883–1935," Ph.D. diss., Duke University, 1966, 211–12.

13. Both Sui's photograph and testimony indicate that her appearance was more Occidental than Oriental.

14. Sui's sister Winnifred adopted a Japanese name, Onoto Watanna, and wrote a large number of stories set in Japan under that pseudonym.

15. Why the nineteenth-century American public had a more favorable impression of the Japanese than the Chinese is a complicated phenomenon. In addition to economic and political reasons, the fact that Japanese immigrants were relatively more Westernized seems to have been an important element in shaping that viewpoint. For a brief yet explicit summary of the issue, see Harry H. L. Kitano, "The Japanese," in *Harvard Encyclopedia of American Ethnic Groups,* ed. Stephan Thernstrom (Cambridge: Harvard University Press, 1980), 561–71.

16. "Sui Sin Far" is the Cantonese pronunciation of "narcissus." She not only used the pseudonym as a pen name but also in everyday life. In an autobiographical letter written to Harold Goddard Rugg, a Dartmouth College student who later became a prominent educator, she remarked, "Perhaps I should say 'they,' as I have both an English and a Chinese name." Sui Sin Far to Harold Goddard Rugg, Jan. 18, 1900, Special Collections: Archives, Manuscripts, Rare Books, Dartmouth College Library, Hanover, N.H. She sometimes also signed her name as "Sui Seen Far," especially for work that appeared in *Land*

*of Sunshine,* a popular magazine published in Los Angeles during the 1890s. Sui Sin Far, "The Chinese Woman in America," *Land of Sunshine* 6 (Jan. 1897), 59–64.

17. Zhou Shuren (1881–1936), one of the greatest modern Chinese writers, acquired his pseudonym, Lu Xun, by combining his mother's maiden name with his childhood nickname. It is thus a tribute to the memory of his mother and his hometown. Leo Ou-fan Lee, *Voices from the Iron House: A Study of Lu Xun* (Bloomington: Indiana University Press, 1987), 3–24.

18. Sui's selection of the Chinese pseudonym is inspired by the Chinese love of nar-cissus. Although she was sometimes called "Chinese Water Lily" by her friends, her Chi-nese pseudonym, Sui Sin Far, actually means "narcissus." It is significant that the two plants have different connotations in traditional Chinese culture. The water lily symbol-izes prosperity, whereas the narcissus represents purity, elegance, and dignity. The nar-cissus is also one of the most popular plants in China, particularly in the southern prov-inces of Guangdong and Fujian. The majority of the earlier Chinese immigrants came from these two provinces and brought their fondness for the plant to America. It is the custom of the Chinese community in Honolulu, for example, to celebrate an annual Narcissus Festival and select a Miss Narcissus. Him Mark Lai, Joe Huang, and Don Wong, *The Chinese of America, 1785–1980* (San Francisco: Chinese Culture Foundation, 1980), 86.

19. For a discussion of Winnifred's motivation in assuming a Japanese identity, see Ling, *Between Worlds,* 30.

20. Sui, "The Half Chinese Writer," 1; S. E. Solberg, "Sui Sin Far/Edith Eaton: First Chinese-American Fictionist," *MELUS* 8 (Spring 1981): 36.

21. Robert McClellan, *The Heathen Chinee: A Study of American Attitudes toward China, 1890–1905* (Columbus: Ohio State University Press, 1971), 31–68; Wu, *The Yellow Peril,* 41–70.

22. William Purviance Fenn, *Ah Sin and His Brethren in American Literature* (Peiping [Beijing]: College of Chinese Studies, 1933), 12.

23. "A New Note in Fiction" [editor's note], *New York Times,* July 7, 1912, 45.

24. I am indebted to Amy Ling for reminding me of this important detail.

25. The fact that many of Sui's stories come out of Chinese folklore and classic litera-ture can be seen as evidence of the influence of Sui's mother, as well as the author's close relationships with Chinese immigrants and her self-education in Chinese studies.

26. Most Chinese immigrant laborers of the era, particularly peasants from rural ar-eas in Guangdong and other provinces in South China, customarily used "Ah" as a prefix before their names (e.g., Ah Sing, Ah Nan, or Ah Hong). The cultural differences between peasants from Guangdong province and other Chinese immigrants are analyzed in Francis L. K. Hsu, *The Challenge of the American Dream: The Chinese in the United States* (Belmont: Wadsworth, 1971), 1–10, 39–51.

27. Sui Sin Far was sometimes also called Chinese Lily by her friends.

28. Editor's Note, *The Independent,* Aug. 15, 1912, 338.

29. Solberg, "Sui Sin Far/Edith Eaton," 34.

30. American barbers were known for being prejudiced against immigrants and mi-norities. For example, Ng Poon Chew (1866–1931), a pioneering Chinese American jour-nalist and a leader of San Francisco's Chinese Christian community, could not find any barber willing to accommodate him when he decided to have his queue cut. Corinne

Hoexter, *From Canton to California: The Epic of Chinese Immigration* (New York: Four Winds Press, 1976), 154–67.

31. The author has made a subtle joke on mainstream American culture in the story. Mrs. Carman (the "Superior Woman") is said to be an Irish immigrant, while the name of the "inferior woman," Alice Winthrop, suggests that she might be of colonial New England descent.

32. The husband's name, Wou Sankwei [Wu Sangui], is in reality that of a famous and highly controversial figure in Chinese history. A well-known Chinese general at the end of the Ming Dynasty, Wou Sankwei (1612–78) surrendered to foreigners (the Manchus) and became one of the first Chinese to adopt such Manchu cultural customs as wearing his hair in a queue and dressing in Manchu-style clothes. It is likely that Sui deliberately selected the name to imply the character's submission to American culture. For information on Wou Sankwei, see Li Zhiting, *Wu Sangui dazhuan* [A biography of Wou Sankwei], (Jilin: Jilin Wenyi, 1990).

33. Lorraine Dong and Marlon K. Hom, "Defiance of Perpetuation: An Analysis of Characters in *Mrs. Spring Fragrance*," *Chinese America: History and Perspectives* (San Francisco: Chinese Historical Society of America, 1987), 150.

34. Pau Lin's mentality is similar to that of Sethe in Toni Morrison's *Beloved*. While Pau Lin poisons her son to stop him from receiving "white education," Sethe kills her baby daughter to save her from slavery. Annette White-Parks, "Journey to the Golden Mountain: Chinese Immigrant Women," in *Women and the Journey: The Female Travel Experience*, ed. Bonnie Frederick and Susan H. McLoed (Pullman: Washington State University Press, 1993), 106.

35. The Three Obediences [*San cong*] enjoined women to obey their fathers at home, their husbands after marriage, and their sons when widowed. The Four Virtues [*Si de*] decreed that a woman be chaste, that her conversation be courteous but not gossip, that her deportment be graceful and not extravagant, and that her leisure be spent in perfecting needlework rather than in outdoor activities. The Seven Grounds [*Qi chu*] sanctioned husbands divorcing wives if they showed no respect to the husbands' parents, had no son, committed adultery, or were jealous, seriously ill, talkative, or a thief. For a brief explanation of the sources of these decrees, see *Ci hai* [the Chinese encyclopedia], (Shanghai: Cisu, 1980), 11, 17, 20. For a comprehensive study of Chinese views of women's experiences in traditional Chinese society, see Li Yu-ning, ed., *Chinese Women through Chinese Eyes* (Armonk: M. E. Sharpe, 1992).

36. Stuart C. Miller, *The Unwelcome Immigrant: The American Image of the Chinese, 1785–1882* (Berkeley: University of California Press, 1969), 192. Also see Dong and Hom, "Defiance of Perpetuation," 164.

37. In his study of Irish immigrants, Oscar Handlin discusses why they hold to the Catholic religion despite strong hostility from Protestants. See Handlin, *Boston's Immigrants: A Study in Acculturation*, rev. ed. (Cambridge: Harvard University Press, 1979).

38. Mark Twain, *Roughing It* (repr. New York: Penguin Books, 1983), 391. Twain's "peculiar" attitude toward Chinese immigrants has been widely discussed by historians as well as literary critics. For example, William P. Fenn considers him to be one of the "chief defenders" of the Chinese among late-nineteenth-century American writers. Fenn, *Ah Sin and His Brethren in American Literature*, 30–36. Significantly, Mark Twain was highly praised by critics in China for his sympathetic views. He is one of the few mainstream American writers whose works were widely read and studied in China after the commu-

nist revolution in 1949. Xiao-huang Yin, "Progress and Problems: American Literary Studies in China during the Post-Mao Era," in *As Others Read Us: International Perspectives on American Literature,* ed. Huck Gutman (Amherst: University of Massachusetts Press, 1991), 49–64.

39. Portrayals of traditional Chinese in "Chinatown fiction" in popular American literature are examined ably and thoroughly in Wu, *The Yellow Peril,* 71–163.

40. Dong and Hom, "Defiance of Perpetuation," 144.

41. Ibid., 153. One also needs to be cautious in making that conclusion, however. Such a "cultural inaccuracy" might be Sui's subtle way of indicating the powerful impact of mainstream culture on the Chinese. According to statistics, the divorce rate of Chinese immigrants in America was much higher than in China; more Chinese women than men filed for divorce (chapter 6).

42. Editors of the magazine also commented that "Sui Sin Far is much more 'on the inside' of her theme than are most of those who pretend to depict the expatriated John." *Land of Sunshine* 6 (Dec. 1896): 32; and Chin et al., eds., *Aiiieeee,* xxi.

43. Until *Loving v. Virginia,* 388 U.S. 1 (1967) nullified all laws forbidding interracial marriage, thirty-seven states had antimiscegenation laws. Originally enacted to prohibit intermarriage between Caucasians and blacks, the laws were later extended to Asians in fifteen states. In California, marriages between whites and "Mongolians" were illegal after 1880. Most of Sui Sin Far's stories on intermarriage, however, cover the period before the 1880s, when Chinese-Caucasian marriages, albeit rare, were still possible. After 1880 some interracial couples in California would register their marriages in states that did not have laws against Asian-Caucasian marriage. Virginia Chin-lan Lee, a Chinese American author, mentions the practice in her novel *The House That Tai Ming Built* (New York: Macmillan, 1963). For more information on interracial marriages between Asians and whites in the earlier years, see Paul R. Spickard, *Mixed Blood: Intermarriage and Ethnic Identity in Twentieth-Century America* (Madison: University of Wisconsin Press, 1989), 25–120; Betty Lee Sung, *Chinese American Intermarriage* (New York: Center for Migration Studies, 1990), 1–19.

44. Katharine D. Newman, "Introduction," in *The American Equation: Literature in a Multi-Ethnic Culture,* ed. Newman (Boston: Allyn and Bacon, 1971), 15–16. Also see Werner Sollors, *Neither Black nor White, Yet Both: Thematic Explorations of Interracial Literature* (New York: Oxford University Press, 1997).

45. Translated literally, "Tie Co" in Chinese may mean "very bitter" or "sorrowful."

46. "A New Note in Fiction," 45.

47. Liu's given name, "Kanghi," implies that he is a "cultivated Chinese." Sui intends to use the "sophisticated" name as a subtle indication to suggest why Liu is more individualistic than his peers and that he is different from tradition-oriented Chinese immigrants, most of them peasants from rural regions in South China.

48. The phenomenon changed in the 1940s, when the "China doll" image put an end to the miscegenation taboo in popular American culture, and the film industry "discovered" that Chinese women lent charm, feeling, and atmosphere to "Oriental" productions (chapter 4).

49. In Bret Harte's "Wan Lee, the Pagan," for example, a Chinese man who is romantically involved with a white woman is killed by a mob. *The Writings of Bret Harte* (Boston: Houghton Mifflin, 1896), 2:262–80. The issue was also the subject of D. W. Griffith's

silent film *Broken Blossoms* (1919). Originally entitled *The Chink and the Child,* the movie paved the way for characterizing future Asian-white love relationships: The "Chinaman" kills himself, for society condemns his affection for the white woman, thereby eradicating a threat to white womanhood. Eugene Franklin Wong, *On Visual Media Racism: Asians in the American Motion Pictures* (New York: Arno Press, 1978), 76–77.

50. To some extent the Boxer Rebellion in China (1898–1900) was caused by the same issue. More than thirty thousand Chinese converts were killed because of their association with foreigners and their belief in Christianity. John King Fairbank, *The Great Chinese Revolution, 1800–1985* (New York: Harper and Row, 1987), 84–140.

51. *Daily Alta California,* May 12, 1851, 2, cited in Ronald Riddle, *Flying Dragons, Flowing Streams: Music in the Life of San Francisco's Chinese* (Westport: Greenwood Press, 1983), 39. Chinese-language writing contains more accounts of violent conflicts between Westernized and traditional Chinese immigrants in America. According to Chinese writers, most Chinese immigrants in the early era could not countenance the outright denial of Chinese values and felt betrayed when they found that some of their countrymen had given up Chinese traditions to adopt Western customs. Chin Mu, *Huaqiao ticai zuopinxuan* [Writings by Chin Mu on Chinese immigrants], (Fuzhou: Fujian Renmin, 1984), 79–218.

52. It is commonly observed that in "cross-caste" marriages between minority men and white women in American society, males are usually well educated and of higher economic status whereas females tend to be from lower socioeconomic backgrounds. Romanzo Adams, *Interracial Marriage in Hawaii* (New York: Macmillan, 1937); also see Sung, *Chinese American Intermarriage,* 20–40.

53. The only story Sui wrote in which interracial contact does not end in tragedy is "Sing-Song Woman." Here, Mag-gee, whose is Eurasian and whose name is a Chinese variation of "Margaret," successfully runs away with her white boy friend. Focusing on the family structure of Chinese Americans, however, the story is only one of Sui's lesser efforts on the theme of intermarriage. In addition, the nontragic end is largely due to Mag-gee's quasi-Chinese yet true Caucasian identity. With blue eyes and blond hair, "she is not Chinese in looks or in any other way" (*MSF* 237). Even so, the fact that the couple must run away, fugitives, instead of having a normal family life indicates the strong public disapproval of such a marriage.

54. John Burt Foster, "China and the Chinese in American Literature, 1850–1950," Ph.D. diss., University of Illinois, 1952, 205, quoted in Solberg, "Sui Sin Far/Edith Eaton," 35. Frank Chin and his colleagues also speak highly of the two stories and have anthologized them. Chan et al., eds., *The Big Aiiieeeee,* 111–38.

55. Werner Sollors, "Intermarriage and Mulattos in the 1920s," [Perugia] *RSA* 5, no. 7 (1989): 269.

56. Quoted in Judy Yung, *Chinese Women of America: A Pictorial History* (Seattle: University of Washington Press, 1986), 89.

57. I am indebted to L. Charles Laferrière, Sui Sin Far's grandnephew, for providing a photograph of her burying place and information that enabled me to visit the Protestant Cemetery in Montreal in 1991.

58. The Chinese Exclusion Act required that a child born in China have special documents to enter the United States, even if his or her parents were American-born citizens or permanent residents.

59. Some Chinese immigrants still believe that Irish Americans are inherently more

racist than other whites. In 1985, for example, I attended a hearing on a case involving an elderly Chinese man who had been severely beaten by a law officer in Boston. When I asked why the officer had been so hostile, I was told by a local Chinese community leader that it was because he was an Irish and the Irish were "more racist than other whites in American society." Such a view is, of course, absolutely wrong.

60. Quoted in Ruthanne Lum McCunn, *Chinese American Portraits: Personal Histories, 1828–1988* (San Francisco: Chronicle Books, 1988), 34.

61. McCunn, *Chinese American Portraits*, 34.

62. Between 20 and 30 percent of the Chinese who lived in Mississippi married black women before 1940. James W. Loewen, *The Mississippi Chinese: Between Black and White*, rev. ed. (Prospect Heights: Waveland Press, 1988), 135–48. The status of Chinese-blacks and their relationship with the Chinese American community in the South are also examined in Sung, *Chinese American Intermarriage*, 32–34.

63. McCunn, *Chinese American Portraits*, 79, 81–84, 87. To be sure, such prejudice is not confined to the Chinese. "It is important to remember," as Werner Sollors points out, "that racial thinking typically only accepted 'pure' races and looked at mixtures with particular suspicion and contempt." Sollors, "Intermarriage and Mulattos in the 1920s," 276.

64. Solberg, "Sui Sin Far/Edith Eaton," 34; also see Dong and Hom, "Defiance of Perpetuation," 162–65.

65. This was the prevailing view throughout the West in Sui's time. For example, according to Lynn Pan, those white women in England who chose to marry Chinese during the early twentieth century did so mainly because they thought them more reliable in terms of providing financial support and sharing housework. Pan also reports that "marrying down" was a common phenomenon in cross-race relationships between Chinese men and white women in England. Although Chinese-Caucasian marriages were quite common in Great Britain at the time, in general most white women who married Chinese men were from blue-collar backgrounds. Pan, *Sons of the Yellow Emperor: A History of the Chinese Diaspora* (New York: Kodansha International, 1994), 91, 272.

66. Quoted in Donald N. Bigelow, "Introduction," in Jacob A. Riis, *How the Other Half Lives* (repr., New York: Hill and Wang, 1957), xiv.

*I marched out of the house insouciant. When I wasn't whistling I was muttering to myself a Jewish slang phrase I had just picked up. It was "Ishkabibble" and it meant that I didn't care. And I didn't until I reached the park where all my most vivid daydreaming periods were spent. There, I broke down and wept. For the first time I admitted to myself the cruel truth—I didn't have a "Chinaman's chance" of becoming President of the United States. . . . But after a good cry I felt better—anyway, I could go to an American school again in the fall.*
—Pardee Lowe

# 4

# Seeking a Place in American Life: The Autobiographical Writing of Second-Generation Chinese

Chinese immigration to the United States was curtailed drastically following the implementation of the Chinese Exclusion Act of 1882.[1] With the decline of immigrants from China, the population of American-born Chinese grew slowly but steadily. The native-born were an insignificant number within the Chinese community at the turn of the century, but by 1920 they made up 30 percent of the population. By 1940, three years before the Chinese Exclusion Act was finally repealed, the figure had reached 52 percent in the continental United States.[2]

American-born Chinese, or "ABCs" as they are more commonly called, have significantly changed the character of the Chinese American community.[3] As native-born, English-speaking citizens, they form a distinct subgroup, have their own subculture and social circles, and tend to think and act differently from their parents, particularly with respect to their relationship with China and America. Whether they were "coolies" or members of the exempt classes, China always had a special place in the hearts of the first generation of immigrants, and they generally chose to maintain a close relationship with the old country. When rejected by American society because of their allegedly alien background, they would either indulge in the illusion that someday they might save enough money to return to the land of their birth and enjoy their accumulation or they would seek spiritual comfort by thinking about the superiority of Chinese cultural tradition. As Gerald W. Haslam finds, the knowledge that China produced one of the greatest civilizations in the world stimulated the ethnic pride of Chinese immigrants, providing them with "an inner resource" in their struggle against racism.[4]

The second generation, however, was different. Although they may also have felt "foreign" because of having distinctive racial characteristics, they could not look to a return to China or find strength in Chinese culture as a possible alternative. For them, the choice between China and America did not exist. Born and raised in the United States, America was their only home; few bonds, cultural, emotional, or economic, linked them to their parents' old country. They were Chinese by race but bore the impact of mainstream American culture. Their English accent was the same as their peers in the larger society, and often they understood more about the United States than they did about China. Educated in American public schools, they had learned and adopted many of the cultural values characteristic of mainstream society and tended to be more individualistic and less imbued with traditional Chinese ethics and morality. Indeed, the process of assimilation for second-generation Chinese was so noticeable that as early as the 1920s they had been labeled "Orientals in appearance but not in reality."[5] As a result, no matter how they might feel about being excluded by American society, their unfamiliarity with a China they had never seen (and a culture they had little enthusiasm to embrace) made them ambivalent about seeking a future there. At a time when the concept of multiculturalism was yet a novelty, what they did in the face of racial prejudice was to redouble their efforts to assimilate and make themselves more acceptable to the dominant race, sometimes at the expense of abandoning their Chinese heritage.[6]

Along with the increase of second-generation Chinese, there emerged a substantial body of publications by them. Written from a totally different perspective, the writing provided fresh information about the lives and experiences of native-born Chinese during the transitional era.[7] Representing a broad spectrum, they illustrate the feelings and thoughts of American-born Chinese before the emergence of the civil rights movement that reshaped the concept of race and ethnicity. Although sensibilities of these authors differ according to their age, background, and individuality, their writing, placed within a historical context, suggests that what the native-born had in common was a desire to summarize their generation's perspective.

Because the saga of the second generation's experience was governed by a profound compulsion to belong to mainstream culture, the struggle to enter the larger society and the quest for a place in American life are the dominant themes of their writing, particularly of their autobiographical works and fictionalized life stories. The themes are expressed in terms of conflicts between East-West cultural values, views on interracial marriages, the generation gap, the pursuit of the American dream, the native-born's imperative to assert Americanness, and the anxiety to demonstrate patriotism as a "loyal minority." Works such as Pardee Lowe's *Father and Glorious Descendant* (1943), Jade Snow Wong's *Fifth Chinese Daughter* (1950), Virginia Chin-lan Lee's *The House That Tai Ming Built* (1963), and Monfoon Leong's *Number One Son* (1975) are all part of the genre.[8]

What their works have in common is a sense of alienation from the Chinese community. For many second-generation Chinese during this period, because of the repressive atmosphere at home and in the Chinese community, teachers and friends in society at large seemed more accepting and encouraging than their own people. In part, that is because until the 1960s the Chinese American community remained predominantly a society of older males brought up in Chinese tradition.[9] Such an environment undoubtedly made further acculturation difficult for the second generation. In addition, contacts with peers in the general population caused dissatisfaction with the idea of spending their lives in the Chinese community, running small, ethnic-oriented family enterprises. Public school education thus provided not only the basis for new ideas that enhanced assimilation but was also a source of social forces that uprooted the second generation from the Chinese community and fostered its ambition to seek opportunities in the larger society and compete with the majority race.

There is another factor that links the second generation: They had almost universally undergone a rebellious phase influenced by American culture. The values—independence, equality, and individuality conflict—with those of a traditional Chinese heritage, which stresses family ties, community dependence, and respect for tradition. Although the second generation was aware of both sets of values, they preferred to achieve individuality rather than work at family or community ties. That preference is apparent in almost all their literary work despite their differences in background and personality. Pardee Lowe, for example, openly rebelled against his father and broke from his family, and Jade Snow Wong went to college as a way of avoiding her repressive home. As an act of defiance against her parents' authority, Virginia Chin-lan Lee's protagonist runs away with a Caucasian boyfriend when her parents oppose their impending marriage, which was then invalidated by California's antimiscegenation law. Of course, youthful rebellion against parents and alienation from ethnic community are nothing new among second-generation immigrants.[10] Considering the strong family ties and patriarchal authority emphasized by Chinese culture, however, the lack of filial piety of native-born Chinese is surprising. They traveled far from their "Oriental roots."

Among the work of second-generation Chinese authors during this period, two books in particular deserve examination: Pardee Lowe's *Father and Glorious Descendant* and Jade Snow Wong's *Fifth Chinese Daughter.* Focusing on the experience of those who grew up during the early twentieth century, Lowe's personal narrative is the first published, book-length literary work by an American-born Chinese. Wong's autobiographical novel, the most influential work by a native-born Chinese until Maxine Hong Kingston's *The Woman Warrior* (1976), reveals the lives of those who came of age around World War II, when the fate of Chinese Americans would be dramatically improved.

Both books were published by major commercial publishers and were well received by mainstream audiences, which reflects the public's increasing interest and gradual shift in favor toward the Chinese since the 1930s. Ironically, the criterion adopted to judge the books' value is related to the argument that Chinese Americans, a "loyal minority," deserve sympathetic treatment—the exact reverse of the previous theory of exclusion.

The substance and imagery of both books are controversial because they suggest that all native-born Chinese are assimilated and unobtrusively American, an outcome of the melting pot process. In retrospect, their idealized picture of American life, which helped win them wide praise, might have reinforced the image of the Chinese as unthreatening ethnic novelties. Hence, their "accommodationist attitude" has brought them criticism by contemporary Chinese American activists and is viewed as evidence that the former generations were "Chinese Uncle Toms" and "'whitewashed' to the extent that their experiences of prejudice and discrimination have been deleted from history."[11]

One way to understand the literary sensibilities behind the writing of second-generation authors, however, is to place them within the social and historical context of their time. The authors lived in an era marked by an emphasis on Americanization and "Chinese American loyalty" and could not have foreseen the ethnic consciousness that would follow the civil rights movement in the late

1960s. Instead of taking them out of historical context, we may regard their work as a mirror, reflecting the process by which native-born Chinese evolved from denial of self to finding a self-image and consciousness. The idea of multiculturalism seems nothing more than common sense now, but in their era the melting pot theory still dominated social consciousness, and they were preoccupied with their designated role of being a "model minority," a fact that is ignored by some contemporary critics.

## *Father and Glorious Descendant:* Breaking away from "Oriental Roots"

Because few firsthand accounts of the lives of second-generation Chinese were available, Pardee Lowe's autobiography, *Father and Glorious Descendant,* was well received when it was published in 1943.[12] Critics found the work rewarding and celebrated it as a solid and significant study of the Chinese American community. It was even hailed as "a Chinese-American *Life with Father.*"[13] The positive response reflected what was then the dramatically changed attitude of the American public toward the Chinese. As a result of U.S. involvement in World War II, China had become an important ally; Chinese Americans were deemed a "loyal minority" group and enjoyed unprecedented popularity.[14] Such a change in the social trend regarding the attitude toward the Chinese is indicated clearly in a critic's comment on Lowe's book: "[The] author's love for America and his respect for his Oriental roots . . . show an excellent blending of the two cultures. The book will contribute greatly toward better understanding of one of *our loyal minority groups.*"[15] The intention to use Lowe's autobiography to satisfy the public's vague notion about "Chinese loyalty" is shown even more conspicuously in advertising copy on the book's jacket. To underscore Lowe's patriotism, the publishers state that he had joined the U.S. Army as soon as he completed the manuscript. What better proof of "Chinese loyalty" could there be than a willingness to fight for Uncle Sam on the battlefield?[16]

Undoubtedly, Lowe's American-style patriotism contributed greatly to his book's popularity. But what the critics and publishers failed to perceive or chose to ignore is that the autobiography was also a frank revelation of the psychology of a second-generation Chinese who faced the formidable pressure of assimilation. Seeking to assert his Americanness, Lowe went to the point of self-negation to deny his ethnic affiliation and derogate his Chinese cultural heritage. Focusing on his efforts to "melt" into the American cauldron, the author in reality articulated the notion that the only way Chinese could become respected figures in American society was to break from their ethnic roots.

Although the quest for a place in American life dominates the lengthy auto-biography, Lowe also presents a penetrating account of the lives and feelings of second-generation Chinese during the early twentieth century. As bitterness, rejoicing, and subtler moods unfold, the book becomes an important reflection of the common experience of American-born Chinese during a period when their fate began to catch the attention of society in general.

Born in 1905, Lowe was one of the few Chinese of his time who were truly native-born.[17] His father was a leading figure in San Francisco's Chinese community. In addition to owning several dry-goods stores that hired nearly fifty employees, the senior Lowe was also the head of a large clan association and held a powerful position in the Chinese Six Companies. Because the clan owned more than a hundred stores scattered in cities from San Diego to Seattle, the Lowe family's influence spread throughout the Pacific Coast. At the age of thirty, his father had already been designated "Ah Kung Ah" [respected great-uncle].

Unlike most of his contemporaries, Lowe grew up in a predominantly white neighborhood in East Belleville across the San Francisco Bay.[18] The fact that the family did not reside in Chinatown was unusual at the time and indicated their degree of Americanization and close relationship with mainstream Americans. Most Chinese of the era were confined to Chinatowns; even as late as the 1950s they still found it difficult to move into middle-class white neighborhoods in California.[19]

Indeed, Lowe's father's enthusiasm for American values clearly surpassed that of most early Chinese immigrants. Instead of naming children in the tradition-al Chinese way, as most of his countrymen insisted upon, he gave them the names of prominent American statesmen. Lowe was named after George C. Pardee, a gesture of respect for the Republican governor of California, and he had siblings named Ted Roosevelt and Taft. Such an endorsement for Republicans resembled the practice of newly emancipated slaves after the Civil War, many of whom named themselves Lincoln to acknowledge the president's role in their freedom.

The senior Lowe's fervor for Republicans was in part stimulated by that party's relatively mild stance on the issue of Chinese immigration in the late nineteenth and early twentieth centuries. Prominent Republicans such as William Henry Seward and Charles Sumner advocated fair treatment for Chinese immigrants, even amid growing anti-Chinese antagonism.[20] As the first president who received representatives of the Chinese community in the White House, Theodore Roosevelt tried to modify the unfair Chinese Exclusion Act, acknowledging that "immigration officers had exhibited regrettable acts of discrimination."[21] As he pointed out in his annual message to the Congress in December 1905, "[In] the effort to carry out the policy of excluding Chinese laborers . . . grave injustice and wrong have been done by this Nation to the people of China, and therefore ultimately to this Nation itself."[22]

Of course, Republican endorsement for a less harsh Chinese immigration policy was largely prompted by the interests of big corporations; railway barons, for example, reaped tremendous profits from Chinese labor. It was the same reason that led Southern Democrats to a more "pro-Chinese" stand. Despite racial tension in the Deep South during Reconstruction, Democrats there insisted on free immigration for Chinese laborers. The author of "Common Sense Applied to the Immigration Question" noted:

> Public opinion in the United States is strangely divided at present [1869] on the subject of Chinese labor on American soil. The Democrat party in California is violently opposed to the presence among us of the Chinese, whose best friends are to be found in the Republican ranks. At the East, the Democrats of the South, accustomed from childhood to the idea of the degradation of manual labor, and determined to find a substitute for the labor of the freedmen, are just now in fever of delight at the prospect of an abundant supply of Chinese labor.[23]

While this is not the place to go into the specific political affiliation of Chinese Americans, it is noteworthy that the way in which the Lowe children were named constituted a radical departure from Chinese custom. In traditional Chinese society, even mentioning a top-ranking official's name was deemed a serious crime that would result in harsh punishment. Thus, Lowe's father's behavior reveals how quickly and profoundly he had adapted to the American cultural environment.

The father's acceptance of American values undoubtedly had a strong impact on the son. He was proud that his father, with his Western dress and manners, was one of the few Chinese in San Francisco respected by mainstream Americans. His father, he recalled, was always greeted politely by whites, who distinguished him from the rest of the Chinese passengers on the ferry across the Bay:

> Tall and brawny and queueless, Father resembled an American . . . I could see it every morning when the conductor and the brakeman, without fail, nodded at Father graciously. They recognized him as an individual worthy of special notice, but their cordial greetings were never given to the others— who, I observed, wore sleek bowler hats, Chinese jackets, Western pants, padded slippers from Canton, and over all, dangling queues, streaked with vermilion braid—and whom they disparagingly called Ah John, Ah Charlie, or Ah Jim.[24]

If Lowe's admiration for American values was deeply rooted in childhood memory of his father's "unusual American qualities," it was further fostered by his public school education. He attended a suburban neighborhood school rather than a segregated classroom in Chinatown. Encouraged by a devoted, idealistic Irish woman known as Miss McIntyre, he became caught up in the American dream early on and consciously identified with mainstream society.[25] He was so completely "brainwashed" that he blindly admired everything American: "I became a walking encyclopedia of American history . . . I knew the vivid, gory details, authentic and apocryphal, of every important military engagement in which Americans took part—and always victoriously" (*Father* 132). Legendary figures such as Buffalo Bill became his heroes. Even the names of American outlaws sounded more heroic and romantic than those of the members of Chinese Tongs:

> The deep, dark way of the tongs continued to remain entirely beyond my ken and experience. Even though at the age of nine I was already an inveterate reader of the blood-and-thunder tales glorifying such fearless men as Buffalo Bill and Wild Bill Hickok, I found the tongs with their plots and counterplots, wicked schemes, scouting parties, ambuscades, armed nests, and the odd nicknames of their hatchet men—such as "Big Queue," "Midget Pete," "Handsome Boy," and "Hot Stuff"—extremely sinister; they did not possess the flesh-and-blood qualities of my American heroes. (93)

When his father took him to the Chinese New Year's party, he found that "the entire performance struck me as being totally alien. Fed up, I informed Father: I like 'Yankee Doodle Dandy' much better'" (*Father* 45).

Of course, Lowe was not alone in his fantasies about the dominant race. In *The Man Who (Thought He) Looked Like Robert Taylor,* Bienvenido N. Santos, a leading Filipino writer, sarcastically describes how Solomon King, a Filipino butcher in Chicago, desperately wishes to look and behave like a white movie star.[26] Malcolm X also recalls in his autobiography how light-skinned black children were favored by their parents and some middle-class blacks "break their backs trying to imitate white people."[27] The reason is simple. Although the contemporary American norm allows for more acceptance of ethnic heritage, in Lowe's time anything not white American was ignored. If, according to W. E. B. Du Bois, "this double-consciousness, this sense of always looking at one's self through the eyes of others, of measuring one's soul by the tape of a world that looks on in amused contempt and pity" has long characterized African Americans, it has also overwhelmed other minorities.[28] In an article published in the *New York Times,* the author has estimated that nearly 40 percent of Native Americans hid their ethnic identities until 1990.[29] Thus, Lowe's self-negation and fanatic admiration for American culture were not exceptional but typical of that culture's powerful impact on second-generation Chinese.

It is surprising to read that Lowe, under the influence of Miss McIntyre, nurtured the lofty illusion of achieving prominence and becoming president of the United States—like any other American child. In a chapter entitled "Father Cures a Presidential Fever" he vividly describes his belief that America was a place of equality where everyone could participate fully in political life and be rewarded in accordance with ability. That illusion is a scathing irony of social reality. Chinese immigrants at the time were robbed of the right to become American citizens because of their alleged inability to assimilate. Stereotypes such as power-hungry Chinatown despots, bloodthirsty tong hatchetmen, sensual sing-song girls, and comical houseboys were all part of the popular image of the Chinese and were drearily familiar to average Americans. Against that background, it is easy to understand why Lowe was met with cynical laughter when he proudly declared to his father's white business associates that his lifelong ambition was to be president of the United States.

Ironically, stereotypes of the Chinese sometimes also victimized mainstream Americans. Lowe tells a story of how his uncle, a "hard-boiled guy" and habitual gambler, could borrow money from white friends because they thought a "Chinaman" could be relied upon to keep his word. After the uncle ran away, his creditors came to Lowe's father, believing naively that "a Chinaman always honors his relatives' debts." To their great disappointment and despite "tearful protestations," Lowe's father denied any liability (*Father* 61). Again, it was not unusual to find white Americans being victimized because of the stereotypes they had created for the Chinese. In one of his frontier stories, Bret Harte has "Chinese coolies" outwit pig-headed California tax-collectors by passing one foreign miner's license among themselves. Tax-collectors could not recognize the difference between one Chinese and another and refused to believe they could be fooled by the "Chinamen."[30]

As an innocent boy filled with bright hopes and the American dream, however, Lowe soon learned the hard way that the ideal (regardless of "race, religion, or national origin") is not always true. No matter how American Lowe felt, he would not be treated as an equal member of society because of his appearance. That cruel lesson was unexpectedly brought to the fore when he tried for the first time to find a summer job outside Chinatown during his high school years. Although he was thoroughly American in name, birth, speech, manner, dress, and education—everything but appearance—Lowe painfully discovered that cultural, ethnic, and social biases were against him, as they were against the first-generation Chinese. Although his white schoolmates found ample job opportunities, he was rejected everywhere he applied and frequently not given a chance for an interview.

In this respect, Lowe was by no means the only second-generation Chinese who encountered obstacles on the American job market. Edward C. Chew, son of Ng Poon Chew—an eminent Chinese American journalist and leader of San Francisco's Chinese Christian community—was denied employment despite making numerous applications and despite an education at the University of California and distinguished service as one of the few Chinese American officers during World War I.[31] To some extent, the more education the Chinese received, the fewer opportunities they found open to them. One mainstream scholar observed in the 1920s that "those [second-generation Chinese] who have graduated with honors from our best universities find it difficult to secure positions—the places which are open to them are of an inferior sort with but limited opportunities for advancement."[32] Warning them not to harbor illusions about employment opportunities, the president of the University of Hawaii, David Crawford, lectured Asian students sternly: "Do not count on education to do too much for you, do not take it too seriously. Do not expect a college degree, an A.B. or a PhD, to get you ahead unduly in this world."[33]

Statistics show that as late as 1940, only 3 percent of the Chinese were engaged in professional and technical occupations. They usually either worked in small-scale, ethnically oriented family enterprises or were confined to positions in Chinatown and had little chance for promotion. The banking business in San Francisco, for example, recognized the capability and effectiveness of Chinese tellers but would not hire them for banks outside Chinatown. When Dolly Gee, a native-born Chinese, distinguished herself at the Bank of America, she was appointed manager of its Oriental branch in 1932. Although her abilities were widely recognized, she was never promoted to a higher position outside Chinatown. It is also ironic that in some cases second-generation Chinese received federal jobs only because immigration authorities needed help in seeking out illegal immigrants.[34]

The obstacles Lowe encountered in the job market also existed for other Asian and minority groups at the time. Nisei (second-generation Japanese) college students, unable to secure jobs that would match their qualifications, were often forced to return to their families' small farms or fruit stands. In one case, a nisei told his friends who planned to go to college, "You may go, but after graduation you fellows will come around to my vegetable stand begging me for a job."[35] Elaine H. Kim, a Korean American scholar, recalls that her mother, a graduate from Mount Holyoke College before World War II, was never able to obtain employment that matched her training. Despite her talent and college education she could only make a living by taking odd jobs, such as selling cosmetics and encyclopedias door to door.[36] The same was true for African Americans. Until the 1960s, black Ph.D.s frequently found they were excluded from teaching positions.

The open and subtle racial prejudice presented Lowe with a very real problem: How should he interpret the contradictions between social reality and the ideal of the American dream, and how should he face the outcome of Americanization if the very American democracy and the equality he admired excluded him? Such a dilemma touched tender spots in the minds of second-generation Chinese. Depressed by rejection from society, they were often disillusioned, and many passed through periods of emotional disturbance. Unlike those who solved the dilemma by returning to the Chinese community and its restraining influence, however, Lowe took a different course. Undoubtedly, the bitter lesson of failing to find a job shattered his "presidential dream." Returning home, his illusions crushed, he came to understand better why his father chose to identify with Chinese cultural tradition albeit adopting American manners.

Lowe's lack of success in the job market did not alter his stubborn, innate desire to follow American ideals, however. He quickly dismissed the lesson and comforted himself with the idea that others had fates similar to his and that he could at least study in an American public school—symbolic and significant progress for the Chinese considering the formerly segregated educational system imposed on them: "In this crash of the lofty hopes which Miss McIntyre had raised, it did not occur to me to reflect that the chances of Francisco Trujillo, Yuri Matsuyama, or Penelope Lincoln were actually no better than mine. But after a good cry I felt better—anyway, I could go to an American school again in the fall" (*Father* 148).[37] Clearly, despite a "crash of the lofty hopes," Lowe was unconvinced that he needed to account for the discrepancy between the promised equality of the American myth and his experience of exclusion, which labeled him as being unequal. The passage's conclusion implies that he continued to see becoming part of mainstream society as his only choice. For him, the only true avenue possible when American doors seemed closed was to redouble efforts to seek accommodation.

Such a reflection today would surely be denounced as Uncle Tomism. Nevertheless, given Lowe's circumstances and era it was an understandable response as well as an approved way to behave. A citizen by birth and a product of American public education, Lowe had few alternatives but to follow the traditional response to exclusion: work harder and seek comfort in those aspects of society that did include him. "[He] was only acting the way he'd been brought up to act," the Japanese American writer Hisaye Yamamoto has commented about a character in her fiction, "the way men were supposed to be."[38] In addition, by demonstrating his resolve to participate in American life, Lowe was also defying a popular belief which held that the Chinese did not wish to assimilate into American society and proving the falsity of discriminatory practices against the Chinese based on that idea.

Lowe's choice to adapt to rather than challenge the racial prejudices that confronted him was also a result of his alienation from Chinese cultural tradition—an outcome of assimilation, unintended perhaps, but seemingly inevitable. His embitterment over being rejected by the dominant race was much less than his frustration with and estrangement from his father. This again shows that he was more rooted in the larger society than the Chinese community. Throughout the autobiography, Lowe's thorough assimilation is interwoven with and contrasted to his father's half-way acculturation. The troubled relationship between the father and the son is another major theme of the volume.

The title of Lowe's autobiography means "Father and Son," but it is far from being a smooth record of a father-son relationship.[39] Lowe's attitude toward his father vacillates between being a "glorious descendant" who is proud of his father's American manners and a furious, rebellious son who is outraged by the father's Chinese way of thinking. Although he gratefully acknowledges his father's strength, talent, and adaptability as giving him substance and shaping and inspiring his continuous pursuit of the American dream, he also admits that the father's "stubborn Chinese mind" was a source of constant conflict between the patriarch and son. As Lowe struggled to break away from the course his father designed for him and from the Chinese cultural heritage he found unacceptable to his Americanized mind, subtle frictions escalated into open confrontation. In Lowe's words, "mutual contempt" dominated much of the father-son relationship.

The opening of the book is poignant and indicative of Lowe's views: "I strongly suspect that my father's life is a fraud" (*Father* 1)—a fraud in the sense that the old man was never truly Americanized despite having adopted the extrinsic traits of American culture. Although the father cut off his queue to symbolize that he had severed links with China—a courageous action at a time when the Manchu court's edict was "no queue, no head"—he did not cast away the cultural heritage he brought from the old country.[40] Throughout his life, the father remained a Chinese. "Father's American ways are not American enough," Lowe complained bitterly, "and as for his Chinese habits and ideas, they are queer, unreasonable, and humiliating!" (175) That is especially clear in the old man's distrust of originality, individuality, and emotional expression compared to his advocacy of sobriety and restraint of affection—the traditional Chinese attitude toward life.

The breaking point of the relationship comes when the father insists on the son attending a Chinese-language school. To be fair, his decision that Lowe "should undertake immediately the study of Chinese" is not caused by fear of losing the son to "barbarian" culture, for he himself was the apostle of Americanization; rather, it is motivated by practical considerations. The father is fully aware that Lowe's illusion about equality will be costly. No matter how Americanized the son might be, there is little chance he will acquire anything other than a menial position outside the Chinese community. Therefore, knowledge of the Chinese language would not only preserve a cultural link with the old country but also be "good job insurance" and provide Lowe with an important means of gaining a China-related profession. The intention is underscored by the fact that although Lowe's father recognizes and encourages assimilation by naming his children after prominent American politicians, he insists with greater vehemence on their acceptance of such Chinese cultural customs as worship of family ancestors. That attitude also explains why he had prevented Lowe in childhood from identifying himself entirely as an American and told him he should eventually go to China for education.

Lowe's father's practice was not unique among first-generation Chinese. Three decades later Maxine Hong Kingston related the same story in *The Woman Warrior:* "Not when we were afraid, but when we were wide awake and lucid, my mother funnelled China into our ears: Kwangtung Province, New Society Village, the river Kwoo, which runs past the village. 'Go the way we came so that you will be able to find our house.' . . . I am to return to China where I have never been."[41] Clearly, despite the passage of time, the mentality of many Chinese immigrants remained unchanged long into the twentieth century.

It was on the issue of Chinese education, however, that Lowe's father met bitter resistance from his "Glorious Descendent." Socially and culturally accustomed to the American way of life, Lowe considered Chinese education a major obstacle that would hamper his effort to become a "real American" and "neutralize" his "excessive Americanism." Although returning to China for education, according to the overseas Chinese tradition, indicates the high social status of a student's family (just as well-to-do Americans used to send their children to Europe for schooling), Lowe objected furiously to his father's plan.[42] "What stood out in my mind then was that Chinese was the most difficult language in the world" and China was a remote and backward country with "no redeeming features," a place where he had no interest in setting down roots (*Father* 139). Influenced by misleading concepts that ignored the role of "the Oriental" in world history, Lowe, and many of his contemporaries, was more enthusiastic about, and familiar with, Anglo-American cultural heritage than that of his father's homeland.[43] According to a study conducted on the West Coast during the 1920s, American-born Asians ranked much higher in knowledge of American history than native white children but knew little about the history of their parents' old countries and cared even less.[44]

Lowe's firm rejection of his Chinese affiliation and his strenuous attempt to assert an American identity indicate how large the gap was between the first and second generations. But such a "treacherous mentality" was not unique to native-born Chinese. Marcus Lee Hanson, for example, has observed that the one characteristic perceived to transcend ethnicity is the second generation's proclivity to "treason."[45] As he points out in an article about Swedish immigrants in the United States, "[The second generation] wanted to forget everything: the foreign language that left an unmistakable trace in his English speech, the religion that continually recalled childhood struggles, the family customs that should have been the happiest of all memories. He wanted to be away from all physical reminders of early days, in an environment so different, so American, that all associates naturally assumed that he was as American as they."[46]

Hanson's argument helps explain why Lowe and second-generation Chinese as a whole were so sensitive about their ethnic identity and tended to react fiercely to their parents' intense pressure to maintain Chinese cultural tradition. Without personal experience with their cultural legacy, the native-born tend to seek a remedy for feelings of abasement in the dominant American culture by accommodating to racial prejudice rather than challenging it.

What further exemplifies the gap between the father and son is Lowe's critical attitude toward Chinese family life. He argues that while affection, creativity, and personal feelings among family members are encouraged and welcomed in general society, they are restrained or even stifled by Chinese tradition. As a result, Lowe and his siblings all "longed to escape" from home. His criticism becomes more intensified and bitter when he turns to parental authoritarianism and filial piety. As he points out, although Chinese immigrants were in a "new land," the influence of the tradition of their old country—including unquestioning acceptance of parental authority—remained.

In Lowe's opinion (another endorsement of mainstream American ideals), the custom of not questioning one's parents thwarted the personal freedom of dutiful children who might otherwise pursue their own happiness. He candidly asserted that if Chinese immigrants in America wanted to achieve equal progress with their European counterparts they would have to abandon various objectionable practices and undesirable customs brought from the "old home." Lowe, however, was not entirely wrong on that issue, and there is at least partial truth in his reasoning. In almost all writing by Chinese Americans, from Sui Sin Far to Maxine Hong Kingston, Amy Tan, and Gish Jen, parents exert unyielding patriarchal or matriarchal authority to force their children to take the course they have chosen for them.

Lowe epitomized the second-generation's experience of assimilation as a process of alienation from traditional Chinese culture. Given that he had become so deeply acculturated, it is only natural that his feelings and attitude toward a Chinese cultural heritage would be drastically different from his father's. The thoroughness of his assimilation is perhaps best evidenced by the fact he married a white woman from an old New England family while attending the Harvard Graduate School of Business Administration. The wedding was held in a Protestant Evangelical church in Brandenburg, Germany, in 1931, and Lowe did not inform his parents or his Chinese friends of the event until two years later. Such deliberate distancing reiterated his intention to separate himself from the Chinese community.

It is noteworthy that the marriage is mentioned only in passing in the autobiography. Although it is not unusual for an author to refrain from discussing his or her marital life in an autobiography, the scarcity of information of such a significant issue, compared with Lowe's detailed, meticulous description of many small events in his family, appears rather suspicious and betrays a sense of uncertainty. Perhaps Lowe feared that a more personal and intimate account of the relationship would embarrass his wife, "a born and bred New Englander" (*Father* 237). Or, he might have been concerned that a detailed account of a romance with a white woman would give rise to negative responses from readers because at the time antimiscegenation sentiment was still strong, and the law remained effective in California.

Although the subsequent years saw Chinese-Caucasian marriages gradually gain more approval, particularly those between Chinese women and Caucasian men, the view that Chinese men constituted a threat to white women remained operative in the mind of the American public for a long time.[47] In any case, at the time of Lowe's marriage in 1931, there was very definite fear among the public about Chinese-Caucasian intermarriage. According to a study conducted by a well-known American sociologist in 1927, only 1 percent of native-born Americans, predominantly white, would willingly have accepted a Chinese as a family member through marriage. In a survey of American high school students fifteen years later, "Orientals" were still considered the second-least marriageable group, next only to blacks on the scale. As late as 1948, despite dramatic changes in social trends after World War II, 65 percent of white Americans still opposed marriages between Caucasians and Chinese.[48]

Unfortunately, Lowe's admiration for mainstream society and anxiety to escape the strictures of Chinese tradition sometimes led him to disparage Chinese culture. Even a casual reader cannot finish the book without feeling the author's intention to delineate the son as a rough rider, overcoming conservative traditional Chinese values with his American pioneering spirit. In that respect Lowe is drastically different from earlier Chinese immigrant authors. Because their purpose was to win American sympathy, they were, understandably, quiet on the less bright aspects of Chinese culture, fearing that the exposure would damage the image of the Chinese in this country. But Lowe's purpose is to justify his break from a cultural legacy that he felt unfitting. So he frequently went as far as ridiculing various Chinese cultural customs, such as the firecrackers that exploded one midnight to mark his aunt's wedding and terrified white neighbors. Mistaking them for a signal of the outbreak of a Tong war, they sounded the alarm and called the police. He also provided a detailed description of how his parents ate a fifty-five-pound wildcat in order to obtain a satisfactory tonic (*Father* 262). This is a rare if not highly exaggerated event. Even if some traditional Chinese herbalists would suggest that a patient eat wildcat as a way to derive the benefits of a tonic, it is doubtful whether they could find a wildcat that weighed more than fifty pounds. On another occasion, when the father explains that "the only reason why Mother and I brought you children into this world was to help you," Lowe retorted, "Neither my brothers nor sisters nor I had ever asked to come into the world" (*Father* 177).

Ironically, that argument is the same one Chinese often quote to exemplify the negative side of American individualism. Wu Tingfang, for example, expressed astonishment when he heard a white boy claim "since he was brought into this world by his parents without his consent, it was their duty to rear him in a proper way."[49] Wu would surely have been stunned had he known that only twenty years later an American-born Chinese would use exactly the same rationalization to challenge his father's demand for loyalty.

Despite the tension and confrontations between Lowe and his father, they eventually reconciled. The father finally realized that his behavior was self-contradictory. If he had shorn his queue as a rebellious gesture against the Manchu court and no longer dreamed of returning to his little village by the Pearl River, how could he demand the absolute loyalty of his son in accordance with the old Chinese tradition? In Lowe's case, it was likely that practical considerations prevailed. His newfound freedom from a repressive father was based on the acceptance of society in general. Because he failed to find a job after graduating from Stanford and Harvard universities, he had to rely on the father's support to make ends meet.

Thus, the mainstream's denial threw Lowe, albeit unwillingly, back upon the Chinese community. On the occasion of his father's sixty-sixth birthday, Lowe lined up with his Caucasian wife and three-year-old son, in accordance with their status in the family rank, and paid the father tribute.[50] Curiously, despite the party's traditional Chinese decorations and ceremony—including enthronement on a *taishi* [an old-fashioned, Chinese-style armchair]—Lowe's father insisted on dressing in a Western suit rather than the traditional Chinese "robes of longevity" required for such an occasion. A bizarre and unharmonic picture was the result, yet it was a symbolic compromise between father and son, East and West.

The contending emotions and the message of the father-son relationship are skillfully superimposed in the autobiography's dramatic ending, which supplies the book's title: "Among our people, children are begotten and nurtured for one purpose—to provide for and *glorify* their parents" (*Father* 322, emphasis added). Although Lowe's father was more Americanized than the average Chinese immigrant, it was the son, a native-born descendant, who accomplished the transformation from being Chinese to being Chinese American and "glorified" the first generation in the United States.

It is significant to note that although Lowe wrote his autobiography as anti-Japanese sentiment in the United States, particularly on the West Coast, was coming to a head, he showed no hostility toward Japanese Americans. Fueled by wartime enthusiasm, Lowe felt impelled to demonstrate "Chinese loyalty" to the United States, but, contrary to the belief that Chinese participated in the anti-Japanese American chorus, a considerably large portion of the book concerns Lowe's friendship with local nisei (second-generation Japanese American) children. This would remind us of the mutual assistance between French and German immigrants in the late 1910s when their old countries had been at war. It appears that any holdover from the historical enmity between China and Japan little affected the relationship between the two groups in American society. Of course, Chinese and Japanese immigrants refused to identify with each other in some individual cases, but in general, as Stanford Lyman finds, "In spite of very many reasons to harbor hatred and contempt for Japanese atrocities in China, very few Chinese Americans joined in the orgy of anti-Japanese activities in America after 1941, and many proved to be quite helpful to Japanese Americans returning to the West Coast after 1945."[51] A mutual identification between the two groups of second-generation Asians was also noted by William C. Smith during the 1920s. The fact that Ronald Takaki, a Japanese American, was adopted in childhood by a Chinese immigrant also proves the point.[52] Lowe's experience seems to indicate that pan-Asian identity existed long before the coining of the term *Asian Americans* in the late 1960s.[53]

Such a phenomenon was not accidental. Chinese Americans were fully aware that anti-Japanese sentiment would bring them little reward because the antagonism could easily shift to the Chinese once the international political structure altered. Rose Hum Lee, a prominent Chinese American scholar, criticized the sharp pendulum swing in attitudes toward the Chinese in 1944: "As violently as the Chinese were once attacked, they are now glorified and mounted on a pedestal. It is impossible to predict how lasting this change will be. . . . Largely grounded on the sandy loam of sentimentality, one is left conjecturing what the tone of literature toward the Chinese will be in 1954."[54] Furthermore, there was an additional complication: The American public for the most part was unable to recognize one Asian group from another. Asian Americans frequently find that mainstream society lumps them together despite the cultural and linguistic differences among them.[55] Fearful of being mistaken for Japanese, Chinese storekeepers posted signs indicating their ethnic background to forestall boycotts, assaults, or robberies during World War II.[56] In order to gain admittance to various public institutions, Joe Chiang, a noted Chinese journalist stationed in Washington, found it necessary to pin a piece of cloth on his suit with the following words: "CHINESE REPORTER. NOT JAPANESE. PLEASE."[57] It is ironic that Ji Hongchang, a Chinese general who fought the Japanese invasion in northern China, wanted to wear an identifying button ("I am Chinese") to avoid being mistaken for a Japanese on his tour of the United States during the winter of 1931. Mary Paik Lee, a Korean American author, recalls being mistaken as Chinese or Japanese when she lived in Hawaii and California early in the twentieth century.[58]

As the first book-length autobiography by an American-born Chinese, the significance of *Father and Glorious Descendant* cannot be underestimated. Despite some inherent weaknesses, it is a testimony revealing the ardent desire of second-generation Chinese to seek admission into American society before the 1960s. Although the author launches an attack on Chinese cultural tradition in order to display his quality as a "real American," we cannot totally dismiss the book's importance. The era's racial bias against Chinese effectively limited the degree to which Lowe could assimilate. Therefore, for him, alienation and self-contempt became the products of Americanization, an unfortunate price he had to pay in the process of gaining a place in the larger society. They were the means—rising from human error—to a goal that is good and worthy of sacrifice. If, as Betty Lee Sung observes, assimilation means embracing most of the mainstream values and concepts, Lowe's social acceptance must be measured against the standard established by Anglo-Americans.[59] It became necessary for him to shed certain traditional Chinese cultural values such as filial piety and family obligation. Furthermore, despite his accommodationist attitude, Lowe related to the general public at a time when second-generation Chinese were still a novelty; the public was unaware of their feelings, thoughts, and determination to be

American. In that concrete, limited sense, Lowe's sensitively written autobiography is a text well worth reading.[60]

### *Fifth Chinese Daughter:* A Story of Success and a Portrait of the "Model Minority"

Not all second-generation Chinese in the earlier era were as critical as Pardee Lowe of the cultural values of their parents. For some, the search for the American dream took a different turn. These were the later-born group of the second generation who came of age around World War II when public opinion had shifted to a more favorable view of China and Chinese Americans. Realizing that their ethnic affiliation was no longer a liability, this group was interested in seeking a thread that could link the American values to which they aspired with the Chinese culture into which they were born. Accepting attitudes popularly ascribed to the Chinese at the time, they strove to turn their ethnic legacy into an advantage that could help them gain admission into general society. By introducing the finer qualities inherent in Chinese American life, they hoped to create a new image of the model minority and win greater acceptance in the mainstream world. Jade Snow Wong's *Fifth Chinese Daughter* is a representative work of such efforts.[61]

Recommended as "required reading for all those who are interested in the Sino-American experience," *Fifth Chinese Daughter* was perhaps the most widely read book by a second-generation Chinese until the publication of Kingston's *The Woman Warrior* in 1976.[62] Narrated in the third person, *Fifth Chinese Daughter* vividly captures the life, aspirations, and triumphs of Wong's first twenty-four years. It is both a story of success and a portrait of the model minority. Published in 1950, it immediately rose to the bestseller lists and stayed there for months—a feat for any first-time author but all the more amazing for the personal story of an ordinary Chinese American woman.[63] It was a selection of the Book-of-the-Month Club and the Christian Herald Family Book Club in that year and awarded the Commonwealth Club's Medal for Non-Fiction in 1951. Since then, the book has undergone many reprintings, been translated into a dozen foreign languages, and sold nearly half a million copies. In 1976 *Fifth Chinese Daughter* was made into a PBS special for the U.S. Bicentennial, which was released nationwide on more than 270 television channels and awarded the highest prize at the 1977 American Film Festival.[64]

At first glance, Wong's background and writing seem almost identical to Lowe's. Like Lowe, Wong was born and grew up in San Francisco and views the experience of being a second-generation Chinese as a continuing effort to attain social recognition. The autobiography also provides a detailed account of her relationship with her father. One story, about how her parents decided to purchase a modern American bathtub after much hesitation, is even similar to an anecdote in Lowe's book. A closer examination reveals, however, that the similarities between the books are not as significant as their differences. Each autobiography is informed by the personal backgrounds of its author and the social milieu of its time.

While Lowe was an aristocrat of sorts and represented a small privileged segment of Chinese Americans, Wong came from a humble background and belonged to the lower stratum of the Chinatown community. Although her father was also a merchant, according to the definition of immigration law, the Wongs owned only a small sweatshop, on the scale of many tiny Chinese laundries or eating places at the time, and constantly struggled on the brink of bankruptcy. In contrast to the Lowe family, which lived a comfortable life in a suburban residential neighborhood, the Wongs could only afford to rent a basement apartment in the heart of San Francisco's Chinatown. Both of Wong's parents worked at sewing machines around the clock to save the family from starvation. Furthermore, in light of Chinese tradition that favors not only male children but also the primogeniture system, Wong's family status as "fifth daughter" was no match for Lowe's place as "number one son." While Lowe was fully supported in everything by his parents and went to study at Stanford University and the Harvard Graduate School of Business Administration, Wong had to take care of the housework from the age of fourteen, cooking, laundering, and buying the groceries for a family of seven. Later, because her parents were neither able nor willing to support her ambition for higher education, she worked as a housekeeper and cook for white American families while attending San Francisco Junior College and then Mills College.[65] The sharp contrast between the lives of Wong and Lowe shows how second-generation Chinese authors differ profoundly in family background and personal experiences despite the fact they are from a small and congenial group.

The authors also diverge in the content and style of their writing. Although Wong and Lowe shared a sustaining desire to secure a place in American life, she took a different approach toward that goal. To justify a position in general society, Lowe pursued an Anglo-American identity. Wong, believing that the true values of the American dream ought to include second-generation Chinese, assumed the role of being one of the model minority. Unlike Lowe, who sought to prove himself as American-born and educated by exposing and attacking conservative aspects of Chinese tradition, Wong remained keenly aware of the opportunities her Chinese heritage could offer and used them to help win acceptance. Discovering through experience that her ethnic background had "created a great deal of favorable interest . . . and [could] be accommodated in the widening knowledge of the Western world," she decided to promote her ethnicity rather than downplay it. To that end, she turned her knowledge of Chinese life into a source of inspiration to achieve success in the larger society. As she recounts, "Jade Snow found that the girls were perpetually curious about her Chinese background . . . she began to formulate in her mind the constructive and delightful aspects of the Chinese culture to present to non-Chinese."[66]

Ironically, Lowe's strenuous efforts to demonstrate his Americanness failed to win much acceptance, but Wong's association with Chinese ethnicity brought her wide recognition. The differences between their approaches to seeking an entry into the mainstream world and their respective outcomes are not entirely related to family background, however. They are chiefly a result of a disparity in age and reflect the impact of a changed mainstream social consciousness on Chinese Americans.

Although their books were published only seven years apart, the two authors are separated by almost a generation (born in 1922, Wong was seventeen years younger than Lowe). When Lowe grew up, anti-Chinese prejudice was still prevalent; Wong reached maturity at a time when the general public had become more sympathetic to China and Chinese Americans. The era around World War II boosted the position of the "loyal minority." As a result, Chinese Americans, once regarded as subhuman and unassimilated, became known for their ability to withstand hardship and were praised for their fidelity to the United States. Through the mass media, the American public endowed them with many admirable characteristics, including patriotism, patience, charm, and the ability to work hard. Articles entitled "Career Girls: Chinese Style" and "A Portrait of an American Family" were not only diametrically opposed in viewpoint to those appearing in the earlier decades but also stimulated interest in Chinese American life. The fact that mainstream magazines, *Life* and *Time* included, all joined the effort to enhance the Chinese image is evidence that to support the Chinese had become very much to go with the flow.[67]

Ironically, even popular American culture had shifted to a more "pro-Chinese" stance. By the time Wong entered college, stereotypes of the Chinese had gone from totally negative to being more "positive." Evidence of the shift is attested to by the rise and fall of the two most publicized fictional Chinese characters: Fu Manchu and Charlie Chan. The diabolical Fu Manchu series, which brought the Chinese image to its height of villainy, was gradually in decline. In contrast, the increasing popularity of the witty and eccentric "Oriental good guy" Charlie Chan indicated that the American public was more willing to accept a benign and benevolent Chinese character. Of course, most Chinese Americans were offended by Chan's reliance on stereotypical humor. As many Chinese American scholars remark, compared to the toughness, daring, and romance that are the mainstays of fictional detectives, the pudgy, seemingly sexless Charlie Chan, speaking heavily accented "fortune-cookie wisdom" and cloaked in inscrutability, is still a racial novelty.[68] In addition, although Chan was played by Caucasians, his sons, who had only minor roles in the films, were portrayed by Chinese actors.

Nonetheless, even the stereotypes have value because their fates are not unrelated to social reality. The role of Fu Manchu combines the sinister Chinese opium smoker and the mysterious image of Oriental herbalist, representing for the American public the terror of the Yellow Peril. Charlie Chan, however, albeit a product of racism, possesses a keen intelligence and the ability to outwit and ridicule dull-minded white policemen, as do other popular American folk heroes.[69] His middle-class position of authority also represents upward mobility, symbolizing at least a small step toward a higher rung on the social ladder. It can be seen as a step forward, however insignificant, in the long march of changes involving the Chinese image in popular American culture. What Tiana [Thi Thanh Nga], a veteran Asian American actress who was a close friend of Bruce Lee, observes in a discussion of Asian stereotypes in film applies to the differences between Fu Manchu and Charlie Chan. In an eloquent argument for *The World of Suzie Wong*, which many Asian Americans criticize as "sentimental, racist, and outdated," she concludes, "Sentimental? Of course. Racist? You bet. Outdated? Like the horse and buggy. But sentimental, racist, and outdated as it was, *Suzie Wong* was a breaking through film in the long march from [Anna May] Wong to [John] Woo." Among other things, it broke a long-established taboo on presenting Asian-Caucasian love affairs on the screen.[70]

In other words, change comes slowly and gradually, and not all the stereotypes have the same implications. That is evident even in the names of the two characters. Fu Manchu has a typical "Chinese" name that contains the meaning of "diabolical Chinese."[71] Charlie Chan, however, is clearly more "Americanized," as shown by his given name and the placing of his surname in accordance with Western custom. Such differences reveal that the images assigned to the Chinese had undergone both dramatic and subtle changes during the World War II era.[72]

Improved status and a more sympathetic reception from general society since the 1930s thus opened a new door into American life for second-generation Chinese such as Wong. They found that what had been considered negative elements in their ethnic background had become favorable, and aspects of their Chinese identity now held great interest for average Americans. As Wong discovered, "Her grades [in college] were constantly higher when she wrote about Chinatown and the people she had known all her life" (*FCD* 132). A paper she wrote on *Chin Pin Mei* [Golden vase plum], a Chinese classic of the sixteenth century, was even recommended by her English professor to be read at a literature conference. Of course, the interest in her essay might be attributed to Wong's choice of that particular novel. Unlike other Chinese classics, *Chin Pin Mei* is a romance about sexual scandals in a corrupt merchant family. A Chinese model of Giovanni Boccaccio's *The Decameron,* it was an effective way to stimulate curiosity about traditional Chinese families and society.

For the most part, Wong's autobiography concerns the common aspects of the Chinese American community rather than the exotic elements in Chinese culture. Publications at the time, such as Nobel Prize–winner Pearl S. Buck's trilogy *The Good Earth* (1931), *Sons* (1932), and *A House Divided* (1935), with its depiction of down-to-earth Chinese peasant life, not only produced popular sympathy for the Chinese but also had a compelling impact on the American public.[73] Thus, readers were newly receptive to more realistic aspects of the Chinese American community. This explains why Wong could entertain readers with familiar things in her life such as cooking, rice-washing, child-rearing, and folk customs.

To be fair, Wong tells a good story, and tells it well. Her lucid and carefully researched account of daily activities in Chinatown deftly outlines a fascinating picture. She examines in detail such varied but typical experiences as mounting a traditional Chinese wedding, treating people with herbal medicine, and staging an annual funeral service. She can also be humorous and visually acute. For example, she describes how, at the birth of her younger brother, she was taught by her mother that babies were "roasted in the hospital ovens" and brought out to the parents by "a lady doctor." There were three different sorts of babies: nearly done ones (the white babies), slightly overdone ones (the black babies), and golden brown ones (the Chinese) (*FCD* 24). Such stories run through Wong's autobiography, making various minor details memorable and the book pleasant reading.

Yet Wong's coverage of Chinese life, no matter how fascinating and emblematic, does not mean she embraced her Chinese heritage. The disposition serves only as a means to accomplish her goal—painting a portrait of the model minority. As she says, "What I intend to do is to help people understand Chinese Americans and show them how good and honest we are."[74] That intention is underscored in her effort to filter the text and establish positive stereotypes of Chinese Americans. Her explanation of the Chinese attitude toward welfare programs is an example. According to Wong, "Being poor did not entitle anyone to benefits" and "the only way to overcome poverty is to work hard." During the depression years, although they were under severe strain and faced extremely grim times, her parents would not apply for relief. As her father declared, "[It] is my desire not to apply for relief, even though we may need it. I do not want my children to experience getting anything without first working for it, for they may become selfish. . . . Selfishness often starts with a spirit of dependency; therefore I want my children to learn to cope with the world, and to understand that they get what they want only after working for it." To make ends meet, the family cut down further on their already meager spending and put the children to work: "He [her father] leased sewing equipment, installed machines in a basement where rent was cheapest, and there he and his family lived and worked. There was no thought that dim and airless quarters were terrible conditions for living and working, or that child labor was unhealthful. The only goal was for all in the family to work, to save, and to become educated."[75]

Wong's description of her family's view of the welfare system and their solution to economic hard times fits the popular belief that "Orientals" tend to be more self-reliant than other ethnic groups. Yet the idea of "Puritans from the Orient" was not always the case in real-life situations. In at least one Chinese community—that of Silver Bow County, Montana—the percentage of Chinese who applied for welfare during the Great Depression was not particularly small.[76] In addition, as Roger Daniels argues convincingly, if Chinese Americans in general have traditionally underused available governmental relief, they did so more for a variety of reasons (ignorance, fear of the authorities, prejudice, and statutory discrimination) rather than simply being motivated by a spirit of self-reliance.[77]

Because she intended to create an image of a model minority, Wong's depiction is inevitably restricted and defined by the social acceptance of Chinese Americans. That means she has to satisfy certain expectations of society in general about that minority. Therefore, Wong is highly selective in how she portrays Chinese American life and identifies only with elements that are considered characteristic of a model minority. In this sense, *Fifth Chinese Daughter* parallels the work of earlier Chinese immigrant authors. Like Lee Yan Phou, Wong devotes a large portion of her work to discussing Chinese food because she, too, finds the topic to be among the most popular aspects of Chinese life. In reality, Chinese food had helped Wong gain a foothold in society: "Jade Snow considered a moment before answering. Certainly she could cook Chinese food, and she remembered a common Chinese saying, 'A Chinese can cook foreign food as well as, if not better than, the foreigners, but a foreigner cannot cook Chinese food fit for the Chinese.' On this reasoning it seemed safe to say 'Yes'" (*FCD* 123). To satisfy the curiosity of readers, Wong describes the details that make Chinese food unique and even includes recipes for such popular dishes as sweet and sour pineapple pork and "fu yoon egg." Considering the soaring interest in Chinese food in American society since the 1940s, this treatment of food would surely make her work more attractive to non-Chinese readers.[78]

The similarity between Wong and earlier immigrant authors is and is not accidental. Wong is tied to them by a common desire to correct the distorted image of the Chinese, but she had no knowledge of their work.[79] Furthermore, while immigrant authors dwelled on experiences of the first generation and tended to look backward to their old home or retreated to the Chinese community when rejected by society at large, Wong's emphasis was on the courage and effort of the native-born in seeking admission into mainstream society. Racial bias only reinforced her determination to acquire a place in American life. "Despite prejudice, I was never discouraged from carrying out my creed," she recalls, "because of prejudice, the effort is ongoing" (FCD xi). When told by a bigoted placement officer at Mills College to give up the attempt to find employment outside Chinatown, Wong remarks, "No, this was one piece of advice she was not going to follow, so opposed was it to her experience and belief. She was more determined to get a job with an American firm" (189).

The gap between Wong and earlier immigrant authors is also reflected in differing views on residence in Chinese enclaves. In general, as a Chinese of Wong's era pointed out, despite many problems there the majority of the first generation preferred life in Chinatown: "Most of us can live a warmer, freer and a more human life among our relatives and friends than among strangers . . . Chinese relations with the population outside Chinatown are likely to be cold, formal, and commercial. It is only in Chinatown that a Chinese immigrant has society, friends and relatives who share his dreams and hopes, his hardships, and adventures. Here he can tell a joke and make everybody laugh with him; here he may hear folktales told which create the illusion that Chinatown is really China."[80] Even now, many new immigrants still choose to live in Chinatowns rather than suburbia for reasons of convenience and a sense of community.[81]

But for second-generation Chinese Americans like Wong, contacts with mainstream society dissatisfied them with the idea of spending their lives in a Chinese community. Working for families outside Chinatown exposed Wong to a new world shunned by the insular first-generation. It was a system in which individuals had more freedom and recognition than she could have imagined. She acknowledges that it was in the larger society that she first experienced "complete privacy . . . and inner peace":

It was a home [the Caucasian family with whom she lived] where children were heard as well as seen; where parents considered who was right or wrong, rather than who should be respected; where birthday parties were a tradition . . . where the husband kissed his wife and the parents kissed their children . . . where the family was actually concerned with having fun together . . . where the problems and difficulties of domestic life and children's discipline were untangled perhaps after tears, but also after explanations; where the husband turned over his pay check to his wife to pay the bills; and where, above all, each member, even down to and including the dog, appeared to have the inalienable right to assert his individuality—in fact, where that was expected—in an atmosphere of natural affection. (*FCD* 113–14)

Such longing and passionate admiration for life in the outside world makes Wong's writing distinct from that of immigrant authors who speak chiefly for the first generation to that of a native-born Chinese American representing the second generation.

The attempt to bolster the image of a model minority also prompted Wong to eulogize unselfish white Americans dedicated to the improvement of the Chinese. Of her experience in college, she recalled, "She had a glimpse of the truth, that the great people of any race are unpretentious, genuinely honest, and nonpatronizing in their interest in other human beings" (*FCD* 173). To indicate her appreciation of such assistance from the larger society, Wong frequently quoted Chinese maxims—"He who does not repay a debt of gratitude cannot claim to be princely," for example, or, "When you drink water, think of its source." To Wong, the source of success for a second-generation Chinese woman was the encouragement and benevolence she received from society in general. As she indicates in the preface of the book: "We who did not choose our ancestry can be grateful for opportunities more expansive in this country than in most others" (*FCD* xi). To be fair, there was ample reason for Wong to praise American opportunities and her birthright. She had been able to obtain support from mainstream society at almost every critical stage of her life. Her education would not have been completed without the help of sympathetic white people, she was trusted by her white supervisor and welcomed by colleagues when she worked at a naval shipyard, and when she established her pottery business her wares were purchased and appreciated by the mainstream. All of her achievements—being class valedictorian or chosen to christen a liberty ship during the war, even the publication of her autobiography—resulted from patronage of the larger society.

Wong's experience thus suggests that equality and self-respect, thanks to a more tolerant social atmosphere, could be achieved by minority women. As she remarks, "In business and in civic work, I had no problem in getting along in a

Caucasian world. If anything, people's interest and cordiality had been heightened by my difference."[82] The fact that her pottery has won numerous awards, been put into various exhibitions, and is part of the collections of more than twenty museums, including the Metropolitan Museum of Art and the Smithsonian Institution, illustrates that Chinese Americans have gradually been accepted as an integrated part of American culture. Opinion polls confirm that fact. Despite the persistence of prejudice and social inequality, average Americans became more sympathetic to the Chinese during Wong's era. In 1927 only 27 percent of white Americans would accept them as fellow workers, 16 percent as neighbors, and fewer than 12 percent as friends or members of their clubs. Two decades later, however, an almost comparable national survey found that 86 percent would work with Chinese; 72 and 77 percent, respectively, would welcome them as neighbors and guests.[83] As one second-generation scholar—and Wong's contemporary—concluded optimistically on the eve of America's entry into World War II: "[Earlier] hostility towards the Chinese has given way to a tolerant, kindly feeling, with instances of admiration and confidence in the daily intercourse among individuals."[84]

A more sympathetic attitude toward Chinese Americans does not, of course, mean that racial bias completely disappeared. No matter what progress American society as a whole has made, there are always individuals who are prejudiced against the Chinese. In her life, Wong, too, encountered racial harassment at various times. At one point, for example, she was taunted by a white boy in school:

> "I've been waiting for a chance like this," Richard said excitedly to Jade Snow. With malicious intent in his eyes, he burst forth, "Chinky, Chinky, Chinaman" . . . Jade Snow decided that it was time to leave. As she went out of the doorway, a second eraser landed squarely on her back. She looked neither to the right nor left, but proceeded sedately down the stairs and out the front door. In a few minutes, her tormentor had caught up with her. Dancing around her in glee, he chortled, "Look at the eraser mark on the yellow Chinaman. Chinky, Chinky, no tickee, no washee, no shirtee!" (*FCD* 68)

Such events would likely elicit furious responses from contemporary Chinese Americans, but Wong tried to cope with the situation rather than fight back. Walking away, she decided to forgive the boy: "Jade Snow thought that he was tiresome and ignorant. Everybody knew that the Chinese people had a superior culture. Her ancestors had created a great art heritage and had made inventions important to world civilization—the compass, gunpowder, paper, and a host of other essentials. She knew, too, that Richard's grades couldn't compare with her own, and his home training was obviously amiss" (*FCD* 68).

That calm, passive tolerance exemplifies the role of a model-minority woman willing to keep quiet in the face of racial harassment to prove she is civilized and would not direct anger or displeasure against those in the mainstream. Undoubtedly, this constitutes a sharp contrast to the attitude of such contemporary Chinese American writers as Frank Chin. While Wong is polite and optimistic, subdued in tone, and restrained even at the moment of humiliation, Chin is dominated by frustration, bitterness, and resentment, particularly when he feels unfairly treated because of his ethnic background.[85]

Although Wong might have reinforced the popular notion that the Chinese are lacking in normal assertiveness and temper, her behavior was typical for its time. As one ethnic studies scholar points out, Chinese Americans were historically sustained throughout various ordeals by finding psychological comfort in the belief that "their ancestors had created a great and complex civilization when the inhabitants of the British Isles still painted their faces blue."[86] In that sense Wong has only followed an old practice and tried to tap an inner resource to imagine her cultural superiority in this racial incident: "They [whites] probably could not help their own insensibility. Mama said they hadn't even learned how to peel a clove of garlic the way the Chinese did" (FCD 69).

Wong's intent to construct an image of the model minority seems to cause her to over-idealize American life. Nevertheless, given the amount of her support and encouragement from society, it is understandable why she writes in this way. As a fifth daughter in a traditional Chinatown family, she owes her accomplishments more to the patronage of a benevolent larger society than to traditional Chinese society, where women are judged by their obedience to men. That oppression of women was prevalent in old China is evidenced in imperial decrees such as Three Obediences, Four Virtues, and Seven Grounds.[87] For more than two thousand years, these decrees remained effective and constituted the only way for women to live, both in and out of the home. Or, as in Maxine Hong Kingston's poignant language, it is the ghost and curse of "No Name Woman" that haunt Chinese daughters who dare challenge the iron rule of being neither heard nor seen. Wong underscores the especially "virulent misogyny" of Chinese tradition by pointing out that even in America's Chinatowns women are still kept at the bottom of society: "She was trapped in a mesh of tradition woven thousands of miles away by ancestors who had no knowledge that someday one generation of their progeny might be raised in another culture" (FCD 110).

Despite the Wong family's striking poverty, her brother was cherished in the best Chinese tradition. He had his own room, kept a German shepherd as a pet, and was tutored by a Chinese scholar and sent to a private college with full financial support from his parents. His privileges were his birthright. The only male child in the family, he was expected to carry on the Wong lineage and likely return to China some day, a legitimate representative of the clan, and pay tribute at ancestral tombs.[88] In contrast, Jade Snow Wong and her sisters had to be content with whatever was left. When she asked her father to help pay for college, she received a stern lecture: "You are quite familiar by now with the fact that it is the sons who perpetuate our ancestral heritage by permanently bearing the Wong family name and transmitting it through their blood line, and therefore the sons must have priority over the daughters" (FCD 108).

Compared with such a tradition, American society in general offers Chinese women a better world than they had experienced in the old country. It gives them individual dignity and rights of their own. The increased equality between the sexes in American society allows them to enjoy the benefits of education, social activities, choosing their own mates, and participating in the workforce. When Dr. Faith Sai Leong, part of the second generation, began to set up her dental clinic in San Francisco in 1905, women in China were still forced to stay home and their feet were bound.[89]

Traditional prejudice against women may also explain in part why Wong's talents have not been truly appreciated by the Chinese community. Despite the fact that her artistic achievement made her "a wonder in the eyes of the Western world," Wong's ceramic work has drawn little interest from Chinatown residents: "Caucasians came from far and near to see her work, and Jade Snow sold all the pottery she could make. . . . But the Chinese did not come to buy one piece from her" (FCD 244). In retrospect, Wong feels fortunate that her father's failed dream of returning to China determined her life: "My father regretted that he had not become rich enough to retire during the depression thirties to his native Chung Shan district . . . If he had returned with me and my siblings, I could never have had my independent career" (FCD x).

It is significant that Wong's strong will to acquire social prominence was a product of acculturation, similar to the mentality and behavior of an American feminist rather than that of a Chinese daughter. According to Confucian doctrine, a woman without talent and ambition is a woman of virtue. That doctrine is based on the assumption that women are generally narrow-minded, shortsighted, and unsuited for mental cultivation. They are everything but intelligent and educable. Therefore, for their own benefit, and in society's best interest, it is better that they be humble and invisible. That idea was so influential that even Earl Derr Biggers, author of the Charlie Chan series, would quote a supposed "Chinese aphorism" in one of his most popular novels: "Three things the wise man does not do. He does not plow the sky. He does not paint pictures on the water. And *he does not argue with a woman.*"[90]

In her family and in the Chinatown community, Wong was repeatedly advised, kindly or contemptuously, to be a modest daughter and stay home rather than be ambitious and mix with "barbarians" in general society. Rather than follow traditional guidelines, however, Wong early made up her mind that she would strive to win respect and honor as a solemn reply to male chauvinism: "In her bitterness, Jade Snow made up a solemn vow to God as she knelt in bedtime prayer. 'To make up for this neglect and prejudice, please help me to do my best in striving to be a person respected and honored . . . when I grow up'" (*FDC* 93). In that sense, Wong's pursuit of success is an open identification with mainstream American culture.

Wong's determination to challenge Chinese tradition is also demonstrated by her active participation in various programs sponsored by the larger society. When an essay on wartime absenteeism won the top prize in a contest, she was given the honor of christening a liberty ship. The image of Wong striking the bow of an ocean-going freighter with a champagne bottle is surely symbolic. It must have been a rare and shocking sight for the insular old men of Chinatown, because in traditional China women were even forbidden to touch a new ship before its first voyage. This taboo is rooted in a long-established superstition that a female presence will bring a curse to a new ship and cause it misfortune.[91] Hence, Wong's sending the giant liberty ship to the sea represented not only a personal honor but also constituted an act of self-assertion and defiance against the weight of historical and societal injunctions on Chinese women. It also deepens an understanding of one of her comments: "As an Asian in Asia, we would not find the freedom of choice which is our particular American birthright" (*FCD* xi). That generalization is proved true—at least in Wong's case. She is often deemed an incarnation of the success Asian women have achieved in the United States. Honors such as the Outstanding Art Achievement Award and the Woman Warrior Award for Outstanding Contribution in Literature have made her one of the best-known and influential Asian women in America. During the 1976 U.S. Bicentennial she was named the person who best represented the Asian American community, and her biography is contained in more than thirty national and international reference books, including *Who's Who in the West, International Author and Writer's Who's Who,* and *Makers of America: Children of the Melting Pot.*

Richly textured in contents and ideals, *Fifth Chinese Daughter* also outshines most other work by second-generation Chinese because of Wong's writing style. Although the popularity of work by her contemporaries waxes and wanes, her work continues to be read. The enthusiastic reception of the reading public and critics to the 1989 edition of *Fifth Chinese Daughter* is a good example.

The vital quality of Wong's literary achievement derives from many aspects. Her ability to appreciate the style of simplicity as an art in writing autobiography seems an important element. The even-tempered, calm, yet lyric narration resembles that of Richard Wright's in *Black Boy* and is illustrated in the refreshing, personal approach of the opening part of the book:

> Hugging the eastern slope of San Francisco's famous Nob Hill is one of the unique spots of this continent. A small, compact area overlooking the busy harbor at its feet, it extends only a few blocks in either direction. Above its narrow, congested streets, the chimes of beautiful Grace Cathedral ring out the quarter hours; and tourists and curio-seekers in a bare three minutes can stroll from the city's fashionable shopping district into the heart of Old China . . .
>
> To this China in the West, there came in the opening decade of this century a young Chinese with his wife and family. There they settled among the other Cantonese, and as the years slipped by, the couple established their place in the community.
>
> I tell the story of their fifth daughter, Jade Snow, born to them in San Francisco. (*FCD* 1–2)

Not the least interesting part of the autobiography are the illustrations by Kathryn Uhl, of which a drawing of Wong working at a pottery wheel in a Chinatown shop window, a large crowd looking on, is perhaps the most fascinating.

Wong's use of third-person narrative is also a key factor in the book's popularity. Ironically, critics believe this is "a typical Chinese style" of autobiographical writing. This erroneous comment is partly caused by Wong's statement that "the third-person-singular style in which I told my story was rooted in Chinese literary form" (*FCD* vii). Wong's crediting the style to "Chinese habit" is somewhat misleading and probably motivated by an intention to make her already colorful writing even more exotic. Given the popular notion that "Orientals" are perpetual foreigners, a claim that a first-person-singular autobiography was written in third-person "Chinese style" would surely help promote the book's sales. Contrary to Wong's statement, however, the style has nothing to do with Chinese literary form. There is no such genre as autobiography in Chinese tradition. Until Western literature was introduced into China around the turn of the twentieth century, any attempt to write personal history would have been considered egocentric, especially an autobiography by a young woman of humble background. In reality, Wong's use of third-person-singular reveals the influence of American autobiographic writing, such as *The Education of Henry Adams*. Therefore, the style itself reflects the impact of mainstream culture on native-born Chinese Americans. That few critics are aware of that point shows that they tend to underestimate the degree of acculturation of second-generation Chinese. Perhaps they are unable to recognize that native-born Chinese are just the same as their peers in the larger society except for their physical characteristics.[92]

As the first American-born Chinese author who gained international popularity, Wong's greatest accomplishment is her successful portrayal of the life of a second-generation Chinese woman who realized her American dream and achieved it through self-struggle. In the process, she provides, perhaps unconsciously, a portrait of the model minority for a general audience. It is a task of redefining Chinese heritage to fit certain expectations of the American public. Her popularity is in part based on roles that correspond to conventional images defined by mainstream culture. For that reason, *Fifth Chinese Daughter* has been disparaged by some Chinese Americans.[93] But the book is also authentic and compelling in its understated way. As a Chinese American woman critic argues, although modest in tone, it reveals the inner fire of a determined second-generation Chinese woman who bested all difficulties, fought substantial prejudice, both within and outside the Chinese community, and achieved ultimate triumph.[94] Despite a tendency to overidealize American life and filter her experience to satisfy the reading public, Wong considers issues indigenous to her historical and cultural milieu and has created a new image of Chinese American women.

Although her portrayal of a docile young woman may have contributed to the creation of a new or strengthened a convention of a Chinese stereotype, it was a step forward and constitutes progress, considering the historical circumstances. The construction of Chinese American stereotypes began long before *Fifth Chinese Daughter* was written. "Oriental" women in popular American culture inevitably appeared as either seductive dragon ladies or sensual geishas. Even in work by other Chinese Americans, such as Lowe's autobiography, they are called "creatures," a term that has sexual implications. By comparison, nearly every aspect of Wong's heroine contrasts sharply with the luscious portrayal of stereotyped Chinese women. Fifth Chinese Daughter, who has a range of human emotions and qualities, is like real Chinese American women.

*Fifth Chinese Daughter,* although perhaps not as powerful and profound as Kingston's *Woman Warrior* or Amy Tan's *Joy Luck Club,* is a serious and engaging account of how an American-born Chinese daughter grew up during a transitional period. For that reason the book has been highly praised by most Chinese American readers and critics. As the editors of the first Asian American anthology comment, "Struggle against being considered just another obedient child among her brothers and sisters, against racial prejudice visited upon her since childhood, against sexual discrimination enforced by family tradition that preferred the male offspring, against parental authoritarianism, and finally against herself in an effort to find meaning for her own life—these are the tensions described in Jade Snow Wong's autobiographical novel."[95] The appeal of the book for a general audience is apparent in a report from one white reader. Wong recalled receiving a long-distance call from a stranger in New York City. She told Wong that she had bought the book in San Francisco, read it aloud as her husband drove across the United States, and finished it by flashlight while he was at the wheel.[96]

More significantly, *Fifth Chinese Daughter* paved the way for a new generation of Chinese American writers. As Wong says proudly, no matter how people criticize it, they have to discuss her book because of its pioneering role.[97] That statement is supported by at least one other prominent woman writer. Praising Wong as the "Mother of Chinese American literature," Kingston recalls that Wong was the only Chinese American author she had read before writing *The Woman Warrior*. It was *Fifth Chinese Daughter* that inspired Kingston to start a literary career: "I found Jade Snow Wong's book myself in the library," she recalls, "and [I] was flabbergasted, helped, inspired, affirmed, made possible as a writer—for the first time I saw a person who looked like me as a heroine of a book, as a maker of a book."[98] Together with Pardee Lowe's autobiography and other work by second-generation Chinese Americans, *Fifth Chinese Daughter* brought native-born experience to public attention before the emergence of the Asian American movement in the late 1960s. It also added to the understanding of Chinatown and its residents and gave rise to a new perspective on Chinese American literature.

### Notes

1. Pardee Lowe, *Father and Glorious Descendant* (Boston: Little, Brown, 1943), 147–48.

2. Him Mark Lai, "The Chinese," in *Harvard Encyclopaedia of American Ethnic Groups,* ed. Stephan Thernstrom (Cambridge: Harvard University Press, 1980), 225. It is necessary to point out, however, that "paper sons" artificially inflated the number of native-born Chinese.

3. Unlike the term *banana* (yellow on the outside but white inside), *ABC* is a neutral term that Asian American scholars use to refer to a subgroup within the Chinese American community, just like *OBC* (overseas-born Chinese) or "1.5 generation"—immigrants who came to America as school children. In other words, ABC is not a negative term unless its use is viewed as divisive and elitist to distinguish the native-born from those who are FOB (fresh off the boat) or to refer to a native-born who retains little except appearance that is Chinese.

4. Gerald W. Haslam, *Forgotten Pages of American Literature* (Boston: Houghton Mifflin, 1970), 80–81.

5. William Carlson Smith, *The Second Generation Oriental in America* (Honolulu: Institute of Pacific Relations, 1927), 5.

6. The mentality of America-born Chinese has undergone dramatic changes since the 1960s. The impact of the civil rights movement, the emergence of the trans-Pacific economic network, and education about multiculturalism have raised ABC interest in Chinese culture and language. For a discussion of the changes of ABC attitudes toward China, see Xiao-huang Yin, "The Growing Influence of Chinese Americans on U.S.-China Relations," in *The Outlook for U.S.-China Relations Following the 1997–1998 Summits,* ed. Peter H. Koehn and Joseph Y. S. Cheng (Hong Kong: Chinese University Press, 1999), 331–49. Also see William Wei, *The Asian American Movement* (Philadelphia: Temple University Press, 1993), 44–71.

7. The transitional era covers roughly the four decades from the 1920s to the early 1960s. The period began when the second generation substantially increased and the status of Chinese Americans gradually improved. It ended on the eve of the civil rights movement, which radically altered the Chinese American community in the ensuing decades.

8. Despite its late date of publication, Monfoon Leong's *Number One Son* was written in the 1950s. He died in a traffic accident in 1964.

9. Victor G. Nee and Brett de Bary Nee, *Longtime Californ': A Documentary Study of an American Chinatown* (repr. Stanford: Stanford University Press, 1986), 182–99, 248–49; Pao-min Chang, *Continuity and Change: A Profile of Chinese Americans* (New York: Vantage Press, 1983), 34–41.

10. Alejandro Portes and Ruben G. Rumbaut, *Immigrant America: A Portrait,* rev. ed. (Berkeley: University of California Press, 1996), 232–68; Werner Sollors, *Beyond Ethnicity: Content and Descent in American Culture* (New York: Oxford University Press, 1985), 149–73.

11. Cited in Melford S. Weiss, *Valley City: A Chinese Community in America* (Cambridge: Schenkman Publishing, 1974), 238; also see Frank Chin, "This Is Not an Autobiography," *Genre* 18 (Summer 1985): 109–30.

12. Although the book was not published until 1943, parts of it appeared in journals and magazines such as the *Atlantic Monthly* and *Yale Review* as early as the 1930s. See Pardee Lowe, "Father's Robes of Immortality," *Atlantic Monthly* 162 (Dec. 1938): 785–92; and Pardee Lowe, "Letters of Hawk Sung," *Yale Review* 28 (Sept. 1938): 69–81.

13. Helen P. Bolman, "Notes: *Father and Glorious Descendant,*" *Library Journal,* April 1, 1943, 287; R.L.B., "The Bookshelf: Meeting of the East and West," *Christian Science Monitor,* April 9, 1943, 12. Also see Elaine H. Kim, *Asian American Literature: An Introduction to the Writings and Their Social Context* (Philadelphia: Temple University Press, 1982), 61.

14. For discussions of the changes in attitude on the part of the average American toward China and Chinese, see Harold R. Isaacs, *Scratches on Our Minds: American Views of China and India,* rev. ed. (Armonk: M. E. Sharpe, 1980), 164–89.

15. Bolman, "Notes: *Father and Glorious Descendant,*" 287, emphasis added. It is important to note the implications of "loyal minority groups" in Bolman's comment. By praising Chinese Americans as a "loyal minority group," she suggested that there were "disloyal" minority groups in America in wartime 1943. It can be seen as her defense for the

administration's decision to send Japanese Americans into internment camps after Japan's attack on Pearl Harbor. For more discussion of the implications of "disloyal minority groups," see Roger Daniels, *Concentration Camps: North America, Japanese in the United States and Canada During World War II*, rev. ed. (Malabar: Robert E. Krieger, 1989), 26–73.

16. Pardee Lowe rose to the rank of lieutenant colonel and was decorated with a Bronze Star for his service during the war. Maria Hong, ed., *Growing Up Asian America: An Anthology* (New York: William Morrow, 1993), 175.

17. Although the native-born accounted for about 10 percent of the Chinese population in America at this time, the actual figure was much smaller. Because the native-born category defined by the U.S. immigration service includes descendants of American citizens born abroad, a significant number of Chinese claimed that derivative citizenship to immigrate to America during the exclusion era. Thus the number of native-born was increased substantially and misleadingly (chapter 1).

18. Lowe's father moved the family to East Belleville after the earthquake destroyed their old home in San Francisco's Chinatown in 1906.

19. Rose Hum Lee, *The Chinese in the United States of America* (Hong Kong: Hong Kong University Press, 1960), 315–19.

20. Otis Gibson, *The Chinese in America* (Cincinnati: Hitchcock, 1877), 1–23.

21. Quoted in Mary Roberts Coolidge, *Chinese Immigration* (New York: Henry Holt, 1909), 477. Also see Sucheng Chan, *Asian Americans: An Interpretive History* (Boston: Twayne Publishers, 1991), 97.

22. Theodore Roosevelt, *Addresses and Papers*, ed. Willis Fletcher Johnson (New York: Sun Dial, 1909), 294. As a mainstream politician, however, Roosevelt's racial views were complex. Although sympathetic with Chinese immigrants, he also signed without protest the extension of the Chinese Exclusion Act in 1902. For more information on Roosevelt's ambivalent attitude toward Asian immigrants, see the discussion of the Progressives in Roger Daniels, *The Politics of Prejudice: The Anti-Japanese Movement in California and the Struggle for Japanese Exclusion* (Berkeley: University of California Press, 1962), 46–91; also see Coolidge, *Chinese Immigration*, 474–77.

23. C. T. Hopkins, quoted in Pearl Ng, "Writings on the Chinese in California," M.A. thesis, University of California, Berkeley, 1939, 16. Also see David J. Hellwig, "Black Reactions to Chinese Immigration and the Anti-Chinese Movement: 1850–1910," *Amerasia* 6, no. 2 (1979): 25–44; and Lucy M. Cohen, *Chinese in the Post–Civil War South: A People without a History* (Baton Rouge: Louisiana State University Press, 1984), 46–104.

24. Lowe, *Father and Glorious Descendant*, 34 (subsequent page citations to *Father* appear in parentheses).

25. Ironically, Lowe's portrayal of Miss McIntyre closely resembles Miss McLeod in Sui Sin Far's "The Gift of Little Me" (chapter 3).

26. Bienvenido N. Santos, *The Man Who (Thought He) Looked Like Robert Taylor* (Quezon City, Philippines: New Day Publishers, 1983).

27. Malcolm X and Alex Haley, *The Autobiography of Malcolm X* (repr. New York: Ballantine Books, 1973), 2–7, 40.

28. W. E. B. Du Bois, *The Souls of Black Folk* (repr. Chicago: A. C. McClurg, 1953), 3.

29. Dirk Johnson, "Census Finds Many Claiming New Identity," *New York Times,* March 5, 1991, A1. One must be cautious, however, in making a conclusion on this issue. The dramatic increase of the Native American population might also be due to changes in self-

identification. Stephan Thernstrom, "American Ethnic Statistics," in *Immigrants in Two Democracies: French and American Experience*, ed. Donald L. Horowitz and Gerard Noiriel (New York: New York University Press, 1992), 80–111.

30. Bret Harte, "See Yup," in *Writings of Bret Harte* (Boston: Houghton Mifflin, 1910), 16:144–60. Also see Robert McClellan, *The Heathen Chinee: A Study of American Attitudes toward China, 1890–1905* (Columbus: Ohio State University Press, 1971), 49–52.

31. Corinne Hoexter, *From Canton to California: The Epic of Chinese Immigration* (New York: Four Winds Press, 1976), 252.

32. Smith, *The Second Generation Oriental in America*, 19.

33. Quoted in Gary Y. Okihiro, *Margins and Mainstreams: Asians in American History and Culture* (Seattle: University of Washington Press, 1994), 169.

34. Chang, *Continuity and Change*, 96–99; Judy Yung, *Chinese Women of America* (Seattle: University of Washington Press, 1986), 53; Him Mark Lai, *Cong huaqiao dao huaren* [From overseas Chinese to Chinese Americans], (Hong Kong: Joint, 1992), 158.

35. Smith, *The Second Generation Oriental in America*, 23.

36. Elaine H. Kim, "Appendix A," in *East to America: Korean American Life Stories*, ed. Elaine H. Kim and Eui-Young Yu (New York: New Press, 1996), 356.

37. The three are, respectively, Mexican, Japanese, and black students in Lowe's class.

38. Charles L. Crow, "A *MELUS* Interview: Hisaye Yamamoto," *MELUS* 14 (Spring 1987): 80.

39. "Glorious Descendant" is a pun containing the literal translation of Lowe's Chinese given name, "Yichang," and symbolizing his subtle relationship with his father. The two Chinese characters mean "a descendant who glorifies his ancestors."

40. Keeping a queue was a cultural custom imposed on the Chinese by the Manchu— a nomadic tribe originating in northeastern China—after they conquered China in the mid-seventeenth century and founded the Qing Dynasty.

41. Maxine Hong Kingston, *The Woman Warrior: Memoirs of a Girlhood among Ghosts* (New York: Alfred Knopf, 1976), 76.

42. C. F. Yong, *The New Gold Mountain: The Chinese in Australia, 1901–1921* (Richmond, S.A.: Raphael Arts, 1977), 211–20. Lowe admits in the autobiography that only wealthy merchants could afford to send their children to China for education.

43. In this respect, second-generation Chinese in America differed profoundly from their peers in Southeast Asia. For the latter, going to China for education was a natural choice and was often expected because China was seen as a culturally superior nation in Asia. But for Chinese born in the United States, the prevailing influence of popular American culture was so powerful that, in general, they were ashamed of China's "backwardness" and had little interest in studying there. For discussions on attitudes of Chinese immigrants toward education in China, see Tu Wei-ming, "Cultural China: Periphery as the Center," in *The Living Tree: The Changing Meaning of Being Chinese Today*, ed. Tu Wei-ming (Stanford: Stanford University Press, 1994), 1–34.

44. Smith, *The Second Generation Oriental in America*, 7.

45. Sollors, *Beyond Ethnicity*, 214.

46. Marcus Lee Hansen, "The Third Generation in America," quoted in Sollors, *Beyond Ethnicity*, 215. Hansen's article, although it treats Scandinavian immigrants generally, is more about Norwegians than any other group. His father was Norwegian and his mother was Danish.

47. Betty Lee Sung, *Chinese American Intermarriage* (New York: Center for Migration Studies, 1990), 1–19, 87–99; Diane Mei Lin Mark and Ginger Chih, *A Place Called Chinese America* (Dubuque: Kendall/Hunt, 1982), 137–43.

48. Emory Stephen Bogardus, *Immigration and Race Attitudes* (New York: D. C. Heath, 1928), 25–26; Sung, *Chinese American Intermarriage,* 49–50; Stanford Lyman, *Chinese Americans* (New York: Random House, 1974), 130; Chang, *Continuity and Change,* 191.

49. Wu Tingfang, *America through the Spectacles of an Oriental Diplomat* (New York: Frederick Stokes, 1914), 125.

50. Lowe's explanation that the sixty-sixth birthday is a special occasion in one's life is not quite correct. According to Chinese tradition, it is the sixtieth birthday that should be greatly celebrated because the figure *60* symbolizes that one has completed a full circle in life. The error can be seen as an example of an ABC's unfamiliarity with traditional Chinese culture.

51. Lyman, *Chinese Americans,* 126. Of course, despite their friendship with and sympathy for Japanese Americans, Chinese in the United States, both native-born and immigrant, strongly supported China's struggle against Japan's invasion in the 1930s and 1940s. Many even went to China to serve in the Chinese army and fight against the Japanese. For information about the Chinese American involvement in China's anti-Japanese war, see Shih-shan H. Tsai, *The Chinese Experience in America* (Bloomington: Indiana University Press, 1986), 120–42; Ren Guixiang, *Huaqiao dierci aiguo gaochao* [The second patriotic movement of overseas Chinese], (Beijing: Zhonggong Dangshi, 1989), 88–128.

52. Smith, *The Second Generation Oriental in America,* 5–26; Ronald Takaki, *Strangers from a Different Shore: A History of Asian Americans* (New York: Penguin Books, 1989), 36, 292, 472–91. Takaki also mentions that like Chinese Americans, most second-generation Koreans had little ill-feeling against Japanese Americans during the World War II era. Also see Chan, *Asian Americans,* 70–73.

53. For discussions of origins of the pan-Asian American identity, see Yen Le Espiritu, *Asian American Panethnicity: Bridging Institutions and Identities* (Philadelphia: Temple University Press, 1992), 1–52. For a somewhat contrasting view, see Roger Daniels, "United States Policy towards Asian Immigrants: Contemporary Developments in Historical Perspective," *International Journal* 60, no. 3 (1993): 310–34.

54. Quoted in Isaacs, *Scratches on Our Minds,* 120.

55. Chan, *Asian Americans,* xiii.

56. Bill Hosokawa, *Nisei: The Quiet Americans* (New York: William Morrow, 1969), 188, 319.

57. "How to Tell Japs from the Chinese," *Life,* Dec. 22, 1941, 81–82.

58. Chen Weihua, "Wo shi zhongguoren" [I am Chinese], [Beijing] *Renmin Ribao* [People's Daily], overseas ed., June 26, 1991, 8; Mary Paik Lee, *Quiet Odyssey: A Pioneer Korean Woman in America,* ed. Sucheng Chan (Seattle: University of Washington Press, 1990), 50–121. Also see Okihiro, *Margins and Mainstreams,* 86–90.

59. Sung, *Chinese American Intermarriage,* 122.

60. The fact that *Father and Glorious Descendant* appears in almost all major anthologies of Asian American literature is evidence of the recognition of the significance of Lowe's writing.

61. Jade Snow Wong, *Fifth Chinese Daughter* (New York: Harper and Row, 1950).

62. Judith Judson, "Child of Two Cultures," *Washington Post*, July 2, 1989, D3.

63. It is surprising to find that many critics, even Asian American scholars, think that *Fifth Chinese Daughter* was first published in 1945. The source of the confusion is perhaps because the book holds a copyright date of 1945. Wong wrote an autobiographical sketch for the Californian magazine *Common Ground* in that year, which was incorporated into the book. The autobiography was not published as a book until 1950, however.

64. One paperback edition of *Fifth Chinese Daughter* was published by the University of Washington Press in 1989; Wong's other work has also enjoyed great popularity. "Puritans from the Orient," a chapter she wrote for *The Immigrant Experience*, ed. Thomas C. Wheeler (New York: Penguin Books, 1971), has been used as a high school text throughout the country, and her memoir *No Chinese Stranger* (New York: Harper and Row, 1975) was reviewed favorably. Compared with *Fifth Chinese Daughter*, however, *No Chinese Stranger* had only limited success; it has never been issued in paperback. In my opinion, this is in part because *No Chinese Stranger* covers too wide a range of subjects, from Wong's marriage and children in the 1950s, to her trips to China and Asia in the 1970s. It is not well focused on a central topic and fails to convey the impact of the profound changes on Chinese Americans after World War II. Thus it lacks the social significance of *Fifth Chinese Daughter*. In addition, written hurridley—Wong finished the memoir within a few weeks—*No Chinese Stranger* does not have the same literary flavor and is not as highly polished as *Fifth Chinese Daughter*.

65. After graduation from junior college, Wong went to Mills College on a combination of savings, scholarships, and more drudge labor as housemaid. In contrast, her brother's college education was financed by the family.

66. Wong, *Fifth Chinese Daughter* (repr. Seattle: University of Washington Press, 1989), 161 (subsequent pages citations to *FCD* appear in parentheses). Mona Chang, a Chinese American girl in Gish Jen's *Mona in the Promised Land*, adopts the same strategy to win favor in school. As a new student and the only Chinese in her high school, Mona uses her Chinese heritage to impress classmates, telling them she knows karate and even offering to "chop" a girl's arm. Jen, *Mona in the Promised Land* (New York: Alfred A. Knop, 1996), 5.

67. Lee, *The Chinese in the United States of America*, 364–65; Isaacs, *Scratches on Our Minds*, 140–75; also see Lyman, *Chinese Americans*, 129; and Amy Ling, *Between Worlds: Women Writers of Chinese Ancestry* (New York: Pergamon Press, 1990), 57.

68. For analyses of differences between Fu Manchu and Charlie Chan, see William F. Wu, *The Yellow Peril: Chinese Americans in American Fiction, 1850–1940* (Hamden: Archon Books, 1982), 164–82; Eugene Franklin Wong, *On Visual Media Racism: Asians in the American Motion Pictures* (New York: Arno Press, 1978), 100–111; and Mark and Chih, *A Place Called Chinese America*, 137–39.

69. My African American students and colleagues have told me they enjoy seeing the Charlie Chan films because they are pleased to see how a Chinese, albeit played by a Caucasian, fools and ridicules white police officers on the screen.

70. Tiana [Thi Thanh Nga], "The Long March: From Wong to Woo: Asians in Hollywood," *Cineaste* 21, no. 4 (1995): 38. To some extent, Charlie Chan movies played a role similar to that of Pearl S. Buck's fiction in that they both helped bring about positive changes in the portrayal of the Chinese in popular American culture.

71. "Fu" in Chinese means "negative," and "Manchu" is the official title of the Qing

Dynasty, which ruled China between 1644 and 1911. The name was originally hyphenated (Fu-Manchu) when it first appeared in the works of the English novelist Sax Rohmer, who created the character. That made it more like the Chinese connotation discussed here, because in Chinese the name would be a compound word.

72. For more discussions on this issue, see Fred Warren Riggs, *Pressures on Congress: A Study of the Repeal of Chinese Exclusion* (New York: Columbia University Press, 1950). For more analyses of the implications of the evolution from Fu Manchu to Charlie Chan, see Isaacs, *Scratches on Our Minds*, 80–91, 116–22. Also see Roger Daniels, *Asian America: Chinese and Japanese in the United States since 1850* (Seattle: University of Washington Press, 1988), 98.

73. Pearl S. Buck (1892–1973), who wrote several dozen books on China and the Chinese and won the Pulitzer Prize in 1935 and the Nobel Prize in 1938, made enormous contributions to reshaping the American image of the Chinese during the 1930s. According to Harold Isaacs, many Americans deemed Buck's novel *The Good Earth* (1931), together with the MGM film of 1937, to be the most influential positive factor that changed their impression of Chinese. "It can almost be said that for a whole generation of Americans she [Pearl Buck] 'created' the Chinese," Isaac points out, "in the same sense that Dickens 'created' for so many of us the people who lived in the slums of Victorian England." Isaacs, *Scratches on Our Minds*, 155.

Significantly, both Jade Snow Wong and Maxine Hong Kingston have acknowledged Buck's writing had a positive impact on them. Wong recalled that Buck's work on China "greatly enriched" her understanding of Chinese culture (author interview with Jade Snow Wong, San Francisco, Feb. 5, 1991); and Kingston said during a visit to Taiwan in 1995, "When I started reading and writing . . . I was lucky to have Jade Snow Wong and Pearl S. Buck." Shan Te-hsing, "An Interview with Maxine Hong Kingston," [Taipei] *Tamkang Review* 27 (Winter 1996): 253. For a discussion of how Buck's writing helped improve the Chinese image in popular American culture, see Peter J. Conn, *Pearl S. Buck: A Cultural Biography* (New York: Cambridge University Press, 1996); also see "China Reevaluates Pearl Buck," [Beijing] *China Today* 40 (May 1991): 61.

74. Author interview with Jade Snow Wong.

75. Wong, "Puritans from the Orient," 110, 54, 109.

76. Rose Hum Lee, *The Growth and Decline of Chinese Communities in the Rocky Mountain Region* (New York: Arno Press, 1978), 84, 288–89. Lee reports that there were thirty-three different applications for relief filed by the Chinese in Silver Bow County, Montana, from the beginning of the depression to 1945. Because the Chinese population there during those years ranged from 155 to 52, that number is not a particularly small one.

77. Daniels, *Asian America*, 88.

78. According to a study conducted in the Boston area, three-quarters of the patrons of Chinese restaurants were non-Chinese after World War II, compared to only one-fourth before the war. Rhoads Murphey, "Boston's Chinatown," *Economic Geography* 28 (April 1952): 244–55.

79. Wong had never read or heard of the work of any Chinese Americans before she wrote *Fifth Chinese Daughter*. Author interview with Jade Snow Wong.

80. Quoted in Ching-Chao Wu, "Chinatowns: A Study in Symbiosis and Assimilation," Ph.D. diss., University of Chicago, 1928, 158.

81. Min Zhou, *Chinatown: The Socioeconomic Potential of an Urban Enclave* (Philadelphia: Temple University Press, 1992), 1–118.

82. Wong, "Puritans from the Orient," 127.

83. Bogardus, *Immigration and Race Attitudes,* 25; Lyman, *Chinese Americans,* 130; Isaacs, *Scratches on Our Minds,* 164–76.

84. Ng, "Writings on the Chinese in California," 46–47.

85. Frank Chin, "Come All Ye Asian American Writers of the Real and the Fake," in *The Big Aiiieeeee: An Anthology of Chinese American and Japanese American Literature,* ed. Jeffery Paul Chan et al. (New York: Meridian, 1991), 1–30. For information on the difference between Chin and Wong, see chapter 7 of this volume.

86. Haslam, *Forgotten Pages of American Literature,* 80.

87. See note 35, chaper 3, for definitions of the imperial decrees.

88. According to traditional Chinese culture, only male children are considered the descendants of a family.

89. Lai, *From Overseas Chinese to Chinese Americans,* 158. The notorious foot-binding custom was not officially abolished until the early twentieth century. The status of Chinese women in American society, however, is a highly controversial issue among Chinese Americans (chapter 7).

90. Earl Derr Biggers, *Keeper of the Keys* (Indianapolis: Bobbs-Merrill, 1932), 307, emphasis added.

91. The same taboo also forbids the female presence on occasions such as an opening ceremony of a new business venture or the first trip of a new cart. For example, Xiangzi, the hero of Lao She's classic *Luotuo Xiangzi* [Rickshaw boy], (repr. Beijing: Renmin Wenxu, 1994), 11, believed that the first customer on his newly purchased rickshaw cart "absolutely must not be a woman" because taking a female for the first trip would bring him misfortune and ruin the new cart.

92. Critical misjudgment of Wong's literary style is by no means the only such case in Chinese American literature. *The Woman Warrior,* for example, has been said to be written in an "exotic foreign style" although Kingston indicated that she modeled the book on William Carlos Williams's *In the American Grain.*

93. For example, Frank Chin calls *Fifth Chinese Daughter* "part cook book" and "food pornography." Chin, *The Chinaman Pacific & Frisco R.R. Co.* (Minneapolis: Coffee House Press, 1988), 3.

94. Scarlet Chen, "The Asian Presence," *Belle Lettres: A Review of Books by Women* 6 (Fall 1990): 22; also see Amy Ling, *Between Worlds: Women Writers of Chinese Ancestry* (New York: Pergamon Press, 1990), 119–30.

95. Kai-yu Hsu and Helen Palubinskas, eds., *Asian-American Authors* (Boston: Houghton Mifflin, 1972), 24.

96. Wong, *Fifth Chinese Daughter,* viii.

97. Author interview with Jade Snow Wong.

98. Maxine Hong Kingston to Amy Ling, April 28, 1988, quoted in Ling, *Between Worlds,* 120. Kingston has also emphasized Wong's influence on her. Author interview with Maxine Hong Kingston, March 7, 1990, Harvard University, Cambridge, Mass.; also see Shan, "An Interview with Maxine Hong Kingston," 251.

# AN ANALYSIS

OF

# THE CHINESE QUESTION.

CONSISTING OF

## A SPECIAL MESSAGE OF THE GOVERNOR,

AND, IN REPLY THERETO,

## TWO LETTERS OF THE CHINAMEN,

AND

## A MEMORIAL OF THE CITIZENS OF SAN FRANCISCO.

..........................................

SAN FRANCISCO:

PRINTED AT THE OFFICE OF THE SAN FRANCISCO HERALD, MONTGOMERY ST.

1852.

Cover of *An Analysis of the Chinese Question* (1852). The pamphlet contains two of the earliest publications by Chinese immigrants in North America: "Letter of the Chinamen to His Excellency, Governor Bigler" (April 29, 1852) and "To His Excellency, Gov. Bigler, from the Chinamen" (May 16, 1852). (Reproduced by permission of The Huntington Library, San Marino, California)

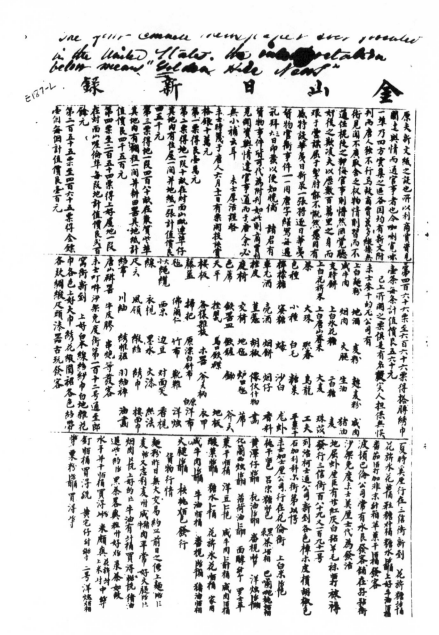

Front page of *Kim Shan Jit San Luk* [Golden Hill News], San Francisco, April 22, 1854, the first Chinese newspaper published in North America. (Courtesy of the Massachusetts Historical Society)

WHEN I WAS

A BOY IN CHINA

BY

YAN PHOU LEE

✳

BOSTON
LOTHROP, LEE & SHEPARD CO., 1887

Lee Yan Phou (1861–1938?) and *When I Was a Boy in China* (1887), the first book in English written by a Chinese immigrant in America. (Courtesy of Harvard College Library)

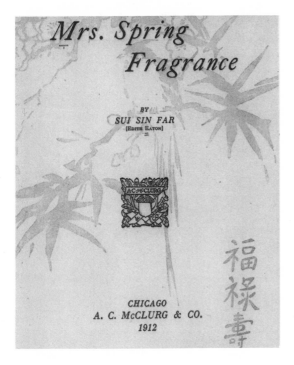

*Mrs. Spring Fragrance* (1912). (Courtesy of Harvard College Library)

Sui Sin Far (Edith Maude Eaton, 1865–1914). (Courtesy of L. Charles Laferrière)

Monument erected by Chinese Americans on the site of the Angel Island Immigration Station (1910–40). The inscription reads: "Leaving old homes / Sailing across the ocean / Only to be detained in wooden cells; / Breaking the earth / Opening the sky / Building up new lives on Gold Mountain."

Angel Island in the San Francisco Bay.

Four among dozens of Chinese-language dailies that are published in the United States; from top: *Sing Tao Daily, International Daily, World Journal,* and *The China Press.* (Courtesy of Louise R. Yuhas)

Yu Lihua in her residence,
Albany, New York.

Books by Chinese immigrant authors in America: *My Forty Years in San Francisco, Black, Black, the Most Beautiful Color, The Ordeal, The American Moon, A Selection of Short Stories by Chinese Immigrant Writers, My Experience as an American Lawyer, Poets and Gay Poets,* and *Break Out.* (Courtesy of Louise R. Yuhas)

Maxine Hong Kingston in her office at the University of California Berkeley. (Courtesy of Jane Scherr)

Below: Amy Tan answers questions during a talk at Occidental College, 1997. (Courtesy of Don Milici)

Frank Chin. (Connie Hwang Photo)

*I tell you, in this country, whether you are right or wrong depends on if
you have tough muscle and dare to fight. . . . Be quiet and patient? Forget
it! If you're modest and self-giving, others will treat you like trash. The
high-sounding Chinese doctrine of endurance, benevolence, and always
putting others before you, doesn't work at all in this place.*
—Zhuang Yin

# 5

## What's in a Name: Chinese-Language
## Literature in America

The birth of Chinese-language writing in America, like that by Chinese Americans in English, can be traced to the mid-nineteenth century.[1] On April 22, 1854, San Francisco saw the publication of *Kim Shan Jit San Luk* [Golden Hill News]—the first Chinese newspaper to appear in North America.[2] During the following decades, Chinese newspapers and periodicals sprang up in major Chinatowns throughout the United States. As early as 1902 the prosperity of Chinese-language publications impressed a mainstream reporter so much that she wrote: "The land of liberty and free speech seemed to offer advantages to the Chinese who would be journalist, and who would say what he would say. In San Francisco there are four Chinese dailies, besides several weeklies."[3]

Although they varied in quality and scope, most Chinese-language newspapers contained some form of literary work as a means of promoting circulation. A few, such as the *Chung Sai Yat Pao* [China-West Daily, 1900–1951], founded by Ng Poon Chew, and *Mon Hing Yat Bo* [Chinese World, 1891–1969], favored by Sui Sin Far, were particularly known for their dedication to literary endeavors and had significant influence on the Chinese American community.[4]

The efflorescence of Chinese-language literature in America is a combination of many factors. Throughout the history of Chinese settlement in America, it has provided a bridge between the Chinese community and the larger society and furnished an interpretive prism through which most immigrants receive information and share experiences of their adopted country. Ordinary Chinese immigrants must rely on it for knowledge about American society because they are unable to understand English. Even those highly proficient in English find Chinese-language literature a significant and convenient vehicle to exchange impressions of American life and communicate feelings about it.[5]

Another critical element leads to the prominence and popularity of Chinese-language literature in America: It provides Chinese immigrants with a sense of community and ethnic unity. Chinese in America are a diverse population, made up of Cantonese from different districts of the Pearl River Delta as well as Hakka, Fujianese, Northerners, and immigrants from other parts of the Chinese world.[6] Spoken Chinese is composed of a variety of mutually incomprehensible dialects; written Chinese, however, is read across linguistic lines and recognized as a common heritage by all Chinese.[7] Thus, Chinese-language publications in America reinforce the ethnic consciousness and solidarity of Chinese immigrants and function as an identity tool that unites them in a strange land.

Despite its popularity and influence, Chinese-language writing is rarely viewed as part of the authentic body of Chinese American literature. In most cases, it receives little analysis save for a few brief comments in Chinese American literary studies.[8] Although that is in part a result of critics' inability to read Chinese, it also derives from the impression that immigrant writers are sojourners who look to their homeland for inspiration. Their work primarily covers events in the old country and thus lacks a genuine Chinese American sensibility. Such views place work by Chinese immigrants in their native tongue on the margins of Chinese American literature and regard them as part of overseas Chinese writing.[9]

In reviewing Chinese-language literature in America, however, we are struck by a binding theme that runs through most of the works: the struggle of Chinese immigrants for survival and success in the new country. Indeed, Chinese-language literature in earlier years served mainly as a means of helping immigrants preserve their memories of the old country. Its tone and themes were similar to literature published in China.[10] Two interrelated trends in terms of themes and subject matter characterized it: teaching traditional Chinese values and a strong sense of sentimental nostalgia for the homeland, which can be summarized in a dictum: "Falling leaves settle on their roots," meaning that those who reside elsewhere should eventually return to their ancestral land. Even stories that seem to be irrelevant to these subjects were penetrated by such messages.

In his study of early Chinese-language publications in America, for example, Hsiao-ming Han discusses one story published in a Chinese newspaper in San Francisco in 1874. The story concerned a Chinese scholar's dramatic experiences in a brothel. Having failed at professional achievement in the "Gold Mountain," he fails yet again when he is turned away by a prostitute who thinks scholars "earn very little" and have no value. Disappointed that even a "street woman" does not welcome him, the man laments that America is not the right place for literary men because "the value of literature turns out to be insultingly cheap here."[11] The story is significant in that its author is suggesting that America is a land of muscle and practical knowledge rather than scholarship and literary delicacy.[12] That message appears frequently in works by early Chinese immigrants and still prevails in contemporary Chinese-language writing. Yet despite its significance, the story falls into the realm of moral teaching and nostalgic, sentimental writing.

That the creative writing of early Chinese immigrants was dominated by didacticism and nostalgia is not surprising. Throughout the history of the Chinese diaspora, immigrant literati assumed the responsibility of interpreting and mediating Chinese culture, particularly ethical doctrines, for compatriots abroad. Elaborations of traditional Chinese values such as filial piety, faithfulness, and righteousness made up a large part of the literary production of Chinese immigrant communities all over the world.[13] That tradition inevitably affected Chinese immigrants when they began their literary endeavors in America. Throughout history, verse contests and poetic couplet competitions sponsored by Chinese literary societies in Chinatowns have raised immigrants' awareness of their cultural heritage and reminded them of their dignity, obligations, and responsibilities as Chinese.[14]

Nostalgia and an emphasis on Chinese culture in early Chinese-language writing were not only shaped by the perceptual baggage the immigrants carried with them but also by their bitter experiences in America. The hardships and racial discrimination they encountered forced them to seek comfort from their Chinese cultural legacy and dream of returning home as a happy ending to their suffering in America. As discussed earlier, even an English-Chinese phrase book was used as an occasion to convey the lessons of Confucianism to immigrants.

Given that the immigrants were shut out of the "melting pot," an emphasis on traditional Chinese values and sentiment for the motherland in early Chinese-language writing was only natural. For Chinese immigrants, identification with Chinese culture in their writing provided the psychological support and group identity denied them by mainstream culture.

The influence of Chinese culture is also reflected in the styles of writing by early Chinese immigrant authors. Their work was modeled closely on classical Chinese literature and traditional Chinese storytellers. Concise sentence structure and a literary vocabulary turned the writing into replicas of classic Chinese literature. Because of these characteristics, Chinese scholars tend to view early Chinese-language writing in America as "overseas Chinese literature" (i.e., an extension of Chinese literature abroad) rather than as part of an authentic body of Chinese American literature.[15]

That trend gradually fell from favor, however, and Chinese-language writers in America turned increasingly to the sensations and conditions of Chinese Americans for ideas in their writing. The change was inevitable. As one prominent Chinese-language writer points out, immigrants cannot "live forever on the memory of the old country, writers especially so."[16] Yu Lihua, another noted Chinese-language author, acknowledges that she has grown increasingly interested in Chinese American life because she understands Chinese in the United States better and more profoundly than their counterparts in China or Taiwan.[17]

The shift in focus has also come about because contemporary Chinese-language writers in America, in contrast to their forebears, no longer desire to return home, choosing instead to settle in the United States. For them, the question of how to adjust to American life assumes more urgency. Therefore, although sentimental nostalgia for the old country is still expressed, endeavoring to define the meaning of Chinese American life now has formed the center of their themes and subject matter. There is a consistent voice in their works, showing awareness of how individual stories can relate and contribute to the commonality of the Chinese American experience. "As an immigrant writer and poet, I cannot forever look to China for ideas in writing," explains Dominic Cheung, author of *Tears of Gold* (1985), a book on Chinese gold miners in the nineteenth century. "I wrote the book because I share with them [earlier immigrants] the same ethnic feelings" and "a common dream."[18]

The sense of an American identity is further evidenced in writing style. Just as the taste of Chinese food changes after the journey across the Pacific, so does the literary flavor of works written in Chinese alter in the United States. A casual conversation about literature with Chinese-language writers could include issues that range from the sensibility of the Lost Generation to the sentence structure in Henry James's fiction to the images in Walt Whitman's poetry. Nie Hua-ling, whose highly acclaimed novel *Mulberry and Peach* (1976) has been trans-lated into English and several other languages, admits that had she not been liv-ing in the United States she would not have written such an epic: "I have acquired lots of Western techniques of creative writing. So my style is quite innovative."[19] Noticeably, the adoption of Western-style expressions and techniques has made the work of Chinese-language writers more appealing, because most of their readers are Chinese immigrants who are familiar with Western literature. "I am pleased to find that she [Yu Lihua] has brought into her writing Western expres-sions and techniques," notes C. N. Yang, a Nobel Laureate in physics. "It has cre-ated a fresh yet serious style of spoken Chinese language."[20]

In other words, for most Chinese-language writers, although they may re-main emotionally associated with China, their identification with America has been increased as they gradually settle down in the United States. Their work, albeit written in Chinese and largely unknown to mainstream readers, demon-strates the influence of American social, cultural, and political thought and is unmistakably American in style and content. The authors' ties to Chinese liter-ature and society continue, but it is the context of Chinese American life that is dominant in shaping their themes and subject matter. The combination has transformed the literature into a unique Chinese American product. In this sense, contemporary Chinese-language writing is neither a microcosm nor an exten-sion of Chinese literature to America. Instead, it represents an integrated part of the Chinese American experience and a gratifying expression of the problems and progress found in Chinese American life.[21]

## Transformations in Chinese-Language Literature since the 1950s

Chinese-language literature in America began a distinctive new phase after World War II as an outcome of historical, social, and cultural forces that dramatically transformed the makeup and dynamics of the Chinese American community. In particular, the decades since the 1950s have witnessed the emergence of a large number of critically acclaimed Chinese-language writers. A series of immigra-tion laws passed by Congress since the late 1940s led to an escalation of Chinese immigration. Their impact was twofold: The Chinese population in the United States grew from about 120,000 in 1950 to more than two million in 1995 while the percentage of the American-born dropped from around 60 percent to 30 percent.[22]

For Chinese-language literature, the numbers are only the tip of an iceberg.

As Roger Daniels points out, new Chinese immigration not only far outstrips the old in size but also represents a more varied group of people.[23] The new immigrants are highly skilled in terms of training and education, reflecting the postwar immigration trend that witnessed thousands of immigrant intellectuals setting down roots in American society. Their arrival created a striking distinction between the new immigration and the old. Although there were Chinese students and scholars in the United States as early as in the mid-nineteenth century, not until after World War II did Chinese student immigration gain momentum.[24] Between the 1950s and the mid-1980s, nearly 150,000 students from Taiwan came to America for graduate education and advanced training, and a large majority settled in the United States after graduation. The decades of the 1980s and 1990s also saw approximately 250,000 students and scholars from the People's Republic of China study in American institutions of higher learning, and more than 50 percent eventually settled in the United States.[25]

That demographic change, especially the growing presence of highly educated immigrants, helped Chinese-language literature develop at an unprecedented rate. The new immigrants have displayed strong interest in and sustaining enthusiasm for works written in Chinese. Consequently, the decades since the 1950s have seen a renaissance of Chinese publications occur in America. Chinese-language journalism demonstrates that trend.[26]

By the early 1940s, many Chinese newspapers had been forced to close because of shrinking subscription rates—a result of the decline of immigration. With the influx of new immigrants, however, readership underwent quantitative and qualitative changes. In addition, the availability of advanced Chinese typesetting techniques reduced production costs and made Chinese publishing businesses more accessible and profitable. America's Chinatowns became the largest centers of Chinese publications outside Asia. As a result, Chinese-language journalism has grown rapidly. The numbers of Chinese newspapers and magazines in America are exceeded only by those in China, Taiwan, and Hong Kong. In New York City alone, Chinese dailies increased from four in the 1940s to seven in 1975 and nine by 1987, most of them with international circulation. Twice as many Chinese newspapers are printed each day in Los Angeles County as there are Chinese households in the area.[27]

The thirst of new immigrants for publications in their mother tongue has caused the flourishing of Chinese-language literature. From the 1950s on, riding the wave of readers' enthusiasm, most Chinese newspapers began to add *fu kan* [literary pages] to promote creative writing and compete for prospective subscribers. That practice attracted more readers. Hu Shi, for example, a prominent Chinese writer and literary critic, showed great interest in poems published in various *fu kan* during his stay in New York in the 1950s.[28]

In many cases, work by Chinese-language writers first appears in Chinese American newspapers before being published in book form in Asia. Yu Lihua's bestseller *Sons and Daughters of the Fu Family,* for example, which deals with the experience of Chinese student immigrants in America, was a hit when it first appeared in serial form in *Xing dao Ribao* [Sing Tao Daily] in New York in 1976. *Breaking Out,* a popular novel by Chen Ruoxi about Chinese immigrants in San Francisco, was carried in serial form in *Shijie Ribao* [World Journal] throughout the United States in 1982 before its simultaneous publication in Hong Kong, Taipei, and Beijing in 1983. *The American Moon,* a bestseller by Cao Youfang about the lives of Chinese restaurant workers in New York City, stimulated such strong interest when serialized in 1985 in *Zhong Bao* [The Central Daily] in New York that the author received telephone calls from readers wanting to share their impressions of the characters with her.[29]

It is noteworthy that the quantitative dimensions of newspaper-reading by Chinese in America is a uniquely "immigrant phenomenon." According to a Gallup study of urban life in China, even in cities that had the nation's highest economic development, only about 42 percent of adults regularly read newspapers or magazines, a rate about the same as Taiwan's.[30] By contrast, nearly 90 percent of Philadelphia's Chinatown residents read Chinese newspapers regularly.[31] "[I] used to hunt Chinese newspapers everywhere just like a hungry wolf," one student immigrant recalls. "Sitting in the basement studio, [I] would read every character in *fu kan* carefully."[32] Maxine Hong Kingston also recounts that her father loved reading the *Gold Mountain News,* a major Chinese-language newspaper on the West Coast: "The one event of the day that made him get up out of his easy chair was the newspaper. He looked forward to it. He opened the front door and looked for it hours before the mailman was due. *The Gold Mountain News . . .* came from San Francisco in a paper sleeve on which his name and address were neatly typed. He put on his gold-rimmed glasses and readied his smoking equipment. . . . He killed several hours reading the paper, scrupulously reading everything, the date on each page, the page numbers, the want ads."[33] To a great extent, the keen interest shown by Chinese immigrants in newspapers in their native language is a familiar phenomenon among immigrant groups across America. "Out of 312 Russian immigrants," a study conducted by sociologist Robert Park finds, "only 16 have regularly read newspapers in Russia. . . . [But] in America all of them are subscribers or readers of Russian newspapers."[34]

The arrival of a large number of student immigrants since the 1950s has dramatically shaped the fate of Chinese-language literature in another way. Although the majority are in the sciences and engineering, a significant number have been writers and literary critics.[35] Little Chinese-language writing is a debut effort. Most represents a continuation of work, albeit with new directions, by authors who had literary careers in the Chinese world. With professionalism, talent, and craft, this cohort of experienced immigrant writers has won critical acclaim and raised the quantity and quality of Chinese-language literature in America.

Globalization is another critical factor that has promoted the rise of Chinese-language literature in America. With the emergence of the trans-Pacific economic and social network, Asia has turned to the West, and work by Chinese immigrant writers in America has filled local bookstores in their old countries. Because most Chinese newspapers in America are subsidiaries of news networks in China, Taiwan, and Hong Kong, being published in them means that writers have gained broad access to markets in Asia.[36] Trans-Pacific migration has also made writing by Chinese immigrants who describe their American experiences appeal to audiences in their native lands. Since the late 1980s, for example, autobiographies and other forms of literature that record Chinese immigrant life in America—such as *A Beijinger in New York* (1991), *Manhattan's China Lady* (1992), and *My Experience as an American Lawyer* (1994)—have been enthusiastically received in China.[37] The rise of transnationalism has thus served the interests of Chinese-language literature in America by helping the authors win a growing readership, which in turn means more profits for publishers.[38]

## Worlds of Difference: Characteristics and Significance of Chinese-Language Literature in America

As a product of the Chinese experience in America, Chinese-language literature understandably shares many qualities with its counterpart in English. For example, the understated confrontation between immigrant parents and their American-born children in Chen Ruoxi's stories, such as "To the Other Side of the Pacific Ocean" (1980), parallels mother-daughter conflicts in Amy Tan's *The Joy Luck Club* (1989). Nie Hualing's *Mulberry and Peach,* featuring a female protagonist restlessly traversing the American landscape to explore the meaning of freedom and identity, brings to mind Maxine Hong Kingston's *Tripmaster Monkey: His Fake Book* (1990). The anger and frustrations frequently part of Chinese male immigrants' work echo Frank Chin's often-bitter voice. Even the details of the two literatures are sometimes similar. The protagonist in Yu Lihua's *Seeing the Palm Trees Again* (1967) enjoys a red bean and ice bar eating contest, and there is a similar scene in David Henry Hwang's play *FOB* (1979). Despite such similarities, however, Chinese-language literature has its own sensibility and perspective and differs profoundly and poignantly from those of English literature.

In general, three points stand out to offer useful glosses to understand the significance and characteristics of Chinese-language literature in America. First and foremost, Chinese-language authors, writing in their native tongue and read mainly by members of their own community, enjoy a high degree of freedom that their counterparts writing in English may not have.[39] Indeed, a hallmark of Chinese-language literature is the liberty it takes with subject matter of great sensitivity while remaining within the general corpus of Chinese American writing. Because most of their readers are Chinese, writers are freed from the social codes of mainstream American society. As a result, their discussions of controversial issues differ from those of Chinese American literature in English and include, for example, the relationships of Chinese with other ethnic and minority groups, the rise of feminist consciousness among Chinese American women, the divided interests of the "uptown" and "downtown" Chinese, the mutual exclusiveness of immigrants and the native-born, and the implications of interracial love affairs.[40]

Chinese American authors who write in English, especially immigrant writers, sometimes (and understandably) are silent on problems in American society and tend to present an image that fits the public's imagination. By contrast, because Chinese-language writers seek affirmation and recognition only from their own community, they do not worry about responses from outsiders. Hence they are more outspoken about problems, both in the Chinese community and society at large. They have consciously created a unique perspective from which to explore the Chinese American experience.

Poverty and crime in Chinatowns, for example, draw considerably more attention from Chinese-language writers than from those who write in English. We are made to see, through their penetrating observations, an entire subgroup of destitute Chinese immigrants that exists below the poverty line. From their work it is clear that not all Chinese Americans are successful or a "model minority" group. In the story "Abortion" (1979), the author examines the lives of sweatshop women in San Francisco's Chinatown and their attitudes toward abortion. Written with bold frankness and robust honesty, the story vividly demonstrates how sexual harassment and economic hardships force working-class Chinese women to choose abortion as a means of surviving their plight in poverty-stricken inner-city ghettos.[41] One doubts that the author would have written so straightforwardly about the polarization of the Chinese community had she published the story in English.

The liberating impact on these writers of knowing that their audience is strictly Chinese is perhaps most apparent in portrayals of interracial affairs. Relationships between men of color and white women have long been a sensitive subject in American literature. A nightmare for many in mainstream society, it was a major source of public anxiety that led to the development of laws against interracial marriage during the late nineteenth and early twentieth centuries. Underlying the discourse on miscegenation was a fear of, and preoccupation with, the rape of white women.[42] Against such a background, interracial love stories in English usually occur between white men and Chinese women. If the romance happens in the "wrong" way, that is, between a white woman and Chinese man, it is usually presented in the context of a working-class woman who falls in love with an upper-class man.[43] That arrangement accords with the idea that the Chinese are an "inferior" people and that a better class of white women would prefer white men.

The work of Chinese-language writers, in contrast, includes sensational descriptions of sex between Chinese men and white women. An account of a Chinese student having sex with a white girl is an example: "It's terrific last night! Sue [a white coed] went to bed with me. Gosh, she is really tender and tasty. The white flesh of her body is so white and the red so red. . . . What a pity she has such strong body odor. But, without that smell, her flesh might not be so juicy!"[44]

Other than attracting readership, such stories also have a social purpose: They represent the authors' efforts to reverse the stereotyped image created by popular American culture. Chinese prostitution has always been a favorite topic in American media, creating a scar in the layers of the collective Chinese American psyche.[45] By writing explicitly of sexual affairs between Chinese men and white women, these writers break down a taboo and offer readers psychological comfort that soothes their wounded feelings. For this reason, although they may fail to disentangle fantasy from reality, they illustrate a point of contrast between works in Chinese and in English.

While it grants its authors a sense of freedom, writing in Chinese has its own set of problems. Because Chinese publications go out to both immigrant readers in America and Chinese in the old countries, Chinese-language writers must satisfy those who are part of the immigrant experience as well as those who are not. Insiders want to read stories that truly reflect American life, whereas outsiders' fantasies about life in the "barbarian paradise" must be catered to. That situation can present a dilemma for Chinese-language writers, as was the case in the controversy over Yu Lihua's short story "A Childish Game" (1969).[46]

The story concerns a group of school children, around thirteen or fourteen, who "accidentally" discover the secret and pleasure of sex by playing a "game." Teenage sex is a common subject in American society, but it is not the case in traditional Chinese literature. Discussion of such a sensitive topic was viewed as violating the moral code of Chinese society, and the story caused controversy when published in Taiwan.[47] Even that controversy, however, indicates that only readers of their own ethnic background question the validity of Chinese-language writing. These authors have no need to fear offending a mainstream American audience. That unique circumstance has influenced the way Chinese-language writers handle certain issues and makes their approach measurably different from that of their counterparts who write in English.

The fact that their prospective readers are Chinese, coupled with an intense desire to explore their own literary paths, has prompted those who write in Chinese to remain closely identified with the immigrant experience in their themes and subject matter. While American-born Chinese writers tend to delve into the broad issues of cultural identity, generation conflicts, and sentiments of the native-born, Chinese-language writers deal more with compelling issues grounded in an immigrant sensibility, such as the agony of displacement, the dilemma of assimilation and alienation, and the hardship and struggle of daily life in a strange land. That is because, for immigrants, the pressing issue is not who they are but rather how to survive in an alien land. Their work possesses more complexity regarding immigrant feelings and provides insights about how race relations, class identification, economic factors, and social environment affect the concerns and consciousness of Chinese immigrants. In "A Visit at Night," for example, Zhuang Yin describes how recent immigrants who have educations and urban backgrounds fit into American society. With a strong desire to succeed in their adopted land, they have become assertive and no longer avoid racial confrontations. In the story, an immigrant father urges his son to challenge anyone who bullies him: "I tell you, in this country, whether you are right or wrong depends on if you have tough muscle and dare to fight. . . . Be quiet and patient? Forget it! If you're modest and self-giving, others will treat you like trash. The high-sounding Chinese doctrine of endurance, benevolence, and always putting others before you, doesn't work at all in this place."[48]

In other words, Chinese-language writers are distinguished by a persistent focus on issues unique to the fate of immigrants. The bewilderment caused by issues of multicultural polarity, the troubles of displacement and expatriation, and the mentality of marginalization provide them with a unique angle from which to observe the losses and gains of life in a new country and also the differences and similarities between the Chinese and other minority groups in multiracial American society.

More significantly, the complexity and diversity of their immigrant-centered subject matter reveal that traditional theories on race and ethnicity based on the experiences of other ethnic and minority groups, such as those of assimilation patterns or structural discrimination, cannot adequately address the Chinese American reality. The theory of ethnic solidarity, for one, holds that a shared history of oppression and discrimination is more important than class identity to members of an ethnic or minority group.[49] But according to the work of Chinese-language authors, there is not much basis for such solidarity in their economically polarized community. Socioeconomic stratification is clear in the depiction of the confrontation between Chinese restaurant workers and their employers in Cao Youfang's novel *The American Moon* as well as in Yi Li's stories of the misery of women in Chinatown sweatshops. It reveals that the disparities between the rich and poor have created two groups among Chinese Americans, the haves and the have-nots. The contingents share few common interests.

Yet the work of Chinese-language writers show that like other ethnic and minority groups, Chinese immigrants also become entangled in the prevailing currents of American life. Their experience has been punctuated by repeated changes since the 1950s, and the extent to which they participate in American society is surprising. Catch-phrases such as "color line" or "glass ceiling" are familiar to them, and the prevailing trends in mainstream culture have left strong traits and been crystallized in their writing.[50] Clearly, the critical factor that prompted a fundamental rethinking of their role in American society was the civil rights movement, and that continues to be the case. It improved in a revolutionary way the status of Chinese immigrants and made them aware of how events in society at large influence their lives. For that reason, contemporary Chinese-language literature has broadened and deepened to embrace increasingly diverse perspectives of the Chinese American experience.

Although earlier authors usually attributed social ills in Chinese life, explicitly or implicitly, to the tyranny of institutional racism, contemporary writers are more balanced in their criticism of problems in American society. They have broadened the discussion to cover not only exposure to racism but also feelings of exile, conflicting interests between rich and poor in the Chinese American community, and the torment of anxieties resulting from the pressure to survive and succeed. Such close attention to the many facets of immigrant life, and the strong concern for it, make Chinese-language literature vitally relevant to the Chinese American reality yet dramatically different from work written in English. In that sense, Chinese-language authors have become spokespersons for Chinese immigrants and contribute a unique perspective that reveals the racial aspects and cultural and socioeconomic underpinnings of Chinese Americans.

It is noteworthy that Chinese-language writers, with a few exceptions, rarely publish in English. That is not because writing in English is the province of the American-born. Many Chinese immigrant writers are well versed in English, as attested to by their translations of Chinese literature, research publications, and occasional creative writing in English. Rather, they argue that until recently, for

Chinese immigrant writers, creative writing in English has often demanded the suppression and distortion of Chinese sensibility, which does not fit into the stereotypical portrayal of "Orientals" in popular American culture.[51]

Such a critical opinion in part comes from their personal experience. Many have encountered difficulty or subtle bias when trying to place work that does not address popular Chinese stereotypes. A case in point concerns Yu Lihua. A prolific writer, she has published more than fifteen volumes, novels as well as collections of short stories, in Chinese since her arrival in America in 1953. Regarded as precursor to the "literature of student immigrants," she employs a wide range of narrative strategies and techniques to trace the lives of Chinese students and faculty on campuses across America and offer glimpses into the world of Chinese immigrant intellectuals, which is little known to the public.

Ironically, Yu Lihua's career as a Chinese writer in America began with the publication of a prize-winning story in English entitled "Sorrow at the End of the Yangtze River." It is a romance about a young woman's journey to find her "lost" father along the river. Shortly before her mother dies, the daughter sets out to look for the father, who left home years before. When she finally finds him, however, he does not recognize her until she plays a touching piano tune he taught her in childhood. The familiar and moving music awakens the father's memory and conscience, and he and the daughter reconcile.[52] The Hollywood-style sentimental story helped Yu Lihua win the prestigious Samuel Goldwyn Creative Writing Award and raised her confidence about pursuing a career as a professional writer of English.

Yu's subsequent writing in English—three novels and several short stories written during the late 1950s and early 1960s about Chinese immigrants in America—were all rejected by various publishers, however. "They [the publishers] were only interested in stories that fit the pattern of Oriental exoticism—the feet-binding of women and the addiction of opium-smoking men," she recalls. "I didn't want to write that stuff. I wanted to write about the struggle of Chinese immigrants in American society."[53] Convinced that only by conforming to these low expectations would she fit the "ethnic niche" of the mainstream publishing market, Yu decided to engage primarily in Chinese writing. To her and her peers, writing in Chinese thus represents a vindication of their artistic integrity.

In many ways, Yu Lihua's experience has provided a more convincing explanation than the enclave theory for understanding why Chinese immigrant writers choose to write in Chinese. According to this theory, Chinese writing in America is largely an outcome of the development of an enclave society. An enclave differs from the more general sociological notion of a ghetto in that a ghetto is rarely seen as having any positive function, whereas an enclave is not necessary to cater exclusively to an internal audience but grants writers freedom in their choice of languages. As such, writers can live within an enclave of ethnic Chinese culture and enjoy writing in Chinese.[54] The cases of Yu Lihua and other Chinese authors, however, reveal that writing in Chinese is not always a true choice. Sometimes it is the result of a limited access to the mainstream publishing market—a product of compromise to relative functionalism and its consequences.[55]

The allegation made by Yu Lihua and her peers that mainstream publishers tend to use their gatekeeping power to control and regulate the access of Chinese immigrant writers is widely shared by Asian American critics and some mainstream scholars. In her review of Frank Chin's work, Sau-ling Cynthia Wong argues that in order to win acceptance from readers, writing about Chinatowns demands suppression or distortion of all individual experiences that do not fit into white society's image of Chinese Americans. A mainstream scholar also agrees that as late as the 1970s it was "still difficult for Chinese American authors to find a publisher; playwrights, a theater; and actors, a stage."[56]

The comments made Yu and other Chinese-language writers are also echoed by the American-born Chinese and Asian authors whose work is exclusively in English.[57] For example, Monfoon Leong (1916–64) recalled that publishers repeatedly rejected his work because they thought his stories had "no readership" and were "not marketable." The collection of his short stories, *Number One Son*, written during the 1950s, was published posthumously in 1975 by an Asian American publisher at the Leong family's expense. Toshio Mori (1910–80), a pioneering nisei writer, produced four novels about Japanese Americans between the 1930s and 1960s but despite repeated efforts could find no publishers interested in the manuscripts.[58] Of course, with social progress and a growing interest in multiculturalism, Chinese and Asian American authors have won more recognition in the mainstream market. This is clearly seen in the enthusiastic reception from critics and the general reading public to work such as Amy Tan's *The Joy Luck Club* (1989), Gus Lee's *China Boy* (1991), and Gish Jen's *Mona in the Promised Land* (1996). The fact that these books, from major commercial publishers, were well reviewed in prestigious journals and newspapers indicates that Chinese American writing has emerged as a distinctive part of mainstream literature. Some Chinese and Asian American writers, however, still feel that when they write in English about Asia and Asian America the expression and effects of their work are restricted to ideas sanctioned by mainstream society. David Mura, a sansei (third-generation) Japanese American author, finds that writing about Japan illustrates a familiar contradiction: "The more people you want to communicate to, the more your descriptions must be ideologically palatable and conform to your reader's expectations of what Japan should be."[59]

Their problematic experiences with some mainstream publishers also explain why Chinese-language writers tend to hold low opinions of some bestsellers written in English by Chinese American authors—immigrants and the native-born. They argue that what these popular writers in English have done is resort to sensational distortion and emphasize the "exotic" aspects of Chinese culture, such as pigtails and bound feet, to attract readers. In their view, the Chineseness in these bestsellers is highly selective and staged, appealing rather than threatening. Although it is the right of individual authors to choose what their readers should know, it is wrong to wrench cultural practices out of context and display them for gain to the curious gaze of outsiders.[60]

Indeed, evidence shows that the themes and subject matters of Chinese immigrant authors who write in English are often affected by mainstream publishers or agents. Zhang Ailing [Eileen Chang, 1920–95], an eminent Chinese immigrant writer, received a plot and outlines from an agent for a novel she wrote in English, *The Rice-Sprout Song* (1956).[61] The agent of Anchee Min, author of the bestselling *Red Azalea* (1994), reportedly suggested that she add a lesbian relationship to her story to make the memoir of her life in China during the Cultural Revolution more captivating.[62] C. Y. Lee [Li Qinyang], author of *Flower Drum Song* (1957), observed that his success as a bestselling writer in English depended on "exposing mysterious elements in Chinatown life, because it can satisfy the curiosity of American readers."[63]

The difference between work that Lin Yutang wrote in Chinese and in English further proves that Chinese immigrant writers, because of their desire to win popularity in mainstream society, are more likely to give up certain principles when they write in English. The author of more than thirty books in English, Lin Yutang (1895–1976) is perhaps the most widely read Chinese writer and was one of the best-known Asian immigrants in America. His fame in the English-speaking world was established with the publication of the bestselling *My Country and My People* (1935). Apparently, Lin Yutang's portrayal of the Chinese in the book as loyal, reserved, modest, obedient to elders, and respectful of authority and his interpretation of Taoism as a philosophy of patience and belief in maintaining a low profile are in keeping with the Western view of "Orientals." For this reason, he was recognized as an exponent of China and Chinese civilization in the West.[64] *My Country and My People* became a record-breaking success for a Chinese writer in America and underwent eleven reprintings within two years.[65] The fact that George Bush quoted the book half a century later in his 1989 State of Union Address to Congress attests to its immense popularity.[66]

Lin Yutang's subsequent writing in English further reinforced Western stereotypes of China and the Chinese. For example, elaborating on "the Chinese way of life" in *Chinatown Family* (1948), he asserted that the Chinese were able to succeed and get along with people everywhere because they knew how to follow Taoist teachings and avoid confrontations: "He [Tom Fong, Sr.] had been pushed about in this country and he had made his way like water, that symbol of Taoist wisdom, seeking the low places and penetrating everywhere . . . Laotse was right; those who occupy the lowly places can never be overthrown."[67]

While Lin Yutang's writing in English is lauded by mainstream readers as a "cultural eye-opener" on China, however, Asian American scholars have accused it of being submissive in tone and representing no more than an effort to exploit "Oriental exoticism" and boost Lin's fame in the West. His writing, they argue, comes from "a white tradition of Chinese novelty literature" and misrepresents the Chinese in precisely the way that Asian Americans find offensive.[68] In fact, despite their conflicting views on many issues, most Asian American scholars are critical of Lin Yutang for capitulating to the "white mentality," being "morally bankrupt," and buying his way into second-class white status.[69]

Although Lin Yutang's English writing seems "whitewashed" to collaborate in rather than challenge the stereotyping of the Chinese in the West, his work written in Chinese assumes a surprisingly opposite role. In contrast to the polite and self-mocking tone, lighthearted jokes, and apolitical attitude that characterize his English writing, his work in Chinese (published during the same period) was often highly political, angry, impassioned, and even rebellious. In a Chinese essay that appeared shortly before *My Country and My People,* Lin expressed concern with sharp and sensitive feeling for the well-being of the Chinese people:

> I am not dreaming: I only wish there were a small piece of peaceful land in China where there are no wars, no exorbitant taxes . . .
>
> I am not dreaming: I only wish there would be a good university run by the Chinese so that our children could have a place to study without having to attend schools taught by *foreign devils* . . .
>
> I am not dreaming: I only wish we Chinese could have the right to vote for and dispose of government officials . . .
>
> I am not dreaming: I only wish China could really ban opium and forbid anyone to use warships to carry opium . . .
>
> I am not dreaming: I only wish there would be no more corrupted and greedy officials and the government would not destroy people's property and lives so casually . . .
>
> I am not dreaming: I only wish the government could truly protect people, and would not tear down people's houses nor impose harsh taxes on peasants.[70]

In another essay, "Guoshi weiyi" [China in crisis], written at the end of 1935 and after the publication of *My Country and My People,* Lin argued emotionally that the only way to save China was to stand up to foreign pressures rather than bow to them and that the government must stop the practice of "spineless diplomacy."[71] In these essays, his bitter criticism of government policies and passionate defense of the rights of the people differed dramatically from his humble tone and the doctrine of "endurance and passivity" he preached in *My Country and My People.*

Lin Yutang became mainly a writer of English after he moved to the United States in 1936. But his occasional writing in Chinese still contained criticism and thorny remarks not seen in English. In an essay for the Chinese press in 1943, for example, Lin commented sarcastically on U.S. presidential elections: "In not too long I will see a presidential election . . . I want to see who tells more lies to the people, the Republican party or the Democratic party. If the Republicans are able to tell more lies, then a Republican president will be elected; if the Democrats are able to tell more lies, then a Democratic president will be elected."[72] These biting remarks presented a sharp contrast to the amiable words and praise of America found in Lin's English writing.

The progressive views in Lin Yutang's Chinese writing were no accident. He was a friend of left-wing Chinese writers such as Lu Xun and Yu Dafu and supported the student movement when he taught at Beijing Women's Normal University in the 1920s. Because of his radical ideas, he was threatened by the warlord regime and had to flee for his life. When the League of Defense for Chinese Democracy, a left-wing organization, was founded in Shanghai in December of 1932, Lin Yutang was an elected member of its standing committee and participated in the organization's activities until he moved to America.[73]

There are various explanations for why Lin Yutang became so "whitewashed" in his English writing, and Lin himself admitted he was "a person full of contradictions."[74] Two factors are particularly worth mentioning, however. First, Lin Yutang was thrilled by the fame and fortune his role as "an interpreter of China to the West" bestowed.[75] Until the 1960s he was the only Asian in America to be included in *The Picture Book of Famous Immigrants,* where his name was listed together with that of Eleutherie Irenee Dupont and Andrew Carnegie. Second, money meant a great deal to Lin, who had grown up in an impoverished family. According to his daughter, Lin Yutang enjoyed enormous financial rewards for his publications in English. He made $36,000 in 1938, $42,000 in 1939, and $46,800 in 1940—extraordinary sums in those days.[76]

Editors and agents also influenced Lin Yutan's writing in English. Particularly influential were Pearl S. Buck, the foremost missionary writer on China, and her husband, Richard J. Walsh, whose publishing house, the John Day Company, brought out most of Lin Yutang's work in English. According to Lin's daughter, Buck and Walsh played an extensive role in her father's choice of subject matter and themes for his work published in English.[77] Lin himself acknowledged this point in the preface to *My Country and My People:* "My thanks are due to Pearl S. Buck who, from the beginning to the end, gave me kind encouragement and who personally read through the entire manuscript before it was sent to the press and *edited it,* to Mr. Richard J. Walsh who offered valuable criticism while the book was in progress."[78] Helen Foster Snow, who befriended Lin Yutang when she worked as a freelance reporter with Edgar Snow in China during the 1920s and 1930s, also recalled that Buck and Walsh "tailor-made Lin's books."[79]

If the gap between Lin Yutang's writing in Chinese and in English constitutes an example of how a Chinese immigrant writer might not say the same thing in each language, the fate of *Luotuo xiangzi* [Rickshaw boy], a modern Chinese classic, in America reveals how a Chinese text can be altered to satisfy readers' sentiments when it is translated into English.

The most successful work of Lao She [Lau Shaw, Shu Qingchun, 1900–1966], the novel was first published in serial form in 1936 in the periodical *Yuzhoufeng,* founded by Lin Yutang in Shanghai.[80] A tragedy and social exposé, it is based on a pessimistic and fatalistic viewpoint—the inevitable downfall and destruction of individuals, honest and hardworking though they may be, in an oppressed and diseased society. At the end of the story, Xiangzi (the hero) dies in poverty and his lover commits suicide after being trapped in a brothel.

The novel was translated into English by Evan King and published in 1945 under the title *Rickshaw Boy* by Reynal and Hitchcock.[81] In the translation, the final two chapters of the novel were completely rewritten, and the story ends with a happy reunion of the two young lovers. Well reviewed in mainstream magazines such as *The New Yorker* and *Saturday Review of Literature,* the novel was celebrated as "a modern novel about China written for the Chinese, of the Chinese, and by a Chinese."[82] Reviewers also praised King's translation: "There remains to say that the translation, sufficiently colloquial to give us the color of pungent Chinese phrases, is simple and pleasant to read."[83] Chosen by the Book-of-the-Month Club, the novel became a runaway bestseller. Ironically, reading public and critics alike favored the sweet, triumphant ending of the English version. Unaware of its differences with Lao She's original theme, reviewers thought the hero rescuing his lover from the brothel was "the climax of the story."[84]

The happy ending clearly undermined the novel's powerful criticism of social injustice and contradicted in every way Lao She's intent in writing the book. Those who read the concluding chapters of King's translation and those of Lao She's original would wonder if they were reading the same book. The Chinese text, translated by Jean M. James, ends in this way: "Handsome, ambitious, dreamer of fine dreams, selfish, individualistic, sturdy, great Hsiang Tzu [Xiang-zi]. No one knows how many funerals he marched in, and no one knows when or where he was able to get himself buried, that degenerate, selfish, unlucky off-spring of society's diseased womb, a ghost caught in Individualism's blind al-ley."[85] King's translation, or rather, rewriting, ends in a dramatic and happy re-union of the hero and his lover: "With quick movements he [Xiangzi] lifted the frail body up, folding the sheet about it, and, crouching to get through the door, he sped as fast as he could across the clearing into the woods. In the mild cool-ness of summer evening the burden in his arm stirred slightly, nestling closer to his body as he ran. She was alive. He was alive. They were free."[86]

The gap between the English and the Chinese versions raises a question, How could there be two entirely different endings for the same work? Most critics suspect that King rewrote the final two chapters without consulting Lao She. But Lao She himself left no record, nor did he make any public statement concern-ing the issue, even though he lived in New York City at the time.[87] During his stay in America (1946–49), King's translation went through at least five editions in New York and London. Furthermore, it is doubtful that King, a career foreign service officer, would have been able to make such a profound change entirely on his own. A former American diplomat to China, he had never engaged in creative writing and did not seem to possess a literary talent. His only previous publication had been a research report on market and business activities in Hong Kong during World War II.[88] Entitled *Hong Kong under Japan's Occupation: A Case Study in the Enemy Techniques of Control* and published by the U.S. Depart-ment of Commerce, the carefully written and well-documented report was no doubt a valuable source of information to businessmen and government bureau-crats. Nevertheless, it was dry and dull and had none of the rich literary flavor and local color of *Rickshaw Boy*. It is difficult to believe, therefore, that King was capable of rewriting the final two chapters of a modern Chinese classic and making the change artistically. The fact that no reviewers discovered flaws or inconsistencies in the chapters attests to the quality of the work. Even Chinese critics agree that the alteration was "masterfully" done.[89]

More significantly, *Rickshaw Boy* was not Lao She's only work that differed substantially between its English and Chinese versions. During his stay in New York, he collaborated with Ida Pruitt to translate his novel *Sishi tongtang* [Four generations under one roof] into English. In rewriting the novel based on sug-gestions from the publisher, Lao She added thirteen episodes—nearly 20 percent of the manuscript—that he had dropped from the Chinese text. The English version, published under the title *The Yellow Storm,* was again chosen by the Book-of-the-Month Club and became a bestseller.[90] As was the case of *Rickshaw*

*Boy,* critics and readers had no way of knowing that *The Yellow Storm* differed significantly from its Chinese text.

It is possible, therefore, that Lao She *might* have advised King, or whoever worked with King, on how to rewrite the concluding part of *Rickshaw Boy* in English. The sentimental ending, especially the rescue scene in which the hero carries his lover in his arms and rushes into the woods, would surely satisfy American readers whose literary taste was heavily influenced by Hollywood-style dramatics. Moreover, the happy ending, the two lovers freed at last, may also have been intended to arouse pro-China sentiments among readers at the time. The English version of the novel was published on the eve of victory in the Pacific War. It was a time when the American public harbored warm feelings toward China and the Chinese. Considering the timing of the publication, Lao She might have agreed that a triumphant ending for *Rickshaw Boy* would abet the image of the Chinese and also imply that China, like the hero of the novel, faced bright prospects and was entering a new phase of hope and prosperity after the decade-long, brutal Japanese invasion.[91]

Such speculation is not far-fetched, as born out by recent studies. For example, Hu Jieqing, Lao She's widow, has recalled that he dropped the tragic ending of the Chinese text when he republished *Rickshaw Boy* in China in 1950. By then Lao She had returned to Beijing and cast his lot with the New China. He might have felt it more appropriate to have "Rickshaw Boy" avoid a tragic ending and even planned to write a happy sequel. "After liberation, Lao She wanted very much to write a sequel to *Luotuo Xiangzi,*" Hu recalled. "He wanted to write the new life of Xiangzi and his happiness."[92] It is also well-known that during the 1950s Lao She changed the sad endings of several of his major works because he thought they were too pessimistic to be consistent with the upbeat atmosphere in China after the communist victory.[93] Although ultimately Lao She's life was tragic (he committed suicide during China's Cultural Revolution in 1966), he was optimistic about the fate of his native land when he was in America. A Chinese immigrant writer who met Lao She shortly before he was repatriated was impressed by the confidence he had in China's future after the civil war.[94]

The fate of *Rickshaw Boy* in America and the discrepancy between writing in Chinese and English by Lin Yutang and others demonstrate that Chinese immigrant writers sometimes assume different identities when working in English. Intending to present the world in the best possible light, they may make conscious choices to provide what they believe mainstream audiences want.[95] In that sense, a comment by Paul Celan, a noted German Jewish poet, can help us understand the significance and characteristics of Chinese-language literature in America. Asked why he still wrote in German after he had left Germany, Celan replied,

"Only in the mother tongue can one speak one's own truth. In a foreign tongue the poet lies."[96]

## Notes

1. The epigraph is from Zhuang Yin, "Yeben" [A visit at night], in *Haiwai huaren zuojia xiaoshuoxuan* [A selection of short stories by Chinese immigrant writers], ed. Li Li [Bao Lili], (Hong Kong: Joint, 1983), 310–11; A Ying [Qian Xingcun], ed., *Fan mei huagong jinyue wenxueji* [Anthology of Chinese literature against the American exclusion of Chinese laborers], (Shanghai: Zhonghua, 1960), 3–26.

2. Li Chunhui et al., *Meizhou huaqiao huaren shi* [A history of Chinese immigration to America], (Beijing: Dongfang, 1990), 250–56; Feng Ziping, *Haiwai chunqiu* [The Chinese diaspora], (Shanghai: Shangwu, 1993), 121–26; Karl Lo and Him Mark Lai, comps., *Chinese Newspapers Published in North America, 1854–1975* (Washington, D.C.: Center for Chinese Research Materials, 1977), 2–3. The Massachusetts Historical Society has a copy of the *Golden Hill News* in its collection.

3. Ednah Robinson, "Chinese Journalism in America," *Current Literature* 32 (Feb. 1902): 325.

4. For discussions of early Chinese-language newspapers in America, see Liu Pei-chi [Liu Baiji], *Meizhou huaqiao yishi* [A history of the Chinese in America], (Taipei: Liming, 1976), 427–52; and Robinson, "Chinese Journalism in America," 325–26. Also see Shih-shan Henry Tsai, *The Chinese Experience in America* (Bloomington: Indiana University Press, 1986), 128–32, 140; Gunther Barth, *Bitter Strength: A Study of the Chinese in the United States, 1850–1870* (Cambridge: Harvard University Press, 1964), 175, 178–213; and Corinne K. Hoexter, *From Canton to California: The Epic of Chinese Immigration* (New York: Four Winds Press, 1976), 168–99.

5. Hsiao-min Han, "Roots and Buds: The Literature of Chinese Americans," Ph.D. diss., Brigham Young University, 1980, 47–58; Karl K. Lo, "The Chinese Vernacular Presses in North America, 1900–1950: Their Role in Social Cohesion," *Annals of the Chinese Historical Society of the Pacific Northwest* (Seattle, 1984), 170–78.

6. I use "the Chinese world" to refer to countries and regions populated by the Chinese. It includes mainland China, Taiwan, Hong Kong, Singapore, and some regions in southeastern Asia. For more discussion of the significance of Chinese-language publications in Chinese immigrant communities, see Lynn Pan, *Sons of the Yellow Emperor: A History of the Chinese Diaspora* (New York: Kodansha International, 1994), 248–53; and Teresita Ang See, ed., *The Chinese Immigrants: Selected Writings of Professor Chinben See* (Manila: Kaisa Para, 1992). Also see Rong Futian, "Taiguo huaren tonghua wenti yanjiu" [A study of assimilation of the Chinese in Thailand], in *Dongnanya huaren shehui yanjiu* [The Chinese communities in Southeast Asia], ed. Li Yiyuan and Guo Zhenyu (Taipei: Academia Sinica, 1985), 2:1–52.

7. For discussions on the transnational nature of Chinese-language literature in America, see Hsin-sheng C. Kao, ed., *Nativism Overseas: Contemporary Chinese Women Writers* (Albany: State University of New York Press, 1993). Also see Aihwa Ong and Donald M. Nonini, eds., *Ungrounded Empires: The Cultural Politics of Modern Chinese Transnationalism* (New York: Routledge, 1997).

8. There are some exceptions in this regard. The growing interest in multilingualism and multiculturalism has brought more attention to Chinese-language writing in America. See, for example, Him Mark Lai, Genny Lim, and Judy Yung, *Island: Poetry and History of Chinese Immigrants on Angel Island, 1910–1940* (repr. Seattle: University of Washington Press, 1991); Marlon K. Hom, ed. and trans., *Songs of Gold Mountain: Cantonese Rhymes from San Francisco Chinatown* (Berkeley: University of California Press, 1987), and Hom, "A Case of Mutual Exclusion: Portrayals by Immigrant and American-born Chinese of Each Other in Literature," *Amerasia Journal* 11, no. 2 (1984): 29–45; Sau-ling Cynthia Wong, "Ethnicizing Gender: An Exploration of Sexuality as Sign in Chinese Immigrant Literature" in *Reading the Literatures of Asian America*, ed. Shirley Grok-lin Lim and Amy Ling (Philadelphia: Temple University Press, 1992), 111–29; and June Mei and Jean Pang Yip with Russell Leong, "The Bitter Society: *Ku Shehui*—A Translation, Chapters 37–46," *Amerasia Journal* 8, no. 1 (1981): 33–67.

9. Frank Chin et al., eds. *Aiiieeeee! An Anthology of Asian-American Writers* (Washington, D.C.: Howard University Press, 1973), xxi–xlvii; Shan Te-hsing, "Redefining Chinese American Literature," in *Multilingual America: Transnationalism, Ethnicity, and the Languages of America*, ed. Werner Sollors (New York: New York University Press, 1998), 112–23.

10. Han, "Roots and Buds," 1–106. Han's study is probably the most comprehensive coverage of early Chinese-language publications in America. For more discussions of early Chinese-language writing, see Him Mark Lai, *Cong huaqiao dao huaren* [From overseas Chinese to Chinese Americans], (Hong Kong: Joint, 1992), 46–66; and David Hsin-Fu Wand, ed., *Asian-American Heritage: An Anthology of Prose and Poetry* (New York: Washington Square Press, 1974), 17.

11. *San Francisco China New*, July 28, 1874, cited in Han, "Roots and Buds," 81–82. I was unable to find this issue of the newspaper.

12. Sui Sin Far also shared such a belief. In her story "Mrs. Spring Fragrance," a Chinese immigrant claims that "a keen eye for business . . . in America is certainly much more desirable than scholarship." Sui Sin Far, *Mrs. Spring Fragrance* (Chicago: A. C. McClurg, 1912), 17.

13. For example, Chinese-language newspapers published in southeastern Asia typically put cultural lessons ahead of daily news. Pan, *Sons of the Yellow Emperor*, 106–27; See, ed., *The Chinese Immigrants*, 119–63.

14. Liu, *A History of the Chinese in America*, 453–60; Lai, *From Overseas Chinese to Chinese Americans*, 46–48; Tsai, *The Chinese Experience in America*, 128.

15. Pan Yatun and Wang Yisheng, *Haiwai huawen wenxue mingjia* [Distinguished Chinese-language writers abroad], (Guangzhou: Jinan, 1994).

16. Chen Ruoxi [Chen Jo-hsi; Lucy Chen], "Haiwai zuojia he bentuxing" [Chinese immigrant writers and their sense of Chineseness], *Xianggang Wenxue* [Hong Kong Literature], Sept. 5, 1988, 21. The English translation of Chen's article appears in Kao, *Nativism Overseas*, 9–19. My translation of Chen's comments here is slightly different from that of Kao's.

17. Cited in Yan Huo [Pan Yaoming], *Haiwai Huaren Zuojia Luying* [Interviews with Chinese immigrant writers], (Hong Kong: Joint, 1984), 41–42.

18. Dominic Cheung [Zhang Cuo], *Huangjin lei* [Tears of gold], (Hong Kong: Joint, 1985), 1; Yan, *Interviews with Chinese Immigrant Writers*, 101.

19. Quoted in Yan, *Interviews with Chinese Immigrant Writers*, 18–19. Also see Nie

Hualing [Hua-ling Nieh], *Sangqing yu taohong* [Mulberry and peach], (Hong Kong: Joint, 1976).

20. C. N. Yang [Chen Ning Yang; Yang Zhenning], "Xu" [Preface], in Yu Lihua, *Kaoyan* [The ordeal], (repr. Hong Kong: Cosmos Books, 1993), i.

21. For discussion of the decline of Chinese influence on immigrants, see Tu Wei-ming, ed., *The Living Tree: The Changing Meaning of Being Chinese Today* (Stanford: Stanford University Press, 1994); and Lai, *From Overseas Chinese to Chinese Americans*, 273–82.

22. The statistics are calculated from the following sources: "Demographics in Southland: Chinese in the Southland," *Los Angeles Times,* June 29, 1997, A32; Edna L. Paisano, ed., *We the American . . . Asians* (Washington, D.C.: Bureau of the Census, 1993), 3; "Huaren renkou laiyuan" [Origins of the Chinese American population], *Nanjiazhou huaren gongshang dianhua haomabu* [Southern California Chinese telephone directory], (Los Angeles, 1994), 85; Roger Daniels, *Asian America: Chinese and Japanese in the United States since 1850* (Seattle: University of Washington Press, 1988), 190, 312; Harry H. L. Kitano and Roger Daniels, *Asian Americans: Emerging Minorities,* 2d ed. (Englewood Cliffs: Prentice-Hall, 1995), 171.

23. Roger Daniels, "The Asian-American Experience: The View from the 1990s," in *Multiculturalism and the Canon of American Culture,* ed. Hans Bak (Amsterdam: VU University Press, 1993), 141–42.

24. I use the term *student immigrant* to refer to a person who enters the United States on student or scholar visa but later adjusts to immigrant status.

25. Peter Kwong, *The New Chinatown* (New York: Noonday Press, 1987), 60–62. Also see Hsiang-shui Chen, *Chinatown No More* (Ithaca: Cornell University Press, 1992), 129; and Qian Ning, *Liuxu Meiguo* [Studying in the USA], (Nanjing: Jiangsu Wenyi, 1996), 277–300.

26. Him Mark Lai, "The Chinese Press in the United States and Canada Since World War II: A Diversity of Voices," *Chinese America: History and Perspectives* (San Francisco: Chinese Historical Society of America, 1990), 107–55.

27. Andy McCue, "Evolving Chinese Language Dailies Serve Immigrants in New York City," *Journalism Quarterly* 52 (Summer 1975): 272–76; Albert Scardino, "A Renaissance for Ethnic Papers," *New York Times,* Aug. 22, 1988, D1, D8; Philip P. Pan, "War of Words—Chinese Style: Papers Fight for Readers amid Rising Competition, Waining Ad Income" *Los Angeles Times,* Sept. 12, 1993, J1; Chen, "Chinese Immigrant Writers," 20.

28. Tang Degang, "Xinshi laozuzong yu disan wenyizhongxin" [Founding father of new poetry and the third center of literature], in *Haiwai huaren zuojia sanwenxuan* [A selection of essays by Chinese immigrant writers], ed. Mu Lingqi (Hong Kong: Joint, 1983), 139–61.

29. Cao Youfang, *Meiguo yueliang* [The American moon], (Hong Kong: Joint, 1986), 159–60.

30. *China: Nationwide Consumer Survey* (Princeton: Gallup Organization, 1994); [Los Angeles] *Zhongguo Daobao* [China Guide], Aug. 26, 1994, 8.

31. Daisy Chang-ling Tseng, "Chinese Newspapers and Immigrant Assimilation in America: A Local Exploratory Study," M.A. thesis, University of Pennsylvania, 1984, 67–70.

32. Yu Lihua, *Youjian zonlu, youjian zonlu* [Seeing the palm trees again], (repr. Beijing: Youyi, 1984), 270.

33. Maxine Hong Kingston, *China Men* (repr. New York: Ballantine Books, 1981), 250.

34. Quoted in Werner Sollors, "Immigrants and Other Americans," in *Columbia Literary History of the United States*, ed. Emory Elliot (New York: Columbia University Press, 1988), 579.

35. Hsien-yung Pai [Bai Xianyong], "Wandering Chinese: Themes of Exile in Taiwan Fiction," *Iowa Review* 7 (Spring–Summer 1976): 205–12; Li Li, "Xu" [Preface], in *Haiwai huaren zuojia xiaoshuoxuan* [A selection of short stories by Chinese immigrant writers], ed. Li Li [Bao Lili], (Hong Kong: Joint, 1983), 1–4; Nie Hualing, *Heise, heise, zuimeili de yanse* [Black, black, the most beautiful color], (Hong Kong: Joint, 1983), 107; Chen, "Chinese Immigrant Writers," 20.

36. Joe Chung Fong, "Transnational Newspapers: The Making of the Post–1965 Globalized/Localized San Gabriel Valley Chinese Community," *Amerasia* 22, no. 3 (1996): 65–77.

37. Cao Guilin [Glen Cao], *Beijingren zai niuyue* [A Beijinger in New York], (Beijing: Zhongguo Wennian, 1991); Zhou Li [Julia Z. Fochler], *Manhadun de zhongguo nuren* [Manhattan's China lady], (Beijing: Beijing Chubanshe, 1992); Zhang Xiaowu [Michael X. Zhang], *Wozai meiguo dang lushi* [My experience as an American lawyer], (Beijing: Beijing Chubanshe, 1994). *A Beijinger in New York* has been adapted into a popular television series and been translated into English and published in the United States. *Manhattan's China Lady* sold out a hundred thousand copies in two months, and *My Experience as an American Lawyer* underwent three printings within a month.

38. Pan, *Sons of the Yellow Emperor*, 372; Lai, *From Overseas Chinese to Chinese Americans*, 423–31. Most Chinese-language works are printed in Hong Kong because of lower manufacturing costs there. The publishing business of American ethnic groups has long been transnational. For example, Lithuanian American writers historically had their works printed or published in Prussia and then shipped to North America for sale. See Werner Sollors, "Introduction: After the Culture Wars; or, from 'English Only' to 'English Plus,'" in Sollors, *Multilingual America*, 1–13.

39. Of course, writing in Chinese has its own set of problems, and Chinese-language authors may feel restricted because of the social codes of traditional Chinese values. See my discussion of this issue in subsequent pages.

40. Socioeconomically, Chinese Americans have now been divided into two distinctive groups: "uptown" and "downtown." The former are Chinese professionals who reside in suburban towns and are well integrated into mainstream society, whereas the latter are predominantly Chinese immigrant laborers struggling for survival in isolated and poverty-stricken urban ghettos. Kwong, *The New Chinatown*, 5.

41. Yi Li [Pan Xiumei], "Duotai" [Abortion], in *Haiwai huaren zuojia xiaoshuoxuan* [A selection of short stories by Chinese immigrant writers], ed. Li Li [Bao Lili], (Hong Kong: Joint, 1983), 84–116.

42. Paul R. Spickard, *Mixed Blood: Intermarriage and Ethnic Identity in Twentieth-Century America* (Madison: University of Wisconsin Press, 1989), 3–20.

43. See the discussion on interracial marriage in chapter 3.

44. Yu Lihua, *Fujia de ernumen* [Sons and daughters of the Fu family], (repr. Hong Kong: Cosmos, 1994), 48.

45. Pan, *The Sons of the Yellow Emperor*, 122–23.

46. Yu Lihua, "Erxi" [A childish game], reprinted in Yu Lihua, *Huichang xianxinji* [Scandals at a conference], (Taipei: Zhiwen, 1972), 51–75.

47. Yu Guangzhong, "Xu" [Preface], and Yu Lihua, "Houji" [Afterword], both in Yu Lihua, *Huichang xianxinji* [Scandals at a conference], (Taipei: Zhiwen, 1972), 3, 200.

48. Zhuang, "A Visit at Night," 310–11.

49. Timothy P. Fong, *The First Suburban Chinatown: The Remaking of Monterey Park, California* (Philadelphia: Temple University Press, 1994), 157–72.

50. Li Li, "Preface," 1–4.

51. Author interview with Yu Lihua, Albany, N.Y., Oct. 13, 1994. Also see Yu, *Seeing the Palm Trees Again,* 158, 270; and Chen, "Chinese Immigrant Writers," 21.

52. Yu Lihua, "Sorrow at the End of the Yangtze River," *UCLA Review* (March 1957): 1–13.

53. Author interview with Yu Lihua. Also see Yu, *The Ordeal,* 1; Huang Wenxiang, *Oumei jiechu huayi nuxing* [Outstanding women of Chinese ancestry in Europe and America], (Hong Kong: Shanghai Book, 1992), 200–201, 206–26; and Yan, *Interviews with Chinese Immigrant Writers,* 32–53. Of course, it is necessary to separate commercial interests from institutionalized racism. Publishers may have rejected Yu Lihua's work for profit-making reasons.

54. Barth, *Bitter Strength,* 157–82. Also see Pan, *Sons of the Yellow Emperor,* 246–74.

55. The theory of "relative functionalism" explains why Asian Americans tend to concentrate in certain fields such as academia. It represents a primarily pragmatic strategy to gain a foothold in the mainstream job market because Asian Americans find that anti-Asian sentiments make it difficult to move upward in other fields. Stanley Sue, "Asian-American Educational Achievements: A Phenomenon in Search of an Explanation," *American Psychologist* 45 (Aug. 1990): 913–20.

56. Sau-ling Cynthia Wong, *Reading Asian American Literature: from Necessity to Extravagance* (Princeton: Princeton University Press, 1993), 177, 180–82; Stanford Lyman, *Chinese Americans* (New York: Random House, 1974), 144. The situation has changed since the publication of Maxine Hong Kingston's *Woman Warrior* in 1976. With the significance of Asian American literature receiving greater recognition, the interest in Chinese American literature has risen dramatically (chapter 7).

57. Chin et al., eds., *Aiiieeeee,* vii–xlvii; Jeffery Paul Chan et al., eds., *The Big Aiiieeeee! An Anthology of Chinese American and Japanese American Literature* (New York: Meridian, 1991), xi–xvi, 1–51.

58. Monfoon Leong, *Number One Son* (San Francisco: East/West, 1975), vii–xiv; Frank Chin and Jeffery Paul Chan, "Racist Love," in *Seeing through Shuck,* ed. Richard Kostelanetz (New York: Ballantine Books, 1972), 77.

59. Quoted in Carlton Sagara, "David Mura's Poetry Links Generations," [Boston] *Sampan,* Nov. 16, 1990, 7.

60. Author interview with Yu Lihua. Also see Chen, "Chinese Immigrant Writers," 21. Their views are strikingly similar to those Frank Chin makes about Chinese American bestsellers (chapter 7).

61. Yu Qing, *Qicai yinu: Zhang Ailing* [Eileen Chang: A talented woman writer], (Jinan: Shandong Huabao, 1995), 122.

62. Anchee Min, *Red Azalea* (New York: Pantheon Books, 1994). I received the information from several friends and colleagues.

63. Shen Zhengrou, "Li Qingyang lishi xiaoshuo xinzuo *Taiping Tianguo* chuban" [C. Y. Lee has written another historical novel *Taiping Heavenly Kingdom*], [New York] *Shijie Ribao* [World Journal], June 18, 1990, A2.

64. Wing-tsit Chan, "Lin Yutang, Critic and Interpreter," *College English* 8 (Jan. 1947): 163–69.

65. Lin Yutang, *My Country and My People* (repr. New York: John Day, 1937), copyright page. Also see Mao-chu Lin, "Identity and Chinese-American Experiences: A Study of Chinatown American Literature since World War II," Ph.D. diss., University of Minnesota, 1987, 73–84.

66. "Bushi shouci guohui lianxi huiyi yanshuo yinyong Lin Yutang *Wuguo yu wumin yu*" [President Bush quotes Lin Yutang's *My Country and My People* in his first State of the Union address to Congress], [New York] *Meizhou Huaqiao Ribao* [Chinese American Daily], Feb. 11, 1989, A1. Also see Pan and Wang, *Distinguished Chinese-Language Writers Abroad*, 240.

67. Lin Yutang, *Chinatown Family* (New York: John Day, 1948), 148.

68. Chin et al., eds., *Aiiieeeee*, x.

69. Ibid., x–xii, xiv; Elaine H. Kim, *Asian American Literature: An Introduction to the Writings and Their Social Context* (Philadelphia: Temple University Press, 1982), 27–29, 104–8. Chinese critics in Lin Yutang's time did not hold his English writing in high estimation either. They thought it elegant in style but superficial in substance. For example, in his novel *Fortress Besieged* (1947) Qian Zhongshu, a renowned Chinese writer and critic, makes humorous yet biting mention of Lin's English writing. He places *My Country and My People* alongside books such as *How to Gain a Husband and Keep Him* and lists them as the favorite readings of a daughter of a Chinese comprador in Shanghai in the late 1930s. Some Chinese critics also dubbed *My Country and My People* as *Selling Country and Selling People* because, phonetically, "my" in Chinese has the same sound as the word "selling" [*mai*]. Qian, *Weicheng* [Fortress besieged], (repr. Beijing: Renmin, 1991), 42; Lin Taiyi [Anor Lin], *Lin Yutang zhuan* [Biography of Lin Yutang], (Beijing: Zhongguo Xiju, 1994), 136.

70. Lin Yutang, "Xinnian zhimeng—zhongguo zhimeng" [New year's dream: My wishes for China], [Shanghai] *Dongfang Zazhi* [Eastern Magazine], 1933, reprinted in Lin Taiyi, *Biography of Lin Yutang*, 104–6, emphasis added. It is significant that Lin Yutang used the term *yang guizi* [foreign devils] in his Chinese writing to refer to Westerners.

71. Reprinted in Lin Taiyi, *Biography of Lin Yutang*, 109–11.

72. Lin Yutang, "Impressions on Reaching America, " in R. David Arkush and Leo Ou-fan Lee, trans. and eds., *Land without Ghosts: Chinese Impressions of America from the Mid-nineteenth Century to the Present* (Berkeley: University of California Press, 1989), 161–62.

73. Wan Pingjin, *Lin Yutang lun* [A study of Lin Yutang], (Xi'an: Renmin, 1987), 15–26.

74. Wan, *A Study of Lin Yutang*, 29–32. Also see Pan and Wang, *Distinguished Chinese-Language Writers Abroad*, 237–46.

75. Wan, *A Study of Lin Yutang*, 29.

76. Lin Taiyi, *Biography of Lin Yutang*, 158, 165, 177.

77. Ibid., 131–49.

78. Lin Yutang, *My Country and My People*, xviii, emphasis added.

79. Helen Foster Snow, *My China Years* (New York: William Morrow, 1984), 121.

80. Lao She and Lin Yutang were close friends. It was no accident that some of Lao She's most important works were first published in magazines founded or edited by Lin Yutang.

81. Evan King is the nom de plume of Robert Spencer Ward. Reynal and Hitchcock is a branch of the John Day Company.

82. Hamilton Basso, "New Bottles, Old Wine," *The New Yorker*, Aug. 11, 1945, 61.

83. Harrison Smith, "Out of the Streets of China," *Saturday Review of Literature*, July 28, 1945, 12.

84. Quoted in George Kao, ed., *Two Writers and the Cultural Revolution* (Hong Kong: Chinese University Press, 1980), 38. Also see Smith, "Out of the Streets of China," 12.

85. Lao She [Lau Shaw, Shu Qingchun], *Rickshaw*, trans. Jean M. James (Honolulu: University of Hawaii Press, 1979), 249. Also see Perry Link, "End of *Rickshaw Boy,*" in *Two Writers and the Cultural Revolution*, ed. Kao, 50.

86. Lao She [Lau Shaw, Shu Qingchun], *Rickshaw Boy,* trans. Evan King (New York: Reynal and Hitchcock, 1945), 384.

87. Wang Runhua, *Lao She xiaoshuo xinlun* [New studies of Lao She's fiction], (Shanghai: Shulin, 1995), 216. Personal memories have not provided much help on this issue. George Kao said that Lao She told him King wrote the last two chapters himself, but Lao She's widow, Hu Jieqing, mentioned nothing of that kind in her memoir, other than a brief yet ambiguous comment: "So far we haven't got much information on Lao She's work during his stay in America." Lin Yutang's daughter, who saw Lao She frequently in New York at that time, has recalled that he seemed pleased by the popularity of *Rickshaw Boy* in America. Kao, ed., *Two Writers and the Cultural Revolution*, 30; Hu Jieqing and Shu Yi, *Sanji Lao She* [Random notes on Lao She], (Beijing: Beijing Renmin, 1986), 281; Lin Taiyi, *Biography of Lin Yutang*, 188.

88. Robert S. Ward [Evan King], *Hong Kong under Japan's Occupation: A Case Study in the Enemy Techniques of Control* (Washington, D.C.: Department of Commerce, 1943).

89. Kao, ed., *Two Writers and the Cultural Revolution*, 38.

90. Hu and Shu, *Random Notes on Lao She*, 278–89; Lao She [Lau Shaw, Shu Qingchun], *The Yellow Storm*, trans. Ida Pruitt (New York: Harcourt, Brace, 1951).

91. The discrepancy between *Rickshaw Boy* in Chinese and English resembles that in writings by Abraham Cahan. A renowned Jewish American writer, Cahan made changes in his Yiddish novel when he turned it into English. Sollors, "After the Culture Wars," 1–13.

92. Hu and Shu, *Random Notes on Lao She*, 154.

93. Ibid., 282–83; Wang, *New Studies of Lao She's Fiction*, 211–13, 216–18.

94. Weng Shaoqiu, *Wozai jiujinshan sishinian* [My forty years in San Francisco], (Shanghai: Renmin, 1988), 36.

95. Discrepancies between Chinese and English versions of the same work can also be found in bilingual Chinese American newspapers, largely because they aim at different readers. For example, the English version of *Sampan,* a Chinese-English weekly published in Boston, usually contains reports on Chinese and Asian cultural events and interviews of Chinese and Asian American celebrities; its Chinese edition focuses more on news about the local Chinese communities.

96. Quoted in John Felstiner, *Paul Celan: Poet, Survivor, Jew* (New Haven: Yale University Press, 1995), 46. Of course, Celan's comment comes from the context of a Jewish writer using the German language after the Holocaust. Furthermore, although there are writers who tend to tell the truth in their mother tongues, others may more likely do that in acquired languages. Sollors, "After the Culture Wars," 1–13.

*"Your husband won't allow you to do that [sterilization]," Mrs. Fu said to Mrs. Chen.*
*"I don't care if he objects. I am the one who suffers [abortion]."*
*"What if you want more children later?" Nifeng [another woman worker] asked.*
*"More children? Three kids are enough for me to be a slave all my life. When they grow up, I'll get old, too. I don't want to condemn my entire life to suffering for them," Mrs. Chen replied.*
—Yi Li

## Immigration Blues: Themes and Subject Matter in Chinese-Language Literature since the 1960s

In identifying themes that are closely related to Chinese America life and affect it, Chinese-language writers have taken on the role of spokespersons for immigrants, and their work is significant to the study of the Chinese American experience.[1] For those who strive to interpret concerns of Chinese immigrants in American society, their literature, especially its themes and subject matter, provides a wealth of information and descriptive detail and offers a valuable conceptual framework. Within that framework, the forces and thoughts that shape and influence the lives of Chinese immigrants can be understood. Although varied in thematic scope and covering a wide range of subject matter, in a broad outline, the work of Chinese-language writers is shaped by three factors: race, class, and gender. *The Ordeal,* a critically acclaimed novel by Yu Lihua on Chinese American academics, is one example of a book defined by those factors.

## *The Ordeal:* The Chinese American Experience in Academe and Views on Jewish Americans

By any count, a disproportionately large number of works by Chinese-language writers deals with the lives of Chinese American faculty and students, especially immigrants. Their strong interest in dissecting the fate of Chinese academics is both personal and communal. Being former student immigrants, they have taken it as their mission to define and reveal the Chinese American experience in the academic world.[2] Furnished with firsthand knowledge gained from personal experience, they have explored the lives of Chinese American academics with affectionate and unsentimental familiarity.

The interest in Chinese American academics also represents an attempt to examine a significant aspect of the broader intellectual milieu of the Chinese community. Academic careers are so pervasive and deeply ingrained in the lives of Chinese immigrants that writing about them speaks to several central issues. Although not offering lucrative occupations, academic careers seem ideal places for aspiring student immigrants from the Chinese world in the overall socioeconomic structure of American society.[3] To anyone conversant with upward mobility and Chinese immigrants' occupational patterns, the significance of the growing Chinese presence in academe evokes ready associations with that of African Americans in sports and the entertainment industry. It is no accident that Chinese Americans have produced large numbers of outstanding scholars, including six Nobel Laureates in science.[4] Indeed, it is primarily their academic accomplishments that have made the Chinese seem a "model minority" in American society.

The relatively large Chinese American presence in academe is only a very recent phenomenon, however. In his fictionalized autobiography *East Goes West* (1937), Younghill Kang (1903–72), a Korean immigrant, recalled sarcastically that Chinese academics before World War II were unable to find positions in their fields and had to wait tables in Chinatown restaurants, using their education for calculating tips: "There were nine waiters [in the Chinese restaurant]. Among these were three Ph.D.s from Columbia, and two more to be next June. . . . One of the waiters, a recent Ph.D., was a real M.D. as well. He studied medicine in Peking, and had come over to take Public Health at Johns Hopkins. He had finished his work, and now preferred waiting on tables. . . . Certainly the boys made tip-getting a matter of fact. So anybody who did not tip well had to be marked. Anybody who did tip well also got marked, just as on a dean's list."[5]

In reality, Chinese student immigrants entered academia in the post–World War II era because they were in the right place at the right time. It was a decidedly golden era in American educational history, and it coincided with the rise of the civil rights movement. The rapid development of higher education in the United States during the 1950s and 1960s and the struggle waged by civil rights activists paved the way for the Chinese in American institutions of higher education.[6]

As they earn distinction in the professions and in academe, Chinese Americans, along with other Asians, are lauded by the media as the latest success story of the American dream. One viewpoint even holds that having an Asian background is a blessing in America's job market. "[The] erstwhile 'yellow peril' is fast becoming the 'yellow blessing,'" claims one Asian immigrant, "because personal characteristics such as education and experience have become more important and institutional barriers no longer exist."[7]

Chinese-language literature shows, however, that the rosy picture is far from true. Although merit has become more important in determining individual success, American reality is still disappointing to those who dream of a level playing field and a color-blind society. Although the "iron cage" (outright exclusion and overtly institutionalized racism) has been dismantled, the glass ceiling (covert, sinister prejudice) remains a problem for the Chinese and for other Asian Americans. Studies conducted by the Census Bureau show that Asian professionals, both immigrants and the native-born, make about 13 percent less in median income than their Caucasian counterparts and have more difficulty breaking into top-ranking administrative and executive positions.[8] Clearly, prejudice has not entirely disappeared, nor have ignorance or bigotry.

Likely the most influential work of its kind, Yu Lihua's novel *The Ordeal* describes the experiences of Chinese Americans in academe and the consequences of the glass ceiling. First published in 1974, the novel centers around the agony caused by the tenure review of Zhong Leping, a physics professor at a state university on the East Coast. The novel is concerned with Zhong's growing awareness of the realities of race and his struggle to find the will to challenge the unfair tenure review process.

A former student immigrant from Taiwan, Zhong is intended to be the epitome of a Chinese American academic. As an accomplished scientist and conscientious teacher, he is a dedicated scholar and never doubts the fairness of the tenure review process. Yet despite his strong record in research and teaching, he is denied tenure because Arnold, the department chair, wants to cut the budget.[9]

Zhong, stunned, looks at Arnold's cold blue eyes and blond hair and cannot believe what has happened: "[Zhong] counts his research papers published over the past two years: fifteen. Tenure appointment is usually based on one's performance in the following areas: research, teaching, and service to the institution. Measured by all three criteria, he is as good as any of his colleagues. . . . Why is he the only one being denied tenure among the three who are currently under tenure review in the department?"[10]

Zhong begins to suspect that it is his racial background that makes tenure appointment unattainable. Yet he still wants to bury his head in the sand. He tries to convince himself that the problem can best be handled by being humble and maintaining a low profile. Indeed, according to the code of traditional Chinese culture under which he was brought up, Zhong does the right thing. "The nest of heaven may have big holes but it never leaks," Chinese philosophy preaches. Good behavior will eventually be rewarded while evil is punished, hence there is no need to fight.

Unfortunately, Zhong's dream is shattered, and his grievance goes unheeded. Outraged and deeply hurt, he finally decides to take control of his fate. Encouraged by a sympathetic Jewish colleague, he hires a Jewish lawyer to appeal his case and finally wins an ugly lawsuit. The victory is proof that assertiveness is necessary in a society that mistakes passivity for submission. It also demonstrates that a new generation of Chinese immigrants will be determined to fight for their rights. It is for this reason that the novel is considered an effective and striking social commentary and has resonated with Chinese immigrant readers.[11]

The bitter fight, however, exacts an enormous price: Zhong's health is ruined, his wife is alienated, and his dream is doomed. In that sense, his experience of tenure review lives up to the novel's title, *The Ordeal,* and symbolically suggests the painful cost Chinese immigrants may have to pay to gain acceptance by mainstream society.

What happens during Zhong's tenure review etches a vivid picture of the hypocrisy of the power establishment of the academic world, the same environment that Jane Smiley describes in her bestseller *Moo* (1995). It is an apt footnote to a comment allegedly made by Henry Kissinger when he taught at Harvard University in the late 1950s: "Academic politics is the dirtiest politics because the stakes are so small." Yu Lihua's novel, however, is more than a social exposé of the schemes and vanities of academic politics. Furthermore, although the author has incorporated some personal elements to give the characters depth and complexity, the novel is not quasi-autobiographic.[12] Rather, it should be read as the author's attempt to report and record the collective experience of the Chinese American academics of her generation, especially that of student immigrants.

Yu Lihua's choice of the seemingly formal and rule-governed process of tenure review as the focus of her novel is significant. Given their emphasis on academic careers, it is natural that Chinese immigrants deem tenure appointment to be a means of guaranteed freedom and employment security, awe-inspiring enough to symbolize the realization of their American dream. By depicting the racial discrimination inflicted on Zhong during his tenure review, the author thus provides an authentic account of the suffering of Chinese American academics and transforms the novel into an anguished, compassionate statement about the need for racial justice in academia.

Zhong's background as a scientist also adds powerful irony to his "ordeal." Statistics show that Chinese student immigrants are heavily concentrated in the sciences and engineering.[13] Among the things that control their pursuit of the sciences, however, are not opportunities to realize individual ambitions but the perception that these arenas offer a world of open and fair competition. They believe that the nature of scientific research enables them to be measured on merit rather than skin color and that the sciences provide them with a better chance to be treated with respect. That is why Zhong's failure to receive a fair tenure review as a physicist touches especially hard on the Chinese immigrant dream and reflects more conspicuously the impact of the American dilemma on minorities, who must live with two different systems of justice.

Surely, not everyone agrees with the author's viewpoint, but many would share her belief that, like Asian application to some elite universities, Chinese and Asian American academics are perhaps judged by harsher criteria in tenure reviews and are more likely to be brought into colleges and universities and then pushed out through "revolving doors." Stories of individual Asian Americans encountering barriers to tenure are common. Although personal accounts may not always be reliable, many reports indicate that denial of tenure occurs more frequently for Asian Americans than other ethnic or racial group.[14]

Why Chinese and Asian Americans have more difficulty receiving tenure is a topic of considerable debate. Some suggest that they are overrepresented in academe and have become unwitting victims of a hidden quota system. Others believe there is a penalty for people who keep to themselves. Being "quiet and unsociable," Asian American academics, the majority of whom are immigrants, do not push as hard as other groups for raises and promotions and are victimized by the system. The American bias against those who are unaggressive thus could be blamed.[15] What happens to Zhong in *The Ordeal*, however, appears to suggest that at least in some cases racial prejudice works against Chinese and Asian Americans in the tenure review system. The evidence of the invisible bias of the glass ceiling is obvious: Despite his accomplishments, Zhong is the only one in the department who is denied tenure.

Ironically, instead of singing praises for how justice prevails, the author distills a dissenting message in Zhong's story—she surprises readers by putting a twist on his victory. At the end of the novel, Zhong decides to give up his hard-won tenure appointment and move to a smaller, more obscure institution to avoid further confrontation with the vengeful department chair. His lack of confidence about claiming his victory leaves unanswered questions and seems to indicate that nonwhites who are under intense pressure may at some deep level become a party to their own capitulation to racial bias.

Zhong's decision must also be seen, however, as an earnest attempt to come to terms with reality; the hostility of departmental and university authorities has made his future doubtful. As a critic points out, the fact that the department chair is unapologetic (he refuses to shake Zhong's hand at a departmental party after the event) suggests that racial animosity will continue despite Zhong's willingness to compromise.[16] Such recognition forces Zhong to give up the victory he has gained through the lawsuit. He is realistic about the odds against him. Transferring to another institution, Zhong reasons, would enable him to calibrate his emotional commitment and protect himself from revenge from the university's administration. Such rationalization, albeit disappointing for his supporters, is close to the truth of Asian American life. For example, in a well-publicized case, Michael Thornton, a Japanese American formerly on the faculty of an Ivy League university, decided to resign rather than to fight the racial prejudice he encountered, because he did not want to stay in a hostile work environment. "It has nothing to do with reality and everything to do with the perception of reality," Thornton commented bitterly in an interview.[17]

While Zhong's struggle for tenure appointment is the major theme of *The Ordeal*, what is equally engaging is the author's portrayal of the Chinese professor's relationship with Jewish colleagues. It brings out another important theme in Chinese-language literature: Chinese views of Jewish Americans. In fact, the novel promises a point of entry to those interested in that topic.

Yu Lihua leaves little doubt about her favorable opinion of Jewish Americans. They play a critical role in Zhong's uphill battle for tenure. It is Bailyn, his Jewish colleague, who first helps him at a critical moment: "If I were you, I'd battle it to the end. . . . I suggest you submit the case to the faculty grievance committee and spend some money to hire a lawyer to sue them" (*Ordeal* 229, 244). Similarly, Levy, Zhong's lawyer, eloquently challenges the unfair tenure review in the hearing. He even provides virtually free legal service: "Don't worry about my fee. When we finish the case, you can pay me a token amount of money. I don't treat every client this way. You are an exception because I am interested in your case" (250).

Yu Lihua's positive accounts of relationships between the Chinese and Jews in *The Ordeal* is by no means unusual but recur frequently in Chinese-language literature.[18] Bai Xianyong's "Night Tune" (1979), Chen Ruoxi's *Breaking Out* (1983), Yi Li's "Professor Fu Doesn't Believe It" (1987), and Zhang Xiguo's "Circumcision" (1971), treating Jewish Americans either as major themes or as background characters, are a few examples.[19] Comments on Jews are even found in commercial Chinese writing; for example, a Chinese-language advertisement for tourism in Southern California contains a favorable account of the Jewish neighborhood of Los Angeles.[20] The wide coverage of Jewish Americans in Chinese-language literature leaves us with a key contextual and analytical question: Why are there such strong interests in Jews in writings about Chinese in America? Certainly, these stories, written in Chinese, are not intended to appeal to Jewish readers or the general public.

Chinese interest in Jewish Americans has many ramifications. In part it reflects Chinese curiosity about Jewish American culture, which seems to resemblance that of the Chinese, but it would be an oversimplification to treat such interest as mere hyperbole about the parallels between the groups. In essence, Chinese perception and portrayals of Jewish Americans exemplify what anthropologists call the "performance of ethnic identity."[21] Chinese-language writers tend to use the Jewish experience as a mirror image against which to redefine and compare their own.[22] Zhong's comments to Levy about Jewish Americans' strong sense of self-esteem illustrate this point: "I agree with you that Chinese and Jews share lots of things in common, but we are far behind you in terms of community unity. . . . There are many Chinese who possess an inferiority complex. This mentality causes them to attack and disparage their own people in front of whites in order to demonstrate how 'un-Chinese' they have become" (*Ordeal* 260, 294).

Coincidentally, parallels between the cultural values of the Chinese and the Jews (such as an emphasis on education) and between their American experiences have long been subjects of scholarly studies and media coverage. In an article "Jew and Chinaman," published in *The North American Review* in 1912, the author carefully examined similarities between the experiences of the two groups in American society and concluded that "[the] Chinaman is the coming Jew [in America]."[23] Others made the same comparison. "I've heard mentioned countless times that there's a bit of Jew in every Chinese person and a bit of Chinese in every Jew," said Rabbi Shmuel Lopin.[24] Theodore von Karman, a Jewish immigrant and pioneer in aviation and space science, mentioned in his autobiography a conversation with a Jewish colleague at the California Institute of Technology: "I remember that Professor Paul S. Epstein of the Physics Department, a great theoretician, once said to me: 'Your student H. S. Tsien is in one of my classes. He is brilliant.' '*Ja*, he is good,' I replied. 'Tell me,' Epstein said with a twinkle in his eye. 'Do you think he has Jewish blood?' "[25]

Historically, however, racist views worldwide have tended to equate the Chinese with the Jews. According to scholars of the Chinese diaspora, anti-Chinese forces in Europe and Southeast Asia liked to place the Chinese in a "Jewish context" in order to solicit popular sentiment against them. One police officer in London remarked during an inspection of Chinatown in 1902, "I had always considered some of the Jewish inhabitants of Whitechapel to be the worst type of humanity I had ever seen." But, he concluded, the Chinese were even "worse" than the Jews.[26] "Jews of the East," a notorious document said to be written by the king of Thailand in 1914, charged that the Chinese, like the Jews, would "endure any privation and perform the vilest deeds [for money]" and accused them of "bleeding Southeast Asia dry."[27]

Considering the anti-Semitic tone of campaigns directed against the Chinese, it is not surprising that many Jews sided with them during the exclusion era (1882–1943). Studies show that although, as a community, Jewish Americans did not associate with the Chinese, they in general expressed sympathy for the suffering of Chinese immigrants during the anti-Chinese movement.[28] In *The Ordeal*, Yu Lihua also indicates that it is the memory of being victimized by racism that makes Zhong's Jewish colleagues feel obliged to support him. Although it varies in particulars, Zhong's agony during the unfair tenure review resembles the Jewish experience in academe of an earlier era. In her autobiography, Adrienne Rich, for example, has provided a touching account of how her father, the first Jew on the faculty of the Johns Hopkins Medical School in the 1930s, was victimized by the biased tenure system.[29]

Understanding that they had been victimized by various forms of bigotry throughout history, Jewish Americans forged a close alliance with minorities in the civil rights movement.[30] That alliance has subsequently changed though, and new studies argue that white ethnic groups may now be more bigoted toward minorities than they have been previously.[31] During the late 1960s, however, when Yu Lihua was writing *The Ordeal*, Jewish Americans were known for being committed to racial harmony and social justice. A comment Bailyn makes to Zhong illustrates that point, as well as the perceived kinship between Chinese and Jewish spiritual life: "Don't be so appreciative." Bailyn says, "I am doing this for justice." Then he adds with a smile, "How about praying to God? Oh, you're not a Christian, neither am I. Otherwise, I'd pray for you" (*Ordeal* 196).

A careful analysis of works by Chinese immigrant writers further reveals that to various degrees and in different ways their observations of Jewish Americans are an attempt to deal with an ever-present and pressing issue—what it means to be a Chinese American in the age of ethnic consciousness. That is apparent in their effort to place the Jewish experience within a coherent overview of how

immigrants can preserve their heritage in American life. The nature of multiracial and multicultural American society has tied Chinese immigrants to the perpetually simmering, if sometimes submerged, issues of cultural and ethnic identity. Although the melting pot metaphor is no longer a dominant social paradigm,
the pressure of Americanization on immigrants remains strong. Most Chinese
immigrants feel that as a marginal group they must choose between being ghettoized and being assimilated—not much of a choice. For this reason, they want
to find a point of balance in the invisible see-saw between being Chinese and
being American. It is such an attempt to explore a new path for the Chinese in
American life that turns Chinese-language writers to Jewish Americans, whose
experience and status are not entirely different from theirs.

Stories about Chinese immigrants by Chen Ruoxi, one of the most popular
Chinese-language writers, are a good example. In her novella "To the Other Side
of the Pacific" (1980), which focuses on Chinese immigrants in San Francisco,
Chen expresses admiration for how Jewish Americans emphasize tradition within
assimilation and successfully maintain their cultural values. This is shown in lively
discussions at family gatherings. Her words are so lucid and compelling that they
are worth quoting here:

> Yizhen can't find any words to argue against [granny's] comment. Jews in
> America are known for their adherence to tradition and their sense of com-
> munity, and they are also highly successful in almost every aspect of life. . . .
> "How about Jews?" Suzhong suddenly raises the question. The topic imme-
> diately catches everyone's attention. They all make comments on Jewish
> Americans. While some are critical, most are favorable. Lao Qiao says: "Jewish
> Americans have a strong sense of unity. I think this is the first and foremost
> thing we should learn from them because we Chinese are a pile of grains of
> sand." Nina suggests: "Chinese should definitely adopt the Jewish strategy
> to attain success. Jews have become Americans but they also remain a hun-
> dred percent Jews in ethnic identity. Isn't this something Chinese immigrants
> always dream of?"[32]

In contrast to Chen Ruoxi's "To the Other Side of the Pacific," "Circumcision" (1971), a widely read story by Zhang Xiguo, is more symbolic yet subtler
in its use of Jewish Americans as role models for Chinese immigrants. Vivid in
tone and accurate in image, the story concerns a bris, the traditional Jewish practice of circumcision, and its impact on the protagonist's ethnic consciousness.

Like Zhong in *The Ordeal,* Song Daduan, the protagonist of the story, is a
former student immigrant. But unlike Zhong, his position as chair of the political science department in a large university indicates his solid, comfortable niche

in the academic hierarchy. Thoroughly Americanized, Song has little interest in Chinese American affairs and strongly opposes his daughter's involvement in activities organized by Chinese students on campus. After witnessing a bris in a Jewish colleague's home, however, "[Song] cannot calm down tonight. What he saw this afternoon has greatly stirred him—the baby's tender and red penis appears again and again in his sight. The baby's penis looks weak and tiny with the skin at the tip peeled off. . . . But Song is aware of the potential strength of the small penis, and he can picture its magnificent shape years later: growing from a defenseless bloody flesh sprout to a giant and powerful root of life."[33] Shocked, he begins to ponder whether to reevaluate his attitude toward Chinese tradition. The circumcision has provided a powerful awakening for Song's long-repressed ethnic consciousness.

The nostalgic account of the protagonist's reviving memories of his early life in China makes the story somewhat oversentimental, but the allegory of the circumcised penis is blunt and unsparing. The story calls to mind a traditional Chinese belief: You cannot deny your ethnic roots because they are intrinsic to your racial descent. What makes the story remarkable is the author's definitive message: As with being Jewish, being Chinese means being a part of an old and valuable culture. If Jews can carry out an ancient tradition in postmodern American society, Chinese immigrants (called by Gish Jen "the new Jews") should be capable of doing likewise.[34] But how can Chinese succeed at this? Zhang Xiguo, like the protagonist in his story, leaves it an open question.

Although they fail to articulate a specific solution to the problem of assimilation, the fact that many prominent Chinese-language writers are impressed by the Jewish American experience is noteworthy. Jewish Americans are important to Chinese immigrants not merely as exemplars of an economically and politically successful group but also because they represent a commitment to affirming ethnic identity within assimilation. If the Jewish experience strikes familiar chords and elicits responses from Chinese immigrant writers, it is because they find that Jews have altered the rule of Americanization and given it new meaning. It no longer equates with assimilation into the WASP culture; rather, it means integration into a diversified society while maintaining one's own roots.[35] As Yu Lihua concluded during an interview, "Jewish Americans have set up schools in their communities all over the country so that their children can study Jewish culture and religion. In many aspects, we Chinese in America are very similar to the Jews. So when we see that Jewish Americans are not only highly successful [in American life] but also able to carry out their cultural traditions, we would like to use them as an example."[36]

Of course, there are occasionally pockets of ambivalence in the coverage of the Jewish experience by Chinese-language writers, reflecting that they are not totally free from the influence of racial bias in American society. In *The Ordeal,* having learned that her husband has hired a Jewish lawyer, Zhong's wife complains, "How can we afford to pay a Jewish lawyer? . . . I mean, Jewish lawyers are usually very expensive. Have you made sure how much he would charge you?" (250). The unconscious bias inherent in an otherwise innocent comment is intrusive upon Yu's smooth narrative, yet it is also testimony to the impact of the immense power of mainstream culture on Chinese immigrants.

A meticulously researched piece of work, *The Ordeal* provides rich details of the Chinese American experience in academia. Well-told and evenly paced, it describes academic life for a broader audience. More significantly, it demonstrates that Chinese Americans, despite being stereotyped as more successful than other Americans, continue to encounter barriers as a result of racial prejudice. Although the novel focuses only on one specific milieu, Chinese American academics, its thorough exploration of the effects of the glass ceiling—a major concern of Asian Americans today—furthers understanding of the contemporary Chinese American experience and provides a fine example of how informative Chinese-language literature can be.

## The Impact of the Struggle for Survival on Chinatown Life

Life in America's urban Chinatowns, especially the impact of the struggle for survival of the "downtown Chinese," is another recurrent theme in Chinese-language literature.[37] Living through the civil rights fervor of the 1960s and galvanized by rising ethnic and class consciousness, Chinese-language writers are sympathetic with their working-class countrymen in America. They also well understand ghetto life: Most worked in Chinatowns to support themselves at one time or another during their studies at American colleges and universities. Their writing demonstrates familiarity with conditions in Chinatowns and shows that despite improvement not every new Chinese immigrant fares well in American society. Moreover, it reveals that the Chinese community has become increasingly polarized since the 1960s.

That poverty coexists with growing prosperity in Chinese American life is not surprising. While recent decades have seen the coming of a different sort of Chinese immigrant, those who are affluent or well educated, immigration laws such as the "family reunion act" and upheavals in Southeastern Asia since the 1960s have brought to the United States large numbers of non-English-speaking, working-class Chinese immigrants and refugees who have few readily transferable skills. As one Chinese woman in Los Angeles says, "It is not true that all Asians come to the United States with suitcases . . . full of cash. I came here with very limited resources."[38] There are also immigrant professionals who, failing to acquire positions in their fields of training, are forced to take manual and service work and become mired in menial positions. As a result, the Chinese American community has been transformed into a bimodal socioeconomic structure composed of two distinct groups: the "uptown" and the "downtown."

Compared with the uptown Chinese, who live comfortably in racially integrated suburbs, downtown Chinese are trapped in urban ghettos. Caught in a world of gangs, drugs, and poverty, they differ dramatically from their uptown counterparts in the American experience.[39] While uptown Chinese feel embittered about the glass ceiling that halts career advancement, downtown Chinese, locked in dead-end jobs and with little chance to move up, are more concerned with immediate survival.

The depression that prevails in the cramped, rundown houses of overcrowded Chinatowns and the daily constraints and hardships of the downtown Chinese are captured vividly by Chinese-language writers. Their stories, set against backdrops of economic difficulties and intertwined with the effects of mass uprooting, provide pathetic, credible, and at times scathing portrayals of Chinatowns as stagnant ponds. Representative sketches of New York's Chinatown by two women writers, Zhou Li and Yu Lihua, demonstrate how the consequences of poverty and alienation have turned ghettos into waste lands and excluded residents from mainstream social, economic, political, and cultural life:

> Chinatown. Hot with the sound of cicadas, dirty streets, gilded gates dotted with red paint. . . . Under the heat, Chinatown residents line up to buy lottery tickets in front of newsstands. If you look closely at their faces, your heart would be filled with sorrow and disappointment: their faces are so rigid and stiff as if they were just carved out of wood. . . . Bearing the burning heat, people stand there quietly. . . . Under the expressionless faces, they are daydreaming of making a big fortune.

> Nighttime in Chinatown. A pedestrian clutches the stub of a cigarette with his tired and numb fingers. A man walks across the street as he spits at the sidewalk. . . . Cluttered shop windows of a curio store. Behind the dimly-lit counters sits a man, indistinguishable as to his age, staring blankly at passersby, yet seemingly not seeing anything. Perhaps he is lost in thinking why he failed to grab a double-dragon card at a mahjong game last night.[40]

Such satirical and gloomy visions drive home the message that although there are individuals who thrive in Chinatowns, immigrants who lack skills or resources can only expect to spend a lifetime scraping and scrimping for a living in poor neighborhoods.

What has caught the attention of Chinese-language writers, however, is the impact of the struggle for survival on downtown Chinese rather than the pervasiveness of poverty in Chinatown life. In fact, a particular strength of their work is that it proves that the contextual forces shaping the problems in Chinatown life are not merely racial in nature. By examining how poverty and the struggle for survival exacerbate sharp divisions, ignite conflicts, and widen the schism among Chinese immigrants, they have demonstrated that the process of racialization is never based on race alone. It is determined by a number of factors, economic conditions among them.

"Two Ways to Eat American Meals" (1984), a short story by Zhou Feili, deals with that aspect of Chinatown life.[41] Like the author, the protagonist is an immigrant from Taiwan and lives in Los Angeles's Chinatown. After being laid off four times within two years in the mainstream job market, he and his wife decide to open a small restaurant with old friends from Taiwan. The growing popularity of Chinese food will, they hope, provide a chance to earn a relatively easier, more stable livelihood.

That is not purely wishful thinking. The spread of Chinese cuisine and the corresponding increase in consumer sophistication have made the Chinese restaurant business boom and given unskilled immigrants an opportunity for economic sufficiency. Unfortunately for the protagonist and his friends, the dream is shattered by ruthless reality. The risk of conducting business in a crime-ridden urban ghetto and cut-throat industry competition soon exhaust their resources and transform the partnership into an ugly game of mutual deception. In order to survive on the knife-edge profits, they resort to cheating and playing tricks on one another. In the end, the protagonist outwits and outmaneuvers his friends in a dramatic gamble and seizes ownership of the restaurant.

The narrator's voice, albeit occasionally staccto, is rich and thought-provoking. It shifts from the emotional to the matter-of-fact and is both comic and coolly illuminating, showing vividly the unpleasant reality of Chinatown life:

> "I have calculated," my wife insisted, "if we don't hire anyone but do everything ourselves, we can net about one thousand dollars more a month from the savings on the labor costs. . . . If we make two hundred dollars more, we may even afford medical insurance. Then we won't fear being sick."
>
> "If we make another one hundred dollars, we can even afford life insurance. Then we won't fear death." I replied in a cynical tone. . . . "[B]ut where can we borrow the money [to buy the restaurant]?"

"How about from your friends?"

"I have only two sorts of friends in this country: those who have money but won't lend it to me and those who want to help me but don't have money."[42]

Beneath the self-mockery and seeming lightheartedness exist layers of doubts, anxiety, and bitterness along with a sense of insecurity. By attributing their agony and moral deterioration to the constraints and hardships in Chinatown life, the author implies that what happens to the characters is a predictable consequence of the struggle for survival. Uprooted from their native land and inserted into an alienating, impoverishing environment, they have failed miserably and are unable to rise above their despair.

The clashes and rivalries among the friends in Zhou's story emphasize that Chinese immigrants, despite sharing a common ethnic background, are divided and do not always live harmoniously. In real life, competition for limited resources turns Chinatowns into places where tensions and mutual distrust flourish. Unable to find the true sources of their problems, residents often blame their own community for deteriorating living environments, slashed wages, and worsening work conditions. The irrational vehemence with which they lash out against each other reflects their frustration over failed expectations and shattered dreams.

The sad phenomenon is frequently seen among immigrants who struggle in poverty. "The people at the bottom tend to strike out at whomever is closest," explains an author of immigration studies. "It is not a rational decision."[43] At one large gathering of garment workers in New York's Chinatown during the early 1990s, for example, discussions of problems in sweatshops quickly turned into an ugly confrontation between legal and illegal immigrants. While the former angrily denounced the latter for their declining wages and demanded that all illegal immigrants be sent home, the latter cried bitterly about being mistreated and exploited, even by other Chinese workers. The emotional dispute almost escalated into violence.[44] The case reveals clearly that competition for scarce opportunities creates discord between Chinatown residents and fragments the community.

The struggle for survival has not only intensified competition for limited resources in Chinatowns but also isolated and thwarted the downtown Chinese from actively participating in fights for racial justice and political rights. Compared to native-born Chinese, immigrants all too often become alienated and passive observers and are less sensitive toward racial prejudice. The controversy over *The Year of the Dragon* is a case in point.[45] Although most American-born

Chinese were outraged by the film's blatant racism and distortion of life in Chinatown, there were immigrants who dismissed the protests against the movie as being overly sensitive.[46]

It is also common to find immigrants shunning discussions of difficulties and racial prejudices in Chinese American life. "I feel uncomfortable with your reports of problems and hardships in American society," complained the reader of a Chinese-language newspaper in California. "There are so many happy and pleasant things in this country. Why don't you write more about pretty scenes or stories of people who have made it?" One new immigrant even claimed that if living in the United States meant being a slave, he was willing to be such a "happy slave."[47]

Some Chinese and Asian American scholars and activists believe that such a mentality is the outcome of an ideology of social control by mainstream society to "whitewash" immigrants and make them conform to dominant institutions. Others think that those who arrived after the 1960s had no experience or memories of living in a land that once openly discriminated against Chinese and Asians. Therefore, they tend to be content with the status quo and lack racial consciousness.[48] As Angela Oh, an articulate Korean American lawyer and community activist, points out, "They [the newly arrived Asian immigrants] don't understand what that concept [of minority] means in terms of historical treatment of non-English-speaking people and people who are racially different."[49]

Although finding a single, satisfactory explanation for the phenomenon is difficult, the portrayal of Chinatown life by Chinese-language writers suggests that the passivity and apolitical tendencies displayed by new immigrants, especially by the downtown Chinese, are results of the survival mentality acquired from their experiences in American society. Poverty and insecurity distract them from fighting for racial equality. Ghettoized spiritually and physically, they are confined to a narrow perspective wherein the struggle for economic efficiency and the fight for political rights seem mutually exclusive. As Qian Ning, author of critically acclaimed reportage on Chinese students and scholars in America, points out, it is the anxiety and deprivation of being new immigrants that force them to repress their political enthusiasm and emotional nature in order to make a living.[50]

Qian's argument resembles Oscar Handlin's use of estrangement as a centerpiece of immigration studies and is supported by extensive surveys and interviews of Chinese student immigrants. In one story in Qian's book, the interviewee describes having strong interest in political events when he first arrived in America, but economic necessity soon reduced his aspirations to a mere desire for survival. Making a living cutting up chickens in a Chinatown restaurant, he has lost enthusiasm for politics. As an Asian immigrant organizer in Los Angeles finds, "Most people in the community don't care about that [Asian American movement]. To them, the question is how to pay the bills."[51]

Ironically, purgatorial suffering notwithstanding, many Chinatown residents still see America as a paradise. The feeling of being elevated in America while living in poverty is not contradictory. Much of it has to do with preimmigration experience and expectations. For immigrant laborers from various parts of the Chinese world, coming to America means that they can now escape starvation and destitution. They find America's promise of material abundance alluring and expect to exploit the opportunities they see around them. That mentality—a "green-card mindset"—is well illustrated in subject matter, theme, and characters in "The Ship of Bananas" (1973), a short story by Zhang Xiguo.

The highly symbolic story centers around a meeting between a sailor who jumps ship and a student immigrant from Taiwan. Asked why he risks being caught entering America illegally, the sailor replies, "Don't laugh at me. There are many Chinese ship-jumping sailors [in New York]. Our wages are too low . . . we all tried to find opportunities to jump ship once we got to New York. . . . Working in a Chinese restaurant here for a year or two, I can save as much as several thousand dollars. It is much better than working on a ship."[52]

The story's title, an allusion to Sebastian Brant's classic *Ship of Fools,* evokes irony concerning the fate of Chinese immigrants in America. Obvious satirical overtones aside, its implication as an incarnation of the Chinese immigrant community is thought-provoking. In a broad sense, as a critic points out, Chinese immigrants such as the nameless sailor and the other characters in the story are "bananas"; they have lost their common sense and fail to understand the reality of American life.[53] This is shown by the death of the sailor at the end of the story—he dies in an accident aboard a ship that carries bananas when he tries to reenter America.

The sailor's dream, albeit ending as tragedy, is shared by many downtown Chinese. Compared to those in their homelands, wage levels for unskilled labor in the United States are strikingly high, making America a "shining Gold Mountain" in the eyes of immigrant laborers. As Mary C. Waters explains, "Four dollars an hour means nothing to us as Americans. [But] it means a lot to somebody for whom it once represented a month's rent [back home]. Even though they're not paying that rent here, they're still using that metric."[54] That mentality is described poignantly in "A Hundred Thousand Dollars" (1987), a short story about Los Angeles's Chinatown, in which a longtime resident tells his newly arrived brother-in-law why he thinks America is a "promised land":

> In America, the most important thing is that you must be willing to work hard and endure more suffering than others. For example, if other people work eight hours a day, we Chinese do sixteen hours; if they can't stand the heat of the stoves in kitchen, we can. . . . There is no paradise, we earned every penny with sweat and blood. . . . This is a wealthy country, and there are too many Americans who just want to eat without having to work. It is under such circumstances that we Chinese have got a chance to make money.[55]

In other words, because most downtown Chinese in their homelands lived in poverty and faced daily, backbreaking physical labor, their expectations for what constitutes a happy life are quite moderate. They greet any improvement in living standards and working conditions, however small, as significant progress. It is such a mentality that makes Chinese immigrant laborers endure more than people should, turns them into hardworking employees, and stifles their aspirations for political rights.

More significantly, the struggle for survival has left a mark on even many Chinese immigrant professionals. This is reflected in their self-chosen "Chineseness" in American life. Unlike their working-class peers, immigrant professionals, especially those from Taiwan and Hong Kong who are accustomed to urban living and Western popular culture, are already highly Westernized upon arrival. For example, growing up in Taiwan inculcates American ideas; from chewing gum to G.I. caps, from pop music to Hollywood movies, the accoutrements of American culture are a familiar part of daily life there. As a character in Yu Lihua's *Seeing the Palm Trees Again* discovers during a visit to Taiwan, "Entering Xilingmen [a posh hotel], he saw the band playing fast-rhythm disco on the stage. The overcrowded dance hall is full of men and women twisting their bodies rapidly and drastically with the mad music, as if they all suddenly had abdominal pain. Were the faces not yellow, he would think this is a night club in Chicago."[56] In short, the trappings of affluent international urban culture in their native lands provide Chinese immigrant professionals with a sophisticated understanding of the West, and they are not at odds with American culture. As a character in David Henry Hwang's play *FOB* observes, "All I am saying is that the people who are coming in now—a lot of them are different—they are already real Westernized. They don't act like they're fresh off the boat."[57]

By comparison, the "Chineseness" of some immigrant professionals can be considered a post-immigration, employment-related choice. America's long interest in China tends to associate the immigrants with an exotic and outlandish culture. As America's demand to understand China grows, however, the bias has also provided Chinese immigrant intellectuals with additional resources for living. The protagonist in *Seeing the Palm Trees Again* discovers the "usefulness" of a Chinese identity for employment in America. Although trained in English literature, to earn a livelihood he abandons that training to switch to teaching Chinese, a subject he is neither knowledgable about nor interested in. For such people, their "Chinese-ness" is a self-made choice to adapt to the job market and a way to make a livelihood in America. As Younghill Kang discovered long ago, "In making a living, *Oriental scholarship* may help you more than American education."[58]

The struggle for survival has made an even more powerful impact on the attitude toward life in America among the ethnic Chinese, especially refugees from Southeastern Asia who constitute a significant part of the Chinatown population since the 1970s. For them, American society is a sheltered realm offering protection unavailable in overseas Chinese communities. That view derives from the unique experience of the Chinese diaspora, which, as defined by Andrew J. Nathan, "is in large part, a story of racist victimization."[59] The government-sanctioned discrimination against ethnic Chinese in Indonesia and the persecution of them helps in understanding that point. "Excluded from politics, the civil service and state companies," a 1997 study reports, "the ethnic Chinese [in Indonesia] must carry national identification cards with a special code. Places at state universities are restricted from the Chinese, forcing them to study at private institutions or abroad."[60] Compared with such blatant racial discrimination, prejudice in American society appears insignificant to these ethnic Chinese immigrants. As one author wrote, "We Chinese living in North America should be grateful that we don't have to fear such ugly anti-Chinese sentiments in our life."[61] Even in Hong Kong, which claimed to be more democratic under British rule than the rest of the Chinese world, Chinese were still treated as second-class citizens. One immigrant recalls:

> I can still remember vividly . . . my first job in Hong Kong as an engineer fresh out of school [in the 1950s]. . . . A fellow white engineer, also freshly out of school from Britain, was paid a salary seven times mine. . . . When I brought this gross discrepancy to the attention of my superior, I was told I can leave the colony if I don't like it there. Till this day I can not believe the gall of this foreigner to tell a local to leave. I was quite pleasantly surprised when I immigrated to Canada in 1972 to find out that whites in Canada and the U.S. do not behave the same way as the British do in Hong Kong.[62]

Such an impression inevitably affects the immigrants' attitude toward American society. It also explains in part why Chinese and other Asian immigrants have a higher rate of naturalization than any other immigrant group. For them, American citizenship symbolizes the right to live in a society where stability and continuity seem unquestioned, which is not the case in their homelands.[63]

The point is sharply illustrated in "The Paradise" (1980), a short story by Yi Li about Chinese refugees from Vietnam. The satirical nature of the work is marked by the author's use of the word *paradise* to refer to the image of America in the eyes of the ethnic Chinese from Southeast Asia. Her lively and artful prose vividly reflects the refugees' mentality and feeling of great relief upon settling in America. Their miserable lives in old homes and refugee camps prompt them to embrace America as a "paradise." "Where can you find such a good government?" exclaims one character when handed a small settlement fee on arrival in America and finding that her family is eligible for welfare benefits.[64]

Thus, overwhelmed by their preimmigration experience, downtown Chinese sometimes fail to understand the significance of the struggle for political rights. Their memories, coupled with their relatively better treatment in America, lead them to approach the issues of racial equality and social justice with modest expectations. As one resident of San Francisco's Chinatown explained, he stayed away from the civil rights movement because "one does not eat butter unless one has had butter before. So if I never had butter it didn't mean a darn thing to me. Whether they allowed us in the Palace Hotel . . . , it didn't matter because I never even tried to enter the place. . . . I accepted a lot of this as natural."[65] That viewpoint, although displaying a problematic and limited vision of racial equality, is highly representative of the opinions of immigrants across racial and ethnic boundaries. Mario Puzo recalls that his mother, a villager from Southern Italy, was always grateful to America even though she could barely survive in the new country. "Never mind about being happy," she told her children. "Be glad you're alive."[66]

It would be wrong, however, to assume that Chinese immigrants will always remain passive toward the struggle for racial equality. On the contrary, most undergo dramatic changes once they secure economic sufficiency. Joan Chen [Chen Chong], a recipient of the prestigious Golden Ring Award for her contributions to Asian-Pacific Arts, is an outstanding example. Although economic necessity forced Chen to play parts that debased the Chinese when she first arrived in America in 1981, as she gradually established herself she became critical of Hollywood's bias against Asians. "Most of my career up until now has been spent playing vulnerable Asian girls," she observed. "As an Asian American actress, I want to win acceptance and recognition based on racial equality. I may never succeed in this goal, but I'll keep fighting for it."[67]

Chen's story exposes the fraudulence of the argument that immigrants cannot appreciate the Chinese American sensibility. It also indicates that economic self-sufficiency, although not leading automatically to the rise of ethnic consciousness, grants immigrants a higher degree of freedom and power to define themselves and challenge racism. In real life, the line between native-born and immigrants on the issue of racial assertiveness is not always clear-cut. While there are native-born Chinese who compete to be "top bananas," a study of Chinese immigrant entrepreneurs in Los Angeles finds that despite having conservative stands on many issues "they do not shy away from asserting themselves, economically, culturally, or politically."[68] Opinion polls also indicate that Asian American professionals, both native- and overseas-born, are more likely to challenge racial discrimination than their working-class counterparts.[69] As William Wei argues, the Asian American movement is essentially a middle-class movement.[70]

By exploring how the struggle for survival frustrates aspirations for political rights, Chinese-language writers have not only associated economic conditions with the rise of racial consciousness but also implied that the gap between rich and poor plays a significant role in dividing the immigrant community. Such an economic interpretation of problems in Chinatown life represents a different perspective than found in theories of ethnic solidarity but parallels traditional Marxist ideology. As Eugene Genovese contends, "All good Marxist writing leads to an explication of class."[71] Judged by that standard, a large part of Chinese-language literature might be considered "good Marxist writing"; its authors seem to argue that class is a critical factor, transcending Chinese identity and affecting community unity. As Yu Lihua notes, "I agree that racial and ethnic conflicts in essence are an issue of class struggle."[72]

Perhaps that is why Yu writes about a conflict between Zhong Leping and Jia, another Chinese American professor, in *The Ordeal*.[73] Described with less detail but equal sharpness, Jia, a whitewashed snob, contrasts with Yu's sympathetic depiction of Zhong. Jia's father was a corrupt official in China who amassed a huge fortune and fled to the United States during the late 1940s. Jia brags that his father's wealth can allow the family to live in luxury for three generations. With money from his father, Jia lives lavishly. He owns summer houses and vacations in posh hotels all over the world.[74] By comparing and contrasting Jia, whose life is one of ultimate privilege, with Zhong, an average, hardworking immigrant intellectual, Yu seems to suggest that the gap in their class background has produced tensions and clashes between them.

Indeed, there persists either a conspicuous or a nearly hidden class struggle in virtually every major Chinese-language work, serving as backgrounds for the dynamic processes of intra-ethnic confrontation. For example, the author of "Abortion" provides snapshots of another side of problems in Chinatown life. The yawning chasm between poor and rich in the story challenges prospects of Chinese unity and the establishment of a single, unified Chinese American agenda. The protagonist's husband, a chef in a Chinatown restaurant, complains bitterly that although he has worked hard for nearly twenty years he cannot afford to pay for medical insurance. His boss, however, has bought a mansion with the money exacted from the toil of the restaurant workers.[75] The gap between the lives of those who enjoy extravagance and those who extract mere sustenance reveals that what happens in Chinatowns is not always a tale of wealthy white Americans taking advantage of helpless immigrants but of Chinese exploiting Chinese.

The bestselling *American Moon* by Cao Youfang makes an even more powerful case: The real division in the Chinese community is often drawn along socioeconomic lines rather than along the immigrant past or degrees of acculturation. Set in New York's Chinatown, the novel tells a moving story of the joys and sorrows of a student-turned-waiter in his American life. Amid the seemingly agreeable and lively scene, the author inserts a deeper story about a labor dispute in a restaurant where the protagonist organizes a union.[76]

Cao's message is clear: It is disparity in economic status rather than difference in birthplace that causes the rift among Chinese immigrants. That argument, although deeply held and strongly felt by many Chinese-language writers, is at odds with that of American-born Chinese writers such as Amy Tan, who sees cultural differences and the generation gap as the major sources of conflicts in the Chinese community. Nevertheless, research conducted by Chinese American scholars on Chinatown politics appears to confirm that the problems in the Chinese community have economic interpretations and that the downtown Chinese are aware of class difference.[77] Indeed, economic status has been a widely used criterion to guide personal relations and measure individuals' positions on the social ladder of Chinatowns, and there is intense antagonism between haves and have-nots. Although rarely reported by the mainstream media, strikes and labor disputes in Chinatown businesses occur quite frequently.[78]

The impact of the struggle for survival on immigrants reflected in Chinese-language literature demonstrates that although racism remains a barrier to Chinese American progress, it is neither the sole nor the unbridled locus of problems in Chinese American life, especially the lives of the downtown Chinese. By examining how the struggle for economic sufficiency, and the gap in class identification, twists and deforms the issue of race, Chinese immigrant writers seem to argue that classism and racism in American society have been compounded. It is difficult to separate one from the other.[79] In other words, challenging racial prejudice requires a self-confidence that many recent immigrants, subjected to the pressures and hardships of earning a livelihood, lack. Life in the isolation and squalor of urban ghettos forces them to remain single-minded in the pursuit of survival. Therefore, a key to the successful integration of downtown Chinese into

American life involves not only a struggle against racism but also efforts to help them, especially those immigrant laborers who are disenfranchised, improve their living conditions and achieve economic equality. Only in that way can China-town residents be organized into an effective, consolidated, and coherent political force in the struggle to ensure Chinese American progress.

## The Role of Gender in Chinese Immigrant Life:
## The "Rise" of Women and the "Fall" of Men

It would be incomplete to treat the enormously complex body of Chinese-language literature as merely a protest against racism or an exposure of economic hardships in immigrant life. The issue of gender, especially the rise of women vis-à-vis men in the Chinese American community, is another essential intertext parallel to the issues of race and class. *The Ordeal* is a case in point. It concerns the struggle of Zhong Leping, a Chinese American professor, for a fair tenure review. But the author skillfully integrates into the plot the awakening and rise of Wu Shiyu's (Zhong's wife) consciousness as a woman.

Although well educated, Wu has given up a promising career to stay at home and raise the couple's children in order to help her husband acquire a better job. She is constantly torn, however, between the desire to be a devoted wife and a yearning for personal fulfillment. Interaction with mainstream society and the conflict between her longing for independence and the traditional responsibility of women toward their families gradually "awaken" her. Unable to contain her will, she grows more determined to create meaning in life by actively involving herself in Zhong's career. In fact, she is the driving force behind his campaign for tenure, by organizing parties to help him win support from friends and colleagues, and constantly encouraging him to keep fighting.

When Zhong chooses to move to another university without consulting her, Wu is so upset that she decides to leave him and pursue her own career. Her act shows that for a new type of Chinese immigrant woman the prospect of marital security is not as vital as individual freedom. What better proof of one's feminist stance than an independent decision to leave a family and search for career advancement? The knowledge that her children need constant care and that they may never recover from the emotional shock she will impose upon them burdens Wu with guilt and makes her break difficult. Nevertheless, she feels she can no longer bear a homemaker's dull, routine life and determines to follow her own calling. In one emotional argument with her husband she says forcefully, "How did you know that once you made up your mind to move, I would follow? . . . Am I not an independent person with feelings of love and hate? Haven't I got my own affections for people I know and the places I like? Do you think I'm only a handkerchief in your pocket? When you need it, you pull it out to clean your glasses, dry your nose, and mop your brow; but when you don't need it, you just keep the handkerchief in your pocket and carry it with you."[80] The fact that her act received harsh comments from critics of the novel in Taiwan also proves how untraditional and "un-Chinese" she has become.[81]

Yu Lihua is not the only Chinese immigrant writer to express a strong feminist view. Yi Li, another woman author, deals with the same theme. In "Dr. Fang's Free Medical Service" (1987), she has created the thematic embodiment of feminist identity: a Chinese immigrant woman—a doctor's wife—who strives to be completely self-confident. A social worker in Los Angeles's Chinatown, she actively participates in various community projects. When her husband asks her to resign and stay home to care for their family, she views the request as an attempt to strip away her individuality and force her to submit to traditional Chinese values. Her feminist viewpoint and sense of social responsibility are illustrated by a comment she makes to her husband, "What do you want me to do at home—cooking, gardening, raising more children? Shall I follow the example of the wives of your colleagues; dress up in fancy clothes and bury myself in fashionable and luxurious furniture?"[82] In the end, like Wu Shiyu in *The Ordeal*, she divorces the husband and pursues a career.

More significantly, according to Chinese-language writing, Chinese women, as a result of settling in America, seem to gain power in relationships with men—a change few could have foreseen before emigrating. This is not only symbolized by their growing presence in professions but also represented by their initiatives in decision-making about family affairs and businesses. It is common in Chinese-language literature to find Chinese immigrant men who may seem to be dominant but are inwardly and emotionally highly dependent upon wives. Sometimes a male protagonist may bluster and swagger, but it is the wife who controls everything in the family. In *The American Moon*, for example, the rituals that the Chinese immigrant couple adopt seem to affirm the husband's authority at home and in business. In reality, as he acknowledges, his wife is the really strong one, holding power and making decisions.

Like the rise of Chinese women, the fall of men is another common theme in work by Chinese immigrant writers. Two stories, albeit extreme examples, come readily to mind. In Chen Ruoxi's *Uncle and Nephew of the Hu Family* (1984), the fate of a husband differs dramatically from that of his wife in America. A factory administrator in China, the husband fails miserably after arriving in San Francisco and finally hangs himself. The wife, however, is highly successful and becomes active in the local Chinese community. In *Sons and Daughters of the Fu Family,* another bestseller by Yu Lihua, a student immigrant from Taiwan commits suicide after he repeatedly suffers setbacks in his new environment; his wife, however, fares well in her career and eventually marries her employer, who is white.[83]

These portrayals of the sharp contrast in the fates of men and women reflect new realities in Chinese immigrant families. As scholars of the Chinese diaspora point out, emigration has frequently created a change in the balance of power in Chinese families, altered certain aspects of gender dynamics, and granted more social and economic options for women. For one thing, Chinese men no longer hold the same power over women as they used to do in their "old home" while the possibility of better economic opportunities for women in the new environment raises their status within the family.[84] For example, as is so often seen in Chinese-language literature about immigrant families in America, husbands who rarely performed domestic chores in the old country are forced to do so because their wives may now earn higher salaries working outside their homes. In "Visitors from the Hometown" (1981), Chen Ruoxi's story set in San Francisco's Chinese community, the husband admits that the wife now supports the family by working as a street vendor at Fisherman's Wharf. "We would have starved if the family had to rely on my income from selling my paintings for a living," he says frankly to old friends from Beijing, who are astonished to find that he stays at home while she goes out to work.[85]

The rising influence of wives and daughters in Chinese families demonstrates the impact of American institutions and values on Chinese immigrants. Despite hostile immigration laws and dehumanizing stereotypes of the Chinese, American institutions deserve credit for being attuned to the needs of women.[86] For Chinese men, especially those who were well established in their native country, emigration to America can mean a leap into peril and a step down, materially and socially. Of course, Chinese women may encounter similar barriers, but they have more choices than they did before emigrating. The choices are not always ideal, but as a female scholar of Chinese immigration points out, at least the new country provides a chance to escape from traditional cultural restrictions on women in Chinese society and allows them to "stand outside convention more easily" than their counterparts in the Chinese world.[87] "This is America. Everyone has her individual rights," a young woman defiantly tells her husband in *The American Moon.* "When I plan to do something in the future," she continues, "you can join me if you want. Otherwise, I'll go ahead alone, and you must not interfere with me."[88]

Some Asian American scholars also argue that if there is indeed an increase in options for Asian women in American society, it is made possible because

"Asian patriarchy was pushed aside or subsumed by an American patriarchy that did not, because of racism, extend its promise to Asian American men."[89] That reality has strong economic and social implications for Chinese immigrants and results in comparative benefits for Chinese women. As a Chinese scholar argues convincingly, emigration to America turns the world of Chinese men upside down. The fact that their patriarchal authority disappears in American life comes as a shock. Not only are they cut off from the collective male history, which was once integral to their identity, but their confidence also erodes as they discover that their economic power has declined dramatically and they are not favored in the mainstream job market.[90] As a result, Chinese immigrant men come to value relationships with their spouses and seek an emotional haven in them.

In other words, the post-immigration experience of many Chinese men consists of a daily attrition of confidence, on-going difficulties in adjustment, and the shock of losing their once treasured male status. By contrast, women, who were not pampered in Chinese society, are less affected by change. Consequently, they often become stronger than men, are better adapted to their new environment, and play more significant roles in family life. Zhou Feili, who writes about Chinese immigrants in Southern California, has commented upon the phenomenon based on his observations: "There has emerged a particularly large number of strong-willed women among new [post 1960s] Chinese immigrants. . . . After they have settled down, women often find men in their families—fathers, husbands, and brothers—are unable to adjust to the new surroundings and fail in their responsibilities to support families. . . . This circumstance forces Chinese women to forge ahead and sharpen their instincts to fight."[91]

Although a single explanation for the increasing empowerment of Chinese women cannot be readily provided and the experiences of Chinese women and men in America cannot be easily compartmentalized, the changes of female and male status in Chinese American life and its implications are widely apparent in Chinese-language literature. What used to be unthinkable in the old country becomes natural for Chinese women in America. The three brothers in *Sons and Daughters of the Fu Family* all appear weak or ineffectual and have lost direction in the new environment. Their wives, however, are capable, resourceful, and function well in their jobs. Above all, they seem determined to succeed in American life, whereas their husbands are frustrated and disillusioned. In "Weekly Event" (1985), a story about Chinese immigrants in Los Angeles, Zhou Feili describes a woman who is the "boss" of her family, managing their toy store and directing her disoriented, embittered husband to work.[92]

Women as central figures of immigrant families are also common in Chinese American literature in English. Maxine Hong Kingston recalls her mother often bitterly comparing her professional status as a doctor in China to that of a laundrywoman in San Francisco's Chinatown: "You have no idea how much I have fallen coming to America." Despite that, however, she is clearly the authority in family affairs and frequently "scolds" her husband to go to work.[93] Such an image of a strong and powerful Chinese woman shatters stereotypes of the passive, submissive, China-doll stereotypes of popular American literature.

Portrayals of strong women and weak men are by no means confined to Chinese American literature. Kim Ronyoung, a Korean American, describes two individuals in *Clay Walls*, a fictionalized autobiography of a Korean family in Los Angeles: a confused, failed husband and a brave wife who corrects his mistakes and supports the family.[94] Hisaye Yamamoto, a nisei, depicts Japanese males in her short stories who have collapsed under pressure and are unable to act or think clearly under adverse conditions.[95]

The exposure of Chinese women to mainstream American culture, especially the contrast of style and manners afforded by the feminist movement, has further contributed to transforming the ideal of womanhood from what it was in the Chinese world. It stimulates their gender consciousness and inspires them to seek personal freedom or succeed on their own in America. Academy Award nominee Joan Chen, for example, has observed that women are a different "race" than men—an idea she has developed since her arrival in America.[96] Similarly, Yu Lihua acknowledges that she considers her writing career the foremost thing in life, affection the second, and marriage the third.[97] Such a list of priorities itself challenges the virtues that traditional Chinese culture defines for women. It is no wonder that one of Yu's female characters criticizes male superiority in memorably earthy language: "You men seem very polite; always open doors for us to get into cars and houses. But what's really on your mind is only one thing: how to open *that door.* . . . and turn us into maids-on-the-bed."[98] Although her satirical comments suffer from being overly transparent, they demonstrate Yu's indictment of male chauvinism and her strong feminist stance—the result of living in America.

Even the high divorce rate among Chinese women in America can be seen as evidence of a heightened capacity for self-determination. Broken marriages are a popular subject in Chinese-language writing, and marital constraints are major themes or the backgrounds of work by almost every major Chinese immigrant writer. The literature reflects the reality. Studies indicate that the divorce rate of Chinese immigrants in America has soared, and more women than men have initiated the separations.[99] Different explanations are given for the cause of the growing numbers of divorces being sought by Chinese women in America. Some believe that marital crisis is a consequence of economic hardship in immigrant families. According to a scholar, there seems to be a pattern for broken marriages among recent Chinese immigrants: Women tend to file for divorce if their husbands fail to find employment in America.[100] That observation is confirmed by Zhou Feili, who notes from personal experience that "poverty likes to destroy marriages."[101] Others think that the high rate of divorce among Chinese immigrants is an outcome of living in America. As one mainstream woman scholar claims, divorce is an "American tradition" and can be viewed as a woman's right. "Isn't divorce as easy as going to restaurant or toilet in America?" the younger brother asks his elder sister in Sons and Daughters of the Fu Family.[102]

Still others, especially women, blame Chinese men for their male chauvinism, which drives their wives to file for divorce. It is a familiar scene under the pen of Chinese women writers that Chinese immigrant men, despite decades of settlement in America, keep a traditional attitude toward women. "Although he has lived in America for so many years, Tao [the protagonist] remains very Chinese in his food tastes and in his views on women. . . . He hates vehemently the shrewdness and calculation that are the characteristics of Chinese women in America," writes Cao Youfang in her bestselling The American Moon.[103] Yet another Chinese immigrant woman writer complained, "He [her former husband] always took everything for granted. He thought that since he was the husband, he should have a dinner ready for him when he returned home. But it never occurred to him that his wife was also an individual person. She had her own hobbies, career; and she, too, had to go to work everyday."[104] Such an indictment of male chauvinism is indirectly confirmed by comments of Chinese men that are often unconsciously revelatory. Asked why he chose to marry his current wife, Wu'er Kaixi, a leading Chinese dissident leader in exile, explained, "I love her because she has the merits held by a *traditional Oriental woman,* and the concern for the society as well as wisdom [of] a modern woman."[105]

Despite controversy about the reasons for the high rate of divorce in the Chinese community, most Chinese immigrant writers seem to agree that the tolerance and respect for privacy in American society provide divorced women with opportunities and benefits without stigmatizing them. In a way, the fact that Chinese women no longer fear the consequences of divorce shows that they enjoy more freedom in America.[106] Until the 1980s, divorced women in China were targets of gossip. Although divorced men or widowers could remarry, it was considered immoral for women to do likewise. The power of social convention was so tyrannical that violating such mores might well make her an outcast. According to one traditional saying rooted in Confucianism, "A man of integrity never leaves his master; a woman of virtue never marries twice." That belief comes from the old-fashioned view that the virtue of women is measured by their chastity and their loyalty to their husbands. "Starving to death is a small matter," a cen-turies-old Chinese maxim claims, "but losing one's chastity is a great calamity." Historically, Chinese emperors and local officials periodically issued decrees in praise of women who committed suicide after the deaths of their husbands—a practice contemporary Chinese scholars condemn as one of the most brutal acts against women in Chinese history.[107]

In contrast, American-style freedom and respect for privacy lift moral restric-tions on Chinese women who are divorced. They are no longer worried about being shunned by their families or the local Chinese communities for violating a taboo. "I have sometimes brought men to bed. . . . This is a good thing about America: people mind only their own business; nobody cares about your private life," comments a woman about her sex life to her newly arrived sister.[108] Of course, the liberty and privacy Chinese women enjoy in their American life are by no means decisive factors in contributing to the high rate of divorce; but as Chinese-language writing reveals, they give Chinese women freedom and the ability to choose to end unhappy marriages. "Worry? You don't need to worry about that [the consequences of divorce] in America," a woman says of her bro-ken marriage in a story by Yuan Zenan. "I fulfilled my duty to Jiangchen [her former husband]; I tried my best to treat him well and I suffered enough. Final-ly, I made up my mind one afternoon. I threw down the mop, and walked out of the kitchen. I have never returned to him since then."[109]

Undoubtedly, living in a society in which women are granted more social, political, and economic power gives Chinese women additional impetus to achieve more and even to brag about doing so. "Asian women who live in the U.S. are the luckiest among their gender," a young Chinese woman proudly claimed. "I had a post-Doc who was a forty-seven-year-old Chinese man report-ing to me for two years. I didn't find it difficult *managing him*."[110] Similar senti-ments are found among women in other ethnic groups. A Japanese woman ob-served, "I'm so lucky to be in the United States. In Japan, I wouldn't have had the chance as a woman."[111] Hasia Diner, who has studied Irish Americans, ar-gues convincingly that despite the burdens of cultural confusion, Irish women also felt that they enjoyed more rights in America.[112]

The advancement of women described in Chinese-language writing is confirmed by studies of the employment patterns and salary levels of Asian women in America. The census shows that college-educated Asian American women, both immigrants and native-born, report earnings comparable to those of white women. That is an impressive accomplishment, given that Asian men earn only 87 percent of the incomes of white men.[113] Perhaps more evidence of their improved status is that there are more Asian American women than men in journalism. Connie Chung, the only Chinese American to become a national network news anchor, observes that women outnumber men on air as reporters and anchors throughout the United States, a finding supported by studies on Asian Americans in journalism.[114] Again, it is noteworthy that the success of Chinese immigrant women is not an isolated phenomenon; it is consistent with the experience of immigrant women from other countries. Statistics show that since the 1960s more female immigrants have engaged in white-collar and professional fields than their male counterparts in the American job market.[115]

Of course, the success of Chinese women in America, however impressive, should not be overestimated. Their progress is largely judged by the standards of Chinese society. It is a comparison that may lower expectations and inflate perceptions of accomplishment. Therefore, the standard of comparison should be set against the mainstream population, especially white males. Measured in that way, Chinese women are far from successful. "As a group, Asian American women are drastically underrepresented in fields such as law and medicine," Elaine H. Kim points out. "[And] few Asian American women are working anywhere as managers or administrators or in the skilled trades."[116] Indeed, for Chinese women, especially those from working-class backgrounds, who dream of America as a paradise for women, illusions can be shattered and American life may be a disappointment.

Studies also find that only those Chinese and Asian women from highly educated and professional backgrounds have enjoyed access to power and liberty in America or reached a level of success that can be defined as being on the rise.[117] Those who live in Chinatowns and are trapped in poverty have made little progress and are more concerned with survival than gender equality.

That theme is treated poignantly in "Abortion," in which Yi Li strives to deal with the gender experience from the perspective of women in Chinatown. Their misery and frustrated aspirations indicate that, similar to the struggle for racial justice, the struggle for gender equality is woven of many strands and that Chinese women in America are divided by economic status. An emigrant from Hong Kong, Yi Li came to the United States to study English in 1973 after working as a nurse in Great Britain for several years. Perhaps because of her familiarity with immigrants from Canton and her career as a social worker, she is deeply interested in Chinatown life and is one of the rare literary voices of working-class Chinese women.[118] Her coverage of their hardships provides a counterpoint to the success stories of other Chinese women and exposes the multileveled complexity of gender issues in Chinese American life.

Set in San Francisco's Chinatown, the plot of "Abortion" is simple. Mrs. Luo, a fifty-year-old sweatshop worker and mother of four, is pregnant. Aware that her family is too poor to support another child, she plans to have an abortion. Unfortunately, her meager salary is barely enough to cover her family's food and rent, never mind the $160 needed for the abortion. Meanwhile, her husband, a chef in a Chinatown restaurant and addicted to gambling, keeps their bank book and refuses to give her money. In the end, it is support from her female co-workers that enables her to pay for the procedure.

The tragedy of Mrs. Luo is not the only drama in the story. Almost all the women around her have suffered a similar fate. Lacking resources and confined to urban ghettos, they have little chance to move upward in American life and are deprived of motherhood by poverty. Asked why they choose abortion, the five women waiting in a Chinatown clinic all answer that economic constraints have forced them to make that decision. As a sweatshop worker who has had several abortions explains, "It's not that I don't want any more [children], but how can I afford to support five kids? If I didn't sew everyday, based on the little money my husband earns, we couldn't even afford to eat congee."[119] Their suffering and the sadness caused by unwanted pregnancies and abortions are exemplified by Mrs. Luo's daughter's traumatic observation: "Mom, why is it always us women [who suffer]?" she cries bitterly after being made pregnant by her boyfriend and having an abortion (105).

Written in a sober tone, the narration of the story is direct and clear. By using abortion as a controlling motif to unfold the stories of her characters, Yi Li describes the tragedy of working-class Chinese women in America. One example of the salience of her message is that she uses a woman's rights poster as an extended metaphor for the gap between Chinatown women and their uptown peers. The slogan on the poster, "Abortion: A Woman's Choice," is consistently linked with the imagery of Mrs. Luo's pregnancy. The irony is that for her and her co-workers, abortion does not involve choice. It is a choiceless decision and a desperate attempt at trying to overcome poverty rather than a volitional act inspired by woman's rights.

Yet the story is not merely a pessimistic account of working-class Chinese women. Although they appear to be indoctrinated with traditional Chinese values and tend to behave in the manner considered proper and desirable by patriarchal culture, their reticence should not be mistaken for passivity or submissiveness. Beneath their acquiescence to the Chinese tradition of duty for women, there is a mood of growing rebellion. After all, they live in America and are influenced by the women's movement, both within the Chinese American community and within society at large. As shown in a casual talk among several sweatshop workers in the story, the rebellious feelings will find outlets and rise in intensity when there is an opportunity:

"Your husband won't allow you to do that [sterilization]," Mrs. Fu said to Mrs. Chen.

"I don't care if he objects. I am the one who suffers [abortion]."

"What if you want more children later?" Nifeng [another woman worker] asked.

"More children? Three kids are enough for me to be a slave all my life. When they grow up, I'll get old, too. I don't want to condemn my entire life to suffering for them," Mrs. Chen replied. (91)

That Mrs. Chen, a peasant from the rural regions of Canton, dares to challenge her husband about the serious matter of sterilization and that she wants to have her own life indicates that, even for working-class Chinese women, emigration to the United States makes a difference to their fate. Their American experience has empowered them with a strong sense of gender consciousness. It is difficult to believe that Mrs. Chen would have acted in the same way had she stayed in her native village in the Pearl River Delta. Her words must stun the men in a milieu where until the mid-twentieth century husbands beat wives as a matter of course.

The web of the plot in "Abortion" is skillfully spun. Each strand weaves itself into the others and is a necessary step toward the eventual thematic conclusion: The rise of Chinese women in America, albeit impressive, has been neither equal nor universal. Yi Li has closely modeled her account on actual life in Chinatowns and filled it with details. The overall edginess and graphic boldness in her portrayal of the agony of women who live in Chinatown has an impact that makes her account seem like raw testimony. When read alongside other Chinese immigrant writers' accounts of professional women, the simple plot in "Abortion," coupled with its true-to-life characters, gives it a momentum that is difficult to forget.

The advancement of Chinese women in America raises another important question: What is the attitude of Chinese men, especially those who are not doing well, toward the success of women? The seemingly straightforward question is difficult to answer, because the work of Chinese-language writers offers a bewildering variety of views. The portrayals of male attitudes toward the role of gender often seem at odds with one another. For some Chinese men, perceptions of feminism are fundamentally confounded by a strong commitment to woman's rights and its progressive nature. They see the progress of Chinese women in America as a sign of strength that benefits the community as a whole. As Lin Yutang observed in 1936, "America gives women the opportunity to develop. Old-world men, especially Asian men, are frequently astonished to hear that women are given this opportunity to develop. . . . After obtaining the opportunity to develop, women have not encountered disaster. . . . They evidently are capable of looking after themselves."[120]

Others have trouble grasping the positive values attached to American feminism. They are unable to appreciate the liberal premises underlying the improved status of Chinese immigrant women, particularly as they are disempowered of their formerly held authority in the family and face the uncertainty and unpredictability of developing careers in American society. A Chinese immigrant complains in *Breaking Out,* Chen Ruoxi's novel about Chinese American professors in a university in the San Francisco Bay area, "The twentieth century is surely already the century of the women. How can there still be so many feminists making a fuss about women's rights? In marital relations, for example, women are always the victors while men have completely surrendered. They are treated like oxen and horses by women, working hard for their families, and they can't have a rest until death. Still, women insist they have not achieved equal status."[121] Others maintain that because social convention and traditional values require men to support women and children, they have become merely money-making tools and have suffered as much as Chinese women: Both are victims of oppression and alienation in American society.

Thus the view of Chinese men concerning the empowerment of women is not merely complex. It is at times incoherent and turns back upon itself. As a result, there is one salient theme about men's attitudes toward the role of gender in Chinese-language literature: ambivalence. "Killing Wife" (1988), a story by Zhang Xiguo, offers observations on the ambiguity and complexity of the mentality of Chinese men who have "gone down" in America.[122] Like many Chinese immigrant writers in his generation, Zhang was born in China, grew up in Taiwan, and came to the United States for graduate studies in the 1960s. Over the years, he has distinguished himself as not only a prolific writer but also as a vigorous and innovative explorer of the boundaries between fiction and reportage.[123]

Told with black humor, the fifty-two-page story covers issues that many similar works have dealt with and can be viewed as a prototypical tale in Chinese-language writing of the male perspective on gender. The plot centers on the enmity between Wu Ziqiao, a disillusioned immigrant headed "downward," and his upwardly mobile and career-oriented wife. Although it was Wu who sponsored the wife to come to America and has found her a job, he now lags far behind her in salary and status. She earns twice as much as he and becomes his supervisor at the company where they both work. Wu feels embittered and even betrayed after the wife files for divorce and allegedly has an affair with her white boss. He begins to fantasize about various ways to kill her as a means of retaliating against society, which he thinks has been unfair to him. At the end of the story, he is confined to an asylum after a court has ruled that he can longer be held accountable for his behavior.

Anchored in absurd fantasy, much like the work of Hunter S. Thompson, the story is poignant if somewhat melodramatic. At the most obvious level, it resembles those emotionally charged men's tales filled with bitterness against "betrayal" by "their" women, as indicated by the story's title and its shocking opening: "Wu Ziqiao has wanted to kill his wife for at least four or five years. The first time he thought in this way, his wife had just been promoted to junior manager of the company and was entertaining guests at their home. . . . Although he never really wants to kill his wife, he has to admit that the thought has brought him a great sense of satisfaction" ("Killing Wife" 155, 157).

However rich in symbolism and ideas, the story is far more than a simple account that sympathetically elucidates the woes of Chinese men, nor is it solely a misogynist fantasy. Zhang is less interested in creating a satiric, Waugh-like portrait of a crazed man than in using Wu's fantasy to expose him as an outsider and misfit, a representative of those Chinese men deprived of masculinity and suffering degradation in their post-immigration experience. For example, the 108 methods Wu thinks up to kill his wife and his interest in kung fu evoke ready association with the legendary 108 outlaws in *The Water Margin*, a sixteenth-century Chinese household classic and a celebrated novel of male heroes.[124] Wu's habit of making "absurd" notations in his diary also parallels the practice of the Madman in "A Madman's Diary" by Lu Xun.[125] Like the 108 outlaws in Chinese folklore who were forced to rebel against the government (and the Madman, who is pushed to the limits by oppressive, traditional Chinese culture), Wu feels himself to be a victim of American society and wants to lash out at that system.[126]

Having worked hard for more than ten years, he remains at the same entry-level position and has little prospect of being promoted, largely because he is a "Chinaman." His frustrations are reflected vividly in his cynicism toward his wife's Americanness: "Why do you think I want to kill her?" Wu asks his sister. "After more than ten years of marriage, have I ever touched her once? She always thinks that the Americans are better, stronger in all ways than the Chinese. That's right, they speak English better than the Chinese, but when they beat their wives, they beat them really hard until blue and green, and sometimes they even beat their wives to death" ("Killing Wife" 179).

In essence, Wu's misery and feeling of oppression, long suppressed, are aimed at mainstream institutions he feels degrade him. This is subtly revealed through the author's use of the image of whiteness and the phrase *snow mountain* to symbolize the wife whenever Wu fantasizes about killing her: "He is watching his plump wife take off clothes one by one and gently slip into the bath tub just like a *pure white* sea lion. . . . His wife's *pure white* body floats on water in the tub, just like a *snow mountain*. . . . He pictures his wife lying in the bath tub. Her *pure white* body submerged in the water just like a *snow mountain*. . . . [He] thrusts the dagger into the *snow mountain*. It collapses" ("Killing Wife" 155, 156, 160, emphasis added). The image of whiteness, together with the number 108 and Wu's absurd diary, lead one to understand that what he really hates is a system that "whitewashes" his life and causes him to fail.

Wu's fantasy is also a convenient fiction that veils more unruly issues in his life, especially his problematic adjustment to the American environment. As he struggles to confront his upwardly mobile wife, his fall becomes inevitable. He lacks the qualities needed to succeed in American life, such as competitiveness, aggressiveness, and confidence. He does not, for example, want to argue with anyone. "Good men don't fight with women" ("Killing Wife" 157), he claims when his wife challenges him about avoiding arguments. The seemingly gentlemanly statement reveals the extent to which Wu refuses to come to terms with reality, let alone overcome the unseen forces that oppress him in America.

His problematic mentality is further mirrored through his oscillation between two sharply contrasting worlds: the illusion of "there" (his steamy, prosperous past as a confident and boisterous man in Taiwan) and the reality of "here" (the chilling and isolated present in America, where he becomes ailing and weak). Always imagining that he will one day regain the affections of his wife, he never understands that what goes on in their marriage reflects his American reality. In that sense, Wu is defeated rather than uplifted by his dreams—he is destroyed by his dysfunctional "cultural baggage" as he struggles in an alien environment.[127] Sympathetic and critical by turns, the author artfully explores Wu's misguided and menacing frustrations and exposes the radical dissonance between his flattering self-image as a kung fu master and the rude reality of his inadequate qualifications to rise in American life.

At the end of story, Wu is shut up in an asylum, where he becomes a "model patient": "Wu Ziqiao behaves well after entering the mental asylum, and becomes the *model patient* of the entire hospital. . . . He always sits on an iron chair in the ward yard. With a camera in hand, he sings an old Chinese tune: 'How fragrant the spring flowers are; How bright the autumn moon is; How happy I am as a young boy; How do you feel my beautiful girl?'" ("Killing Wife" 206–7, emphasis added). The sarcastic tone seems to indicate that the asylum is the only place for Wu; there he can live forever in his memories of the "good old days." The scene also assumes multiple meanings within the Chinese and Asian American social setting. That Wu becomes a "model patient" in the asylum is an ultimate irony because Asians are praised for being the "model minority" in American society. It also resembles an episode in Kingston's *Woman Warrior*. Like "crazy" Aunt Moon Orchid, Wu enjoys asylum life.[128] Despite the difference in gender between the two characters, they both are misfits in American society and victims of it.

The narrative of the story is befuddled yet has raw power. It underscores a mentality that is both fundamental and common to those Chinese men whose position in America is deteriorating. Like the protagonist, they find that their status has declined from "family heads" to "family maids" and that their world has been knocked off-center. Instead of appealing to their taste for sympathy, however, the author makes a conscious effort to show, through the tragedy of the protagonist, that blaming women for men's failure in America obscures the real problem, and that escaping to a world of traditional Chinese culture cannot help either. But what is the solution? As he does in other stories such as "Circumcision" and "The Ship of Bananas," Zhang leaves the question unanswered. Such a way to respond to and prefigure the recurrent concern of the implications of the "rise" of Chinese American women and the "fall" of men is keenly felt by readers. As one critic has pointed out, "Zhang Xiguo's representative work, 'Killing Wife,' is not a simple story of conflicts between men and women nor a dramatic confrontation between husbands and wives. Its underlying message exposes the anxiety of Chinese men, their feelings of being oppressed and emasculated in American life, and their problematic adjustment to an alien culture. Its real theme is: where is the way out for Chinese men in America?"[129]

Discussion of the role of gender by Chinese immigrant writers reflects more than a social-realist view of gender issues in Chinese American life. Although much of the argument has to do with the controversy over changing relations between Chinese men and women in America, what makes the discussion of gender worth reading is a quality that transcends a male-versus-female perspective and demonstrates that the experience of Chinese immigrants is not isolated. Rather, it is tied to prevailing social, economic, political, and cultural trends in American society.

Depicting the role of gender in Chinese-language literature raises a critical issue: What actual power do Chinese men and women wield or lack in American life? It demonstrates that gender is relational and that Chinese men and women do not live in a vacuum. The rise of Chinese women and the fall of men make sense only in how they react with each other and by comparing their status in China and in American society. If the prospects of Chinese immigrant men in America are not as promising as those of Chinese women, that has nothing to do with the ascent of women. It is a complex product of dehumanizing pressure on the immigrants in American life.

In addition, as Yi Li's story "Abortion" indicates, the struggle for woman's rights is an issue of gender and class. The socioeconomic burden on women in Chinatowns means that working-class women are still far from gaining equality, despite an active struggle waged by the feminist movement that has succeeded in improving their conditions substantially. Only with economic equality can they cease being entrapped and become self-assertive enough to confront sexism within and outside of the Chinese American community. In this sense, it is hardly an overstatement to say that Chinese-language literature has broken a new path in exploring the role of gender in American culture.

### Notes

1. Yi Li [Pan Xiumei], "Duotai" [Abortion], in *Haiwai huaren zuojia xiaoshuoxuan* [A selection of short stories by Chinese immigrant writers], ed. Li Li [Bao Lili], (Hong Kong: Joint, 1983), 91.

2. Many Chinese-language writers are also faculty members at American colleges and universities. Bai Xianyong, for example, is a professor at the University of California, San Diego; Nie Hualing has been on the faculty of the University of Iowa since the 1960s; Yu Lihua taught Chinese at the State University of New York, Albany, until her retirement in the early 1990s; and Zhang Xiguo is on the faculty of the University of Pittsburgh.

3. For Chinese immigrants, there is also a Confucian aspect in their pursuit of academic careers. In traditional Chinese society, having wealth was not as prestigious as being a scholar, because the layers of hierarchy in the imperial system were: scholar, farmer, artisan, and merchant. That tradition has left a mark on the mentality of Chinese immigrants.

4. There are six Chinese American Nobel Laureates—for physics, 1957: C. N. Yang [Chen Ning Yang; Yang Zhenning], 1922– , and T. D. Lee [Tsung Dao Lee; Li Zhengdao], 1926– ; for physics, 1976: Samuel Chao Chung Ting [Ding Zhaozhong], 1936– ; for chemistry, 1986: Yuan Tze Lee [Li Yuanzhe], 1936– ; for physics, 1997: Steven Chu [Zhu Diwen], 1948– ; and for physics, 1998: Daniel C. Tsui [Cui Qi], 1939– .

5. Younghill Kang (1903–72), *East Goes West* (New York: Charles Scribner, 1937), 87, 89. A Korean student immigrant, Kang, like many Korean intellectuals of his time, was well educated in traditional Chinese culture. He maintained a close relationship with the Chinese American community and married an American-born Chinese. Elaine H. Kim, *Asian American Literature: An Introduction to the Writings and Their Social Context* (Philadelphia: Temple University Press, 1982), 32–43.

6. Some Chinese immigrant writers argue that minorities can enter higher education more easily than used to be the case because declining faculty salaries have made academic careers less attractive to many in mainstream society. Chen Ruoxi, *Tuwei* [Break out], (repr. Hong Kong: Joint, 1983), 26; Yi Li, *Shiwan Meijin* [A hundred thousand dollars], (Hong Kong: Joint, 1987), 63.

7. Won Lee, "Second Generation Korean American," [Korean American Friendship Society] *Pacific Bridge* 3 (Winter 1994): 2–3.

8. Census Bureau report cited in "U.S. Asians Earning Less Than Whites," *Los Angeles Times,* Dec. 9, 1995, D2. Also see "Glass Ceiling? It's More Like a Steel Cage," *Los Angeles Times,* March 20, 1995, B4.

9. Arnold's name is based on the pronunciation of the character's surname in Chinese. Chinese authors usually give only surnames to non-Asian characters.

10. Yu Lihua, *Kaoyan* [The ordeal], (repr. Hong Kong: Cosmos Books, 1993), 89 (subsequent page citations to *Ordeal* appear in parentheses).

11. A Chinese American professor has told me that the novel moved him when he read it before being denied tenure at an Ivy League university during the 1970s. Author interview, Cambridge, Mass., Nov. 19, 1997.

12. It is difficult to measure the full impact of Yu Lihua's experience in academe on shaping the plot and details of the novel, but she incorporated personal information to make the story closer to reportage than imaginative literature. Similar to Zhong, Yu Lihua's former husband is a Chinese American physicist and was once denied tenure. Like the author, Zhong's wife (the female protagonist) was born and grew up in southeastern China, received a college education in Taiwan, and came to America for graduate studies. Also like the author, the Zhongs have three children—two daughters and a son. How Yu Lihua's personal philosophy affects the development of feminist consciousness in Zhong's wife is a matter of speculation. Like Yu, after a period of painful bewilderment she finally decides to leave Zhong. Zhong Meiyin, "Xiezuo wuru jieshu nan" [An introduction to *Kaoyan*], in Yu Lihua *The Ordeal* (repr. Hong Kong: Cosmos Books, 1993), 6–14; Li Ziyun, "Yu Lihua he tade xiaoshuo 'Jiemeiyin'" [Yu Lihua and her story "Two Sisters"], [Shanghai] *Xiaoshuo Jie* [Fiction World] 4 (1988): 176; Huang Wenxiang, *Oumei jiechu huayi nuxing* [Outstanding women of Chinese ancestry in Europe and America], (Hong Kong: Shanghai Book, 1992), 198–226.

13. Jayjia Hsia, *Asian Americans in Higher Education and at Work* (Hillsdale: Lawrence Erlbaum, 1988), 127–32; [New York] *Shijie Ribao* [World Journal], Oct. 21, 1994, A2.

14. William Wei, *The Asian American Movement* (Philadelphia: Temple University Press, 1993), 158–59. Also see Linda Greenhouse, "Shield of Secrecy in Tenure Disputes," *New York Times,* Jan. 10, 1990, B1; Chang-lin Tien, "A View from Berkeley," *New York Times,* March 31, 1996, A30; and Kaori Tanegashima, "College Courses in Asian Studies," *Los Angeles Times,* Jan. 25, 1996, B8.

15. Wei, *The Asian American Movement,* 158–61.

16. Hsin-sheng C. Kao, ed., *Nativism Overseas: Contemporary Chinese Women Writers* (Albany: State University of New York Press, 1993), 88.

17. Quoted in Samantha Young, "Interview," [Boston], *Sampan,* June 20, 1997, 3.

18. Discussion of the relationship between the Chinese and the Jews is also common in Chinese American literature in English. See, for example, Jeffery Paul Chan, "The Chinese in Haifa," in Frank Chin et al., eds., *Aiiieeeee! An Anthology of Asian American Writers* (Washington, D.C.: Howard University Press, 1974), 12–29; and Gish Jen, *Mona in the Promised Land* (New York: Alfred A. Knopf, 1996).

19. Bai Xianyong, "Yequ" [Night tune], and Zhang Xiguo, "Geli" [Circumcision], both in *Haiwai huaren zuojia xiaoshuoxuan* [A selection of short stories by Chinese immigrant writers], ed. Li Li [Bao Lili], (Hong Kong: Joint, 1983), 67–83, 291–306; Chen, *Breaking Out,* 50–52, 70–74, 91–96; Yi Li, "Fu jjiaoshou bufu" [Professor Fu doesn't believe it], in Yi, *A Hundred Thousand Dollars* (Hong Kong: Joint, 1987), 149–52. There is also strong interest in Jewish American literature among critics and readers in China. Xiao-huang Yin, "Progress and Problems: American Literary Studies in China during the Post-Mao Era," in *As Others Read Us: International Perspectives on American Literature,* ed. Huck Gutman (Amherst: University of Massachusetts Press, 1991), 49–64.

20. "Liuyou pian" [Tourism in Los Angeles], *Nanjiazhou huaren gongshang dianhua haomabu* [Southern California Chinese telephone directory], (Los Angeles, 1994), 45.

21. Susan Kalcik, "Ethnic Foodways in America: Symbol and the Performance of Identity," in *Ethnic and Regional Foodways in the United States: The Performance of Group Identity*, ed. Linda Keller Brown and Kay Mussell (Knoxville: University of Tennessee Press, 1984), 37, 44–61 (also see "Introduction," 3–15).

22. I am indebted to Tu Wei-ming for this observation.

23. William Trant, "Jew and Chinaman," *North American Review* 195 (Feb. 1912): 249–60. There are similar interests in comparative studies of the Chinese and Jews among scholars in China. Jiang Wenhan, *Zhongguo gudai jidujio ji Kaifeng youtairen* [Christianity in ancient China and Jews at Kaifeng], (Shanghai: Zhishi, 1982), 143–201.

24. Quoted in Larry Tye, "Hong Kong New Year: Tradition, Informality," *Boston Globe*, Sept. 6, 1994, A2.

25. Theodore von Karman with Lee Edson, *The Wind and Beyond: Theodore von Karman: Pioneer in Aviation and Pathfinder in Space* (Boston: Little, Brown, 1967), 309.

26. Quoted in Lynn Pan, *Sons of the Yellow Emperor: A History of the Chinese Diaspora* (New York: Kodansha International, 1994), 88, 152.

27. Garth Alexander, *The Invisible China: The Overseas Chinese and the Politics of Southeast Asia* (New York: Macmillan, 1974), 30–48, 59, 213–24.

28. Rudolf Glanz, "Jews and Chinese in America," in Glanz, *Studies in Judaica Americana* (New York: KTAV, 1970), 314–29. I am indebted to Marc Shell for this information. Also see Trant, "Jew and Chinaman," 249–60.

29. Adrienne Rich, "Split at the Root: An Essay on Jewish Identity," in *Visions of America: Personal Narratives from the Promised Land*, ed. Wesley Brown and Amy Ling (New York: Persea Books, 1993), 91–92.

30. For more information, see John Higham, *Send These to Me: Jews and Other Immigrants in Urban America* (New York: Athenaeum, 1975). Also see Ronald Takaki, *A Different Mirror: A History of Multicultural America* (Boston: Little, Brown, 1993), 277–310.

31. James W. Loewen, *The Mississippi Chinese: Between Black and White*, rev. ed. (Prospect Heights: Waveland, 1988), 185–202; Marvin Hightower, "Interview: The Counterpoint of Race and Ethnicity," *Harvard Gazette*, Nov. 12, 1993, 5. Also see Mary C. Waters, *Ethnic Options: Choosing Identities in America* (Berkeley: University of California Press, 1990); and Jonathan Kaufman, *Broken Alliance: The Turbulent Times between Blacks and Jews in America* (New York: Charles Scribners Sons, 1996).

32. Chen Ruoxi, "Xiangzhuo taipingyang bi'an" [To the other side of the Pacific], in *Haiwai huaren zuojia xiaoshuoxuan* [A selection of short stories by Chinese immigrant writers], ed. Li Li [Bao Lili], (Hong Kong: Joint, 1983), 243, 269.

33. Zhang Xiguo, "Circumcision," 300.

34. Cited in Richard Eder, "A WASP-Free America," *Los Angeles Times Book Review*, May 26, 1996, 2. Also see Eric Liu, *The Accidental Asian: Notes of a Native Speaker* (New York: Random House, 1998), 145.

35. The view is also apparent in Chinese American literature in English. Amy Ling, *Between Worlds: Women Writers of Chinese Ancestry* (New York: Pergamon Press, 1990), 1–20.

36. Quoted in Yan Huo [Pan Yaoming], *Haiwai huaren zuojia luying* [Interviews with Chinese immigrant writers], (Hong Kong: Joint, 1984), 52–53. Of course, in their use of Jewish Americans as role models for Chinese immigrants, Chinese-language writers may have idealized the Jewish experience.

37. I use the term *downtown Chinese* to refer to economically disadvantaged residents of Chinatowns. Overwhelmingly foreign-born, they are on the lowest rungs of the job ladder in the Chinese American community. For information on the backgrounds and socioeconomic statuses of the Chinatown population, see Chalsa M. Loo, *Chinatown: Most Time, Hard Time* (New York: Praeger, 1992).

38. Quoted in Timothy P. Fong, *The First Suburban Chinatown: The Remaking of Monterey Park, California* (Philadelphia: Temple University Press, 1994), 70.

39. Peter Kwong, *The New Chinatown* (New York: Noonday Press, 1987), 3–10.

40. The first passage is quoted from Zhou Li [Julia Z. Fochler], *Manhadun de zhongguo nuren* [Manhattan's China lady], (Beijing: Beijing Chubanshe, 1992), 322; the second is from Yu, *The Ordeal*, 373.

41. Zhou Feili [Philip Chou], "Yangfan erchi" [Two ways to eat American meals], in Zhou, *Yangfan erchi* [Two ways to eat American meals], (repr. Taipei: Erya, 1987), 1–24.

42. Zhou, "Two Ways to Eat American Meals," 9.

43. Peter A. Quinn, quoted in Patrick J. McDonnell, "Connecting the Past and Present," *Los Angeles Times*, March 11, 1995, B3.

44. "Feifa renshe yuanyuan jinru Meiguo" [Illegal immigrants continuously enter America], [Boston] *Yamei Shibao* [Asian American Times], Sept. 24, 1993, 11. For information on the issue of division in (and fragmentation of) Chinese communities, see Fong, *The First Suburban Chinatown;* 138–56; Kwong, *The New Chinatown*, 81–106; and Victor G. Nee and Brett de Bary Nee, *Longtime Californ': A Documentary Study of an American Chinatown* (repr. Stanford: Stanford University Press, 1986), 289–319. The fact that Chinese and Asian Americans were highly divided on issues such as the Affirmative Action Program is also evidence of community fragmentation. Cecilia Wong, "Asians and Affirmative Action: Two Views," *Sampan*, April 3, 1998, 3–5.

45. Directed by Oliver Stone, *Year of the Dragon* (1985) was adapted from the bestseller by Robert Daley, a former New York City police commissioner. By exploiting gangs in Chinatowns, the film portrays the Chinese American community as a den of criminal aliens and a center of international drug networking. The film's violence and bloody gun play resemble Hollywood's depiction of the Tong wars during the 1920s and 1930s. The hero, a white police detective, is worshipped by a young Chinese American woman reporter, and they have an affair. *Year of the Dragon* projected a negative image of Chinatowns and Chinese Americans and caused wide protest in the Chinese and Asian American communities. Kwong, *The New Chinatown*, 116–17; Wei, *The Asian American Movement*, 260.

46. Chen Ruoxi, *Zhihun* [Paper marriage], (repr. Hong Kong: Joint, 1987), 193–94. Also see Kwong, *The New Chinatown*, 116–23.

47. Zhu Ying, "Bie laoxiang geiren chi yikufan" [Don't always feed us with bitter stories about American life], [Los Angeles] *Xin Dalu* [New Continent], Aug. 1, 1994, 16; Pangzi, "I Am a Happy Slave," *Chinese Community Forum*, no. 9808, March 11, 1998. *Chinese Community Forum* [CCF] is an electronic journal sponsored by Chinese students and scholars in America and published on China-Net. Its Web site is at [http://www.cnd.org].

48. Fong, *The First Suburban Chinatown*, 157–77; K. Connie Kang, "Chinese in the Southland: A Changing Picture," *Los Angeles Times*, June 29, 1997, A1. Also see Carla Rivera, "Asians Say They Fare Better than Other Minorities," *Los Angeles Times*, Aug. 20, 1993, A1; and "Wu Jiawei fouren qishi xianxiang pubian" [Wu Jiawei denies racial discrimination is a common phenomenon], [New York] *Zhong Bao* [Central Daily], Nov. 19, 1987, A3.

49. Angela Oh and Nancy Yoshihara, "Adding an Asian American Voice to the Race Debate," *Los Angeles Times*, July 13, 1997, M3.

50. Qian Ning, *Liuxu Meiguo* [Studying in the USA], (Nanjing: Jiangsu Wenyi, 1996), 174–92.

51. Quoted in Susan Moffat, "Splintered Society: U.S. Asians," *Los Angeles Times*, July 13, 1992, A1, A20.

52. Zhang Xiguo, "Xiangjiao chuan" [The ship of banana], in *Zhang Xiguo ji* [Selected stories of Zhang Xiguo], ed. Chen Wanyi (Taipei: Qianwei, 1993), 112–13.

53. Yang Mu, "Zhang Xiguo de guanxin yu yishu" [Zhang Xiguo's concerns and arts of literature], in *Zhang Xiguo ji* [Selected stories of Zhang Xiguo], ed. Chen Wanyi (Taipei: Qianwei, 1993), 245–47. Also see Pan Yatun and Wang Yisheng, *Haiwai huawen wenxue mingjia* [Distinguished Chinese-language writers abroad], (Guangzhou: Jinan, 1994), 176–79.

54. Quoted in Hightower, "The Counterpoint of Race and Ethnicity," 5. Also see Zhou, "Two Ways to Eat American Meals," 18.

55. Yi Li, *Shiwan meijin* [A hundred thousand dollars], (Hong Kong: Joint, 1987), 138.

56. Yu Lihua, *Youjian zonlu, youjian zonlu* [Seeing the palm trees again], (repr. Beijing: Youyi, 1984), 31. Also see Pan, *Sons of the Yellow Emperor*, 375–79. Purchases of American musical tapes and CDs in Asia made up a quarter of American music record sales in 1994. Maggie Farley, "MTV Hopes Chinese Will Be Staring," *Los Angeles Times*, June 20, 1995, D1.

57. David Henry Hwang, *FOB and Other Plays* (repr. New York: New American Library, 1990), 38.

58. Kang, *East Goes West*, 276, emphasis added.

59. Andrew J. Nathan, "But How Chinese Are They?" *New York Times Book Review*, Dec. 9, 1990, 26. Also see Alexander, *The Invisible China*, 150–66.

60. "Ethnic Chinese in Indonesia," *South China Morning Post*, Hong Kong, May 29, 1997, A1. The ethnic Chinese make up about 4 percent of Indonesia's population of 202 million. Although a few are among the richest people in Indonesia, the majority are small businessmen or peddlers. They are often made scapegoats, however, during economic crises in that country. Mely G. Tan, "The Ethnic Chinese in Indonesia," in *Ethnic Chinese as Southeast Asians*, ed. Leo Suryadinata (Singapore: Institute of Southeast Asian Studies, 1997), 33–65; Stephen Fitzgerald, *China and the Overseas Chinese* (New York: Cambridge University Press, 1972), 1–11, 74–101. Also see "Indonesian Mobs Loot and Attack Chinese Merchants," *Boston Globe*, Feb. 15, 1998, A4.

61. Kong Xiangjiong, "Huaren shouxi cheng daizui gaoyang" [Ethnic Chinese again become scapegoats in Indonesia], [New York] *Haojiao* [Herald Monthly] 11 (April 1998): 2.

62. Zhifu Du, "6.5 Million Hong Kong People Returning to the Communist Motherland," *Chinese Community Forum*, no. 9733, July 1, 1997.

63. Around 76 percent of Chinese immigrants become naturalized American citizens after their eligibility. By comparison, only about 44 percent of European immigrants apply for American citizenship when they become eligible. Harry H. L. Kitano and Roger Daniels, *Asian Americans: Emerging Minorities*, 2d ed. (Englewood Cliffs: Prentice-Hall, 1995), 183. Also see Elliot R. Barkan, *Asian and Pacific Islander Migration to the United States: A Model of New Global Patterns* (Westport: Greenwood Press, 1992), 69–77.

64. Yi Li, "Tiantang" [Paradise, 1980], in Yi, *A Hundred Thousand Dollars* (Hong Kong: Joint, 1987), 116–20.

65. Quoted in Nee and Nee, *Longtime Californ'*, 245–46. Of course, in participating in political movement in American society, Chinese immigrants are also handicapped by their "alien" status because they may be deported for allegedly radical views. One Chinese writer, for example, recalls in her fictionalized autobiography being deported to China in 1954 for her left-wing ideology during the wave of anticommunist hysteria that swept America. See Wang Ying, *Liangzhong meiguoren* [Two different kinds of Americans], (Beijing: Zhongguo Qingnian, 1980). See also L. Ling-chi Wang, "Roots and the Changing Identity of the Chinese in the United States," in *The Living Tree: The Changing Meaning of Being Chinese Today*, ed. Tu Wei-ming (Stanford: Stanford University Press, 1994), 185–212.

66. Mario Puzo, "Choosing a Dream: Italians in Hell's Kitchen," in *Visions of America: Personal Narratives from the Promised Land*, ed. Wesley Brown and Amy Ling (New York: Persea Books, 1993), 58.

67. Quoted in Yan Geling, *Chen Chong—helihuo de zhongguo nuren* [Joan Chen: A Chinese woman in Hollywood], (Hong Kong: Cosmos, 1995), 200, 221. In this respect, Chen seems to have followed in the footsteps of Anna May Wong, a pioneer Asian American actor who became critical of the racial prejudice in Hollywood once she had made a name in the entertainment industry. Tiana [Thi Thanh Nga], "The Long March: From Wong to Woo," *Cineaste* 21, no. 4 (1995): 38–40; Philip Leibfred, "Anna May Wong," *Films in Review* 38 (March 1987): 146–52; Edward Sakamoto, "Anna May Wong and the Dragon-lady Syndrome," *Los Angeles Times Calendar*, July 12, 1987, 40.

68. Fong, *The First Suburban Chinatown*, 154. Also see Angelina T. Wong, "The Contest to Become Top Banana: Chinese Students at Canadian Universities," *Canadian Ethnic Studies* 11, no. 2 (1979): 63–69.

69. Kang, "Chinese in the Southland"; also see Rivera, "Asians Say They Fare Better than Other Minorities."

70. Wei, *The Asian American Movement*, 1–43; also see Gary Y. Okihiro, *Margins and Mainstreams: Asians in American History and Culture* (Seattle: University of Washington Press, 1994), 148–75.

71. Quoted in Arif Dirlik, "Asians on the Rim: Transnational Capital and Local Community in the Making of Contemporary Asian America," *Amerasia Journal* 22, no. 3 (1996): 7. Chinese American scholars also argue that conflicts in economic interests are a primary source of tensions within the Chinese American community. L. Ling-chi Wang, "The Politics of Ethnic Identity and Empowerment: The Asian American Community since the 1960s," *Asian American Policy Review* 2 (Spring 1991): 43–56. Also see Fong, *The First Suburban Chinatown*, 138–56; and Kwong, *The New Chinatown*, 81–106. The interest of Chinese immigrant writers in Marxist views is also a result of the influence on them of American academicians. For a general discussion of the influence of Marxism on the humanities and social science in American academia, see Dario Fernandez-Morera, *American Academia and the Survival of Marxist Ideas* (New York: Praeger, 1996).

72. Author interview with Yu Lihua, Albany, N.Y., Oct. 13, 1994.

73. His name *Jia* ["fake"] reveals the author's subtle indication that he is a *jia yangguizi* [a "pseudo-foreign devil"].

74. Yu, *The Ordeal*, 192–93, 252–53.

75. Yi, "Abortion," 102–3.

76. Cao Youfang, *Meiguo yueliang* [The American moon], (Hong Kong: Joint, 1986), 4–6.

77. Wang, "The Politics of Ethnic Identity and Empowerment," 45–54; Fong, *The First Suburban Chinatown;* 138–56; Kwong, *The New Chinatown,* 81–106.

78. "Opinion: When Restaurants Fail, Who Pays the Workers?" *Sampan,* Feb. 20, 1998, 7; also see Wang, "The Politics of Ethnic Identity and Empowerment," 45–54.

79. Many Asian American activists and scholars have expressed similar views. Oh and Yoshihara, "Adding an Asian American Voice to the Race Debate," M3; Yen Le Espiritu, *Asian American Women and Men: Labor, Laws, and Love* (Thousand Oaks: Sage Publications, 1997), 113–16.

80. Yu, *The Ordeal,* 400–401.

81. Zhong, "An Introduction to *Kaoyan,*" 6–14. Yu Lihua admits being influenced by the feminist movement, which gained momentum in American society when she was writing the novel during the early 1970s.

82. Yi Li, "Fang yisheng yizhen" [Dr. Fang's free medical service], in Yi, *A Hundred Thousand Dollars* (Hong Kong: Joint, 1987), 104.

83. Chen Ruoxi, *Er Hu* [Uncle and nephew of the Hu family], (repr. Hong Kong: Joint, 1986), 7–8, 219–27; 233–34; Yu Lihua, *Fujia de ernumen* [Sons and daughters of the Fu family], (repr. Hong Kong: Cosmos, 1994), 256–57. Although the two novels are fictional portrayals, there are frequent reports of such tragedies in real life. See Yungui Ding and Wei Lin, "Unemployed Man Killed Daughter and Self," *China News Digest,* U.S. regional, no. 97027, Sept. 4, 1997. Also see Chris Poore, "A Tragedy at Quiet Berea College, Kentucky," *Herald-Leader,* reprinted in *China News Digest,* U.S. regional, no. 9405, Jan. 29, 1994. The *China News Digest* is another major Chinese community–based electronic journal in America. Its Web site is at http://www.cnd.org; or ftp://ftp.cnd.org.

84. Pan, *Sons of the Yellow Emperor,* 191–201; Qian, *Studying in the USA,* 207–19. There are similar changes in the relationship between men and women in the Chinese communities in Southeastern Asia. See Wang Gungwu, *A Short History of the Nanyang Chinese* (Singapore: Eastern Universities Press, 1959); and Teresita Ang See, ed., *The Chinese Immigrants: Selected Writings of Professor Chinben See* (Manila: Kaisa Para, 1992), 91–271.

85. Chen Ruoxi, "Kezi guxiang lai" [Visitors from the hometown], in Chen, *Chengli chengwai* [In and outside the wall], (Taipei: Shibao, 1981),185.

86. See chapter 4 for a discussion of Jade Snow Wong. For more information on the experience of immigrant women in American society, see Donna Gabaccia, ed., *Seeking Common Ground: Multidisciplinary Studies of Immigrant Women in the United States* (Westport: Greenwood, 1992).

87. Pan, *Sons of the Yellow Emperor,* 191. Also see Li Yiyuan and Guo Zhenyu, eds., *Dongnanya huaren shehui yanjiu* [The Chinese communities in Southeast Asia], (Taipei: Academia Sinica, 1985), 2:144–61; and Ling, *Between Worlds,* 104–57.

88. Cao, *The American Moon,* 94–95.

89. Elaine H. Kim, "Such Opposite Creatures: Men and Women in Asian American Literature," *Michigan Quarterly Review* 29 (Winter 1990): 75. Also see Okihiro, *Margins and Mainstreams,* 64–92.

90. Qian, *Studying in the USA,* 209. Qian's analysis of changes in the marital relationship in Chinese student immigrant families is perhaps the best work on this subject that has been published in Chinese. The fact that the book has been highly praised by both Chinese readers and the mainstream American media is rare. For a review of Qian's work,

see Patrick E. Tyler, "A Chinese View of Life in the United States," *New York Times,* July 21, 1997, A1.

91. Quoted in Tian Xinbin, "Laobang shengzhu de wentan xinxiu" [A new star in the writers' circle], in Zhou Feili, *Yangfan erchi* [Two ways to eat American meals], (repr. Taipei: Erya, 1987), 239. For more discussion on the role of women in the Chinese American community, also see Rose Hum Lee, *The Chinese in the United States of America* (Hong Kong: Hong Kong University Press, 1960), 185–230; Roger Daniels, *Asian America: Chinese and Japanese in the United States since 1850* (Seattle: University of Washington Press, 1988), 78, 82–3; and Judy Yung, *Unbound Feet: A Social History of Chinese Women in San Francisco* (Berkeley: University of California Press, 1995), 52–105.

92. Zhou Feili, "Yizhou dashi" [Weekly event], in Zhou Feili, *Yangfan erchi* [Two ways to eat American meals], (repr. Taipei: Erya, 1987),25–49.

93. Maxine Hong Kingston, *The Woman Warrior* (repr. New York: Vintage, 1989), 77; Kingston, *China Men,* 246–47.

94. Kim Ronyoung, *Clay Walls* (repr. Seattle: University of Washington Press, 1990).

95. Hisaye Yamamoto, *Seventeen Syllables and Other Stories* (Latham: Kitchen Table, 1988).

96. Yan, *Joan Chen,* 202.

97. Shu Fei, "Xiezuo, aiqing, hunyin—ji Yu Lihua" [Writing, love, and marriage: My impression of Yu Lihua], [Shanghai] *Wenhui* [Enchanter Monthly] 85 (June 1987): 61. Also see Huang, *Outstanding Women of Chinese Ancestry in Europe and America,* 207.

98. Yu, *Sons and Daughters of the Fu Family,* 200.

99. Qian, *Studying in the USA,* 207–41. Some prominent Chinese women such as Yu Lihua and Joan Chen went through divorce in America. Chinese women also have the highest divorce rate of any ethnic group in Australia. Coral O'Connor, "Survey Reveals Chinese Immigrants in Australia Divorce Most," *South China Morning Post,* Hong Kong, July 24, 1994, A4. The phenomenon is also seen among Korean immigrants in America. Lawrence K. Hong, "The Korean Family in Los Angeles," in *Koreans in Los Angeles,* ed. Eui-Young Yu, Earl H. Phillips, and Eun Sik Yang (Los Angeles: Center for Korean-American and Korean Studies, California State University, 1982), 99–132.

100. Qian, *Studying in the USA,* 213–14.

101. Zhou, *Two Ways to Eat American Meals,* 236.

102. Yu, *Sons and Daughters of the Fu Family,* 436.

103. Cao, *The American Moon,* 18.

104. Quoted in Huang, *Outstanding Women of Chinese Ancestry in Europe and America,* 207.

105. Quoted in "Chinese Protester, Taiwan Woman Wed," *Boston Globe,* Aug. 31, 1994, A15, emphasis added.

106. Qian, *Studying in the USA,* 216–21.

107. Chen Junjie, "Ming Qing shiren jieceng nuzi shoujie xianxiang" [The Ming and Qing intelligentsia and the moral imposition on widows], [Hong Kong] *Ershiyi Shiji* [The Twenty-first Century] 27 (Feb. 1995): 98–107. Also see Tseng Pao-sun [P. S. Tseng], "The Chinese Women: Past and Present," in *Chinese Women through Chinese Eyes,* ed. Li Yuning (Armonk: M. E. Sharpe, 1992), 72–86.

108. Yu, *Sons and Daughters of the Fu Family,* 314–15.

109. Yuan Zenan [Yuan Zhihui], *Bujian busan* [Until we meet], (Hong Kong: Joint, 1985), 33.

110. Jin Hallock, "Show Your Abilities and Intelligence," *Chinese Community Forum*, no. 9723, May 14, 1997, emphasis added. Also see Morrison G. Wong, "A Look at Intermarriage among the Chinese in the United States in 1980," *Sociological Perspectives* 32, no. 1 (1989): 87–107.

111. Quoted in Okihiro, *Margins and Mainstreams*, 84.

112. Hasia R. Diner, *Erin's Daughters in America* (Baltimore: Johns Hopkins University Press, 1983).

113. U.S. Bureau of the Census report, cited in "U.S. Asians Earning Less Than Whites," *Los Angeles Times*, Dec. 9, 1995, D2.

114. John Koch, "Interview with Connie Chung," *Boston Globe Magazine*, June 29, 1997, 12. Also see Edgar P. Trotter, *The Asian American Journalist: Results of a National Survey* (Fullerton: California State University, Institute for Media-Society Studies, 1987), 13–15; and Cecilia Wong, "Asian Americans in the Newsroom," *Sampan*, Aug. 1, 1997, 4–5.

115. Gabaccia, *Seeking Common Ground*, 33.

116. Elaine H. Kim, ed., *With Silk Wings: Asian American Women at Work* (San Francisco: Asian Women United of California, 1983), 131. Also see Espiritu, *Asian American Women and Men*, 71–77.

117. Espiritu, *Asian American Women and Men*, 61–85; Lisa Lowe, *Immigrant Acts: On Asian American Cultural Politics* (Durham: Duke University Press, 1996), 154–73.

118. Xia Yun, "Xie Yi" [My impression of Yi Li], in Yi, *A Hundred Thousand Dollars* (Hong Kong: Joint, 1987), 1–3.

119. Yi, "Abortion," 90, subsequent page citations to "Abortion" appear in parentheses.

120. Lin Yutang, "Impressions on Reaching America," in *Land without Ghosts: Chinese Impressions of America from the Mid-Nineteenth Century to the Present*, trans. and ed. R. David Arkush and Leo Ou-fan Lee (Berkeley: University of California Press, 1989), 162. Lin's liberal stance on the issue of woman's rights was a major factor in his two daughters' career success; one became an accomplished writer, and the other is a prominent scientist. For more information on Lin Yutang's views on women, see Lin Taiyi [Anor Lin], *Lin Yutang zuan* [Biography of Lin Yutang], (Beijing: Zhongguo Xiju, 1994), 122–30.

121. Chen, *Breaking Out*, 149.

122. Zhang Xiguo, "Shaqi" [Killing wife], in *Zhang Xiguo ji* [Selected stories of Zhang Xiguo], ed. Chen Wanyi (Taipei: Qianwei, 1993), 115–207, subsequent page citations to "Killing Wife" appear in parentheses.

123. Yang, "Zhang Xiguo's Concerns and Arts of Literature," *ibid.*, 239–49.

124. Shi Nai'an, *Shuihu zhuan* [The water margin: Outlaws of the marsh], a sixteenth-century classic, is perhaps the most "masculine" novel in Chinese literary history. In several famous episodes, male heroes such as Song Jiang, Yang Xiong, and Lu Junyi kill their unfaithful wives and seek revenge for social injustice. Their deeds are household stories in China. There are several different English translations of this classic, including one by Pearl S. Buck: *All Men Are Brothers* (New York: John Day, 1933).

125. For an English version of Lu Xun's "A Madman's Diary" (1918), see *The Complete Stories of Lu Xun*, trans. Yan Xianyi and Gladys Yang (Bloomington: Indiana University Press, 1987), 1–12. For discussion of the story, see Leo Ou-fan Lee, *Voices from the Iron House: A Study of Lu Xun* (Bloomington: Indiana University Press, 1987), 49–109.

126. Frank Chin, a leading voice among Chinese American male writers in English, acknowledges that he loves reading stories of outlaws in *The Water Margin*. The number

108 appears frequently as an important symbol in his novel *Donald Duck* (Minneapolis: Coffee House Press, 1991). Also see Chin's written statement for a press release, courtesy of the Cultural Studies Office of Occidental College, Nov. 6, 1995, 2; and Robert Murray Davis, "Frank Chin: An Interview with Robert Murray Davis," *Amerasia Journal* 14, no. 2 (1988): 91.

127. The term *cultural baggage* is a complicated concept. As Sau-ling Cynthia Wong argues, socialization requires confidence in dealing with one's surroundings and resisting the stereotyping of others. Chinese immigrants, however, marginalized and denied full membership in American society throughout history, never possessed the power to define their personalities or enjoy the freedom to participate in the host society, as other groups did. Sau-ling Cynthia Wong, *Reading Asian American Literature: From Necessity to Extravagance* (Princeton: Princeton University Press, 1993), 85.

128. Kingston, *The Woman Warrior*, 159–60.

129. Chen Wanyi, "Xu" [Preface], in *Zhang Xiguo ji* [Selected stories of Zhang Xiguo], ed. Chen Wanyi (Taipei: Qianwei, 1993), 12.

*Today, almost every month, a wonderful new book by an Asian American is published. . . . I can't keep up reading all of them. When I started reading and writing. . . . I was lucky to have Jade Snow Wong and Pearl S. Buck. I think that my role in Asian American literature is that I write in such a way that it helps our work to be taken seriously as literature, not merely as anthropology, entertainment, exotics.*
—Maxine Hong Kingston

*Good or bad, the stereotypical Asian is nothing as a man. . . . he is womanly, effeminate, devoid of all the traditionally masculine qualities of originality, daring, physical courage, and creativity. The mere fact that four out of five American-born Chinese-American writers are women reinforces this aspect of the stereotype.*
—Frank Chin et al.

# 7.

# Multiple Voices and the "War of Words": Contemporary Chinese American Literature

The decade of the 1960s changed the Chinese American literary scene forever.[1] While the struggle for racial equality initiated by the civil rights movement raised the ethnic consciousness of Chinese Americans, new immigration laws led to a dramatic increase in, and diversity of, the Chinese population in the United States. Other events of the decade, such as the anti-war movement, the rise of feminism, ethnic literary activism, and the emergence of the Asian American movement, also had an impact on Chinese American literature. More Chinese Americans were led to participate in creating literature that had expanded readership, a broadened scope, and reshaped thematic concerns. As a result, Chinese American literature entered a distinctively new phase of development.

Among Chinese American writers since the 1960s, Frank Chin and Maxine Hong Kingston stand out as the two most influential. While Chin strives to shatter racial stereotypes and define a new form of Chinese American masculinity, Kingston delves into the lives of Chinese women and voices strong feminist concerns. In particular, the staging of Chin's plays *Chickencoop Chinaman* (1972) and *The Year of the Dragon* (1974) and the publication of Kingston's books *The Woman Warrior: Memoirs of a Girlhood among Ghosts* (1976) and *China Men* (1980) were landmarks in the history of Chinese American literature. Despite their efforts to improve the image of the Chinese, earlier writers such as Yung Wing and Pardee Lowe reinforced stereotypes of Chinese Americans as being completely assimilated and unobtrusively American—models of the melting-pot process.

But the strident words of Chin's "Chinatown cowboys" and the defiant imagery of Kingston's "warrior women" mark a departure from the self-controlled tone and restraint that characterized many early Chinese American publications. Rather than presenting a portrait of humble, loyal, Americanized, and law-abiding immigrants or an image of passive, obedient, disciplined, and hardworking American-born Chinese, Chin and Kingston demonstrate ethnic pride as they recount and redefine the Chinese American experience. In doing so, they have made groundbreaking contributions to the creation of a new Chinese American sensibility and embarked upon new paths, to be followed by others. David Henry Hwang, for example, has acknowledged that he was inspired and influenced by Kingston and Chin when he began his career as a playwright.[2]

A leading voice of the "angry young men" of the 1960s, Frank Chin is deliberately anti-nostalgic, anti-exotic, and unsentimental in his writing. Left-wing radicalism and a strong anti-elite ideology have led him to "kick the ass of the establishment" and write about the feelings of average Chinese Americans, especially the frustration and bitterness of downtown Chinese.[3] Speaking through Tam Lum, a Chinese American writer in *Chickencoop Chinaman*, Chin claims, "I am the natural born ragmouth speaking the motherless bloody tongue."[4]

Chin's audaciously frank observations and fierce descriptions of Chinese American life expose not only the visible obstacles that Chinese face in American society but also the invisible yet powerful psychological effects of ghettoization on Chinatown residents. In Chin's plays and stories, Chinese Americans struggle hopelessly in a suffocating, paralyzing "chickencoop," gloomy urban ghettos surrounded by "dark streets full of dead lettuce and trampled carrot tops."[5] Even those who have been successful in American society seem cynical and pessimistic about the Chinese American reality. "Look at me. I eat, dress, act, and talk like a fool. I smell like [a] rotten flower shop," says a "professional Christian Chinese" in "The Only Real Day" (1974). "I'm becoming [an] American citizen, not because I want to be like them, but because it's good business. . . . They like the Chinese better than Negroes because we're not many and we're not black. . . . They like us better than Jews because we can't be white like the Jews and disappear. . . . But! They don't like a Chinaman being Chinese about life."[6]

Chin's desire to "torpedo" racial stereotypes, especially that of the "emasculated Chinamen," leads him to use violent images and language intended to shock. His graphic portrayal of intercourse between a "Chinaman" and a white former nun, symbolically named Lily, in "The Eat and Run Midnight People" (1976) is a case in point: "I rolled over onto her sandy breasts, her sandy belly, her sandy thighs, and stuck it in. . . . Inside her twat was like I was mixing concrete. . . . I moved back and then I moved in, in cold blood, in and out, fascinated with the motion."[7] Although such graphic accounts can hardly succeed in constructing a new Chinese American manhood, they have stirred controversy by presenting a profoundly ironic and belligerent view of Chinese Americans as a model minority. It is a very different sensibility from that of Pardee Lowe and Jade Snow Wong. Indeed, Chin's quarrel with society yields moving expressions of anger and irony and has a social component, as demonstrated in his refusal to be categorized and thereby counter the racial stereotypes endorsed by mainstream critics and readers.

Sharing a similar background, yet differing widely from Chin in her writing philosophy, Maxine Hong Kingston is another prominent figure among contemporary Chinese American writers.[8] Her representative work *The Woman Warrior,* which has been called a "fantasy autobiography," is the most widely read work by an Asian American writer.[9] Rich in literary flavor and social significance, the book is an intricate and brilliant web of differing versions of the American dream mixed with the Chinese American reality. The confrontation and reconciliation between a rebellious Chinese American daughter and her strong-willed mother saturate almost every page of the book, and Kingston eventually resolves the identity crisis of the protagonist to create an epic of Chinese American life and the place of women in it.

More significantly, Kingston's "talk stories" about various "crazy women" established a new kind of female image in American literature. Although the crazy woman is an old and familiar character in both Western and Eastern literature, Kingston adds a new dimension to that image. Her colorful portrayal of a wide range of women, from the No-Name aunt to Crazy Mary, is meaningful. Each can be singled out, through careful reading of the text and analysis of the background, as a clue toward a better understanding of her intention: to present women as victims and victors. At the same time, such a portrayal is a master motif that unifies the events that occur in seemingly different and unrelated scenarios.

It is common in classic Western and Chinese literature, for example, for "fallen women" to commit suicide. They are described as having brought disgrace and shame to themselves and their families, and suicide is seen as both a punishment and a perverse triumph for them.[10] But in *The Woman Warrior,* the No-Name aunt, who commits suicide by jumping into the family well, transforms herself into a powerful and revengeful "weeping ghost" that will haunt those who victimized her. According to Chinese superstition, as Kingston explains, a drowned woman will emerge from the water to exact vengeance on her enemies.[11] That image of victim becoming victor differs significantly from the tragedies of traditional crazy women and moves the theme and formula for female empowerment a step forward.

A brilliant wordsmith, Kingston is also a great stylist. *The Woman Warrior* is so complex and subtle in symbolism that, despite careful studies, there are symbols and metaphors that still remain to be decoded. For example, the poetic force of Kingston's beautifully rendered writing in the chapter "White Tigers" creates an imagined world where fantasy, myth, and history converge to form a lyrical image of Fa Mulan, the legendary Chinese swordswoman. Critics and readers alike, however, have failed to perceive that the chapter's title also alludes to the influence of Western culture on Chinese Americans. According to ancient Chinese mythology, white tigers symbolize divine forces from the West. In the practice of divination, Chinese fortune-tellers refer to the constellation in the West as the white tiger.[12] By naming the chapter "White Tigers," Kingston thus implies that her Fa Mulan story is not a Chinese legend but a Chinese American allegory, or, as Kingston says, a Chinese myth "transformed by America."[13]

Like Chin and Kingston, Amy Tan is another pathfinder who deserves a special place in the study of contemporary Chinese American literature. Her immensely popular debut novel, *The Joy Luck Club* (1989), focuses on four Chinese immigrant mothers and their American-born daughters and explores the generation gap, a traditional theme in Chinese American literature, from a new perspective. Amid agreeably picturesque and lively family scenes, Tan inserts a deeper message by describing changes in the Chinese American experience and underscoring the differences between new immigrants' views of American life and those of their forebears.

Unlike the parents of Wong and Kingston, who strove to keep China in their children's minds, *The Joy Luck Club* mothers, albeit immigrants, well understand that their children's future is not in China but in America, where they consciously put down roots. Recognizing the urgency of integration into mainstream society, they push their daughters to succeed. As a result, the tensions in *The Joy Luck Club* families are produced not by conflicts between preserving the old and adapting to the new but by parental pressure to succeed. Jing-mei Woo, a daughter in the novel confesses, "And after seeing my mother's disappointed face once again, something inside of me began to die. I hated the tests, the raised hopes and failed expectations."[14] In other words, in uptown Chinese immigrant families the generation gap is no longer caused by differences in cultural allegiance. Instead, the disparity between parental hopes and children's failures brings about tensions, like they do in most other American families.

The enormous popularity of *The Joy Luck Club* signals an important transition in contemporary Chinese American literature: The success of Chinese American writers now depends less on their ethnicity than on thematic content.[15] The rich diversity of themes and styles of writing has cut across lines of color, gender, and class. "Everyone [in America] relates to parental hopes and dreams," commented Elaine Dutka about the film adaptation of Tan's novel, "'Joy Luck' is no more a 'Chinese' picture than 'Terms of Endearment' is a 'Caucasian' film." In the words of Orville Schell, Tan's work has begun to "create what is, in effect, a new genre of American fiction."[16]

Other writers have also left their imprint on the contemporary Chinese American cultural milieu. Some, contemporaries of Chin and Kingston, such as Laurence Yep, Eleanor Wong Telamaque, David Henry Hwang, and Shawn Hsu Wong, have helped enrich Chinese American writing in theme and genre and thus been among those who have moved the literature to a new stage. For example, Yep achieved a breakthrough for Chinese Americans in children's literature with *Dragonwings* (1975), a fascinating account of a Chinese boy in San Francisco who dreams of building and flying an airplane during the early 1900s. A gifted story-teller, Yep creates the child's world with clarity and brilliance. The intertwining and fusion of fantasy with reality demonstrate his literary sophistication and fiction-writing skills. In *It's Crazy to Stay Chinese in Minnesota* (1978), Telamaque explores the sentiments of a Chinese girl who lives in a small midwestern town. The story replaces the exotic China-doll stereotype with a realistic, flesh-and-blood Chinese woman. The antithesis of passive, she is witty, smart, opinionated, and driven by curiosity and ambition. Lonely and bored with small-town life, she is at the same time "crazy" and feels intrigued and even elated by being a racial novelty in the eyes of the townspeople. It is apparent that the author has been influenced by classics such as Sinclair Lewis's *Main Street,* Sherwood Anderson's *Winesburg, Ohio,* and Theodore Dreiser's *Sister Carrie.* Hwang's play *FOB* (1979) is a thought-provoking story of how post–1965 Chinese immigrants struggle to find identities and adjust culturally and psychologically to the American environment. A conflict of ideas between an FOB man and an ABC woman vividly exposes the profound changes that the Chinese American community has undergone since the 1960s. In *Homebase* (1979), Wong skillfully entwines the concepts of nostalgia and alienation and the effects of conflicts and reconciliation between father and son in a fourth-generation Chinese American family. His use of the ailanthus—a plant originating in South China, the home of most early Chinese immigrants, but flourishing in California—as a metaphor enriches the image of Chinese pioneers who survived and succeeded despite the adverse conditions of the West.

That Chinese American writers are now capable of dealing with broad and universal themes is reflected even more conspicuously in the poetry they write. Instead of probing the "immigrant memory" for Chinese American themes, Mei-mei Berssenbrugge, a leading contemporary poet, dedicates herself to writing primarily about nature and its attraction to human beings. Alex Kuo, another prominent poet, describes the beauty of the New England wilderness in his collection *The Window Tree* (1971), and his work shows the influence of American Romanticists. David Rafael Wang [David Hsin-Fu Wand] expresses in *The Intercourse* (1975), a trilogy of poems, awe at being able to enjoy sex. The three-part poetic work—"The Thrusts," "The Insertions," and "The Withdrawal"—contains wonder at sexual power and its symbolic significance but little immigrant sentiment.[17]

Greatly divergent and individually oriented in terms of themes, imagery, genre, styles, and temperament, the Chinese American literature since the 1960s is more complex than it has ever been. It includes a multiplicity of viewpoints about Chinese American life and accurately expresses a diversity of experiences and sensibilities. As one critic points out, changes in the Chinese and Asian American communities "have transformed the nature and locus of literary production, creating a highly stratified, uneven and heterogeneous formation, that cannot easily be contained within the models of essentialized or pluralized ethnic identity suggested by the rubric Asian American literature."[18] To borrow a traditional Chinese phrase, the literature has entered a stage in which "a hundred flowers bloom and a hundred schools contend." Although its proliferation and diversity make generalities difficult, the work of contemporary Chinese American writers cuts across lines of age, ethnicity, and gender and has achieved a high degree of acceptance in mainstream culture.

## Kwan Kung versus Fa Mulan: The War of Words between Chin and Kingston

While the accomplishments of contemporary Chinese American writers are impressive, a deep controversy among Chinese Americans over the role of gender and ideology in creative writing is equally significant. Much of the dispute is the result of conflicting views about Kingston's innovative way of presenting

Chinese culture in *The Woman Warrior*.[19] The book, which has won wide praise from the general public, has also generated controversy within the Chinese community (and more generally the Asian American communities) for allegedly distorting and misrepresenting Chinese history and culture. Some critics believe that Kingston "exaggerated" Chinese patriarchal practices and makes Chinese society appear, among other things, misogynistic and void of ethics. It has also been suggested that Kingston's presentation of Chinese culture demonstrates a sense of "positional superiority," a term Edward Said has coined to refer to the Orientalist approach toward Asian studies.[20]

Because the most vociferous critic has been Frank Chin, the controversy has been labeled as a "war of words" between Kwan Kung and Fa Mulan, two icons appropriated by Chin and Kingston to represent, respectively, Chinese American men and women.[21] Protesting what he considers an attempt to feminize Chinese American literature, Chin accuses Kingston of being a "yellow agent of the stereotype" and calls her (as well as several other prominent Chinese women writers, including Jade Snow Wong and Amy Tan) an enemy. In his opinion, they demonstrate a vested interest in casting Chinese men in the worst possible light and have perpetuated the stereotype of a misogynistic, and therefore inferior, Chinese society. Such practices, Chin believes, spring from intentions to promote their work at the expense of Chinese men. For that reason, he warns, "I have no advice for young yellow writers, only a warning and a promise: as long as I live, if you fake it, I will name you and your fake tradition."[22]

Few Chinese Americans agree with Chin's personal attack on Kingston and other Chinese women writers, but some argue that the exposure of misogyny in Chinese culture by the women is indeed simplistic and often removed from sociohistorical context.[23] For example, although women in traditional Chinese society, as Kingston correctly points out, were addressed as *"nu"* [slaves] and deprived of independent status after marriage, Chinese men of lower social status were also "nameless" and did not possess an identity. They had to call themselves either *xiaoren* [a worthless person] or *nucai* [slaves].

Similarly, although it is true that traditional Chinese culture oppressed women, it also produced a large number of "warrior women." Chinese literary history records 3,500 women poets in the two dynasties of Ming and Qing alone (1366–1911).[24] That paradox can be explained by the fact that the hierarchy of traditional Chinese society was generally based more on class than on gender. For instance, in sharp contrast to working-class women, most upper-class women kept their names after marriage and enjoyed considerable freedom, such as access to social life and education. Li Qinzhao (1084–1156), a great Chinese woman poet from an aristocratic family, is a case in point.[25]

That class status affected a woman's fate was also reflected in the notorious practice of foot-binding, allegedly "invented" by Emperor Li Yu of the Later Tang Dynasty (923–936). Ironically, in this case it was the working women in China who fared better than their wealthier counterparts. In general, the practice was applied to upper-class women. The poor were able to escape the torture, largely because they were needed by their families to work at home and in the fields. In other words, the practice was a "luxury" that most working-class women could not afford.[26] The fact that class distinctions transcended gender divisions in traditional Chinese society in part explains why women scholars in China tend to hold views that are different from those of Western feminists about the sources of women's oppression. They argue forcefully that Western feminists have sometimes ignored realities elsewhere in the world, especially in developing countries.[27]

In the case of Chinese Americans, the gender issue is further complicated by race. Historically, Chinese of both sexes were equally powerless in American society. Given the hardships and racial discrimination that immigrants encountered in America, male privilege, at least for Chinese laborers, was extremely limited. For that reason, some Chinese women activists argue that among Chinese Americans, racial consciousness must come before women's rights. "If I am forced to choose to fight against racism or sexism," Ying Lee Kelly declares, "my first battle must be to fight racism."[28] Even women who are angered by Chin's comments and find them offensive agree that classic feminist theory does not always apply to the Chinese and Asian Americans. Because racial policies have "limited Asian American men's social power," the construction of gender in Asian American communities must be placed in a sociohistorical context that differs from that of mainstream society.[29]

Similarly, Chin's observation that women writers tend to treat Chinese men unfairly in their writing has reverberated among some Chinese and Asian Americans.[30] In most writing by Asian American women, men have only negative or passive roles and serve as conservative forces against women's pursuit of selfhood and progress.[31] In *The Joy Luck Club*, Tan's male characters, Chinese national and Chinese American alike, are all unsavory and confirm some of the mainstream media's worst stereotypes of Chinese men. Her women characters, however, are positive and upbeat. The negative portrayal contradicts reality, because the relationship between Chinese and Asian American men and women is not a zero-sum game. Women's gains are by no means men's losses. On the contrary, Chinese American women and men are generally mutually supportive and frequently join forces to combat racism.[32] For that reason, one Asian American college student has expressed anger at what he regards as Tan's "male bashing": "The men in *The Joy Luck Club* are either misogynist or aloof, domineering or clueless. . . . Why is it that an Asian man can't be a heroic figure unless he stays within his cultural idiom?"[33] Even Janet Maslin, an influential mainstream critic, was bothered by the unfavorable imagery of Chinese men in the film based on the novel: "[The] husbands and boyfriends are all such cads or fools . . . [the] daughters barely seem to have fathers at all."[34]

One cannot underestimate the influence of the portrayal of Fu Manchu–style "bad Chinese guys" in the literary work of Chinese women. Because the depiction of "Oriental" men as villains is still socially, politically, and culturally acceptable in American life, and Asian men are more likely than the women to be victims of racially motivated violence, it is possible that the negative role of Chinese men in work by women of their own race could further stereotypes and perpetuate other damaging images.[35] The concern is not unwarranted. Shawn Hsu Wong, who teaches Asian American studies at the University of Washington, finds that most Asian women students have unfavorable impressions of Asian males because of the "confusion, racism, and contradictions that surround the image of Asian American men in the media. Asian men are very rarely portrayed as husbands, fathers or lovers in television and movies," Wong points out. "Most often they are portrayed as gardeners, houseboys, ruthless foreign businessmen, cooks . . . or martial-arts specialists who in recent years can't even beat an Italian-American teenager known as the Karate Kid."[36]

A controversial article published in the campus magazine *Momentum* at the University of California at San Diego tends to support these observations. In an opinion essay entitled "A Little 'Mail,'" Ivy Lee, a Chinese American student, recorded her impressions of Asian males: "Asian American males are extremely short. . . . No wonder Asian American men exemplify the ideal women as petite, thin and delicate. Doing so probably makes them feel more masculine, much like a Chihuahua would seem when standing next to a baby chick. As for physical build? Practically non-existent. It's safe to say that most Asian men are skinny to the point of scrawniness . . . he probably has a small penis. And doesn't that just say it all?"[37] Her "opinion" might be seen as a sign of how Asian male-bashing has affected the attitude of younger Chinese women toward Chinese men. Even women scholars who are critical of Chin feel somewhat ambivalent about the male-female dispute. "Their [Chinese men's] response is understandable," writes King-Kok Cheung. "Asian American men have suffered deeply from racial oppression. When Asian American women seek to expose anti-female prejudices in their own ethnic community, the men are likely to feel betrayed."[38]

Of course, that does not mean that Chin's attack on women writers can be justified. To many Chinese Americans, both female and male, his comments, especially labeling Kingston's writing as "border town whore talk," are offensive and amount to nothing more than personal insult.[39] For most Chinese American women, Chin's indiscriminate accusations against a wide range of female authors represent an attempt to assert male authority at the expense of women. His criticism that Chinese American women writers have aligned themselves with the mass market is seen as an attempt to discredit and silence women, which implies that they do not have the same right as men to speak out.[40] Chin's assault is also unwise and counterproductive. In an era that has witnessed an upsurge of feminist consciousness, few Chinese American women want to be told by a "Chinatown cowboy" what they should or should not write. Virginia Chinlan Lee, whom Chin criticized for her portrayal of "wishy-washy" Chinatown boys in her novel *The House That Tai Ming Built* (1964), makes that point clear.[41] She asserts that she wrote about the Chinese American experience as she saw and understood it; those who have different perceptions should come forth with them rather than disparage her way of writing.[42]

Even Chinese American men who share Chin's views disagree with his denial of the presence of male chauvinism in traditional Chinese culture and his criticism that Kingston deliberately omits men from her work. On the contrary, they argue that Kingston is one of the women writers who acknowledges male contributions to Chinese American life. She has openly admitted that her father played a critical role in her development as a writer and that she acquired knowledge of "enwording" Chinese American lives and images from the work of both women and men, including Lin Yutang.[43] "Men are important to me," she declares. "I want to see and appreciate the 'other'."[44]

Kingston's second book *China Men,* written and dedicated to her "immigrant fathers," was originally entitled *Gold Mountain Heroes.* "I'd entitled my book *Gold Mountain Heroes* . . . to find a name for the pioneers," she explained. "But the year that *China Men* came out, there were quite a few books being published with the words 'mountain' or 'gold' in their titles. So my editor and I settled on *China Men.*"[45] She chose the book's title because it emphasizes the subtle yet significant difference between the way Chinese immigrant men viewed themselves and the derogatory term *Chinamen.* To make her intention known, Kingston retains the original title, *Gold Mountain Heroes,* on a seal that is written in Chinese and printed on the cover and opening page of every chapter. This can be considered an important symbol of her respect for "China Men."

Similarly, Chin's allegation that the popularity of Chinese women writers is exploited by mainstream readers, especially by rapacious and uncouth white men, seems to lack credence.[46] One measure of its validity can be challenged by the success of Chinese immigrant women writers who publish in Chinese. Their work is read by people of their own race rather than by white men, but many are well received and more popular than their male counterparts.[47] In reality, it is the rise of women's consciousness and the increased interest in (and appreciation of) cultural pluralism and diversity in American society that have inspired more Chinese American women than men to pursue literary careers and find popular success.

Some Asian American scholars have speculated that Chin's anger toward women writers, especially those who have succeeded in the mainstream market, in part grows out of personal jealousy.[48] Although he has gained fame in Asian American communities, Chin has never achieved the same degree of popularity as many women writers. In his criticism of Kingston, he mentions a bit sourly that 450,000 copies of *The Woman Warrior* were sold between 1976 and 1991—an extraordinary figure by any standard.[49] Chin's bitterness may have also been intensified by a sense of betrayal. A gifted writer, he could have used his talent to pursue success in the mainstream market. Instead, Chin has chosen to work to establish a record of Chinese manhood and yet has not made much progress or been appreciated in his efforts. Perhaps the many embittered and resentful male protagonists in his work can be viewed as the frustrated author, who complains that he is unable to stand on an equal footing with popular writers despite his pioneering role in Chinese American literature and his status as a fifth-generation Chinese American.[50]

Even if one could prove that mainstream critics and readers tend to favor Chinese women while ignoring male writers, it is misguided to aim one's anger at women authors. Both Chinese American women and men are victims of misdirected public rancor and racism. Those in power are generally white males, and they may feel more comfortable dealing with Chinese women, who pose little threat to their positions.[51] "Just three things I look for in hiring . . . small, foreign, and female," claims a Caucasian manager at a Silicon Valley assembly shop. "You find those three things and you're pretty much automatically guaranteed the right kind of workforce. These little foreign gals are grateful to be hired—very, very grateful—no matter what."[52] By comparison, the presence of Chinese men can constitute a challenge to white men. In that sense, ironically, Asian women are favored for the same reason that Asian men are rejected—to serve the interests of white superiority. It is mainstream culture rather than Chinese women writers that should be blamed for perpetuating the images of effeminate Chinese males or of exotic, mysterious, and erotic stereotypes of "Oriental" customs in American culture.[53]

## The Debate over Chinese American Literary Sensibility

Despite Chin's bias against many Chinese American women writers, it would be overly simplistic and misleading to view the Chin-Kingston controversy merely as a war drawn along gender lines or to accuse Chin of conducting an antifeminist vendetta.[54] For one thing, he is equally critical of a great number of male writers, from earlier authors Yung Wing, Lin Yutang, Pardee Lowe, and C. Y. Lee to the younger generation of Chinese American writers, David Henry Hwang and Gus Lee.[55] It is also significant that Chin, despite harsh criticism of Kingston and Tan, included Asian American women such as Sui Sin Far, Monica Sone, and Hisaye Yamamoto in an anthology, *The Big Aiiieeeee*, which he coedited with several other Asian American writers. In addition, not all Asian women writers are critical of Chin. Jessica Hagedorn, a prominent Filipina writer, refers to him in an anthology of Asian American fiction she edited. Praising the publication of Chin's *Aiiieeeee! An Anthology of Asian-American Writers* in 1974 as "an absolute breakthrough for Asian Americans," she recalls that "receiving my copy [of *Aiiieeeee*] as a gift from Frank Chin . . . proved a joyous revelation."[56] In essence, the controversy exemplifies the complexity of the Chinese American experience in literary production, and it has highlighted a deep-seated argument among Chinese Americans about writing philosophy. The significance of the Chin-Kingston "feud" cannot be fully understood apart from this background. As Chin asserts, "We have to make the difference between the real and the fake," meaning to establish standards to judge works that possess a true Chinese American sensibility.[57]

According to William Wei, with the emergence of the Asian American movement in the 1960s there developed two competing yet interrelated approaches to creative writing among Chinese Americans. One emphasizes the importance of social and ideological factors and the other stresses the significance of aesthetics and individual freedom.[58] Specifically, the socioideological approach views Chinese American writers as members of a racially discriminated against, culturally distorted ethnic group who bear moral concerns and have a social responsibility to speak on behalf of the community. It is their mission to illuminate the Chinese American experience and prove the fraudulence of racial stereotypes created by mainstream culture. The aesthetic-individual approach, in contrast, is more in keeping with American-style individualism and supports the idea that creative activities in literature should be individually oriented and based on the development of a writer's personal preferences in terms of themes, styles, and techniques. Supporters of that approach believe Chinese American writers ought to enjoy the same artistic freedom as their counterparts in the larger society and that authors should find their own subject matter. Although freedom must be accompanied by responsibility, the distinction between "real" or "fake" Chinese American writing, if it exists at all, should be judged by time and readership rather than by a criterion established by any single group of individuals.[59]

The dichotomy between the two approaches has been blurred since the 1980s, and not everyone takes a side in the argument. Between those who passionately advocate writers' social responsibilities and those who support aesthetic dimensions and artistic freedom in creative writing lies a wide, neutral spectrum of Chinese American authors and critics.[60] In general, Frank Chin is a leading voice of the socioideological approach. "The subject matter of minority literature is social history," he declares, "there is responsibility for a minority writer." Based on that view, Chin insists that in "reclaiming" the Chinese American experience, authors must choose to write from a Chinese American perspective or conform to popular expectations and stereotypes. "Writing is fighting," he claims. It is a political act by which a writer can and should combat racial stereotypes.[61]

Chin underscores this theory when he contends that Kingston reinvented Chinese myths for *The Woman Warrior*, David Henry Hwang revised Chinese history for his plays, and Amy Tan used "fake" Chinese fairy tales in her novels. Pointing out their errors in "recycling" Chinese history and culture, Chin argues: "Their elaboration of this version of history . . . is simply a device for destroying history and literature." What they have done is to wrench cultural practices out of context and display them to the curious gaze of outsiders—a white-pleasing practice.[62]

According to Chin, the "fake" writers have capitalized on their "Orientalness" to gain popularity in mainstream society, and their Chinese-Americanness is highly selective and staged, appealing rather than threatening. His criticism of the "Christian soldiers" (another of his labels for Kingston, Hwang, Tan, Gus Lee, and others) is identical to a comment he made in 1972 about "whitewashed" Chinese, long before the beginning of the debate with Kingston: "They bought their way into second-class white status by humiliating their whole race and people and history and fucking up the future. This is exactly what white culture has demanded. . . . Writing is white, the standards of art and culture are white, and this tyranny of culture by the whites has been an oppressive force on non-white arts."[63]

The individual-aesthetic approach to writing is favored, understandably, by Kingston and Tan. In responding to criticism of her work, Kingston maintains that she believes in "the timelessness and universality of individual vision" and "does not want to be measured by a false standard at all."[64] Advocating individually oriented artistic freedom, she emphasizes that as a Chinese American writer she has transformed Chinese culture into American life rather than recount Chinese history or legends. Her social commentary and ideology are integrated into the words and actions of her characters. If people misunderstand her, that is their problem. "I am not a sociologist who measures truth by the percentage of times behavior takes place," she elaborated. "Those critics who do not explore why and how this book [*The Woman Warrior*] is different but merely point out its difference as a flaw have a very disturbing idea about the role of the writer. Why must I 'represent' anyone besides myself? Why should I be denied an individual artistic vision?"[65]

A significant number of other Chinese American writers, especially those who have distinguished themselves in the larger society, share Kingston's views. Amy Tan, for example, made similar comments in an acid retort to Chin's accusation: "What bothers me about Frank Chin's stance is his tendency to interpret literature as a representation of life, and therefore, writers have an obligation to think of how their work is going to be interpreted or misinterpreted by a larger audience," she said in 1997. "I consider myself an American writer. I have the freedom to write whatever I want to write, what is close to me."[66]

To be sure, the aesthetic-individual approach is not flawless. Its emphasis on creative freedom can confuse readers unfamiliar with Chinese Americans. Unaware that what she has done is to reinvent Chinese myths, readers may regard Kingston's talk stories as truths. In a discussion of *The Woman Warrior,* one Chinese American scholar cites ample cases of non-Asian students who developed critical opinions of Chinese American culture after reading the book.[67] For that reason the San Francisco Association of Chinese Teachers has warned, "Especially for students unfamiliar with the Chinese background, it [*The Woman Warrior*] could give an overly negative impression of the Chinese American experience."[68] Even a Chinese American woman scholar who is sympathetic toward Kingston in the dispute feels that "for a 'minority' author to exercise such artistic freedom is perilous business because white critics and reviewers persist in seeing creative expressions by her [Kingston] as no more than cultural history."[69]

Similarly, Tan's audience may find that her writing reinforces stereotypes about Chinese and Chinese Americans. "What fascinates [about Tan's writing] is not only the insistent story telling, but the details of Chinese life and tradition," observes Nancy Forbes Romano.[70] Unfortunately, she fails to understand that many aspects of Chinese life and tradition in Tan's work have never existed in the real world but were invented to advance plots. The comments by another mainstream critic are even more disturbing: "Each [mother] recalled the events of her life in *lavish and exotic detail,* and *those events had a way of teaching lessons.*"[71] Such misperceptions upset even those scholars who are supportive of Tan, because they feel that she presents Chinese culture in a loose manner. As Sauling Cynthia Wong points out, "[T]here are many details [in *The Joy Luck Club* and *The Kitchen God's Wife*] whose existence cannot be justified on structural or informational grounds, but whose function seems to be to announce 'We are Oriental' to the 'mainstream' reader."[72]

Writers, however, must not be held responsible when their work is misunderstood. Good literature always produces multiple and even conflicting interpretations, and critics' opinions should reveal an author's message to the reading public. Furthermore, if the aesthetic-individual approach is controversial, the socioideological approach is also problematic. Criteria for a Chinese American sensibility based on such an approach are inevitably subjective. Different writers can have different perceptions of what constitutes moral concerns and social responsibilities, and class and gender may have greater impacts than race on a writer's attitude toward Chinese American life.

Freed from the poverty and segregation that restricted their predecessors' experience, younger-generation Chinese Americans may respond in different ways to the responsibility of being a writer. Having experienced much more acceptance from mainstream society and been exposed to cultures that are widely diverse, they are more interested in claiming and projecting individuality than in committing themselves to the search for an authentically Chinese cultural identity. Gish Jen, author of *Typical American* (1989) and *Mona in a Promised Land* (1996), is one example. She was born into a family of university professors and grew up in a white, middle-class suburban town in New York. After graduating from Harvard College, she studied law at Stanford University, taught English for a year in a coal-mining city in northern China, and married an Irish American computer specialist. Cosmopolitan, transcultural, and easy-going, her ideas about ethnic identity and the responsibility of being a minority writer differ significantly from those of Chin. It is no accident that she has been outspoken in explaining her writing philosophy: "I don't know if there is a PC way to write about all the different groups reacting to each other. . . . It would have to be like the UN. Very boring."[73]

Some Chinese American scholars contend that Chin's views on the role of literature in Chinese American life were influenced by the Red Guard movement of the Chinese Cultural Revolution (1966–76). His emphasis on the social responsibilities of writers, clearly a product of the 1960s, resembles Mao Zedong's well-known slogan that literature and the arts must serve the interests of the working class.[74] (Curiously, Chin's belief that "writing is fighting" also bears traits of the Puritan doctrine, which is known for its rigid stance regarding the didactic purpose of literature.)

The socioideological approach Chin advocates may have helped mobilize the Chinese American community during the 1960s, when there was intense struggle against racism and social injustice, but it has lost its appeal and urgency in the 1990s. Both the Chinese American community and the society in general underwent a dramatic transformation during those thirty years, and a "true"

Chinese American sensibility is increasingly difficult to define. In the past, the Chinese constituted a predominantly "downtown" population in America; since the 1970s, however, that population has become highly polarized. The Chinese American experience has constantly and continuously changed and been modified. What is regarded as authentic art can quickly become dated in a way similar to past seasons' fashion, and what is considered as real Chinese American sensibility by a fifth-generation "uptown" Chinese professional may appear a sham to an immigrant laborer still struggling to survive in a Chinatown workshop. After all, as Michael Fischer argues convincingly, ethnic identity in American society is "something reinvented and reinterpreted in each generation by each individual," making ethnic writing highly inclusive rather than exclusive.[75] In that sense, it is baffling and even absurd to think that there can be an adequate and unitary standard by which to measure the literary sensibility produced by a vastly diversified and rapidly changing Chinese American reality. As Jade Snow Wong asked pointedly, "What are exactly Chin's criteria for categorizing the 'real' and 'fake' Chinese American writers?"[76]

Chin's dilemma concerns how to define an authentic Chinese American literary sensibility based on a socioideological approach. As much as he advocated that mission, he has not achieved much success in doing so, and his stance has shifted. In *Donald Duck* (1991), for example, his ideas on such issues as the sources of tensions in Chinese American families and solutions to racial problems differ considerably from those in his plays and stories of the early 1970s. Frustration has been replaced by a sense of humor, racial conflicts are resolved through compromise, and the generation gap is presented from a point of view that is more sympathetic to parents. The changes are so profound that they have moved Chin closer to those whom he has accused of being fake and made him "kinder" and "gentler"; as Amy Ling observes, he seems to begin "making his peace with the world, with the demons of his past."[77]

Ironically, Chin's vigorous efforts to expose the mispresentations of fake Chinese American writers have been undermined by his own misreading of Chinese culture. If Kingston's "recycling" of the Fa Mulan story constitutes a "fake," Chin's translation and explanation of the "Ballad of Mulan" and various Chinese classics are also inaccurate.[78] Given that he and Kingston share many of the same "errors" in presenting traditional Chinese culture, it seems likely that the conflict between them is more rhetorical and personal than substantial.

Since the mid-1980s, Chin has also stressed the Chinese contributions to Chinese American identity. He now feels that the ideal audience for his work are bilingual Chinese immigrants and that the American-born may be confused by his message because of their inability to understand the subtleties of Chinese classics. "Nobody knows enough to understand what I am writing about or from except the immigrants," Chin has declared. "Immigrants who know *Three Kingdoms* and *The Water Margin* have enjoyed my work."[79] That notion greatly contradicts his earlier belief that only the American-born could appreciate a Chinese American sensibility.

The departure can be seen as an effort to re-connect with Chinese tradition under different social and historical contexts.[80] It also indicates that perhaps Chin has finally come to recognize that the Chinese American experience is not static or monolithic but fluid and unfixed. Time is not kind to those unable or unwilling to transcend the limits of their own generations. It may be necessary for Chin to follow changing realities in order to retain the spell of his ideas.

The dispute between Chin and Kingston has evolved into a "feud." In addition to his frequent attacks, Chin has written a story, "Unmanly Warrior," to parody Kingston's bestseller.[81] Most Chinese and Asian Americans are critical of Chin's remarks, but some have been disappointed by what they view as Kingston's overreaction to the dispute. Despite her denial, there is little doubt that Wittman Ah Sing, the protagonist of *Tripmaster Monkey,* seems to be modeled after Chin—the character encompasses the shadow of Chin. What Amy Ling says in a review of the novel can be regarded as representing the disapproval of Kingston's practice: "We, poor mortals, don't read Kingston in order to watch her out-chinning Chin. We read her to hear the voice of Maxine Hong Kingston, and we wish there were more of that voice in this book."[82]

The effort to define a Chinese American literary sensibility is neither easy nor simple, and the controversy over standards, however unpleasant, symbolizes the highly polarized and vastly diversified contemporary Chinese American experience.[83] For one thing, as a product of the social environment wherein Chinese American life has undergone dramatic changes, literature deeply rooted in life will also inevitably be reinvented—its meanings revised and its sensibility redefined. In other words, that contemporary Chinese American literature consists of many individual and conflicting visions is not surprising. Although it may have begun as a means of defending the community against anti-Chinese propaganda, it has developed into a serious exploration of the complexity and diversity of changing realities of Chinese Americans and provided a forum in which to present a rising ethnic consciousness. While Chinese American literature continues to record the Chinese experience in the United States and define a unique culture, its authors do not necessarily follow the same form, depth, scope, and standards of their predecessors. Nor do they always speak with the same voice. Although it is disappointing that the advocates of each side of the argument tend to focus only on elements that support their views, they do have something in common: In their own respective ways, Chin and Kingston each strive to challenge the Orientalist discourse of the Chinese American experience.[84] Their persistent determination to create and exhibit a new form of Chinese American cultural identity makes them more like two sides of one coin rather than true foes.

Furthermore, despite their claimed differences, Chin and Kingston have both demonstrated the influence of earlier Chinese American authors. A careful study shows that Chin's "Chinatown cowboys" inherited the fighting spirit of the Chinese laundryman Lee Chew and speak in the same angry voice as the Angel Island poets. Similarly, Kingston's "warrior women" share the frustrations expressed by Yan Phou Lee and Pardee Lowe and triumphantly travel the same journey begun by Mrs. Spring Fragrance and the Fifth Chinese Daughter. Indeed, both Chin and Kingston have acknowledged that their careers were inspired by the pioneering role of earlier Chinese American writers. In turn, their accomplishments have encouraged more Chinese Americans to participate in literary activities.[85]

Thematic similarities are discernible within Chinese American literature, as is the influence of Chinese American writers on one another. This is seen in the consistency of stylistic features and the similarities of descriptions of characters. For example, one can easily detect the ghost from *The Woman Warrior* in *The Joy Luck Club*'s mothers and daughters. Like Kingston's No-Name aunt, An-Mei Hsu's mother in Tan's novel is also shrouded in silence and forbidden to be mentioned in her family because of her "shameful behavior." "Never say her name," Popo [grandma] warns, "to say her name is to spit on your father's grave." In addition to having her name being lost, the suicide-turned-revenge story of An-Mei's mother bears a striking resemblance to that of the No-Name aunt: They both commit suicide to avenge themselves on those who persecuted and victimized them. Like Kingston's No-Name aunt, who turns herself into a ghost to "get out of the water to haunt" her enemies, the soul of An-Mei's mother "comes back to settle scores."[86]

Finally, although the war of words may have weakened the strength of Chinese American writers as spokespersons for the community, it is also a sign of the maturing of Chinese American literature. Because the conflict has been drawn on the basis of individual views and personal interests rather than along a rigid gender or class line or as an attempt to follow fashions in mainstream society, the division represents a more diversified and balanced opinion of Chinese Americans in terms of the authenticity, representation, and creativity of their writing. In that sense, the controversy represents a multidimensioned Chinese American sensibility and demonstrates that the literature has finally come of age and become an organic part of the Chinese American experience.

## Notes

1. The epigraphs are from Shan Te-hsing, "An Interview with Maxine Hong Kingston," [Taipei] *Tamkang Review* 27 (Winter 1996): 253, and Frank Chin et al., eds. *Aiiieeeee! An Anthology of Asian-American Writers* (Washington, D.C.: Howard University Press, 1974), xxx.

2. David Henry Hwang, *Broken Promises: Four Plays* (New York: Avon Books, 1983), 3; Edward Iwata, "Word Warriors," *Los Angeles Times,* June 24, 1990, E1, E9.

3. Robert Murray Davis, "Frank Chin: An Interview with Robert Murray Davis," *Amerasia* 14, no. 2 (1988): 94.

4. Frank Chin, Chickencoop Chinaman *and* The Year of the Dragon: *Two Plays by Frank Chin* (Seattle: University of Washington Press, 1981), 7.

5. Frank Chin, "The Railroad Standard Time" (1978), in Chin, *The Chinaman Pacific & Frisco R.R. Co.* (Minneapolis: Coffee House Press, 1988), 7.

6. Frank Chin, "The Only Real Day," in Chin, *The Chinaman Pacific & Frisco R.R. Co.* (Minneapolis: Coffee House Press, 1988), 69.

7. Frank Chin, "The Eat and Run Midnight People," in Chin, *The Chinaman Pacific & Frisco R.R. Co.* (Minneapolis: Coffee House Press, 1988), 13.

8. Chin and Kingston were both born in the Year of the Dragon (1940). Both are also descendants of Cantonese immigrants, studied at the University of California at Berkeley in the 1960s, and plunged into the politics of that decade. Coincidentally, Amy Tan was also born in the Year of the Dragon (1952) a cycle later. (The Chinese lunar calendar defines every twelve years as a cycle.)

9. Sidonie Smith, *A Poetics of Women's Autobiography: Marginality and the Fictions of Self-Representation* (Bloomington: Indiana University Press, 1987), 159.

10. The tragic ends of the female protagonists in Gustave Flaubert's *Madam Bovary* (1857), Leo Tolstoy's *Anna Karenina* (1886), and Kate Chopin's *The Awakening* (1899) are three ready examples.

11. Maxine Hong Kingston, *The Woman Warrior: Memoirs of a Girlhood among Ghosts* (repr. New York: Vintage, 1989), 16. As in her other talk stories, Kingston reinvents the Chinese myth in this case. Traditional Chinese culture believes that anyone who dies of a violent death, not necessarily by drowning, is *yuan sigui* [a ghost of abnormal death] and will seek a substitute in order to quickly gain rebirth.

12. Chinese classics on divination claim that the White Tiger, Red Bird, Blue Dragon, and Black Turtle embody the constellations of the four directions of the universe. White Tiger represents the West (right), Blue Dragon the East (left), Red Bird the South (front), and Black Turtle the North (back). For a brief explanation of the symbolism of the four, see *Ci hai* [The Chinese encyclopedia], (Shanghai: Cisu, 1980), 80.

13. Maxine Hong Kingston, "Cultural Mis-readings by American Reviewers," in *Asian and Western Writers in Dialogue,* ed. Guy Amirthanayagam (London: Macmillan Press, 1982), 57.

14. Amy Tan, *The Joy Luck Club* (repr. New York: Ivy Books, 1992), 144.

15. *The Joy Luck Club* stayed on the *New York Times* bestseller list for seventy-seven weeks and sold more than a quarter million hard-cover copies. Janice Simpson, "Fresh Voices above the Noisy Din," *Time,* June 3, 1991, 66.

16. Elaine Dutka, " 'Joy Luck': A New Challenge in Disney's World," *Los Angeles Times,*

August 31, 1993, F1; Orville Schell, "Your Mother Is in Your Bones," *The New York Times Book Review,* March 19, 1989, 3.

17. Mei-mei Berssenbrugge, *Summits Move with the Tide* (Greenfield Center: Greenfield Review Press, 1974), and *The Heat Bird* (Providence: Burning Deck, 1983); Alex Kuo, *The Window Tree* (Peterborough: Windy Row Press, 1971); and David Rafael Wang [David Hsin-Fu Wand], *The Intercourse* (Greenfield Center: Greenfield Review Press, 1975). Kuo has also published extensively on modern China.

18. Susan Koshy, "The Fiction of Asian American Literature," *Yale Journal of Criticism* 9 (Fall 1996), 315–16.

19. Kwan Kung [Guan Gong; Lord Guan], the god of war and literature worshipped by early Chinese immigrants, is identified by Chin as the incarnation of Chinese manhood. Fa Mulan [Hua Mulan], a legendary swordswoman, is hailed by Kingston as the embodiment of Chinese warrior women.

20. Toming Jun Liu, "The Problematics of Kingston's 'Cultural Translation,'" [Ankara] *Journal of American Studies of Turkey* 4 (Fall 1996): 17. For the definition of "positional superiority," see Edward W. Said, *Orientalism* (New York: Pantheon Books, 1978), 7–8.

21. For feminist critiques of Chin's view on Chinese American women writers, see King-Kok Cheung, *"The Woman Warrior* versus *The Chinaman Pacific:* Must a Chinese American Critic Choose between Feminism and Heroism?" in *Conflicts in Feminism,* ed. Marianne Hirsch and Evelyn Fox Keller (New York: Routledge, 1990), 234–51. For a report on the origins of the Chin-Kingston dispute, see Iwata, "Word Warriors," E1, E9. Elaine H. Kim has also presented an explicit analysis of Chin's argument. Kim, "Such Opposite Creatures: Men and Women in Asian American Literature," *Michigan Quarterly Review* 29 (Winter 1990): 68–93.

22. Frank Chin, "This Is Not an Autobiography," *Genre* 18 (Summer 1985): 110; and "Come All Ye Asian American Writers of the Real and the Fake," in *The Big Aiiieeeee: An Anthology of Chinese American and Japanese American Literature,* ed. Jeffery Paul Chan et al. (New York: Meridian, 1991), 2–3. Chin's attack on Chinese women writers began long before Kingston's work appeared. He first made accusations against women writers, including Jade Snow Wong, Virginia Lee, and Betty Lee Sung, in an essay he coauthored with Jeffery Paul Chan in 1972. Chin and Chan, "Racist Love," in *Seeing through Shuck,* ed. Richard Kostelanetz (New York: Ballantine Books, 1972), 68. Since then, Chin has reiterated his criticism, and the list of his "women enemies" keeps growing. In many ways, his criticism of Chinese women writers seems to parallel that by Ishmael Reed on Alice Walker and Toni Morrison, whom Reed views as perpetuating an invidious stereotype of African American men. Noticeably, Chin lists Reed as a reference on his resume. Press release, courtesy of the Cultural Studies Office of Occidental College, Los Angeles, Nov. 6, 1995.

23. Liu, "The Problematics of Kingston's 'Cultural Translation,'" 15. Also see Maureen Dezell, "The Tug of 'Warrior,'" *Boston Globe,* Sept. 23, 1994, 49, 57.

24. Chang Phong [Zhang Feng], "Cong 'Chen-Liu qingyuan' kan Ming Qing funu shici" [Ming and Qing women poetry as reflected in the romance of Chen Tzu-lung and Liu Ru-shi], [Hong Kong] *Ershiyi Shiji* [Twenty-first Century] 27 (Feb. 1995): 71. Also see Kang-I Sun Chang, *The Late-Ming Poet Chen Tzu-lung: Crises of Love and Loyalism* (New Haven: Yale University Press, 1991); Ellen Widmer and Kang-I Sun Chang, eds., *Writing Women in Late Imperial China* (Stanford: Stanford University Press, 1997); and Hu Shih, "Women's Place in Chinese History," in *Chinese Women through Chinese Eyes,* ed. Li Yu-ning (Armonk: M. E. Sharpe, 1992), 3–15.

25. For a brief yet explicit summary of Li Qingzhao's life and career, see Lu Guocai and Zhong Yuren, *Zhongguo wenxue jingdu* [A digest of Chinese literary history], rev. ed. (Hong Kong: Dangdai Jiaoyu, 1987), 2:49–51.

26. Thus far there are no quantitative studies on the relationship between class status and the practice of foot binding in traditional Chinese society, but personal stories and the memories of working-class women in China seem to support that conclusion. For example, my paternal grandmother, born into an average peasant family in 1901, never had her feet bound. When I asked her the question, she explained matter-of-factly, "My parents expected that I had to work when I grew up." For more information and different views on women's status and footbinding in traditional Chinese society, see Ono Kazuko, "Women Who Took to Battle Dress" and "Between Footbinding and Nationhood," in *Chinese Women in a Century of Revolution, 1850–1950*, ed. Joshua A. Fogel (Stanford: Stanford University Press, 1978), 1–46; Patricia Ebrey, "Women, Marriage, and the Family in Chinese History," in *Heritage of China: Contemporary Perspectives on Chinese Civilization*, ed. Paul S. Ropp (Berkeley: University of California Press, 1990), 197–223; Howard S. Levy, *The Lotus Lovers: The Complete History of the Curious Erotic Custom of Footbinding in China* (Buffalo: Prometheus Books, 1992); and Li, *Chinese Women through Chinese Eyes*, xiii–xxx, 1–122.

27. Christina K. Gilmartin et al., eds., *Engendering China: Women, Culture, and the State* (Cambridge: Harvard University Press, 1994), 6, 69–97, 279–338, 360–82.

28. Quoted in Kathryn M. Fong, "Feminism Is Fine, but What's It Done for Asian America?" *Bridge: An Asian American Perspective* 6 (Winter 1978): 21–22. Significantly, Gwendolyn Brooks has made similar comments on the role of feminism in the African American women's lives. For more discussion of feminism and Asian American women, see Gary Y. Okihiro, *Margins and Mainstreams: Asians in American History and Culture* (Seattle: University of Washington Press, 1994), 64–92; and William Wei, *The Asian American Movement* (Philadelphia: Temple University Press, 1993), 72–100.

29. Kim, "Such Opposite Creatures," 74; Cheung, "*The Woman Warrior* versus *The Chinaman Pacific*," 239.

30. Liu, "The Problematics of Kingston's 'Cultural Translation,'" 18. Also see Dezell, "The Tug of 'Warrior,'" 57.

31. Kim, "Such Opposite Creatures," 84–92.

32. Fong, "Feminism Is Fine," 21–22. Also see Tiana [Thi Thanh Nga], "The Long March: From Wong to Woo: Asians in Hollywood," *Cineaste* 21, no. 4 (1995): 38–40.

33. Allen C. Soong, "Unaccepted Images," [Harvard University] *Crimson*, Oct. 8, 1993, A2.

34. Janet Maslin, "Intimate Family Lessons, Available to All," *New York Times*, Sept. 8, 1993, B1.

35. The brutal murders of Vincent Chin in Detroit in 1982 and Jim Ming Hai Loo in Raleigh, North Carolina, in 1989 are two prominent cases involving racially motivated hate crimes against Asian American men. According to U.S. Civil Rights Commission reports, violent hate crimes against Asian Americans have been on the rise since the 1980s. *Civil Rights Issues Facing Asian Americans in the 1990s* (Washington, D.C.: U.S. Commission on Civil Rights, 1992), 25–48. Also see Leonard Dinnerstein and David M. Reimers, *Ethnic Americans: A History of Immigration*, 3d ed. (New York: HarperCollins, 1988), 198.

36. Shawn Hsu Wong, "Beyond Bruce Lee," *Essence* 24 (Nov. 1993): 64.

37. Cited in M. L. Stein, "Opinion Piece Upsets Students," *Editor and Publisher*, Dec.

18, 1993, 24. For an analysis of views of Chinese American women on Chinese men, see Morrison G. Wong, "A Look at the Intermarriage among the Chinese in the United States in 1980," *Sociological Perspectives* 32, no. 1 (1989): 87–107.

38. Cheung, *"The Woman Warrior* versus *The Chinaman Pacific,"* 239.

39. Quoted in William Wei, *The Asian American Movement* (Philadelphia: Temple University Press, 1993), 69.

40. Kim, "Such Opposite Creatures," 80; John Liu, "Towards an Understanding of the Internal Colonial Model," in *Counterpoint: Perspectives on Asian America,* ed. Emma Gee (Los Angeles: Asian American Studies Center, UCLA, 1976), 160–68.

41. Virginia Chin-lan Lee, *The House That Tai Ming Built* (New York: Macmillan, 1964). Lee's novel focusing on the life of a third-generation Chinese girl in San Francisco during the World War II era describes a sentimental interracial love story and the enormous price exacted by efforts to gain admission to mainstream society.

42. Kai-yu Hsu and Helen Palubinskas, eds., *Asian American Authors* (Boston: Houghton Mifflin, 1972), 1–2, 10.

43. Helen Lee, "A Writer Visits High School," [Boston] *Sampan,* Oct. 24, 1994, 5; Shan, "An Interview with Kingston," 250–251.

44. Quoted in Kim, "Such Opposite Creatures," 89; Lisa Lowe, *Immigrant Acts: On Asian American Cultural Politics* (Durham: Duke University Press, 1996), 76–83.

45. Shan, "An Interview with Kingston," 246; Huang Wenxiang, *Oumei Jiechu Huayi Nuxing* [Outstanding women of Chinese ancestry in Europe and America], (Hong Kong: Shanghai Book, 1992), 174–78.

46. Chin, "Come All Ye Asian American Writers of the Real and the Fake," 2. Also see Wei, *Asian American Movement,* 69.

47. Women who write in the Chinese language are also highly critical of sexism in literary circles. They argue that it is often difficult for men to understand the barriers that women writers encounter in their careers. "Sexism is shown right in the term 'women writers,'" Nie Hualing says sarcastically, "because there is not such a term 'men writers.'" Nie, "Nu zuojia" [Women writers], in Nie, *Heise, heise, zuimeili de yanse* [Black, black, the most beautiful color], (Hong Kong: Joint, 1983), 196.

48. Wei, *Asian American Movement,* 69; Kim, "Such Opposite Creatures," 79.

49. Chin, "Come All Ye Asian American Writers," 2.

50. By claiming he is a fifth-generation Chinese American, Chin uses his maternal lineage to account for his status. This is a rather unconventional practice in traditional Chinese culture, which counts the family tree from the paternal side.

51. A 1995 study reports that despite the progress made by women and minorities since the 1960s, among the top five hundred U.S. businesses more than 94 percent of positions at the level of vice president and above are held by white males. They are the real power-holders in American society. "Glass Ceiling? It's More Like a Steel Cage," *Los Angeles Times,* March 20, 1995, B4. According to one study, Asian Americans account for only 0.5 percent of the officers and directors of the thousand largest U.S. firms. Kitano and Daniels, *Asian Americans,* 181.

52. Quoted in Yen Le Espiritu, *Asian American Women and Men: Labor, Laws, and Love* (Thousand Oaks: Sage Publications, 1997), 74.

53. Kim, "Such Opposite Creatures," 70; Judy Yung, *Unbound Feet: A Social History of Chinese Women in San Francisco* (Berkeley: University of California Press, 1995), 1–13.

54. There are similar debates in other Asian American groups. I have concentrated on Chinese American writers only because I have drawn most of my examples from Chinese American literature. For more discussions on the argument among Asian American writers, see Sau-ling Cynthia Wong, *Reading Asian American Literature: From Necessity to Extravagance* (Princeton: Princeton University Press, 1993), 3–17; Amy Ling, "Maxine Hong Kingston and the Dialogic Dilemma of Asian American Writers," paper presented at the Tenth Conference of the Association for Asian American Studies, Cornell University, June 1993; and Koshy, "The Fiction of Asian American Literature," 324–30.

55. Frank Chin, "Rendezvous," *Conjunctions* 19 (Fall 1993): 295; Chin, "Come All Ye Asian American Writers of the Real and the Fake," 8.

56. Jessica Hagedorn, "Introduction," in *Charlie Chan Is Dead: An Anthology of Contemporary Asian American Fiction*, ed. Hagedorn (New York: Penguin Books, 1993), xxvi.

57. Chin, "Rendezvous," 291.

58. Wei, *Asian American Movement*, 64–71. Wei provides an explicit analysis of the sources and development of the two approaches. Although I find his discussion thought-provoking and rich, I hold different views about the origins of the two approaches and the backgrounds of the writers involved in the argument. I also believe that the controversy is related to different visions about the roots of discrimination against the Chinese in American society. Some stress the historic political and economic oppression of the Chinese, whereas others perceive the more critical area of oppression as racial and cultural. Victor G. Nee and Brett de Bary Nee, *Longtime Californ': A Documentary Study of an American Chinatown* (Stanford: Stanford University Press, 1986), 355–60.

59. Asian American scholars have used different terms to refer to the controversy. Some call it an argument between nationalism and assimilation, whereas others consider it a debate about identity and difference. Lowe, *Immigrant Acts*, 60–83; Wong, *Reading Asian American Literature*, 35–37.

60. King-Kok Cheung, for example, feels that she wavers between both sides of the argument, although on the whole she is more sympathetic to Kingston. Cheung, *"The Woman Warrior* versus *The Chinaman Pacific,"* 234–51. Also see Hagedorn, *Charlie Chan Is Dead*, xxvi–xxvii; and Mao-chu Lin, "Identity and Chinese-American Experiences: A Study of Chinatown American Literature since World War II," Ph.D. diss., University of Minnesota, 1987, xiv.

61. Chin, "This Is Not an Autobiography," 129; Chin, "Rendezvous," 291.

62. Chin, "Come All Ye Asian American Writers," 3.

63. Chin, "Rendezvous," 295. Chin is quoted in Nee and Nee, *Longtime Californ'*, 385.

64. Kingston, "Cultural Mis-readings," 57, 65.

65. Ibid., 63. Also see Shan, "An Interview with Kingston"; and Zhang Ziqing, "Transplantation and Transfiguration of Eastern and Western Myths: Interview with Maxine Hong Kingston," [Taipei] *Fiction and Drama* 9 (1997): 19–26.

66. Quoted in Heather Tang, "An Interview with Amy Tan," *The Occidental*, April 14, 1997, 3.

67. Liu, "The Problematics of Kingston's 'Cultural Translation,'" 17–19. It is important to note that Kingston herself complains, however, about being misread; see "Cultural Mis-readings," 55.

68. Ibid., 62.

69. Cheung, *"The Woman Warrior* versus *The Chinaman Pacific,"* 239.

70. Nancy Forbes Romano, "The Disorientation of Pearl and Kai," *Los Angeles Times Book Review*, June 16, 1991, 2.

71. Maslin, "Intimate Family Lessons," B1, emphasis added.

72. Sau-ling Cynthia Wong, "'Sugar Sisterhood': Situating the Amy Tan Phenomenon," in *The Ethnic Canon: Histories, Institutions, and Interventions*, ed. David Palumbo-Liu (Minneapolis: University of Minnesota Press, 1995), 188.

73. Quoted in Matthew Gilbert, "Novelist Jen Takes Wry Look at Diversity," *Boston Globe*, June 4, 1996, 58. Also see Elizabeth Mehren, "Dodging Literary Labels," *Los Angeles Times*, April 29, 1991, E1. When asked the same question at a panel discussion on Asian American studies at Harvard University on April 21, 1998, however, Jen seemingly modified her opinion and stated that she was sometimes misquoted by reporters and that she thought minority writers had social responsibilities.

74. Nee and Nee, *Longtime Californ'*, 377–89; Wei, *Asian American Movement*, 64–71; Cheung, "*The Woman Warrior* versus *The Chinaman Pacific*," 235–38.

75. Michael Fischer, quoted in Werner Sollors, "Introduction," in *The Invention of Ethnicity*, ed. Sollors (New York: Oxford University Press, 1989), xi. Also see Sollors, *Beyond Ethnicity: Consent and Descent in American Culture* (New York: Oxford University Press, 1986), 241–47.

76. Author interview with Jade Snow Wong, San Francisco, Feb. 5, 1991.

77. Amy Ling, "A Kinder, Gentler Frank Chin," *The World and I* 6 (April 1991): 401, 408.

78. For Chin's translation of "Ballad of Mulan" and explanation of Chinese literature and history, see "Come All Ye Asian American Writers," 4–52; and "This Is Not An Autobiography," 113–30. For discussions of Chin's "misreading" of Chinese classics, see Liu, "The Problematics of Kingston's 'Cultural Translation,'" 19; Shan Te-hsing, "Writing Asian American Literary History: A Case of Study of Frank Chin"; and Zhang Qionghui, "Who's Afraid of Frank Chin." Shan and Zhang's papers were presented at the Fifth Conference on American Literature and Thoughts, Taipei, Oct. 1995.

A sixth-century Chinese poem based on a legend and written by an anonymous author, the sources of the Fa Mulan story are controversial even among Chinese historians and literary critics, and it is difficult to present an authentic interpretation of the poem.

79. Davis, "Frank Chin: An Interview," 91. Kingston also implies that only bilingual readers can fully appreciate the subtlety of her work. Of *Woman Warrior*, she says, "There are puns for Chinese speakers only, and I do not point them out for non-Chinese speakers. There are some visual puns best appreciated by those who write Chinese." Kingston, "Cultural Mis-readings," 65.

80. Shan Te-hsing, "Redefining Chinese American Literature," in *Multilingual America: Transnationalism, Ethnicity, and the languages of America*, ed. Werner Sollors (New York: New York University Press, 1998), 112–23; Koshy, "The Fiction of Asian American Literature," 314, 335–39; Cheung, "*The Woman Warrior* versus *The Chinaman Pacific*," 235–238.

81. Frank Chin, "Unmanly Warrior," in Chin, *The Chinaman Pacific & Frisco R.R. Co.* (Minneapolis: Coffee House Press, 1988), ii–v.

82. Amy Ling, "A Kiss and a Tweak," [New York] *New Asian Times*, June 1989, 9. Also see Ling, *Between Worlds: Women Writers of Chinese Ancestry* (New York: Pergamon Press, 1990), 149; and Kim, "Such Opposite Creatures," 87. Kingston has strongly denied, however, that there is any connection between the novel and Frank Chin. She has said that the protagonist has the traits of a cousin in China, whom she met during her visit to her

parents' village in Guangdong in the early 1980s and who immediately impressed her with his "Tripmaster Monkey–style" dynamics. Author interview with Maxine Hong Kingston, Cambridge, Mass., March 7, 1990.

83. There is also a similar, albeit less publicized, argument among Chinese-language writers. See Chen Rouxi, "Haiwai zuojia he bentuxing" [Chinese immigrant writers and their sense of Chineseness], *Xianggang Wenxue* [Hong Kong Literature], Sept. 5, 1988, 21.

84. David Leiwei Li, "The Formation of Frank Chin and Formations of Chinese American Literature," in *Asian Americans: Comparative and Global Perspectives*, ed. Shirley Hune et al. (Pullman: Washington State University Press, 1991), 211–23.

85. There is also the influence of earlier writers on the younger generation in Chinese-language literature. For example, Cao Guilin acknowledges that he is deeply moved by Yu Lihua's *Seeing the Palm Trees Again*. Cao Guilin [Glen Cao], *Beijingren zai niuyue* [A Beijinger in New York], (Beijing: Zhongguo Wenlian, 1991), 1–2.

86. Tan, *The Joy Luck Club*, 34, 271.

# Epilogue

A retrospective look at Chinese American literature allows certain conclusions about the writing and provides an opportunity to see a multifaceted reflection of Chinese life in America. In defining the Chinese American experience, the writing exhibits some unique features and reveals a context that differs even on subtle points from that of mainstream literature. Historically, Chinese immigrants were seen as being unassimilable: They were alleged to be self-disqualified from becoming Americans for their sojourner mentality, questionable economic motives, and alien cultural traditions. To be sure, nearly every immigrant group coming to the United States has encountered problems. Yet the Chinese experience is distinctive. What occurred at Ellis Island left unhappy memories for many Europeans, but the mistreatment Chinese immigrants received at Angel Island, as indicated in their poems written at the detention center, demonstrates a deeper psychological wound that continues to haunt Chinese Americans today.[1]

The Chinese not only faced greater difficulty in entering America but also had to deal with more obstacles in their new life than were likely to be encountered by other ethnic groups. In one book of life stories of immigrants from various parts of the world, an English immigrant calls America "a home away from home" and a Swedish farmer praises the absence of aristocrats in the New World and the freedom of not having to take off his hat to anyone. A Chinese laundry worker, however, complains that this is a hierarchical society based on race and that "Chinamen" are kept at the bottom of the social ladder because they have the "wrong skin color."[2] This aspect of Chinese American experience not only restricts the scope of their choice and freedom in real life but also decides the content and form of their writing.

In other words, there is a feeling—recurrent in the writing of Chinese Americans—that theirs is a unique racial background. For example, few other immigrants produced such a large body of writing pleading for tolerance and protesting against injustice. As "strangers from a different shore," Chinese immigrants had to make a special effort to win acceptance and strive hard to demonstrate their ability to be good Americans. Their pleading appeal for sympathy and the bitter voices heard in their complaints about racial prejudice are rarely seen in writing of other immigrant groups. For that reason, Robert Blauner's observation on black migrants who moved to the North also applies to the Chinese: "All groups started at the bottom, but the bottom has by no means been the same for all groups."[3] Like blacks, Chinese immigrants were stamped with a permanent racial visibility, were victims of legally sanctioned color prejudice, and had to start at a bottom far lower than that of their white counterparts.

What happened to Chinese immigrants also occurred to their American-born children. As the autobiography of Pardee Lowe and the work of other second-generation authors show, despite their enthusiastic embracing of mainstream culture native-born Chinese were rebuffed and frustrated in their pursuit of the American dream and forced to remain in segregated Chinatowns with little chance to move upward and outward. Their bitterness and disappointment are vividly revealed in a comment of one Chinatown resident: "It's as if I thought all whites had it easy. Not had it easy, but they didn't have the same kind of hardship and they did not even deal with it in the same way, they didn't overcome it in the same way as Chinese."[4]

The Chinese American experience has undergone dramatic transformation since the 1960s. Together with changes in the larger society, the progress they have made guarantees that never again will Chinese Americans suffer the mistreatment that characterized their life previously. To those who believe that racism has disappeared, however, the writing of contemporary Chinese American authors, both in English and in Chinese, shows that prejudice is not a thing of the past. An illustrative and thought-provoking dialogue occurs in Kingston's *China Men*. Her brother, an America-born college graduate, is praised by white people for speaking good English. "Thank you, so do you," the brother sarcastically returns the supposed compliment.[5]

Despite the passage of time, frustration over obstacles the Chinese encounter in social advancement remains a major theme in Chinese American literature. As two contemporary scholars point out, the disillusionment that Pardee Lowe described in his autobiography "has been taken seriously by, and continues to cause great concern among, Asian Americans."[6] Racism, be it overt or covert, is a critical element that leads to a sense of skepticism among Chinese Americans about whether they can duplicate the assimilation of white ethnic groups. "Just a human being in this culture, in this society, is a white man, he can disappear," one Chinese American complains. "I couldn't disappear, no matter how enlightened I was, no matter how straight my English was. Someone, just because they saw my skin color, would detect an accent."[7] What reflects in their writing thus demonstrates that although the Chinese American experience is now identified in many ways with that of their counterparts in the larger society, it still takes on a different form, and its manifestations are not always the same as those of their white peers. W. E. B. Du Bois's insight, "The problem of the twentieth century is the problem of the color-line," is proved true by Chinese American writing.[8]

The fact that the Chinese are the "ultimate foreigners" in the United States gives their writing another unique characteristic. It tends to be anthropologically oriented and contain detailed introductions to aspects of Chinese civilization. Particularly among the early Chinese immigrant authors, Chinese life was something that had to be explained. It would be hardly necessary for their European counterparts to write in that way because they shared a point of origin with mainstream Americans. By contrast, the ignorance of the average American on China made the Chinese predicament *sui generis.* Because the unfamiliarity of the public with Chinese American heritage causes much misunderstanding and produces racial friction and bias, Chinese American authors, especially in the earlier years, considered it as their primary task to help Americans understand their culture. To that end, virtually all their literary work elaborates on Chinese cultural customs and traditions. The cultural handicap confronting early Chinese American authors is still experienced by contemporary writers. As Maxine Hong Kingston remarked about readers' comments on *The Woman Warrior,* "They praised the wrong things. . . . I had not calculated how blinding stereotyping is, how stupefying."[9]

In other words, unlike mainstream writers, who "can get away with writing for [themselves], knowing full well [they live] in a society run by people like [themselves]," a Chinese American author often feels that he or she has to act as a native informant because of the racially based cultural blindness of the audience.[10] The public has not yet been capable of understanding Chinese American culture and tends to associate it with racial stereotypes. When Frank Chin's play *Chickencoop Chinaman* was first staged, critics complained that its characters did not "look like Orientals."[11] As long as such blindness remains, Chinese American writers will have to explain the anthropological and ethnographic aspect of their writing. It is difficult to understand the characteristics of Chinese American literature fully unless that is first understood.

Despite racial and cultural differences, however, Chinese American authors have spoken in unison with writers of other ethnic groups on some common issues, such as cultural conflict, the consequences of Americanization, and the role of class and gender in American life. Although there are specific characteristics peculiar to their backgrounds that bring them the distinction of being viewed as "strangers," there are also things they share with other Americans. Chinese Americans, under the influence of mainstream culture, have gone through a series of stages that has gradually transformed them from being Chinese into being Chinese American. The fact that a significant proportion of Chinese American authors, both native-born and immigrants, are women is a clear indication of their Americanization.[12] It highlights the dramatic changes Chinese women have gone through in the Gold Mountain. It is American life that gives them status equal to that of men and imbues a strong sense of the women's consciousness. In that, Chinese women share a common lot with numerous other aspiring immigrant and minority women in American society. As Gish Jen asserts, being a woman is a "big, big, big shaping thing, probably more than my race."[13]

Even the complaints and protests of the early Chinese immigrants against racial prejudice, so profoundly uttered in their writing, yielded not only moving expressions of anger and frustration but also strong evidence of Americanness. That they expected to be treated equally with immigrants from Europe (and that they believed they should be accorded the same rights as the mainstream) indicates that from the very beginning, Chinese immigrants appreciated the American principle of justice and democracy. This phenomenon, as Marlon K. Hom argues, can be seen as a crude sign of their Americanization.[14]

Works by second-generation Chinese further illustrate similarities between Chinese American writing and that of other ethnic groups. Like their European counterparts during the melting-pot era, second-generation Chinese before the 1960s were more oriented toward mainstream society than their own community. Although Chinese immigrant authors may have dreamed of returning to their old home and expressed that desire through their work, the second generation aimed at full participation in American life and revealed in its writing a strong desire to be "real Americans." For them, there was little impulse to become high-minded defenders of Chinese cultural heritage. Rather than being torn between the two worlds, they tried hard to demolish their "Chinese self" and were rarely troubled by the question of how to keep their Chinese heritage.

The sense of Americanness for contemporary Chinese American writers is even more self-evident. Their emphasis on creative freedom and individualism is unmistakably American, as is their strenuous search for a Chinese American cultural identity. Nowhere but in American society are people so obsessed with the identity issue. It is the rise of multiculturalism that has encouraged them to explore the meaning of being a Chinese American, and it is under the American influence that the Chinese have come to be more appreciative of the values of their tradition and culture. Lynn Pan, a Chinese British writer, admits that the ethnic consciousness of the Chinese in Great Britain is not yet awakened and that Chinese there have a long way to go to catch up to their Chinese American peers.[15] In short, Chinese American writing, from immigrant authors' demands for American-style justice, to the second-generation's pursuit of the American dream, to the search for an identity by contemporary writers, demonstrates that no matter how different the Chinese appear to be, they will inevitably undergo the same process of acculturation and integration that led David Levinsky to "rise" in metropolitan New York and Willa Cather's Ántonia to succeed on the Great Plains.

In terms of writing techniques and artistic forms, Chinese American literature appears to resemble that of mainstream society rather than the writing of their old home. It is true that Chinese Americans have inherited the literary tradition and cultural legacy of their ancestral land. Unlike some minority groups such as African Americans, who were deprived of their cultural identity and lost much of their heritage during their brutal uprooting from Africa, the Chinese are fortunate in having retained a rich culture that helped them endure difficult conditions and buoyed them, even in the most adverse circumstances.

Yet Chinese American authors have long been subjected to the powerful influence of mainstream American culture and affected by the literary trends of the larger society, making it difficult for them to retain their heritage. As a result, although their writing is "Chinese" in content and origin, it is "American" in style and literary sensibility. That duality is especially apparent in the writing of cultivated Chinese, whose autobiographies and narrative methods bear a conspicuous American influence. It is also reflected in work by Chinese-language writers; their employment of Western-style techniques and expressions demonstrates that there is not much "Chineseness" in their writing style, other than the use of the language.

The traits of an American influence are more obvious in contemporary Chinese American writing. Although there are many "crazy women" in classic Chinese literature, Kingston claims she was inspired by Hester Prynne in *The Scarlet Letter* in writing about the No-Name Woman. "My heritage is Shakespeare and Walt Whitman," she declares proudly. "The first story about the aunt in *Woman Warrior* is straight out of *The Scarlet Letter*. . . . My experimentation with time and space, straight from James Joyce and Virginia Woolf. I consider the Beat writers—Kerouac, Ginsberg—they are my teachers."[16] Ironically, despite his dispute with Kingston, Frank Chin may share more with her than he wants to ad-mit—he, too, is strongly influenced by Anglo-American literature in style and temperament. Chin has acknowledged that one of his favorite writers stylistically is Jonathan Swift.[17]

Given that it has lost most of the stylistic characteristics of Chinese litera-ture and that it has been more American than Chinese in themes and subject matter, it is perhaps safe to conclude that Chinese American writing, in the pro-cess of being uprooted and resettled, has emerged as a distinctive part of Amer-ican literature and made an undeniable imprint on U.S. culture.[18] In that sense, when Kingston in *The Woman Warrior* comforts her mother over the loss of fam-ily property in China, her comments also symbolize the changed position of Chinese American literature: "We belong to the planet now, Mama. Does it make sense to you that if we're no longer attached to one piece of land, we belong to the planet? Wherever we happen to be standing, why, that spot belongs to us as much as any other spot."[19]

## Notes

1. Him Mark Lai, Genny Lim, and Judy Yung, *Island: Poetry and History of Chinese Immigrants on Angel Island, 1910–1940* (repr. Seattle: University of Washington Press, 1991), 8–28.

2. Hamilton Holt, ed., *The Life Stories of Undistinguished Americans as Told by Them-selves* (New York: Potts, 1906), 295–99.

3. Robert Blauner, *Racial Oppression in America* (New York: Harper and Row, 1972), 63. Also see Carlos Marks, *Farewell—We're Good and Gone: The Great Black Migration* (Bloomington: Indiana University Press, 1989), 13.

4. Quoted in Victor G. Nee and Brett de Bary Nee, *Longtime Californ': A Documentary Study of an American Chinatown* (repr. Stanford: Stanford University Press, 1986), 164.

5. Maxine Hong Kingston, *China Men* (repr. New York: Ballentine Books, 1981), 291.

6. Kai-yu Hsu and Helen Palubinskas, eds., *Asian American Authors* (Boston: Houghton Mifflin, 1972), 16.

7. Quoted in Nee and Nee, *Longtime Californ',* 383.

8. Quoted in Gary Y. Okihiro, *Margins and Mainstreams: Asians in American History and Culture* (Seattle: University of Washington Press, 1994), 129.

9. Maxine Hong Kingston, "Cultural Mis-readings by American Reviewers," in *Asian ad Western Writers in Dialogue,* ed. Guy Amirthanayagam (London: Macmillan, 1982), 55.

10. Frank Chin et al., eds., *Aiiieeeee! An Anthology of Asian-American Writers* (Wash-ington, D.C.: Howard University Press, 1974), xxxv. Also see Amy Ling, "Maxine Hong Kingston and the Dialogic Dilemma of Asian American Writers," paper presented at the Tenth Conference of the Association for Asian American Studies, Cornell University, June 1993, 1–3.

11. Author interview with Frank Chin, Los Angeles, Nov. 6, 1995; Elaine H. Kim, *Asian American Literature: An Introduction to Its Social Context* (Philadelphia: Temple University Press, 1982), xv.

12. There is also an economic factor that has brought about so many women writers in the Chinese American community. Chen Ruoxi recalls that her son was stunned when he learned how small her income from writing was and thought her foolish to be a writer, even though he had taken great pride in having a "writer mom." Chen Ruoxi, "Haiwai zuojia he bentuxing" [Chinese immigrant writers and their sense of Chineseness], *Xianggang Wenxue* [Hong Kong Literature], Sept. 5, 1988, 20.

Kingston also explains the difficulty of being a writer: "Now, practically, a writer, like everybody in this world, has to figure out a way to make a living. There is a statistic that in the United States only a hundred writers can live on their book earnings. . . . A writer should learn to live with few material needs." Maxine Hong Kingston, "Writer," in *With Silk Wings: Asian American Women at Work,* ed. Elaine H. Kim (San Francisco: Asian Women United of California, 1983), 116.

Because writers' incomes are so low, many talented Chinese American males who aspire to write feel they cannot afford a literary career but instead must dedicate themselves to achieving a middle-class standard of living. Zhou Feili notes that his wife and daughter are upset by his interest in writing because they feel he should work to support the family. In comparison, Chinese women in America may not have to conceive of literary success in financial terms, because traditional biases place less pressure on women for family livelihoods. Zhou Feili, "Yangfan erchi" [Two ways to eat American meals], in Zhou, *Yangfan erchi* [Two ways to eat American meals], (Taipei: Erya, 1987), 124.

13. Quoted in Matthew Gilbert, "Novelist Jen Takes Wry Look at Diversity," *Boston Globe,* June 4, 1996, 58.

14. Marlon K. Hom, ed. and trans., *Songs of Gold Mountain: Cantonese Rhymes from San Francisco Chinatown* (Berkeley: University of California Press, 1987), 73. Lynn Pan made similar comments in her study on Chinese immigrants in America, see *Sons of the Yellow Emperor: A History of the Chinese Diaspora* (New York: Kodansha International, 1994), 293.

15. Pan, *Sons of the Yellow Emperor,* xiii, 295, 381–89.

16. Helen Lee, "A Writer Visits High School," [Boston] *Sampan,* Oct. 24, 1994, 5; Shan, "An Interview with Kingston," 250–51.

17. Robert Murray Davis, "Frank Chin: An Interview with Robert Murray Davis," *Amerasia* 14, no. 2 (1988): 94.

18. One example to support the argument is that when Maxine Hong Kingston's *Woman Warrior* and *China Men* were first translated and published in China they were introduced as representative works of contemporary American literature and appeared in the journal *Foreign Literature* in Shanghai. For Chinese critics, Kingston's writing is stylistically and thematically closer to American literature than that of the Chinese.

19. Maxine Hong Kingston, *The Woman Warrior: Memoirs of a Girlhood among Ghosts* (repr. New York: Alfred Knopf, 1976), 107.

# Glossary

Asing, Norman　袁生
Bai Xianyong [Hsian-yung Pai]　白先勇
Cao Guilin [Glen Cao]　曹桂林
Cao Guipeng　曹桂鵬
Cao Youfang　曹又方
Chen Chong [Joan Chen]　陳沖
Chen, Jack　陳依范
Chen Ruoxi [Jo-hsi Chen, Lucy Chen]　陳若曦
Chew, Edward C.　伍朗光
Chew, Ng Poon　伍盤照
Chin, Frank　趙健秀
Chinese Consolidated Benevolent Association　中華會館
Chinese Six Companies　中華總會館
*Chung Sai Yat Pao* [China-West Daily]　中西日報
*Ci hai* [Chinese Encyclopedia]　辭海
fu kan　副刊
Fa Mulan [Hua Mulan]　花木蘭
Gee, Dolly　纯荷珠
Hakka [Kejia]　客家
*Haojiao* [Herald Monthly]　號角
*Hua Xia Wenzhai* [China News Digest]　華夏文摘
Huie Kin　許芹
Hu Shi　胡適
Jen, Gish　任壁蓮
Ji Hongchang　吉鴻昌
*Jinshan Shibao* [Gold Mountain News]　金山時報
Joint Publishing Company　三聯書店

*Kim Shan Jit San Luk* [Golden Hill News]     金山新聞 錄

Kingston, Maxine Hong     湯亭亭

*Ku Shehui* [Bitter Society]     苦 社會

Kwan Kung [Guan Gong, Lord Guan]     關公 [關羽]

Lao She [Lao Shaw, Shu Qingchun]     老舍 [舒慶春 ]

Lee, C. Y. [Li Jinyang]     黎錦揚

Lee, Rose Hum     譚金美

Lee Tsung Dao [Li Zhengdao]     李政道

Lee Yan Phou     李彥富

Lee Yuan Tze [Li Yuanzhe]     李遠哲

Leung, Faith Sai     梁細蘇

Li Li [Bao Lili]     李黎 [包莉莉]

Lin Taiyi [Anor Lin]     林太乙

Lin Yutang     林語堂

Lou Sing Kee     劉成記

Lowe, Pardee     劉裔昌

*Meizhou Huaqiao Ribao* [Chinese American Daily]     美洲 華僑日報

Ng Poon Chew [Wu Panzhao]     伍盤照

Nie Hualing     聶華苓

Park No-yong [Bao Narong]     鮑納榮

pinyin     拼音 [漢字拼音]

*Qiao Bao* [The China Press]     僑報

*Renmin Ribao* [People's Daily]     人 民日報

*Sampan*     舢舨

*Shijie Ribao* [World Journal]     世 界日報

*Shuihu zhuan* [The water margin]     水滸傳

*Sing Tao Daily*     星島日報

Sui Sin Far [Edith Maude Eaton]     水仙花

Tan, Amy     譚思美

Tape, Joseph     趙洽

Tien, Chang-Lin     田長霖

Ting, Samuel Chao Chung [Ding Zhaozhong]     丁肇中

Tong, K. Achick     唐茂枝

Tow, Julius Su [Tu Rusu]     屠汝涑

Tsui, Daniel C. [Cui Qi]     崔琦

Wong, Anna May     黃柳霜

Wong, Jade Snow     黃玉雪

Wong, Shawn Hsu     徐忠雄

Woo, Hong Neok [Wu Hongyu]     吳宏雨

Wu Tingfang     伍廷芳

Xiangshan [Zhongshan]     香山縣 [中山縣]

*Xin Dalu* [New Continent]     新大陸

*Yamei Shibao* [Asian American Times]     亞美時報

Yang, C. N. [Yang Zhenning]     楊振寧

Yi Li [Pan Xiumei]     伊犁 [潘秀媚 ]

Yu Lihua [Li-hua Yu]     於梨華

Yung Wing     容閎
Zhang Ailing [Eileen Chang]     張愛玲
Zhang Xiguo     張系國
Zhen Yatong     甄亞彤
*Zhong Bao* [Central Daily]     中報
*Zhongguo Daobao* [China Guide]     中國導報
Zhu Diwen [Stephan Chu]     朱棣文

# English Bibliography

## Books and Articles Published in English

Adams, Romanzo. *Interracial Marriage in Hawaii.* New York: Macmillan, 1937.

Alexander, Garth. *The Invisible China: The Overseas Chinese and the Politics of Southeast Asia.* New York: Macmillan, 1974.

*An Analysis of the Chinese Question.* San Francisco: Office of the *San Francisco Herald,* 1852.

Arkush, R. David, and Leo Ou-fan Lee, trans. and eds. *Land without Ghosts: Chinese Impressions of America from the Mid-Nineteenth Century to the Present.* Berkeley: University of California Press, 1989.

Asing, Norman. "To His Excellency Governor Bigler." *Daily Alta California,* May 5, 1852, 2.

Baker, Houston A., Jr. *Three American Literatures: Essays in Chicano, Native American, and Asian-American Literature for Teachers of American Literature.* New York: Modern Language Association, 1982.

Barkan, Elliot R. *Asian and Pacific Islander Migration to the United States: A Model of New Global Patterns.* Westport: Greenwood Press, 1992.

———. "Whom Shall We Integrate? A Comparative Analysis of the Immigration and Naturalization Trends of Asians before and after the 1965 Immigration Act (1951–1978)." *Journal of American Ethnic History* 3, no. 1 (1983): 29–57.

Barth, Gunther. *Bitter Strength: A History of the Chinese in the United States, 1850–1870.* Cambridge: Harvard University Press, 1964.

Basso, Hamilton. "New Bottles, Old Wine." *The New Yorker,* Aug. 11, 1945, 61–63.

Baum, Dale. "Women Suffrage and the 'Chinese Question': The Limits of Radical Republicanism in Massachesetts, 1865–1976." *New England Quarterly* 56, no. 1 (1983): 60–77.

Berssenbrugge, Mei-mei. *The Heat Bird.* Providence: Burning Deck, 1983.

———. *Summits Move with the Tide.* Greenfield Center: Greenfield Review Press, 1974.

Berthoff, Warner. *The Ferment of Realism: American Literature, 1884–1919.* New York: Cambridge University Press, 1965.

Bigelow, Donald N. Introduction. In Jacob A. Riis, *How the Other Half Lives,* vii–xiv. Reprint. New York: Hill and Wang, 1957.

Biggers, Earl Derr. *Keeper of the Keys*. Indianapolis: Bobbs-Merrill, 1932.

Bigler, John. "Governor's Special Message." *Daily Alta California*, May 1, 1852, 1.

Blackburn, George M., and Sherman L. Richard. "The Prostitutes and Gamblers of Virginia City, Nevada: 1870." *Pacific Historical Review* 48 (May 1979): 239–58.

Blake, Nelson M. *Novelists' America: Fiction as History, 1910–1940*. Syracuse: Syracuse University Press, 1969.

Blauner, Robert. *Racial Oppression in America*. New York: Harper and Row, 1972.

Blicksilver, Edith, ed. *The Ethnic American Women*. Dubuque: Kendall-Hunt, 1978.

Blinde, Patricia Lin. "Icicle in the Desert: Form and Perspective in the Works of Two Chinese-American Women Writers." *MELUS* 6, no. 3 (1979): 51–72.

Bode, William Walter. *Lights and Shadows of Chinatown*. San Francisco: H. S. Crocker, 1896.

Bogardus, Emory Stephen. *Immigration and Race Attitudes*. New York: D. C. Heath, 1928.

Bolman, Helen P. "Notes: *Father and Glorious Descendant*." *Library Journal*, April 1, 1943, 287.

Brooks, Benjamin. *The Chinese in California*. San Francisco: n.p., 1877.

Brooks, Gwendolyn. *Blacks*. Chicago: Third World Press, 1987.

Brown, Wesley, and Amy Ling, eds. *Imagining America: Stories from the Promised Land*. New York: Persea Books, 1991.

————. *Visions of America: Personal Narratives from the Promised Land*. New York: Persea Books, 1993.

Buck, Pearl S. *All Men Are Brothers*. New York: John Day, 1933.

Bullock, Mary Brown. "American Exchanges with China: Revisted." In *Educational Exchanges: Essays on the Sino-American Experience*, ed. Joyce K. Kallgren and Denis Fred Simon, 23–44. Berkeley: University of California Press, 1987.

Burton, William L. *Melting Pot Soldiers: The Union's Ethnic Regiments*. Ames: Iowa State University Press, 1988.

Buttlar, Lois. "Multicultural Education: A Guide to Reference Sources." *Ethnic Forum* 7, no. 1 (1987): 77–96.

Carnes, Mark. *Secret Ritual and Manhood in Victorian America*. Berkeley: University of California Press, 1989.

Chacon, Ramon D. "The Beginning of Racial Segmentation: The Chinese in West Fresno and Chinatown's Role as Red Light District, 1870s–1920s." *Southern California Quarterly* 70 (Winter 1988): 371–98.

Chan, Anthony M. "Born-Again Asians: The Making of a New Literature." *Journal of Ethnic Studies* 11 (Winter 1984): 57–73.

Chan, Jeffrey Paul, Frank Chin, Lawson Fusao Inada, and Shawn Wong, eds. *The Big Aiiieeeee! An Anthology of Chinese American and Japanese American Literature*. New York: Meridian, 1991.

————. "Chinese in Haifa." In *Aiiieeeee! An Anthology of Asian-American Writers*, ed. Frank Chi et al., 12–29. Washington, D.C.: Howard University Press, 1974.

————. "Resources for Chinese American Literary Traditions." In *The Chinese American Experience: Papers from the Second National Conference on Chinese American Studies (1980)*, ed. Genny Lim, 241–43. San Francisco: Chinese Historical Society of America, 1984.

Chan, Sucheng. *Asian Americans: An Interpretive History*. Boston: Twayne Publishers, 1991.

——. *This Bitter Sweet Soil: The Chinese in California Agriculture, 1860–1910.* Berkeley: University of California Press.

——, ed. *Entry Denied: Exclusion and the Chinese Community in America, 1882–1943.* Philadelphia: Temple University Press, 1991.

Chan, Wing-tsit. "Lin Yutang, Critic and Interpreter." *College English* 8 (Jan. 1947): 163–69.

Chang, Diana. *The Frontiers of Love.* New York: Random House, 1956.

——. *A Woman of Thirty.* New York: Random House, 1959.

Chang, Gordon. "Asian Immigrants and American Foreign Relations." In *Pacific Passage: The Study of American–East Asian Relations on the Eve of the Twenty-first Century,* ed. Warren I. Cohen, 103–18. New York: Columbia University Press, 1996.

Chang, Kang-I Sun. *The Late-Ming Poet Chen Tzu-lung: Crises of Love and Loyalism.* New Haven: Yale University Press, 1991.

Chang, Pao-min. *Continuity and Change: A Profile of Chinese Americans.* New York: Vantage Press, 1983.

Char, Tin-Yuke. *The Sandalwood Mountains.* Honolulu: University of Hawaii Press, 1975.

Cheng, Lok Chua. "Golden Mountain: Chinese Versions of the American Dream in Lin Yutang, Louis Chu, and Maxine Hong Kingston." *Ethnic Groups* 4, nos. 1–2 (1982): 33–59.

Chen, Hsiang-shui. *Chinatown No More.* Ithaca: Cornell University Press, 1992.

Chen, Jack. *The Chinese of America.* New York: Harper and Row, 1980.

Chennault, Anna. *A Thousand Springs: The Biography of a Marriage.* New York: Paul S. Eriksson, 1962.

Chen, Scarlet. "The Asian Presence." *Belle Lettres: A Review of Books by Women* 6 (Fall 1990): 22.

Cheung, King-kok. *Articulate Silences: Hisaye Yamamoto, Maxine Hong Kingston, Joy Kogawa.* Ithaca: Cornell University Press, 1993.

——. *"The Woman Warrior* versus *The Chinaman Pacific:* Must a Chinese American Critic Choose between Feminism and Heroism?" In *Conflicts in Feminism,* ed. Marianne Hirsch and Evelyn Fox Keller, 234–51. New York: Routledge, 1990.

——, and Stan Yogi, comps. *Asian American Literature: An Annotated Bibliography.* New York: Modern Language Association, 1988.

Chiang, Monlin. *Tides from the West: A Chinese Autobiography.* New Haven: Yale University Press, 1947.

Chiang Yee. *A Chinese Childhood.* New York: John Day, 1940.

——. *The Chinese Eye.* New York: Frederick A. Stokes, 1936.

——. *The Silent Traveler in Boston.* New York: W. W. Norton, 1959.

——. *The Silent Traveler in New York.* New York: John Day, 1950.

——. *The Silent Traveler in San Francisco.* New York: W. W. Norton, 1959.

Chih, Andre. *L'Occident "Chretien" vu par les Chinois ver la fin du XIXme siècle* [The "Christian" West as seen by the Chinese around the end of the nineteenth century]. Paris: Presses Universitaires de France, 1962.

Chin, Frank. Chickencoop Chinaman *and* The Year of the Dragon: *Two Plays by Frank Chin.* Reprint. Seattle: University of Washington Press, 1981.

——. *The Chinaman Pacific and Frisco R.R. Co.* Minneapolis: Coffee House Press, 1988.

——. "Come All Ye Asian American Writers of the Real and the Fake." In *The Big*

*Aiiieeeee: An Anthology of Chinese American and Japanese American Literature,* ed. Jeffery Paul Chan et al., 1–30. New York: Meridian, 1991.

———. *Donald Duck.* Minneapolis: Coffee House Press, 1991.

———. "Rendezvous." *Conjunctions* 19 (Fall 1993): 291–302.

———. "This Is Not an Autobiography." *Genre* 18 (Summer 1985): 109–30.

———, et al., eds. *Aiiieeeee! An Anthology of Asian-American Writers.* Washington, D.C.: Howard University Press, 1974.

———, and Jeffery Paul Chan. "Racist Love." In *Seeing through Shuck,* ed. Richard Kostelanetz, 68–77. New York: Ballantine Books, 1972.

*China: Nationwide Consumer Survey.* Princeton: Gallup Organization, 1994.

"China Reevaluates Pearl Buck." [Beijing] *China Today* 40 (May 1991): 61.

*Chinese and Japanese in America.* Philadelphia: American Academy of Political and Social Sciences, 1909.

*The Chinese Experience in Arizona and Northern Mexico: 1870–1940.* Tucson: Arizona Historical Society, 1980.

"Chinese Protester, Taiwan Women Wed." *Boston Globe,* Aug. 31, 1994, A15.

Chock, Eric, et al., eds. *Talk Story: An Anthology of Hawaii's Local Writers.* Honolulu: Petronium Press, 1978.

Chou, Cynthia. *My Life in the United States.* North Quincy: Christopher Publishing House, 1970.

Chu, Bernice, ed. *The Asian American Media Reference Guide.* New York: Asian CineVision, 1986.

Chu, Doris. *Chinese in Massachusetts: Their Experiences and Contributions.* Boston: Chinese Culture Institute, 1987.

Chu, Louis. *Eat a Bowl of Tea.* New York: Lyle Stuart, 1961.

Chung, Sue Fawn. "From Fu Manchu, Evil Genius to James Lee Wong, Popular Hero: A Study of the Chinese American in Popular Periodical Fiction from 1920 to 1940." *Journal of Popular Culture* 10, no. 3 (1976): 534–47.

———. "Their Changing World: Chinese Women on the Comstock, 1860–1910." In *Comstock Women: The Making of a Mining Community,* ed. Ronald M. James and C. Elizabeth Raymond, 203–28. Reno: University of Nevada Press, 1998.

Clarke, James Freeman. *Sermons of James Freeman Clarke.* Reprint. Boston: George H. Ellis, 1912.

Clar, Reva, and William M. Kramer. "Chinese-Jewish Relations in the Far West: 1850–1950." *Western States Jewish History* 21 (Oct. 1988): 12–35.

Cohen, Lucy M. *Chinese in the Post–Civil War South: A People without a History.* Baton Rouge: Louisiana State University Press, 1984.

Collins, Sheila D. *From Melting Pot to Rainbow Connection: The Future of Race in Amerian Politics.* New York: Monthly Review Press, 1986.

Conn, J. Peter. *Pearl S. Buck: A Cultural Biography.* New York: Cambridge University Press, 1996.

Coolidge, Mary Roberts. *Chinese Immigration.* New York: Henry Holt, 1909.

"Cosmopolitan Heroes." *New York Times,* May 4, 1919, sec. 2, 1.

Crow, Charles L. "A *MELUS* Interview: Hisaye Yamamoto." *MELUS* 14 (Spring 1987): 80.

Daniels, Roger. *Asian America: Chinese and Japanese in the United States since 1850.* Seattle: University of Washington Press, 1988.

———. "The Asian-American Experience: The View from the 1990s." In *Multiculturalism and the Canon of American Culture,* ed. Hans Bak, 131–45. Amsterdam: VU University Press, 1993.

———. *Concentration Camps: North America, Japanese in the United States and Canada during World War II.* Rev. ed. Malabar: Robert E. Krieger, 1989.

———. "The Japanese." In *Ethnic Leadership in America,* ed. John Higham, 36–63. Baltimore: Johns Hopkins University Press, 1979.

———. "No Lamps Were Lit for Them: Angel Island and the Historiography of Asian American Immigration." *Journal of American Ethnic History* 17, no. 1 (1997): 3–18.

———. "North American Scholarship and Asian Immigration, 1974–1979." *Immigration History Newsletter* 11, no. 1 (1979): 8–11.

———. *The Politics of Prejudice: The Anti-Japanese Movement in California and the Struggle for Japanese Exclusion.* Berkeley: University of California Press, 1962.

———. "United States Policy towards Asian Immigrants: Contemporary Developments in Historical Perspective." *International Journal* 60, no. 8 (1993): 310–34.

———, ed. *Anti-Chinese Violence in North America.* New York: Arno Press, 1978.

Danton, George Henry. *The Chinese: New Problems and Old Backgrounds.* Boston: Marchall Jones, 1938.

Davis, Horace. *Chinese Immigration: Speech of Hon. Horace Davis of California in the House of Representatives.* Washington, D.C.: n.p., 1878.

Davis, Robert Murray. "Frank Chin: An Interview with Robert Murray Davis." *Amerasia Journal* 14, no. 2 (1988): 81–95.

D'Emilio, Frances. "The Secret Hell of Angel Island." *American West* 21 (May–June 1984): 44–51.

Desnoyers, Charles. "'The Thin Edge of the Wedge': The Chinese Educational Mission and Diplomatic Representation in the Americas, 1872–1875." *Pacific Historical Review* 61, no. 2 (1992): 241–63.

Dezell, Maureen. "The Tug of 'Warrior.'" *Boston Globe,* Sept. 23, 1994, 49, 57.

Diner, Hasia R. *Erin's Daughters in America.* Baltimore: Johns Hopkins University Press, 1983.

Dinnerstein, Leonard, and David M. Reimers. *Ethnic Americans: A History of Immigration.* 3d ed. New York: HarperCollins, 1988.

*Directory of Chinese Business Houses.* San Francisco: Wells Fargo, 1878.

Dirlik, Arif. "Asians on the Rim: Transnational Capital and Local Community in the Making of Contemporary Asian America." *Amerasia Journal* 22, no. 3 (1996): 1–24.

Dong, Lorraine, and Marlon K. Hom. "Defiance of Perpetuation: An Analysis of Characters in *Mrs. Spring Fragrance.*" In *Chinese America: History and Perspectives, 1987,* 139–68. San Francisco: Chinese Historical Society of America, 1987.

Dower, John W. *War without Mercy: Race and Power in the Pacific War.* New York: Pantheon Books, 1986.

Du Bois, W. E. B. *The Souls of Black Folk.* Reprint. Chicago: A. C. McClurg, 1953.

Dutka, Elaine. "'Joy Luck': A New Challenge in Disney's World." *Los Angeles Times,* Aug. 31, 1993, F1.

Du Zhifu. "6.5 Million Hong Kong People Returning to the communist Motherland." *Chinese Community Forum* no. 9733, July 1, 1997.

Ebrey, Patricia. "Women, Marriage, and the Family in Chinese History." In *Heritage of*

*China: Contemporary Perspectives on Chinese Civilization,* ed. Paul S. Ropp, 197–223. Berkeley: University of California Press, 1990.

Eder, Richard. "A WASP-free America." *Los Angeles Times Book Review,* May 26, 1996, 2.

"Edith Eaton Dead: Author of Chinese Stories under the Name of Sui Sin Far." *New York Times,* April 9, 1914, 11.

Elliot, Emory, ed. *Columbia Literary History of the United States.* New York: Columbia University Press, 1988.

Endo, Russell. "Bibliographic Materials on Asian and Pacific Americans." *Ethnic Forum* 3 (Fall 1983): 94–107.

Espiritu, Yen Le. *Asian American Panethnicity: Bridging Institutions and Identities.* Philadelphia: Temple University Press, 1992.

——. *Asian American Women and Men: Labor, Laws, and Love.* Thousand Oaks: Sage Publications, 1997.

Ewen, Elizabeth. *Immigrant Women in the Land of Dollars: Life and Culture on the Lower East Side, 1890–1925.* New York: Monthly Review Press, 1985.

Fairbank, John King. *The Great Chinese Revolution, 1800–1985.* New York: Harper and Row, 1987.

Farquhar, Judith, and Mary L. Doi, "Bruce Lee vs. Fu Manchu: Kung Fu Films and Asian American Stereotypes in America." *Bridge Magazine* 6 (Fall 1978): 23–40.

Felstiner, John. *Paul Celan: Poet, Survivor, Jew.* New Haven: Yale University Press, 1995.

Fenn, William Purviance. *Ah Sin and His Brethren in American Literature.* Peiping [Beijing]: College of Chinese Studies, 1933.

Fernandez-Morera, Dario. *American Academia and the Survival of Marxist Ideas.* New York: Praeger, 1996.

Fessler, Loren W., ed. *Chinese in America: Stereotyped Past, Changing Present.* New York: Vantage Press, 1983.

Fitzgerald, Stephen. *China and the Overseas Chinese.* New York: Cambridge University Press, 1972.

Fong, Joe Chung. "Transnational Newspapers: The Making of the Post-1965 Globalized/ Localized San Gabriel Valley Chinese Community." *Amerasia Journal* 22, no. 3 (1996): 65–77.

Fong, Kathryn M. "Feminism Is Fine, but What's It Done for Asian America?" *Bridge: An Asian American Perspective* 6 (Winter 1978): 21–22.

Fong, Timothy P. *The First Suburban Chinatown: The Remaking of Monterey Park, California.* Philadelphia: Temple University Press, 1994.

Freeman, James M. *Hearts of Sorrow: Vietnamese-American Lives.* Stanford: Stanford University Press, 1989.

Fritz, Christian G. "Due Process, Treaty Rights, and Chinese Exclusion." In *Entry Denied: Exclusion and the Chinese Community in America, 1882–1943,* ed. Sucheng Chan, 25–56. Philadelphia: Temple University Press, 1991.

Fu Chi Hao. "My Reception in America." *Outlook* 86 (Aug. 1907): 770–73.

Gabaccia, Donna, ed. *Seeking Common Ground: Multidisciplinary Studies of Immigrant Women in the United States.* Westport: Greenwood Press, 1992.

Gee, Emma, ed. *Counterpoint: Perspectives on Asian America.* Los Angeles: Asian American Studies Center, UCLA, 1976.

Gibson, Otis. *The Chinese in America.* Cincinnati: Hitchcock and Walden, 1877.

Gilbert, Matthew. "Novelist Jen Takes Wry Look at Diversity." *Boston Globe,* June 4, 1996, 53, 58.

Gilmartin, Christina K., et al., eds. *Engendering China: Women, Culture, and the State.* Cambridge: Harvard University Press, 1994.

Ging Hawk Club. "Ging Hawk Club Essay Contest: 'Does My Future Lie in China or America?'" In *Chinese America: History and Perspectives, 1992,* 149–75. San Francisco: Chinese Historical Society of America, 1992.

Glanz, Rudolf. "Jews and Chinese in America." In *Studies in Judaica American,* ed. Rudolf Glanz. 314–29. New York: KTAV, 1970.

"Glass Ceiling? It's More Like a Steel Cage." *Los Angeles Times,* March 20, 1995, B4.

Glazer, Nathan, and Daniel Patrick Moynihan. *Behind the Melting Pot: The Negroes, Puerto Ricans, Jews, Italians, and Irish of New York City.* Cambridge: MIT Press, 1963.

Gong, Eng Ying, and Bruce Grant. *Tong War!* New York: Nicholas L. Brown, 1930.

Gong, Ted. "Approaching Cultural Change through Literature: From Chinese to Chinese American." *Amerasia Journal* 7, no. 1 (1980): 73–86.

Gossett, Thomas F. *Race: The History of an Idea in America.* Dallas: Southern Methodist University Press, 1963.

Gould, Stephen Jay. *The Mismeasure of Man.* New York: W. W. Norton, 1981.

Gratton, Henry Pearson, ed. *As a Chinaman Saw Us: Passages from His Letters to a Friend at Home.* New York: D. Appleton, 1904.

Greenhouse, Linda. "Shield of Secrecy in Tenure Disputes." *New York Times,* Jan. 10, 1998, B1.

Greenwood, Roberta S. "The Overseas Chinese at Home: Life in a Nineteenth Century Chinatown in California." *Archaeology* 31 (Sept.–Oct. 1978): 42–48.

Gregorovich, Andrew. *Gum Sam: Images of the Gold Mountain, 1886–1947.* Vancouver: The Gallery, 1985.

Hagedorn, Jessica, ed. *Charlie Chan Is Dead: An Anthology of Contemporary Asian American Fiction.* New York: Penguin, 1994.

Hallock, Jin. "Show Your Abilities and Intelligence." *Chinese Community Forum* no. 9723, May 14, 1997.

Handlin, Oscar. *Boston's Immigrants: A Study in Acculturation.* Rev. ed. Cambridge: Harvard University Press, 1979.

Hansen, Marcus Lee. "The Third Generation in America." *Commentary* 14 (Nov. 1952): 492–500.

Han Suyin. *A Many-Splendored Thing.* Boston: Little, Brown, 1952.

Hao Fu Chi. "My Reception in America." *Outlook* 86 (Aug. 1907): 770–73.

Harte, Bret. "An Episode of Fiddletown." In *Writings of Bret Harte,* 2:121–70. Boston: Houghton Mifflin, 1896.

———. "Wan Lee, the Pagan." In *Writings of Bret Harte,* 2:262–80. Boston: Houghton Mifflin, 1896.

Haslam, Gerald W. *Forgotten Pages of American Literature.* Boston: Houghton Mifflin, 1970.

Hellwig, David J. "Black Reactions to Chinese Immigration and the Anti-Chinese Movement: 1850–1910." *Amerasia Journal* 6, no. 2 (1979): 25–44.

Higham, John. *Send These to Me: Jews and Other Immigrants in Urban America.* New York: Athenaeum, 1975.

———. *Strangers in the Land: Patterns of American Nativism, 1860–1925.* Reprint. New York: Atheneum, 1963.

———, ed. *Ethnic Leadership in America.* Reprint. Baltimore: Johns Hopkins University Press, 1979.

Hightower, Marvin. "The Counterpoint of Race and Ethnicity." *Harvard Gazette,* Nov. 12, 1993, 5, 10.

Hing, Bill Ong. *Making and Remaking Asian America through Immigration Policy, 1850–1990.* Stanford: Stanford University Press, 1993.

Hiraoka, Jesse. "A Sense of Place." *Journal of Ethnic Studies* 4 (Winter 1977): 72–84.

Hirata, Lucie Cheng [Lucie Cheng]. "The Chinese American in Sociology." In *Counterpoint: Perspectives on Asian America,* ed. Emma Gee, 20–26. Los Angeles: Asian American Studies Center, UCLA, 1976.

———. "Chinese Immigrant Women in Nineteenth Century California." In *Women of America: A History,* ed. Carol Ruth Berkin and Mary Beth Norton, 223–44. Boston: Houghton Mifflin, 1979.

———. "Free, Indentured, Enslaved: Chinese Prostitutes in Nineteenth Century America." *Signs* 5, no. 1 (1979): 3–29.

Hoexter, Corinne K. *From Canton to California: The Epic of Chinese Immigration.* New York: Four Winds Press, 1976.

Holt, Hamilton, ed. *The Life Stories of Undistinguished Americans as Told by Themselves.* New York: Potts, 1906.

Hom, Marlon K. "A Case of Mutual Exclusion: Portrayals by Immigrant and American-born Chinese of Each Other in Literature." *Amerasia Journal* 11, no. 2 (1984): 29–45.

———, ed. and trans. *Songs of Gold Mountain: Cantonese Rhymes from San Francisco Chinatown.* Berkeley: University of California Press, 1987.

Hong, Lawrence. "The Korean Family in Los Angeles." In *Koreans in Los Angeles,* ed. Eui-Young Yu, Earl H. Phillips, and Eun Sik Yang, 99–132. Los Angeles: Center for Korean-American and Korean Studies, California State University, 1982.

Hong, Maria, ed. *Growing Up Asian America: An Anthology.* New York: William Morrow, 1993.

Hongo, Garrett, ed. *Under Western Eyes: Personal Essays from Asian America.* New York: Anchor Books, 1995.

Hosmer, Margaret Kerr. *You-Sing: The Chinaman in California: A True Story of the Sacramento Flood.* Philadelphia: Presbyterian Publication Committee, 1868.

Hosokawa, Bill. *Nisei: The Quiet Americans.* New York: William Morrow, 1969.

Houston, Jeanne Wakatsuki, and James D. Houston. *Farewell to Manzanar.* Reprint. New York: Bantam Books, 1974.

How, Lee Ming, et al. "To His Excellency U.S. Grant, President of the United States." In *Facts upon the Other Side of the Chinese Question,* ed. Augustus Layres, 20–24. San Francisco: n.p., 1876.

"How to Tell Japs from the Chinese." *Life* magazine, Dec. 22, 1941, 81–82.

Ho Yow. "Chinese Exclusion: A Benefit or a Harm?" *North American Review* 173 (Sept. 1901): 314–30

Hsia, Jayjia. *Asian Americans in Higher Education and at Work.* Hillsdale: Lawrence Erlbaum, 1988.

Hsu, Francis L. K. *The Challenge of the American Dream: The Chinese in the United States.* Belmont: Wadsworth, 1971.

Hsu, Kai-yu, and Helen Palubinskas, eds. *Asian-American Authors.* Boston: Houghton Mifflin, 1972.

Huang, Tsen-ming. *The Legal Status of the Chinese Abroad.* Taipei: China Cultural Service, 1954.

Huie, Kin. *Reminiscences.* Peiping [Beijing]: San Su Press, 1932.

Hundley, Norris, Jr., ed. *The Asian American.* Santa Barbara: Clio Press, 1976.

Hune, Shirley. "Politics of Chinese Exclusion: Legislative Executive Conflict 1876–1882." *Amerasia Journal* 9, no. 1 (1982): 5–27.

———, Hyung-chan Kim, Stephen S. Fugita, and Amy Ling, eds. *Asian Americans: Comparative and Global Perspectives.* Pullman: Washington State University Press, 1991.

Hunter, Jane. *The Gospels of Gentility: American Women Missionaries in Turn-of-the-Century China.* Reprint. New Haven: Yale University Press, 1989.

Hu Shih. "Women's Place in Chinese History." In *Chinese Women through Chinese Eyes,* ed. Li Yu-ning, 3–15. Armonk: M. E. Sharpe, 1992.

Hwang, David Henry. *Broken Promises: Four Plays.* New York: Avon Books, 1983.

———. *FOB and Other Plays.* Reprint. New York: New American Library, 1990.

Irick, Robert L. *Ch'ing Policy toward the Coolie Trade, 1847–1878.* San Francisco: Chinese Materials Center, 1982.

Iriye, Akira. *Power and Culture: The Japanese-American War, 1941–1945.* Cambridge, Harvard University Press, 1981.

Isaacs, Harold R. *Scratches on Our Minds: American Views of China and India.* Reprint. Armonk: M. E. Sharpe, 1980.

Iwata, Edward. "Word Warriors." *Los Angeles Times,* June 24, 1990, E1, E9.

Jen, Gish. *Mona in the Promised Land.* New York: Alfred A. Knopf, 1996.

———. *Typical Amercan.* Boston: Houghton Mifflin, 1991.

Jewett, Sarah Orne. *The Country of the Pointed Firs.* Reprint. New York: Doubleday, 1956.

Johnson, Dick. "Census Finds Many Claiming New Identity." *New York Times,* March 5, 1991, A1.

Johnson, Marjorie R. *Chinatown Stories.* New York: Dodge Publishing, 1900.

Judson, Judith. "Child of Two Cultures." *Washington Post,* July 2, 1989, D3.

Kalcik, Susan. "Ethnic Foodways in America: Symbol and the Performance of Identity." In *Ethnic and Regional Foodways in the United States: The Performance of Group Identity,* ed. Linda Keller Brown and Kay Mussell, 37–65. Knoxville: University of Tennessee Press, 1984.

Kang, Connie K. "Chinese in the Southland: A Changing Picture." *Los Angeles Times,* June 29, 1997, A1, A32.

Kang, Younghill. *East Goes West.* New York: Charles Scribner's Sons, 1937.

Kao, George, ed. *Two Writers and the Cultural Revolution.* Hong Kong: Chinese University Press, 1980.

Kao, Hsin-sheng C., ed. *Nativism Overseas: Contemporary Chinese Women Writers.* Albany: State University of New York Press, 1993.

Kashima, Tetsuden. *Buddhism in America: The Social Organization of an Ethnic Religious Institution.* Westport: Greenwood Press, 1977.

Kaufman, Jonathan. *Broken Alliance: The Turbulent Times between Blacks and Jews in America.* New York: Charles Scribner's Sons, 1996.

Kim, Elaine H. "Appendix A." In *East to America: Korean American Life Stories.* Ed. Elaine H. Kim and Eui-Young Yu, 353–58. New York: New Press, 1996.

———. "Asian American Literature and the Importance of Social Context." *ADE Bulletin* 80 (Spring 1985): 34–41.

———. *Asian American Literature: An Introduction to the Writings and Their Social Context.* Philadelphia: Temple University Press, 1982.

———. "Such Opposite Creatures: Men and Women in Asian American Literature." *Michigan Quarterly Review* 29 (Winter 1990): 68–93.

———, ed. *With Silk Wings: Asian American Women at Work.* San Francisco: Asian Women Union of California, 1983.

Kim, Hyung-chan, ed. *Asian American Studies: An Annotated Bibliography and Research Guide.* Westport: Greenwood Press, 1989.

Kim Ronyoung. *Clay Walls.* Reprint. Seattle: University of Washington Press, 1990.

Kingston, Maxine Hong. *China Men.* Reprint. New York: Ballentine Books, 1981.

———. "Cultural Mis-readings by American Reviewers." In *Asian and Western Writers in Dialogue,* ed. Guy Amirthanayagam, 55–65. London: Macmillan, 1982.

———. *Tripmaster Monkey: His Fake Book.* New York: Vintage, 1990.

———. *The Woman Warrior: Memoirs of a Girlhood among Ghosts.* New York: Alfred A. Knopf, 1976.

Kitano, Harry H. L. "The Japanese." In *Harvard Encyclopedia of American Ethnic Groups,* ed. Stephan Thernstrom, 561–71. Cambridge: Harvard University Press, 1980.

Kitano, Harry H. L., et al. "Asian-American Interracial Marriage." *Journal of Marriage and the Family* 46 (Feb. 1984): 179–90.

———, and Roger Daniels. *Asian Americans: Emerging Minorities.* 2d ed. Englewood Cliffs: Prentice-Hall, 1995.

Knoll, Tricia. *Becoming Americans: Asian Sojourners, Immigrants, and Refugees in the Western United States.* Portland: Coast to Coast Books, 1982.

Koch, John. "Interview with Connie Chung." *Boston Globe Magazine,* June 29, 1997, 12.

Koo, Hui-lan. *Hui-lan Koo: An Autobiography.* New York: Dial, 1943.

Koshy, Susan. "The Fiction of Asian American Literature." *Yale Journal of Criticism* 9 (Fall 1996): 315–46.

Kulik, Gary. "Representing the Railroad." *Gettysburg Review* 2, no. 3 (1989): 495–510.

Kumagai, Gloria L. "The Asian Women in America." *Bridge Magazine* 6 (Winter 1978): 16–20.

Kung, S. W. *Chinese in American Life: Some Aspects of Their History, Status, Problems, and Contributions.* Seattle: University of Washington Press, 1962.

Kuo, Alex. *The Window Tree.* Peterborough: Windy Row Press, 1971.

Kuo, Helena. *I've Come a Long Way.* New York: D. Appleton, 1942.

Kwok, Munson A., and Ella Yee Quan, eds. *Origins and Destinations: Forty-one Essays on Chinese America.* Los Angeles: Chinese Historical Society of Southern California and Asian American Studies Center, UCLA, 1994.

Kwong, Peter. *The New Chinatown.* New York: Noonday Press, 1987.

La Fargue, Thomas E. *China's First Hundred.* Pullman: State College of Washington Press, 1942.

Lai Chun Chuen. "Remarks of the Chinese Merchants of San Francisco, upon Governor Bigler's Message and Some Common Objections." [San Francisco] *The Oriental*, Feb. 1, 1855, 1.

Lai, Him Mark. "The Chinese." In *Harvard Encyclopedia of American Ethnic Groups*, ed. Stephan Thernstrom, 217–34. Cambridge: Harvard University Press.

———. "The Chinese Language Sources Bibliography Project: Preliminary Findings." *Amerasia Journal* 5 (Fall 1978): 66–88.

———. "The Chinese Press in the United States and Canada since World War II: A Diversity of Voices." In *Chinese America: History and Perspectives, 1990*, 107–55. San Francisco: Chinese Historical Society of America, 1990.

———. *A History Reclaimed: An Annotated Bibliography of Chinese Language Materials on the Chinese of America*. Los Angeles: Asian American Studies Center, UCLA, 1986.

———. "The Ups and Downs of the Chinese Press in the U.S." *East West* 10 (Nov. 1986): 9–12.

———, Genny Lim, and Judy Yung. *Island: Poetry and History of Chinese Immigrants on Angel Island, 1910–1940*. Reprint. Seattle: University of Washington Press, 1989.

———, Joe Huang, and Don Wong. *The Chinese of America: 1785–1980*. San Francisco: Chinese Culture Foundation, 1980.

Lai, Yong, et al. "The Chinese Question from a Chinese Standpoint." In Otis Gibson, *The Chinese in America*, 285–92. Cincinnati: Hitchcock and Walden, 1877.

Lao She [Lau Shu; Shu Qingchun]. *Rickshaw Boy*. Trans. Evan King. Reprint. New York: Reynal and Hitchcock, 1945.

———. *Rickshaw*. Trans. Jean M. James. Honolulu: University of Hawaii Press, 1979.

———. *The Yellow Storm*. Trans. Ida Pruitt. New York: Harcourt, Brace, 1951.

Lau, Alan Chong. *Songs for Jadina*. New York: Greenfield Review Press, 1980.

Lauter, Paul, et al., eds. *The Heath Anthology of American Literature*. Vol. 2. Lexington: D. C. Heath, 1994.

Lee Chew. "The Life Story of a Chinaman." In *The Life Stories of Undistinguished Americans as Told by Themselves*, ed. Hamilton Holt, 281–99. New York: Potts, 1906.

Lee, C. Y. [Chin Yang Lee; Li Qinyang]. *Days of the Tong War*. New York: Ballantine Books, 1974.

———. *Flower Drum Song*. New York: Farrar and Cudhay, 1957.

———. *Lover's Point*. New York: Farrar and Cudhay, 1958.

Lee, Helen. "A Writer Visits High School." [Boston] *Sampan*, Oct. 24, 1994, 5.

Lee, Joann Faung Jean, ed. *Asian Americans: Oral Histories of First to Fourth Generation Americans from China, the Philippines, Japan, India, the Pacific Islands, Vietnam and Cambodia*. New York: New Press, 1991.

Lee, Leo Ou-fan. *Voices from the Iron House: A Study of Lu Xun*. Bloomington: Indiana University Press, 1987.

Lee, Mary Paik. *Quiet Odyssey: A Pioneer Korean Woman in America*. Seattle: University of Washington Press, 1990.

Lee, Rose Hum. *The Chinese in the United States of America*. Hong Kong: Hong Kong University Press, 1960.

———. *The Growth and Decline of Chinese Communities in the Rocky Mountain Region*. New York: Arno Press, 1978.

Lee, Virginia Chin-lan. *The House That Tai Ming Built*. New York: Macmillan, 1963.

Lee, Won. "Second Generation Korean Americans." [Korean American Friendship Society] *Pacific Bridge* 3 (Winter 1994): 2–3.

Lee Yan Phou. "The Chinese Must Stay." *North American Review* 148 (April 1889): 476–83.

———. *The Fiftieth Year Record of the Class of 1887.* Yale University, 1938.

———. *When I Was a Boy in China.* Boston: Lothrop, 1887.

Leibfred, Philip. "Anna May Wong." *Films in Review* 38 (March 1987): 146–52.

Leland, Charles Godfrey. *Fusang: The Discovery of America by Chinese Buddhist Priests in the Fifth Century.* New York: J. W. Bouton, 1975.

Leon, George. *A Lone Bamboo Doesn't Come from Jackson St.* San Francisco: Isthmus Press, 1977.

Leong, Monfoon. *Number One Son.* San Francisco: East/West, 1975.

Leong, Pui Chee. Muk Yee: *Wooden Fish Poems.* Hong Kong: Hong Kong University Press, 1976.

Leung, Edwin Pak-wah. "The Education of Early Chinese Students in America." In *The Chinese American Experience: Papers from the Second National Conference on Chinese American Studies (1980),* ed. Genny Lim, 203–10. San Francisco: Chinese Historical Society of America, 1984.

Levy, S. Howard. *The Lotus Lovers: The Complete History of the Curious Erotic Custom of Footbinding in China.* Buffalo: Prometheus Books, 1992.

Li, David Leiwei. "The Formation of Frank Chin and Formations of Chinese American Literature." In *Asian Americans: Comparative and Global Perspectives,* ed. Shirley Hune et al., 211–23. Pullman: Washington State University Press, 1991.

———. *Imagining the Nation: Asian American Literature and Cultural Consent.* Stanford: Stanford University Press, 1998.

———. The Naming of a Chinese American 'I': Cross-Cultural Sign/ifications in *The Woman Warrior. Criticism* 30 (Fall 1988): 497–515.

Li Ling Ai. *Life Is for a Long Time.* New York: Hastings House, 1972.

Lim, Genny, ed. *The Chinese American Experience: Papers from the Second National Conference on Chinese American Studies (1980).* San Francisco: Chinese Historical Society of America, 1984.

Lim, Shirley Geok-lin, and Amy Ling, eds. *Reading the Literature of Asian America.* Philadelphia: Temple University Press, 1992.

———, Mayumi Tsutakawa, and Margarita Donnelly, eds. *The Forbidden Stitch: An Asian American Women's Anthology.* Corvallis: Calyx Books, 1989.

Lin, Adet, and Lin Anor [Lin Taiyi]. *Our Family.* New York: John Day, 1939.

Lin, Anor [Lin Taiyi]. *The Eavesdropper.* Cleveland: World, 1959.

———. *Lin Yutang zhuan* [Biography of Lin Yutang]. Beijing: Zhongguo Xiju, 1994.

Ling, Amy. *Between Worlds: Women Writers of Chinese Ancestry.* New York: Pergamon Press, 1990.

———. "A Kinder, Gentler Frank Chin." *World and I* 6 (April 1991): 401–12.

———. "A Kiss and a Tweak." [New York] *New Asian Times,* June 1989, 9.

Ling, Kwang Chang. "Why Should the Chinese Go?" [San Francisco] *The Argonault,* Aug. 7, 1878, 1.

Link, Perry. "End of *Rickshaw Boy.*" In *Two Writers and the Cultural Revolution,* ed. George Kao, 39–50. Hong Kong: Chinese University Press, 1980.

Lin Yutang. *Chinatown Family.* New York: John Day, 1948.

———. *The Importance of Living.* New York: John Day, 1937.

———. "Impressions on Reaching America." In *Land without Ghosts: Chinese Impressions of American from the mid-Nineteenth Century to the Present,* trans. and ed. R. David Arkush and Leo Ou-fan Lee, 159–63. Berkeley: University of California Press, 1989.

———. *My Country and My People.* New York: John Day, 1935.

———. *On the Wisdom of America.* New York: John Day, 1950.

Liu, Eric. *The Accidental Asian: Notes from a Native Speaker.* New York: Random House, 1998.

———, ed. *Next: Young American Writers on the New Generation.* New York: W. W. Norton, 1994.

Liu, Haiming. "The Trans-Pacific Family: A Case Study of Sam Chang's Family History." *Amerasia Journal* 18, no. 2 (1992): 1–34.

Liu, John. "Towards an Understanding of the Internal Colonial Model." In *Counterpoint: Perspectives on Asian America,* ed. Emma Gee, 160–68. Los Angeles: Asian American Studies Center, UCLA, 1976.

Liu, Kwang-Ching. *Americans and Chinese: A Historical Essay and Bibliography.* Cambridge: Harvard University Press, 1963.

———. *Anglo-American Steamship Rivalry in China, 1862–1874.* Cambridge: Harvard University Press, 1962.

Liu, Toming Jun. "The Problematics of Kingston's 'Cultural Translation.'" *Journal of American Studies of Turkey* 4 (Fall 1996): 15–26.

Liu Zongren. *Two Years in the Melting Pot.* San Francisco: China Books, 1984.

Li Yu-ning, ed., *Chinese Women through Chinese Eyes.* Armonk: M. E. Sharpe, 1992.

Loewen, James W. *The Mississippi Chinese: Between Black and White.* Rev. ed. Prospect Heights: Waveland Press, 1988.

Lo Hsiang-lin. "Yung Wing: First Chinese Graduate from a U.S. University." In *The Life, Influence, and the Role of the Chinese in the United States, 1776–1960: Proceedings, Papers of the National Conference Held at the University of San Francisco,* 207–15. San Francisco: Chinese Historical Society of America, 1976.

Lo, Karl. "The Chinese Vernacular Presses in North America, 1900–1950: Their Role in Social Cohesion." In *Annals of the Chinese Historical Society of the Pacific Northwest,* 170–78. Seattle: Chinese Historical Society of the Pacific Northwest, 1984.

———, and Him Mark Lai, comps. *Chinese Newspapers Published in North America, 1854–1975.* Washington, D.C.: Center for Chinese Research Materials, 1977.

London, Jack. *Tales of the Fish Patrol.* New York: Macmillan, 1905.

Loo, Chalsa M. *Chinatown: Most Time, Hard Time.* New York: Praeger, 1992.

Lowe, Lisa. *Immigrant Acts: On Asian American Cultural Politics.* Durham: Duke University Press, 1996.

Lowe, Pardee. *Father and Glorious Descendent.* Boston: Little, Brown, 1943.

———. "Father's Robes of Immortality." *Atlantic Monthly* 162 (Dec. 1938): 785–92.

———. "Letters of Hawk Sung." *Yale Review* 28 (Sept. 1938): 69–81.

Low, Victor. *The Unimpressible Race: A Century of Educational Struggle by the Chinese in San Francisco.* San Francisco: East/West Publishing, 1982.

Lu Xun. "A Madman's Diary." In *The Complete Stories of Lu Xun,* trans. Yang Xianyi and Gladys Yang, 1–12. Bloomington: Indiana Unviersity Press, 1987.

Lyman, Stanford. *Chinese Americans.* New York: Random House, 1974.

Magnaghi, Russell M. "Virginia City's Chinese Community, 1860–1880." *Nevada Historical Society Quarterly* 24 (Summer 1981): 130–57.

Ma, L. Eve Armentrout. "Chinatown Organizations and the Anti-Chinese Movement,
1882–1914." In *Entry Denied: Exclusion and the Chinese Community in American,
1882–1943,* ed. Sucheng Chan, 147–69. Philadelphia: Temple University Press, 1991.

Mark, Diane Mei Lin, and Ginger Chih. *A Place Called Chinese America.* Rev. ed. Dubuque:
Kendall-Hunt, 1985.

Marks, Carlos. *Farewell—We're Good and Gone: The Great Black Migration.* Bloomington: Indiana University Press, 1989.

Maslin, Janet. "Intimate Family Lessons, Available to All." *New York Times,* Sept. 8, 1993,
B1.

Mason, Richard. *The World of Suzie Wong.* New York: World Publishing Company, 1957.

Maykovich, Minako K. "To Stay or Not to Stay: Dimensions of Ethnic Assimilation." *International Migration Review* 10, no. 3 (1976): 377–87.

McClain, Charles J. *In Search of Equality: The Chinese Struggle Against Discrimination in
Nineteenth-Century America.* Berkeley: University of California Press, 1994.

McClellan, Robert. *The Heathen Chinee: A Study of American Attitudes toward China,
1890–1905.* Columbus: Ohio State University Press, 1971.

McCue, Andy. "Evolving Chinese Language Dailies Serve Immigrants in New York City."
*Journalism Quarterly* 52 (Summer 1975): 272–76.

McCunn, Ruthanne Lum. *Chinese American Portraits: Personal Histories, 1828–1988.* San
Francisco: Chronicle Books, 1988.

———. *Thousand Pieces of Gold.* San Francisco: Design Enterprises, 1981.

McDonnell, Patrick J. "Connecting the Past and Present." *Los Angeles Times,* March 11,
1995, B3.

Mehren, Elizabeth. "Dodging Literary Labels." *Los Angeles Times,* April 29, 1991, E1.

Mei, June, Jean Pang Yip, and Russell Leong. "The Bitter Society: *Ku Shehui*—A Translation, Chapters 37–46." *Amerasia Journal* 8, no. 1 (1981): 33–67.

Melendy, H. Brett. *The Oriental Americans.* New York: Twayne Publishers, 1972.

Miller, Joaquin [Cincinnatus Hiner Miller]. *First Fam'lies of the Sierras.* Chicago: Jansen,
McClurg, and Cox, 1876.

Miller, Stuart C. *The Unwelcome Immigrant: The American Image of the Chinese, 1785–
1882.* Berkeley: University of California Press, 1969.

Min, Anchee. *Red Azalea.* New York: Pantheon Books, 1994.

Moffatt, Susan. "Splintered Society." *Los Angeles Times,* July 13, 1992, A1.

Mori, Toshio. *Yokohomo, California.* Caldwell: Caxton Printers, 1949.

Morris, Edmund. "Books: Short and Simple Annuals." *The New Yorker,* June 11, 1990, 101–
2.

Mura, David. *Turning Japanese: Memories of Sansei.* Boston: Atlantic Monthly Press, 1991.

Murphey, Rhoads. "Boston's Chinatown." *Economic Geography* 28 (April 1952): 244–55.

Nathan, Andrew J. "But How Chinese Are They?" *New York Times Book Review,* Dec. 9,
1990, 26.

Nee, Victor, and Brett de Barry Nee. *Longtime Californ': A Documentary Study of an American Chinatown.* Reprint. Stanford: Stanford University Press, 1986.

Newman, Katherine D., ed. *The American Equation: Literature in a Multi-Ethnic Culture.*
Boston: Allyn and Bacon, 1971.

————. *Ethnic American Short Stories.* New York: Washington Square Press, 1975.

"A New Note in Fiction" [editor's note]. *New York Times,* July 7, 1912, 45.

New, Peter Kong-ming. "Footnotes on a Yankee Chinese: Letters of Shang-chow New, 1913–1917." *Amerasia* 11, no. 2 (1984): 81–96.

Ng, Franklin. "The Sojourner, Return Migration, and Immigration History." In *Chinese America: History and Perspective, 1987,* 53–72. San Francisco: Chinese Historical Society of America, 1987.

————. "The Western Military Academy in Fesno." In *Origins and Destinations: Forty-one Essays on Chinese America,* ed. Munson A. Kwok and Ella Yee Quan, 153–75. Los Angeles: Chinese Historical Society of Southern California and Asian American Studies Center, UCLA, 1994.

Ngon, Fong Kun. "The Chinese Six Companies." *Overland Monthly* 23 (1894): 519–21.

Ng Poon Chew. "Chinaman in America." *The Independent,* April 3, 1902, 801–3.

————. "The Chinese in Los Angeles." *Land of Sunshine* 1 (Oct. 1894): 102–3.

————. *The Treatment of the Exempt Classes of Chinese in the United States.* San Francisco: Office of *Chung Sai Yat Po,* 1908.

Ng, Wendy L., et al., eds. *Reviewing Asian America Locating Diversity.* Pullman: Washington State University Press, 1995.

O'Connor, Coral. "Servey Reveals Chinese Immigrants in Australia Divorce Most." [Hong Kong] *South China Morning Post,* July 24, 1994, A4.

Oh, Angela, and Nancy Yoshihara. "Adding an Asian American Voice to the Race Debate." *Los Angeles Times,* July 13, 1997, M3.

Okihiro, Gary Y. *Margins and Mainstreams: Asians in American History and Culture.* Seattle: University of Washington Press, 1994.

Ong, Aihwa, and Donald M. Nonini, eds. *Ungrounded Empires: The Cultural Politics of Modern Chinese Transnationalism.* New York: Routledge, 1997.

Ong, Paul, et al., eds. *The New Asian Immigration in Los Angeles and Global Restructuring.* Philadelphia: Temple University Press, 1994.

Ono, Kazuko. "Between Footbinding and Nationhood." In *Chinese Women in a Century of Revolution, 1850–1950,* ed. Joshua A. Fogel, 23–46. Stanford: Stanford University Press, 1978.

————. "Women Who Took to Battle Dress." In *Chinese Women in a Century of Revolution, 1850–1950,* ed. Joshua A. Fogel, 1–22. Stanford: Stanford University Press, 1978.

"Opinion: When Restaurants Fail, Who Pays the Workers?" [Boston] *Sampan,* Feb. 20, 1998, 7.

Pai, Hsian-yung [Bai Xianyong]. "The Wandering Chinese: Themes of Exile in Taiwan Fiction." *Iowa Review* 7 (Spring–Summer 1976): 205–12.

Paisano, Edna L. *We the American . . . Asians.* Washington: Bureau of the Census, 1993.

Palumbo-Liu, David, ed. *The Ethnic Canon: Histories, Institutions, and Interventions.* San Paul: University of Minneapolis Press, 1995.

Pangzi. "I Am a Happy Slave." *Chinese Community Forum* no. 9808, March 11, 1998.

Pan, Lynn. *Sons of the Yellow Emperor: A History of the Chinese Diaspora.* New York: Kodansha International, 1994.

Pan, Philip P. "War of Words—Chinese Style: Papers Fight for Readers amid Rising Competition." *Los Angeles Times,* Sept. 12, 1993, J1, J3.

Park, [Pao] No-yong [Bao Narong]. *An Oriental View of American Civilization.* Boston: Hale, Cushman and Flint, 1934.

————. *A Squint-eye View of America*. Boston: Meador, 1951.

Pascoe, Peggy. "Gender Systems in Conflict: The Marriages of Mission-Educated Chinese American Women, 1847–1939." In *Unequal Sisters: A Multicultural Reader in U.S. Women's History*, ed. Ellen Carol Dubois and Vicki L. Ruiz, 123–40. New York: Routledge, 1990.

Pfaff, Timothy. "Talk with Mrs. Kingston." *New York Times Book Review*, June 15, 1980, 25.

Poore, Chris. "A Tragedy at Quiet Berea College, Kentucky," *China News Digest* no. 9405, Jan. 29, 1994.

Portes, Alejandro, and Ruben G. Rumbaut. *Immigrant America: A Portrait*. Rev. ed. Berkeley: University of California Press, 1996.

Puzo, Mario. "Choosing a Dream: Italians in Hell's Kitchen." In *Visions of America: Personal Narratives from the Promised Land*, ed. Wesley Brown and Amy Ling, 48–59. New York: Persea Books, 1993.

Quan, Robert Seto. *Lotus among the Magnolias: The Mississippi Chinese*. Jackson: University Press of Mississippi, 1982.

Rich, Adrienne. "Split at the Root: An Essay on Jewish Identity." In *Visions of America: Personal Narratives from the Promised Land*, ed. Wesley Brown and Amy Ling, 90–105. New York: Persea Books, 1934.

Riddle, Ronald. *Flying Dragons, Flowing Streams: Music in the Life of San Francisco's Chinese*. Westport: Greenwood Press, 1983.

Riggs, Fred Warren. *Pressures on Congress: A Study of the Repeal of Chinese Exclusion*. New York: Columbia University Press, 1950.

Riis, Jacob A. *How the Other Half Lives*. Reprint. New York: Hill and Wang, 1957.

Rivera, Carla. "Asians Say They Fare Better Than Other Minorities." *Los Angeles Times*, Aug. 20, 1993, A1, A20.

R.L.B. "The Bookshelf: Meeting of the East and West." *Christian Science Monitor*, April 9, 1943, 12.

Robinson, Ednah. "Chinese Journalism in America." *Current Literature* 32 (Feb. 1902): 325–26.

Rohmer, Sax. *The Insidious Dr. Fu Manchu*. New York: McBride, 1913.

Romano, Nancy Forbes. "The Disorientation of Pearl and Kai." *Los Angeles Times Book Review*, June 16, 1991, 2.

Roosevelt, Theodore. *Addresses and Papers*. Ed. Willis Fletcher Johnson. New York: Sun Dial, 1909.

Rudolph, Frederick. "Chinamen in Yankeedom: Anti-Unionism in Massachusetts in 1870." *American Historical Review* 80, no. 3 (1947): 1–29.

Rustomji-Kerns, Roshni, ed. *Living in America: Poetry and Fiction by South Asian American Writers*. Boulder: Westview Press, 1995.

Sagara, Carlton. "David Mura's Poetry Links Generations." [Boston] *Sampan*, Nov. 16, 1990, 6–7.

Said, Edward W. *Orientalism*. New York: Pantheon Books, 1978.

Sakamoto, Edward. "Anna May Wong and the Dragon-lady Syndrome." *Los Angeles Times Sunday Magazine*, July 12, 1987, 40.

Sandmeyer, Elmer C. *The Anti-Chinese Movement in California*. Reprint. Urbana: University of Illinois Press, 1973.

Santos, Bienvenido N. *The Man Who (Thought He) Looked Like Robert Taylor.* Quezon City, Philippines: New Day Publishers, 1983.

Scardino, Albert. "A Renaissance for Ethnic Papers." *New York Times,* Aug. 22, 1988, D1, D8.

Schell, Orville. "Your Mother Is in Your Bones." *New York Times Book Review,* March 19, 1989, 3.

Schrieke, Bertram J. O. *Alien Americans: A Study of Race Relations.* New York: Viking Press, 1936.

Schwendinger, Robert L. "Investigating Chinese Immigrant Ships and Sailors." In *The Chinese American Experience: Papers from the Second National Conference on Chinese American Studies (1980),* ed. Genny Lim, 16–25. San Francisco: Chinese Historical Society of America, 1984.

See, Lisa. *On Gold Mountain: The One-Hundred-Year Odyssey of My Chinese-American Family.* New York: St. Martin's Press, 1995.

See, Teresita Ang. *The Chinese Immigrants: Selected Writings of Professor Chinben See.* Manila: Kaisa Para, 1992.

Seword, George. *Chinese Immigration: Its Social and Historical Aspects.* Reprint. New York: Arno Press, 1970.

Shan Te-hsing. "An Interview with Maxine Hong Kingston." [Taipei] *Tamkang Review* 27 (Winter 1996): 244–54.

———. "Redefining Chinese American Literature." In *Multilingual America: Transnationalism, Ethnicity, and the Languages of America,* ed. Werner Sollors, 112–23. New York: New York University Press, 1998.

Shepherd, Charles R. *The Ways of Ah Sin.* New York: Fleming H. Revell, 1932.

Simpson, Janice. "Fresh Voices above the Noisy Din." *Time,* June 3, 1991, 66–67.

Siu, Paul P. C. *The Chinese Laundryman: A Study in Social Isolation.* New York: New York University Press, 1987.

Skardal, Dorothy B. *The Divided Heart: Scandinavian Immigrant Experience through Literary Sources.* Lincoln: University of Nebraska Press, 1974.

Sledge, Linda Ching. "Teaching Asian American Literature." *ADE Bulletin* 80 (Spring 1985): 42–45.

Smith, Harrison. "Out of the Streets of China." *Saturday Review of Literature,* July 28, 1945, 11–12.

Smith, Sidonie. *A Poetics of Women's Autobiography: Marginality and the Fictions of Self-Representation.* Bloomington: Indiana University Press, 1987.

Smith, William Carlson. *Americans in Process: A Study of Our Citizens of Oriental Citizenry and Ancestry.* Ann Arbor: Edward Brothers, 1937.

———. *The Second Generation Oriental in America.* Honolulu: Institute of Pacific Relations, 1927.

Snow, Helen Foster. *My China Years.* New York: William Morrow, 1984.

Solberg, S. E. "Sui Sin Far/Edith Eaton: First Chinese-American Fictionist." *MELUS* 8 (Spring 1981): 27–39.

———. "Sui, the Storyteller." In *Turn Shadows into Light: Art and Culture of the Northwest's Early Asian Community,* ed. Mayumi Tsutakawa and Alan Chong Lau, 85–87. Seattle: Young Pine Press, 1982.

Sollors, Werner. "After the Culture Wars." In *Multilingual America: Transnationalism,*

*Ethnicity, and the Languages of American Literature,* ed. Sollors, 1–13. New York: New York University Press, 1998.

———. *Beyond Ethnicity: Consent and Descent in American Culture.* New York: Oxford University Press, 1986.

———. "Forward: From the Bottom Up." In *The Life Stories of Undistinguished Americans, as Told by Themselves,* ed. Hamilton Holt, xi–xxviii. 2d ed. New York: Routledge, 1990.

———. "Immigrants and Other Americans." In *Columbia Literary History of the United States,* ed. Emory Elliot, 569–88. New York: Columbia University Press, 1988.

———. "Intermarriage and Mulattos in the 1920s." [Perugia] *RSA* 5, no. 7 (1989): 269–87.

———. *Neither Black nor White, yet Both: Thematic Explorations of Interracial Literature.* New York: Oxford University Press, 1997.

———. "Nine Suggestions for Historians of American Ethnic Literature." *MELUS* 11, no. 1 (1984): 95–96.

———, ed. *The Invention of Ethnicity.* New York: Oxford University Press, 1989.

———, ed. *Multilingual America: Transnationalism, Ethnicity, and the Languages of American Literature.* New York: New York University Press, 1998.

Soong, Allen C. "Unaccepted Images." *Harvard Crimson,* Oct. 8, 1993, A2.

Sowell, Thomas. *Ethnic America.* New York: Basic Books, 1981.

Speer, William. *The Oldest and Newest Empire: China and the United States.* Hartford: Scranton, 1870.

Spence, Jonathan. *To Change China: Western Advisers in China, 1620–1960.* Rev. ed. New York: Penguin Books, 1980.

Spickard, Paul R. *Mixed Blood: Intermarriage and Ethnic Identity in Twentieth-Century America.* Madison: University of Wisconsin Press, 1989.

Stahler, Michael L. "William Speer: Champion of California's Chinese, 1852–57." *Journal of Presbyterian History* 48 (1970): 113–28.

Stein, M. L. "Opinion Piece Upsets Students." *Editor and Publisher,* Dec. 18, 1993, 24–25.

Steiner, Stan. *Fusang: The Chinese Who Built America.* New York: Harper and Row, 1979.

Sue, Stanley. "Asian-American Educational Achievements: A Phenomenon in Search of an Explanation." *American Psychologist* 45 (Aug. 1990): 913–20.

———, and Harry H. L. Kitano. "Stereotypes as a Measure of Success." *Journal of Social Issues* 29, no. 2 (1973): 83–98.

"Sui Sin Far" [publisher's note]. *New York Times,* July 7, 1912, 45.

"Sui Sin Far, the Half Chinese Writer, Tells of Her Career." *Boston Globe,* May 5, 1912, 1.

Sui Sin Far [Edith Maude Eaton]. "Chinese Workmen in America." *The Independent,* July 3, 1913, 56.

———. "Leaves from the Mental Portfolio of a Eurasian." *The Independent,* Jan. 21, 1909, 125–32.

———. *Mrs. Spring Fragrance.* Chicago: A. C. McClug, 1912.

———. *Mrs. Spring Fragrance and Other Writings,* ed. Amy Ling and Annette White-Parks. Urbana: University of Illinois Press, 1995.

Sung, Betty Lee. *Chinese American Intermarriage.* New York: Center for Migration Studies, 1990.

———. *Racial and Ethnic Group Population.* New York: City College of New York, 1974.

———. *The Story of the Chinese in America.* Rev. ed. New York: Macmillan, 1975.

Suryadinata, Leo, ed. *Ethnic Chinese as Southeast Asians.* Singapore: Institute of Southeast Asian Studies, 1997.

Sze Mai-mai. *Echo of a Cry.* New York: Harcourt, 1945.

Takaki, Ronald. *A Different Mirror: A History of Multicultural America.* Boston: Little, Brown, 1993.

———. *Strangers from a Different Shore: A History of Asian Americans.* Boston: Little, Brown, 1989.

Tan, Amy. *The Joy Luck Club.* New York: Putnam's Sons, 1989.

———. *The Kitchen God's Wife.* New York: Putnam, 1991.

Tanegashima, Kaori. "College Courses in Asian Studies." *Los Angeles Times,* Jan. 25, 1996, B8.

Tan, Mely G. "The Ethnic Chinese in Indonesia." In *Ethnic Chinese as Southeast Asians,* ed. Leo Suryadinata, 33–65. Singapore: Institute of Southeast Asian Studies, 1997.

Tang, Heather. "An Interview with Amy Tan." *The Occidental,* April 14, 1997, 3.

Tape, Mary. "A Letter to San Francisco Board of Education." *Daily Alta California,* April 16, 1885, 1.

Telamaque, Eleanor Wong. *It's Crazy to Stay Chinese in Minnesota.* New York: Thomas Nelson, 1978.

Teng, Ssu-yu, and John K. Fairbank. *China's Response to the West: A Documentary Survey, 1839–1923.* New York: Atheneum, 1967.

Thernstrom, Stephan. "American Ethnic Statistics." In *Immigrants in Two Democracies: French and American Experience,* ed. Donald L. Horowitz and Gerard Noiriel, 80–111. New York: New York University Press, 1992.

———. *The Other Bostonians: Poverty and Progress in the American Metropolis, 1880–1970.* Cambridge: Harvard University Press, 1973.

———. *Poverty and Progress: Social Mobility in a Nineteenth-Century City.* Cambridge: Harvard University Press, 1964.

———, ed. *Harvard Encyclopaedia of American Ethnic Groups.* Cambridge: Harvard University Press, 1980.

Thomson, James, Jr., Peter Stanley, and John Perry. *Sentimental Imperialists: The American Experience in East Asia.* New York: Harper and Row, 1981.

Tiana [Thi Thanh Nga]. "The Long March: From Wong to Woo." *Cineaste* 21, no. 4 (1995): 38–40.

Tien, Chang-Lin. "A View from Berkeley." *New York Times,* March 31, 1996, A30.

Tong K. Achick, and Hab Wa. "Letter of the Chinamen to His Excellency, Governor Bigler." In *An Analysis of the Chinese Question,* 5–8. San Francisco: Office of the *San Francisco Herald,* 1852.

Tow, Julius Su. *The Real Chinese in America.* Orange: Academy Press, 1923.

Trant, William. "Jew and Chinaman." *North American Review* 195 (Feb. 1912): 249–60.

Trotter, Edgar P. *The Asian American Journalist: Results of a National Survey.* Fullerton: Institute for Media-Society Studies, California State University, 1987.

Trueba, Henry T., Cheng Li Rong Lilly, and Kenji Ima, eds. *Myth or Reality: Adaptive Strategies of Asian Americans in California.* Washington D.C.: Falmer Press, 1993.

Tsai, Shih-shan Henry. *The Chinese Experience in America.* Bloomington: Indiana University Press, 1986.

Tseng Pao-Sun [P. S. Tseng]. "The Chinese Women: Past and Present." In *Chinese Women through Chinese Eyes*, ed. Li Yu-ning, 72–86. Armonk: M. E. Sharpe, 1992.

Tsutakawa, Mayumi, and Alan Chong Lau, eds. *Turning Shadows into Light: Art and Culture of the Northwest's Early Asian/Pacific Community*. Seattle: Young Pine Press, 1982.

Tung, William L. *The Chinese in America 1820–1973: A Chronology and Fact Book.* New York: Oceana, 1974.

Tu Wei-ming. "Cultural China: Periphery as the Center." In *The Living Tree: The Changing Meaning of Being Chinese Today*, ed. Tu Wei-ming, 1–34. Stanford: Stanford University Press, 1994.

———, ed. *The Living Tree: The Changing Meaning of Being Chinese Today.* Stanford: Stanford University Press, 1994.

Twain, Mark. *Roughing It.* Reprint. New York: Penguin Books, 1983.

Twichell, Joseph H. "Appendix." In Wing Yung, *My Life in China and America*, 247–73. New York: Holt, 1909.

Tye, Larry. "Hong Kong New Year: Tradition, Informality." *Boston Globe*, Sept. 6, 1994, A2.

Tyler, Patrick E. "A Chinese View of Life in the United States." *New York Times*, July 21, 1997, A1.

"U.S. Asians Earning Less Than Whites," *Los Angeles Times*, Dec. 9, 1995, D2.

U.S. Bureau of the Census. *U.S. Census: General Population Characteristics, 1900–1970.* Washington, D.C.: Government Printing Office, 1971.

U.S. Commission on Civil Rights. *Civil Rights Issues of Asian and Pacific Americans: Myths and Realities.* Washington, D.C.: Government Printing Office, 1980.

———. *Civil Rights Issues Facing Asian Americans in the 1990s.* Washington, D.C.: Government Printing Office, 1992.

von Karman, Theodore, with Lee Edson. *The Wind and Beyond: Theodore von Karman: Pioneer in Aviation and Pathfinder in Space.* Boston: Little, Brown, 1967.

Wakeman, Frederic E. *Strangers at the Gate: Social Disorder in South China, 1839–1861.* Berkeley: University of California Press, 1966.

Wand, David Hsin-Fu [David Rafael Wang], ed. *Asian-American Heritage: An Anthology of Prose and Poetry.* New York: Washington Square Press, 1975.

———. *The Intercourse.* Greenfield Center, N.Y.: Greenfield Review Press.

Wang Gungwu. *A Short History of the Nanyang Chinese.* Singapore: Eastern Universities Press, 1959.

Wang, L. Ling-chi. "Asian American Studies." *American Quarterly* 33, no. 3 (1981): 339–55.

———. "The Politics of Ethnic Identity and Empowerment: The Asian American Community since the 1960s." *Asian American Policy Review* 2 (Spring 1991): 43–56.

———. "Roots and the Changing Identify of the Chinese in the United States." In *The Living Tree: The Changing Meaning of Being Chinese Today*, ed. Tu Wei-ming, 185–212. Stanford: Stanford University Press, 1994.

Watanabe, Sylvia, and Carol Bruchac, eds. *Into the Fire: Asian American Prose.* New York: Greenfield Review Press, 1996.

Waters, Mary C. *Ethnic Options: Choosing Identities in America.* Berkeley: University of California Press, 1990.

Weiss, Melford S. *Valley City: A Chinese Community in America.* Cambridge: Schenkman Publishing, 1974.

Wei, William. *The Asian American Movement.* Philadelphia: Temple University Press, 1993.

Wheeler, Linda. "Forty-seven Chinese Men Served in U.S. Civil War." *Washington Post,* May 12, 1999, A18.

White-Parks, Annette. "Journey to the Golden Mountain: Chinese Immigrant Women." In *Women and the Journey: The Female Travel Experience,* ed. Bonnie Frederick and Susan H. McLoed, 101–17. Pullman: Washington State University Press, 1993.

———. *Sui Sin Far/Edith Maude Eaton: A Literary Biography.* Urbana: University of Illinois Press, 1995.

Widmer, Ellen, and Kang-I Sun Chang, eds. *Writing Women in Late Imperial China.* Stanford: Stanford University Press, 1997.

Williams, Frederick Wells. *Anson Burlingame and the First Chinese Mission to Foreign Powers.* New York: Charles Scribner's Sons.

Wong, Angelina T. "The Contest to Become Top Banana: Chinese Students at Canadian Universities." *Canadian Ethnic Studies* 11, no. 2 (1979): 63–69.

Wong, Cecilia. "Asian Americans in the Newsroom." [Boston] *Sampan,* Aug. 1, 1997, 4–6.

———. "Asians and Affirmative Action: Two Views." *Sampan,* April 3, 1998, 3–5.

Wong, Eugene Franklin. "Asian American Middleman Minority Theory: The Framework of an American Myth." *Journal of Ethnic Studies* 13 (Spring 1985): 51–88.

———. *On Visual Media Racism: Asians in the American Motion Pictures.* New York: Arno Press, 1978.

Wong, Jade Snow. *Fifth Chinese Daughter.* Reprint. Seattle: University of Washington Press, 1989.

———. *No Chinese Stranger.* New York: Harper and Row, 1975.

———. "Puritans from the Orient." In *The Immigrant Experience,* ed. Thomas C. Wheeler, 107–32. New York: Penguin Books, 1971.

Wong, Laura L. "Chinese Immigration and Its Relationship to European Development of Colonies and Frontiers." In *The Chinese American Experience: Papers from the Second National Conference on Chinese American Studies (1980),* ed. Genny Lim, 34–43. San Francisco: Chinese Historical Society of America, 1984.

Wong, Morrison G. "A Look at Intermarriage among the Chinese in the United States in 1980." *Sociological Perspectives* 32, no. 1 (1989): 87–107.

Wong, Nellie. *Dreams in Harrison Railroad Park.* Berkeley: Kelsey Press, 1977.

Wong, Sam. *An English-Chinese Phrase Book Together with the Vocabulary of Trade, Law, etc.* San Francisco: Cubery, 1875.

Wong, Sau-ling Cynthia. "Ethnicizing Gender: An Exploration of Sexuality as Sign in Chinese Immigrant Literature." In *Reading the Literatures of Asian America,* ed. Shirley Grok-lin Lim and Amy Ling, 111–29. Philadelphia: Temple University Press, 1992.

———. *Reading Asian American Literature: From Necessity to Extravagance.* Princeton: Princeton University Press, 1993.

———. "'Sugar Sisterhood': Situating the Amy Tan Phenomenon." In *The Ethnic Canon: Histories, Institutions, and Interventions,* ed. David Palumbo-Liu, 174–210. Minneapolis: University of Minnesota Press, 1995.

Wong, Shawn Hsu. "Beyond Bruce Lee." *Essence* 24 (Nov. 1993): 64, 164, 165.

———. *Homebase.* New York: I. Reed Books, 1979.

———, ed. *Asian American Literature: A Brief Introduction and Anthology.* New York: HarperCollins, 1996.

Woo, Wesley. "Chinese Protestants in the San Francisco Bay Area." In *Entry Denied: Exclusion and the Chinese Community in America, 1882–1943,* ed. Sucheng Chan, 213–45. Philadelphia: Temple University Press, 1991.

Worner, William Frederick. "A Chinese Soldier in the Civil War." *Journal of the Lancaster County Historical Society* 25 (1921): 52–55.

Wu Cheng-Tsu, ed. *Chink! A Documentary History of Anti-Chinese Prejudice in America.* New York: World Publishing, 1972.

Wunder, John R. "Law and the Chinese in Frontier Montana." *Montana* 30 (Summer 1980): 18–30.

Wu Tingfang. *America through the Spectacles of an Oriental Diplomat.* New York: Frederick A. Stokes, 1914.

Wu, William F. *The Yellow Peril: Chinese Americans in American Fiction, 1850–1940.* Hamden: Archon Books, 1982.

X, Malcolm, and Alex Haley. *The Autobiography of Malcolm X.* Reprint. New York: Ballentine Books, 1973.

Yamamoto, Hisaye. *Seventeen Syllables and Other Stories.* Latham: Kitchen Table, 1988.

Yep, Laurence. *Dragonwings.* New York: Harper and Row, 1975.

Yeun, Kevin, ed. *Hanai: An Anthology of Asian American Writings.* Berkeley: University of California Press, 1980.

Yin, Xiao-huang. "Between the East and West: Sui Sin Far—the First Chinese American Woman Writer." *Arizona Quarterly* 47 (Winter 1991): 49–84.

———. "China's Gilded Age." *Atlantic Monthly* 273 (April 1994): 42–53.

———. "The Growing Influence of Chinese Americans on U.S.–China Relations." In *The Outlook for U.S.-China Relations Following the 1997–1998 Summits,* ed. Peter H. Koehn and Joseph Y. S. Cheng, 331–49. Hong Kong: Chinese University Press, 1999.

———. "Immigration and the Asian American Experience." *The World and I* 13 (Feb. 1998): 330–37.

———. "The Population Pattern and Occupational Structure of Boston's Chinese Community." *Maryland Historian* 20 (Spring 1990): 59–69.

———. "Progress and Problems: American Literary Studies in China during the Post-Mao Era." In *As Others Read Us: International Perspectives on American Literature,* ed. Huck Gutman, 49–64. Amherst: University of Massachusetts Press, 1991.

———. "The Rise of Anti-Chinese Sentiment and Formation of America's Chinatowns." In *Asian Americans: The Year 2000 and Beyond,* ed. Jenn-Yun Tein and Thomas K. Nakayama, 13–22. Tempe: Arizona State University, 1996.

———. "The Voice of a 'Cultivated Asian.'" In *Origins and Destinations: Forty-one Essays on Chinese America,* ed. Munson A. Kwok and Ella Yee Quan, 337–45. Los Angeles: Chinese Historical Society of Southern California and Asian American Studies Center, UCLA, 1994.

———. "Worlds of Difference: Lin Yutang, Lao She, and the Significance of Chinese-language Writing in America." In *Multilingual America: Transnationalism, Ethnicity, and the Languages of America,* ed. Werner Sollors, 176–87. New York: New York University Press, 1998.

Yong, C. F. *The New Gold Mountain: The Chinese in Australia: 1901–1921.* Richmond, Australia: Raphael Arts, 1977.

Young, Samantha. "Interview." [Boston] *Sampan,* June 20, 1997, 3.

Yu, Eui-Young, Earl H. Phillips, and Eun Sik Yang, eds. *Koreans in Los Angeles*. Los Angeles: Center for Korean-American and Korean Studies, California State University, 1982.

Yu, Li-hua. "Sorrow at the End of the Yangtze River." *UCLA Review* (March 1957): 1–13.

Yu, Lucy C. "Acculturation and Stress within Chinese American Families." *Journal of Comparative Family Studies* 15 (Spring 1984): 77–94.

Yung, Judy. *Chinese Women of America: A Pictorial History*. Seattle: University of Washington Press, 1986.

———. *Unbound Feet: A Social History of Chinese Women in San Francisco*. Berkeley: University of California Press, 1995.

Yung Wing. *My Life in China and America*. New York: Holt, 1909.

Zhang Yinhuan. "Chinese in America." In *Land without Ghosts: Chinese Impressions of America from the Mid-Nineteenth Century to the Present*, ed. and trans. R. David Arkush and Leo Ou-fan Lee, 71–76. Berkeley: University of California Press, 1989.

Zhang Ziqing. "Transplantation and Transfiguration of Eastern and Western Myths: Interview with Maxine Hong Kingston." [Taipei] *Fiction and Drama* 9 (1997): 19–26.

Zhou, Min. *Chinatown: The Socioeconomic Potential of an Urban Enclave*. Philadelphia: Temple University Press, 1992.

## Manuscripts, Dissertations, and Theses

Auyang, Grace. "Structural and Processional Change in Philadelphia's Chinatown and among Suburban Chinese." Ph.D. diss., Temple University, 1978.

Barlow, Janelle M. "The Images of the Chinese, Japanese, and Koreans in American Secondary School Textbooks, 1900–1970." Ph.D. diss., University of California, 1972.

Becker, Jules. "The Course of Exclusion, 1882–1924: San Francisco Newspaper Coverage of the Chinese and Japanese in the United States." Ph.D. diss., University of California, Berkeley, 1986.

BeDunnah, Gary. "A History of the Chinese in Nevada: 1855–1904." M.A. thesis, University of Nevada, Reno, 1966.

Chang, Cordelia J. "Chinese-American Culture and Literature, 1943–1969: The Best of East and West." Unpublished paper. Berkeley: Asian American Studies Library, 1969.

Chang, Lydia Liang-Hwa. "Acculturation and Emotional Adjestments of Chinese Women Immigrants." D.S.W. diss., Columbia University, 1980.

Chan, Kai-tin. "Intermarriage and Assimilation of Chinese Americans." M.A. thesis, Michigan State University, 1988.

Chan, Kim Man. "Mandarins in America: The Early Chinese Ministers to the United States, 1878–1907." Ph.D. diss., University of Hawaii, 1981.

Chu, Limin. "The Images of China and the Chinese in the *Overland Monthly*, 1868–1875, 1883–1935." Ph.D. diss., Duke University, 1966.

Demirturk, Emine Lale. "The Female Identity in Cross-Cultural Perspectives: Immigrant Women's Autobiographies." Ph.D. diss., University of Iowa, 1986.

Foster, John Burt. "China and the Chinese in American Literature, 1850–1950." Ph.D. diss., University of Illinois, 1952.

Ger, Yeing-Kuang. "Ethnic Identity and Ethnic Political Development: The Experience of Chinese Americans." Ph.D. diss., University of Wisconsin, 1985.

Han, Hsiao-min. "Roots and Buds: The Literature of Chinese Americans." Ph.D. diss., Brigham Young University, 1980.

Hsaio, Ruth Yu. "The Stages of Development in American Ethnic Literature: Jewish and Chinese American Literatures." Ph.D. diss., Tufts University, 1986.

Huang, Wei-Chiao. "A Study of the Indirect Immigration of Professional Manpower to the United States." Ph.D. diss., University of California, Santa Barbara, 1984.

Jung, Henry. "The Relationship of Kung-Fu Movie Viewing to Acculturation among Chinese American Men." Ed.D. diss., University of Massachusetts, Amherst, 1985.

Lai, Him Mark. "A Short History of the Jop Sen Tong." Unpublished paper, San Francisco.

Lee, Marjorie. "He-Jee: The Forgotten Second Generation of Chinese America, 1930–1950." M.A. thesis, University of California, Los Angeles, 1984.

Ling, Amy. "Maxine Hong Kingston and the Dialogic Dilemma of Asian American Writers." Presented at the Tenth Conference of the Association for Asian American Studies, Cornell University, June 1993.

Lin, Mao-Chu. "Identity and Chinese-American Experience: A Study of Chinatown American Literature since World War II." Ph.D. diss., University of Minnesota, 1987.

Li Xiaolin. "Images of Early (1848–1945) Chinese in Literary Works Written by Chinese American Authors." M.A. thesis, University of California, Los Angeles, 1983.

Ng, Pearl. "Writings on the Chinese in California." M.A. thesis, University of California, Berkeley, 1939.

Qian Jun. "Lin Yutang: Negotiating Modernity between East and West." Ph.D. diss., University of California, Berkeley, 1996.

Shan, Te-hsing. "An Island Where Angels Fear to Tread: Reinscribing Angel Island Poetry in Chinese and English." Unpublished paper, Taipei.

———. "Writing Asian American Literary History: A Case Study of Frank Chin." Presented at the Fifth Conference on American Literature and Thoughts, Taipei, Oct. 1995.

Shin, Linda P. "China in Transition: The Role of Wu T'ing-fang." Ph.D. diss., University of California, Los Angeles, 1970.

Su Hongjun. "Strangers within Our Gates: A Study of Four First-Generation Chinese Immigrant Men's Autobiography, 1930s–1940s." Ph.D. diss., University of Iowa, 1996.

Teng, Jinhua Emma. "The 'Writer as Fighter': Frank Chin and the Construction of a New Asian American Male Identity." Unpublished paper.

Tseng, Daisy Chang-Ling. "Chinese Newspapers and Immigrant Assimilation in America: A Local Exploratory Study." M.A. thesis, University of Pennsylvania, 1984.

Wu, Ching-Chao. "Chinatowns: A Study in Symbiosis and Assimilation." Ph.D. diss., University of Chicago, 1928.

Zhang, Qionghui. "Who's Afraid of Frank Chin?" Presented at the Fifth Conference on American Literature and Thoughts, Taipei, Oct. 1995.

# Chinese Bibliography

A Ying [Qian Xingcun] 阿英 [錢杏邨]. *Fanmei huagong jinyue wenxueji* 反美華工禁約文學集 [Anthology of Chinese literature against the American exclusion of Chinese laborers]. Shanghai: Zhonghua, 1960.

Bai Xianyong [Hsien-yung Pai] 白先勇. *Zhe xian ji* 謫仙記 [Falling to the earth]. Taipei: Wenxing, 1967.

——. "Yequ" 夜曲 [Night tune]. In *Haiwai huaren zuojia xiaoshuoxuan* 海外華人作家小說選 [A selection of short stories by Chinese immigrant writers], ed. Li Li 李黎, 67–83. Hong Kong; Joint, 1983.

"Bushi shouci guohui lianxi huiyi yanshuo yinyong Lin Yutang *Wugou yu wumin* yu" 布什首次國會聯席會議演說引用林語堂 "吾國與吾民" 語 [President Bush quotes Lin Yutang's *My Country and My People* in his first State of Union address to Congress]. [New York] *Meizhou Huaqiao Ribao* 美洲華僑日報 [Chinese American Daily], Feb. 11, 1989, A1.

Cao Guilin [Cao, Glen] 曹桂林. *Beijingren zai niuyue* 北京人在紐約 [A Beijinger in New York]. Beijing: Zhongguo wennian, 1991.

Cao Youfang 曹又方. *Meiguo yueliang* 美國月亮 [The American moon]. Reprint. Hong Kong: Joint, 1986.

Chang Phong [Zhang Feng] 張鳳. "Cong 'Chen-Liu qingyuan' kan Ming Qing funu shi-ci" 從陳柳情緣看明清婦女詩詞 [Ming and Qing women poetry as reflected in the romance of Chen Tzu-lung and Liu Ru-shi]. *Ershiyi shiji* 二十一世紀 [Twenty-First Century Bimonthly; Hong Kong] No. 27 (February 1995), 68–72.

Chen Junjie 陳俊杰. "Ming Qing shiren jieceng nuzi shoujie xianxiang" 明清士人階層女子守節現象 [The Ming-Qing intelligentsia and the moral imposition on widows]. *Ershiyi shiji* 二十一世紀 [Twenty-First Century Bimonthly; Hong Kong], No. 27 (February 1995), 98–107.

Chen Ruoxi [Chen, Jo-hsi; Chen, Lucy] 陳若曦. *Chen Ruoxi duanpian xiaoshuo xuan* 陳若曦短篇小說選 [Short stories by Chen Ruoxi]. Reprint. Beijing: Guangbo, 1983.

————. *Chengli chengwai* 城裡城外 [Inside and outside the wall]. Taipei: Shibao, 1981.

————. *Er Hu* 二 胡 [Uncle and nephew of the Hu family]. Hong Kong: Joint, 1986.

————. "Haiwai zuojia he bentuxing" 海外作 家和 本 土性 [Chinese immigrant writers and their sense of Chinese-ness]. *Xianggang wenxue* 香港文學 [Hong Kong Literature], September 5, 1988, 18–21.

————. "Kezi guxiang lai" 客自故 鄉 來 [Visitors from the hometown]. In Chen, *Inside and Outside the Wall*, 162–88. Taipei: Shibao, 1981.

————. *Tuwei* 突圍 [Break out]. Hong Kong: Joint, 1987.

————. "Xiangzhe taipingyang bi'an" 向 着太平洋彼岸 [To the other side of the Pacific]. In *Haiwai huaren zuojia xiaoshuoxuan* 海外華人作 家小說選 [A selection of short stories by Chinese immigrant writers], ed. Li Li 李黎, 67–83. Hong Kong; Joint, 1983.

————. *Zhihun* 紙婚 [Paper marriage]. Hong Kong: Joint, 1986.

Chen Wanyi 陳萬益. "Xu" 序 [Preface]. In *Zhang Xiguo ji* 張系國集 [Selected stories of Zhang Xiguo], ed. Chen Wanyi, 9–12. Taipei: Qianwei, 1993.

Chen Weihua 陳偉華. "Wo shi zhongguoren" 我是中國人 [I am Chinese]. [Beijing] *Renmin Ribao* 人民日報 [People's Daily], overseas ed., June 26, 1991, 8.

Chen, Yanni 陳燕妮. *Zaoyu meiguo: wushige zhongguoren de jingli* 遭 遇美國： 五十 個中國人的經歷 [The American experience of fifty Chinese immigrants]. Beijing: Shehui kexue, 1997.

Cheung, Dominic [Zhang Cuo] 張錯. *Huangjin lei* 黃金淚 [Tears of gold]. Hong Kong: Joint, 1985.

Chin Mu 秦牧. *Huaqiao ticai zuopinxuan* 華僑題 材作 品選 [Writings by Chin Mu on Chinese immigrants]. Fuzhou: Renmin, 1984.

Fang Jigen, and Hu Wenying 方紀根, 胡文英. *Haiwai huawen baokan de lishi he xian-zhuang* 海外華文報刊的歷史和 現狀 [Chinese-language newspapers and journals abroad: Past and present]. Beijing: Xinhua, 1989.

"Feifa renshe yuanyuan jinru meiguo" 非 法人蛇 源源進入美國 [Illegal immigrants continuously enter America]. [Boston] *Yamei Shibao* 亞美時報 [Asian American Times], Sept. 24, 1993, 11.

Feng Ziping 馮子平. *Haiwai chunqiu* 海外春 秋 [The Chinese diaspora]. Shanghai: Shangwu, 1993.

Hu Jieqing, and Shu Yi 胡潔清 ,舒乙 . *Sanji Lao She* 散記 老舍 [Random notes on Lao She]. Beijing: Beijing renmin, 1986.

Huang Lianzhi 黃連枝. *Dongnanya huazu shehui fazhanlun* 東南亞華族社會發展論 [The development of ethnic Chinese communities in Southeast Asia]. Shanghai: Shehui kexue, 1992.

Huang Wenxiang 黃文湘. *Oumei jiechu huayi nuxing* 歐美杰 出 華裔女性 [Outstanding women of Chinese ancestry in Europe and America]. Hong Kong: Shanghai Book, 1992.

Jian Wan 簡婉. *Yuyu huanxiu* 欲語還休 [Beyond words]. Taipei: Weilai, 1985.

Jiang Wenhan 江文漢. *Zhongguo gudai jidujiao ji Kaifeng youtairen* 中國古代 基督教 及開封猶太人 [Christianity in ancient China and Jews at Kaifeng]. Shanghai: Zhishi, 1982.

Kong Xiangjiong 孔祥炯. "Huaren shouxi cheng daizui gaoyang" 華人 受襲成代罪 羔羊 [Ethnic Chinese again become scapegoats in Indonesia]. *Haojiao* 號角 [Herald Monthly] 11 (April 1988): 2.

Lai, Him Mark 麥禮謙. *Cong huaqiao dao huaren* 從華僑到華人 [From overseas Chinese to Chinese Americans]. Hong Kong: Joint, 1992.

Lao She [Lau Shaw; Shu Qingchun] 老舍 [舒慶春]. *Luotuo xiangzi* 駱駝 祥子 [Rickshaw boy]. Reprint. Beijing: Renmin, 1991.

Li Chunhui, et al. 李春 輝, 等. *Meizhou huaqiao huaren shi* 美洲 華僑華人 史 [A history of Chinese immigration to North and South America]. Beijing: Dongfang, 1990.

Li Li [Bao Lili] 李黎 [包莉莉]. *Haiwai huaren zuojia xiaoshuoxuan* 海外華人 作 家 小說選 [A selection of short stories by Chinese immigrant writers]. Hong Kong: Joint, 1983.

Lin Taiyi [Anor Lin] 林太乙. *Lin Yutang zhuan* 林語堂傳 [Biography of Lin Yutang]. Beijing: Zhongguo xiju, 1994.

Lin Yutang 林語堂. "Guoshi weiyi" 國事危 矣 [China in crisis]. In Lin Taiyi, *Biography of Lin Yutang*. 109–11. Beijing: Zhongguo xiju, 1994.

———. "Xinnian zhimeng—Zhongguo zhimeng" 新年 之夢—中國之夢 [New year's dream: My wishes for China]. In Lin Taiyi, *Lin Yutang zhuan* 林語堂傳 [Biography of Lin Yutang]. 104–6. Beijing: Zhongguo xiju, 1994.

Liu Pei-chi [Liu Baiji] 劉 伯 驥. *Meizhou huaqiao yishi* 美洲 華僑逸史 [A history of the Chinese in America]. Taipei: Liming, 1976.

Li Yiyuan, and Guo Zhenyu 李亦園, 郭振羽. *Dongnanya huaren shehui yanjiu* 東 南 亞華人 社會研究 [The Chinese communities in Southeast Asia]. Taipei: Academia Sinica, 1985.

Li Ziyun, 李子云. "Yu Lihua he tade xiaoshuo 'Jiemeiyin'" 於梨華和 她的小說《 姐 妹吟》 [Yu Lihua and her story "Two sisters"]. [Shanghai] *Xiaoshuo jie* 小說界 [Fiction World] 4 (1988): 176–177.

Lu Guocai, and Zhong Yuren 魯國才, 鐘玉仁. *Zhongguo wenxue jingdu* 中國文學精讀 [A digest of Chinese literary history]. Hong Kong: Dangdai jiaoyu, 1987.

Mu Lingqi 木令 耆, ed. *Haiwai huaren zuojia sanwenxuan* 海外華人 作 家散文選 [A selection of essays by Chinese immigrant writers]. Hong Kong: Joint, 1983.

Nie Hualing [Hua-ling Nieh] 聶華苓. *Heise, heise, zuimeili de yanse* 黑色, 黑色, 最美 麗 的顏 色 [Black, black, the most beautiful color]. Hong Kong: Joint, 1983.

———. *Iowa zaji* 愛 荷華雜記 [Life in Iowa]. Hong Kong: Joint, 1983.

———. *Sangqing yu taohong* 桑青 與桃紅 [Mulberry and peach]. Hong Kong: Joint, 1976.

Ouyang Zi. 歐陽 子. *Ouyang Zi ji* 歐陽 子集 [Selected stories of Ouyang Zi]. Taipei: Qianwei, 1993.

Pan Yatun, and Wang Yisheng 潘 亞暾, 汪 義生. *Haiwai huawen wenxue mingjia* 海外 華文文學名 家 [Distinguished Chinese-language writers abroad]. Guangzhou: Jinan, 1994.

Qian Ning 錢寧. *Liuxue meiguo* 留學美國 [Studying in the USA]. Nanjing: Jiangsu wenyi, 1996.

Qian Zhongshu 錢鐘書. *Weicheng* 圍城 [Fortress besieged]. Reprint. Beijing: Renmin, 1990.

Ren Guixiang 任貴 祥. *Huaqiao dierci aiguo gaochao* 華僑第二 次愛 國高潮 [The second patriotic movement of overseas Chinese]. Beijing: Zhonggong dangshi, 1989.

Rong Futian 戎撫天. "Taiguo huaren tonghua wenti yanjiu" 泰國華人同化問題研究 [A study of assimilation of the Chinese in Thailand]. In *Dongnanya huaren shehui yanjiu* 東南亞華人社會研究 [The Chinese communities in Southeast Asia], ed. Li Yiyuan and Guo Zhenyu 李亦园, 郭振羽,1–52. Taipei: Academia Sinica. 1985.

Shan Te-hsing 單德興. "Yiwo ailun ru quanfu" 憶我愛倫如蜷伏 [An island where angels fear to tread]. In *Zaixian zhengzhi yu huayi meiguo wenxue* 再現政治與華裔美國文學 [Reexamining the relationship between politics and Chinese American literature], ed. He Wenjing and Shan Te-hsing 何文敬, 單德興, 1–56. Taipei: Academia Sinica, 1996.

Shen I-yao 沈亦堯. *Haiwai paihua bainianshi* 海外排華百年史 [One-hundred-year history of the anti-Chinese movement abroad]. Beijing: Shehui kexue, 1985.

Shen Zhengrou 沈正柔. "Li Qingyang lishi xiaoshuo xinzuo *Taiping Tianguo* chuban" 黎清揚歷史小說新作 "太平天國" 出版[C.Y. Lee has written another historical novel *Taiping Heavenly Kingdom*]. [New York] *Shijie Ribao* 世界日報 [World Journal], June 18, 1990, A2.

Shu Fei 舒菲. "Xiezuo, aiqing, hunyin—ji Yu Lihua" 寫作, 愛情, 婚姻—記於梨華 [Writing, love, and marriage: My impression of Yu Lihua]. [Shanghai] *Wenhui* 文匯 [Enchanter Monthly] 85 (June 1987): 60–61.

Tang Degang 唐德剛. "Xinshi laozuzong yu disan wenyizhongxin" 新詩老祖宗與第三文藝中心 [Founding father of new poety and the third center of literature]. In *Haiwai huaren zuojia sanwenxuan* 海外華人作家散文選 [A selection of essays by Chinese immigrant writers], ed. Mu Lingqi 木令耆, 139–61. Hong Kong: Joint, 1983.

Tian Xinbin 田新彬. "Laobang shengzhu de wentan xinxiu" 老蚌生珠的文壇新秀 [A new star in the writers' circle]. In Zhou Feili 周腓力, *Yangfan erchi* 洋飯二吃 [Two ways to eat American meals], 233–48. Taipei: Erya, 1987.

Wang Runhua 王潤華. *Lao She xiaoshuo xinlun* 老舍小說新論 [New studies of Lao She's fiction]. Shanghai: Shulin, 1995.

Wang Ying 王穎. *Liangzhong meiguoren* 兩種美國人 [Two kinds of Americans]. Beijing: Zhongguo qingnian, 1980.

Wang Zaomin 王造民. *Meiguo wanhuatong* 美國萬花筒 [The American kaleidoscope: A Chinese view]. Beijing: Shehui kexue, 1985.

Wan Pingjin 萬平近. *Lin Yutang lun* 林語堂論 [A study of Lin Yutang]. Xi'an: Renmin, 1987.

Weng Shaoqiu 翁紹裘. *Wo zai jiujinshan sishinian* 我在舊金山四十年 [My forty years in San Francisco]. Shanghai: Renmin, 1988.

Wu Fangbin 吳方賓. *Qiyue huagongshi* 契約華工史 [A history of Chinese contract laborers]. Nanchang: Renmin, 1988.

"Wu Jiawei fouren qishi xianxiang pubian" 吳家偉否認歧視現象普遍 [Wu Jiawei denies racial discrimination is a common phenomenon]. [New York] *Zhong Bao* 中報 [Central Daily], Nov. 19, 1987, A3.

Xia Yun 夏云. "Xie Yi" 寫伊 [My impression of Yi Li]. In Yi Li 伊犁, *Shiwan meijin* 十萬美金 [A hundred thousand dollars], 1–3. Hong Kong: Joint, 1987.

Xu Mingqian 徐銘謙. *Jiujinshan zasui* 舊金山雜碎 [San Francisco chop suey]. Hong Kong: Joint, 1987.

Yang, C. N. [Yang Zhenning] 楊振寧. "Xu" [Preface]. In Yu Lihua 於梨華, *Kaoyan* 考驗 [The ordeal], 1. Reprint. Hong Kong: Cosmos Books, 1993.

Yan Geling 嚴歌苓. *Chen Chong—Helihuo de zhongguo nuren* 陳沖 —荷里活的中國女人 [Joan Chen: A Chinese woman in Hollywood]. Hong Kong: Cosmos, 1995.

Yang Guobiao, Liu Hanbiao, and Yang Anyao 楊國標,劉漢標,楊安耀. *Meiguo huaqiao shi* 美國華僑史 [A history of the Chinese in the United States]. Guangzhou: Guangdong jiaoyu, 1989.

Yang Mu 楊牧. "Zhang Xiguo de guanxin yu yishu" 張系國的關心與藝術 [Zhang Xiguo's concerns and arts of literature]. In *Zhang Xiguo ji* 張系國集 [Selected stories of Zhang Xiguo], ed. Chen Wanyi 陳萬益, 239–55. Taipei: Qianwei, 1993.

Yan Huo [Pan Yaoming] 彥火 [潘耀明]. *Haiwai huaren zuojia lueying* 海外華人作家掠影 [Interviews with Chinese immigrant writers]. Hong Kong: Joint, 1984.

Yan Zi 炎子. "Zhongguo liuxue di yi ren" 中國留學第一人 [The first Chinese college student in America]. [Beijing] *Renmin Ribao* 人民日報 [People's Daily], overseas ed., May 5, 1992,8.

Yi Li [Pan Xiumei] 伊犁 [潘秀媚]. "Duotai" 墮胎 [Abortion]. In *Haiwai huaren zuojia xiaoshuoxuan* 海外華人作家小說選 [A selection of short stories by Chinese immigrant writers], ed. Li Li 李黎, 84–116. Hong Kong: Joint, 1983.

———. "Fang yisheng yizhen" 方醫生義診 [Dr. Fang's free medical service]. In Yi Li, *A Hundred Thousand Dollars*, 101–15. Hong Kong: Joint, 1987.

———. "Fu jiaoshou bufu" 服教授不服 [Professor Fu doesn't believe it]. In Yi Li, *A Hundred Thousand Dollars*, 149–52. Hong Kong: Joint, 1987.

———. *Shiwan meijin* 十萬美金 [A hundred thousand dollars]. Hong Kong: Joint, 1987.

———. "Tiantang" 天堂 [Paradise]. In Yi Li, *A Hundred Thousand Dollars*, 116–20. Hong Kong: Joint, 1987.

Yuan Zenan [Yuan Zhihui] 袁則難 [袁志惠]. *Bujian busan* 不見不散 [Until we meet]. Hong Kong: Joint, 1985.

Yu Guangzhong 余光中. "Xu" 序 [Preface]. In Yu Lihua 於梨華, *Huichang xianxingji* 會場現形記 [Scandals at a conference], 1–4. Taipei: Zhiwen, 1972.

Yu Lihua [Li-hua Yu] 於梨華. "Erxi" 兒戲 [A childish game]. In Yu Lihua, *Scandals at a Conference*, 51–75. Taipei: Zhiwen, 1972.

———. *Fujia de ernumen* 傅家的兒女們 [Sons and daughters of the Fu family]. Reprint. Hong Kong: Cosmos, 1994.

———. *Huichang xianxingji* 會場現形記 [Scandals at a conference]. Taipei: Zhiwen, 1972.

———. *Kaoyan* 考驗 [The ordeal]. Reprint. Hong Kong: Cosmos, 1994.

———. *Youjian zonglu, youjian zonglu* 又見棕櫚,又見棕櫚 [Seeing the palm trees again]. Reprint. Beijing: Youyi, 1984.

Yu Qing 于青. *Qicai yinu—Zhang Ailing* 奇才逸女 —張愛玲 [Zhang Ailing: A talented woman writer]. Jinan: Shandong huabao, 1995.

Zhang Huilan 張惠蘭. *Xifang shehui mantan* 西方社會漫談 [Random talks about Western society]. Beijing: Qunzhong, 1985.

Zhang Xiaowu 張曉武. *Wozai meiguo dang lushi* 我在美國當律師 [My experience as an American lawyer]. Beijing: Beijing chubenshe, 1994.

Zhang Xiguo 張系國. "Geli" 割礼 [Circumcision]. In *Haiwai huaren zoujia xiaoshuo-xuan* 海外華人作家小說選 [A selection of short stories by Chinese immigrant writers], ed. Li Li 李黎, 291–306. Hong Kong: Joint, 1983.

———. "Shaqi" 殺妻 [Killing wife]. In *Selected Stories of Zhang Xiguo*, ed. Chen Wanyi, 155–207. Taipei: Qianwei, 1993.

———. "Xiangjiaochuan" 香蕉船 [The ship of bananas]. In *Selected Stories of Zhang Xiguo*, ed. Chen Wanyi, 109–19. Taipei: Qianwei, 1993.

———. *Zhang Xiguo ji* 張系國集 [Selected stories of Zhang Xiguo], ed. Chen Wanyi. Taipei: Qianwei, 1993.

Zhong Meiyin 鐘梅音. "Xiezuo wuru jieshu nan" 寫作無如結束難 [An introduction to Kaoyan]. In Yu Lihua 於梨華, *Kaoyan* 考驗 [The ordeal], 1–15. Reprint. Hong Kong: Cosmos Books, 1994.

Zhou Feili [Philip Chou] 周腓力. *Yangfan erchi* 洋飯二吃 [Two ways to eat American meals]. Taipei: Erya, 1987.

———. "Yizhou dashi" 一周大事 [Weekly event]. In Zhou Feili, *Two Ways to Eat American Meals*, 25–49. Taipei: Erya, 1987.

Zhou Li [Julia Zhou Fochler] 周勵. *Manhadun de zhongguo nuren* 曼哈頓的中國女人 [Manhattan's China lady]. Beijing: Beijing chubanshe, 1992.

Zhuang Yin 莊因. "Ye Ben" 夜奔 [A visit at night]. In *Haiwai huaren zuojia xiaoshuo-xuan* 海外華人作家小說選 [A selection of short stories by Chinese immigrant writers], ed. Li Li 李黎, 307–322. Hong Kong: Joint, 1983.

Zhu Ying 朱英. "Bie laoxiang geiren chi yikufan" 別老想給人吃忆苦飯 [Don't always feed us with bitter stories about American life]. [Los Angeles] *Xin Dalu* 新大陸 [New Continent], Aug. 1, 1994, 16.

# Index

Xiao-huang Yin [Yin Xiaohuang] is an associate professor and chair of the American Studies Program at Occidental College. In addition to his scholarly publications on Asian Americans and U.S.–China relations, he has also written articles and essays on China and Chinese Americans for magazines and newspapers such as the *Atlantic Monthly, Los Angeles Times, Boston Globe, Philadelphia Inquirer,* and *Il Mondo* [Italy].

The Asian American Experience

Typeset in 10/13 Minion
with Helvetica Neue display
Designed by Paula Newcomb
Composed by Jim Proefrock
at the University of Illinois Press
Manufactured by Thomson-Shore, Inc.

University of Illinois Press
1325 South Oak Street
Champaign, IL 61820-6903
www.press.uillinois.edu